16

The Judges and The Judged

THE JUDGES
AND
THE JUDGED

*

Edgar Lustgarten

ODHAMS PRESS LIMITED

LONG ACRE, LONDON

FOR CHARLES CURRAN,
JOHN JUNOR AND CHARLES WINTOUR,
MY EDITORS

Second impression 1961

Made and printed in Great Britain by
Cox and Wyman Limited
London, Fakenham and Reading
T.1161. R1. L.

Contents

CONTENTS

PART THREE
WITNESSES—EXPERT AND OTHERWISE

CONTENTS

7

CONTENTS

Foreword

IF I assert—as I unhesitatingly do—that, for arousing interest and awakening emotion, a trial may eclipse any contrived spectacle, please do not read into this assertion a meaning beyond that which the words will bear. It is not *all* trials, *most* trials, even *many* trials, that realize a particle of this potentiality. The staple fare at your local County Court—or, for that matter, at the Royal Courts of Justice—understandably attract few onlookers, and those are far less often thrilled than bored.

The potentiality always exists, however; and, given favourable circumstances, will achieve fulfilment. To create a real impact, in terms of human drama, a trial, whether criminal or civil, must involve either important issues or vivid personalities; preferably—a rather rare conjunction—both. Then one does occasionally find such a wide variety of absorbing elements woven into a single forensic pattern that eye and ear and mind are almost spoilt for choice. As the conflict unfolds and mounts towards a climax, it requires alert thinking to concentrate on essentials

But the reward for such watchfulness is rich. No matter where the spotlight falls in the course of a great trial, it beats with a white and penetrative intensity unknown in the artificial theatre, or elsewhere. This spotlight of the courts, operating unseen and only upon the challenge and pressure of events, possesses a unique diagnostic power that discloses in their naked truth both character and temperament—often of the cross-examiner as well as of the cross-examined, often of the judges as well as of the judged. Anyone, for instance, who was present at the trial of Alma Rattenbury would come away knowing that unhappy woman better, in some vital respects, than he would know his wife. Anyone who was present at the Hartopp divorce suit would come away knowing the intervener, Mrs. Sands, better, in some vital respects, than he would know his sister. Anyone who was present at Professor Harold Laski's famous libel action would come away knowing not only the Professor, but also Lord Goddard and Sir Patrick Hastings, better, in some vital respects, than he would know his father or his brother or his son.

More than the stories told by witnesses (though these are often poignant or amusing), more than the skill exhibited by counsel (though this is sometimes technically exquisite), more even than the efforts usually made by both judges and juries to do justice (though these efforts evoke the deepest admiration), it is this closer knowledge gained about one's fellow beings—the clever and the stupid, the evil and the good—that for me constitutes the fascination of the courts.

It has been my prime purpose to convey and to share that abiding fascination with those who honour me by reading the succeeding pages.

E. L.

PART ONE

THE JUDGES

Mr. Justice Avory tries
Sergeant Goddard

I DO not suppose for a moment that Mr. Justice Avory, who despised pretensions and detested histrionics, ever consciously cast himself in the role of Nemesis. That he not only fulfilled, but was seen to fulfil, that role more strikingly than any among his contemporaries is an indisputable fact that must be attributed to nature. Cast of mind and cast of features alike equipped him for the part.

It has been said—and perhaps with truth—that an innocent prisoner could count himself lucky to be tried by Avory. It has also been said—and perhaps with equal truth—that a guilty prisoner would get a gentler deal from almost any other judge.

He was technically fair and meticulously correct; he firmly grasped and faithfully applied the legal rules; his conduct of his trials repeatedly gained approval from the Court of Criminal Appeal. But—always strictly within procedural limits—Avory often gave rein to that trait of character by which he is now most vividly remembered: a trait of relentlessness, of implacability.

He did no more injustice—and, in some cases, far less—than judges of a milder temperament and aspect. He seldom, if ever, sought to secure convictions that were not thoroughly and patently deserved. The worst that can be said of him is that he appeared even keener to punish the guilty than to protect the innocent. Aloof and icy, unchanging in expression, with skin like old parchment and pale, piercing eyes, Avory looked—as he was—the embodiment of retribution.

Few knew that better, even before his trial—certainly none knew it better afterwards—than the sacked police officer to whom posterity has restored his forfeit title, and still calls him "Sergeant Goddard".

Policemen are vocationally exposed to great temptation—the wonder is they yield to it so little, not so much—but Goddard was offered more than his reasonable share. Joining the Metropolitan force within a few months of the day when Avory ascended to the Bench in 1910, he inspired such confidence among his seniors that, only eight years later, they entrusted him with the highly responsible plain clothes job of investigating allegations against night clubs and other West End places of resort.

Such allegations were not lacking—nor justification for them. In the hectic, characteristically post-war, saturnalia—only finally dispatched by the Depression of the Thirties—throughout the W.1 district establishments sprang into existence which depended, for their popular success

13

and commercial profit, on violation of the licensing laws, if on nothing worse. These establishments fell under Goddard's particular surveillance; during his tour of duty he took part in more than a hundred raids, and his valuable work in suppressing law-breakers won him many compliments and eulogies in court.

Two or three places, however, although persistently the subject of complaint and gossip, seemed to be more than a match for Sergeant Goddard's zeal.

There was Mrs. Meyrick's "43" Club in Gerrard Street, described by one unknown correspondent of the Yard as "a sink of iniquity, at which young men of means are filled with drink, petted by prostitutes, and robbed".

There was Uncle's Club in Albemarle Street, run by Luigi Ribuffi, former boss of Victor's Club in Leicester Square (which had been raided), and whose new premises soon boasted a police file well filled with unsigned charges of drunkenness and disorder.

Less prominent and pseudo-smart than these notorious haunts, but also buttressed by a band of loyal patrons, there was a bawdy-house in Greek Street, managed by a Mrs. Gadda, which welfare organizations diligently watched and the Westminster Housing authority viewed with strong suspicion.

Goddard, though, never furnished his superiors with the evidence required to institute proceedings against any one of them. On each successive complaint passed to him, he reported back that his inquiries had turned out negative, and that for the present no action could be taken.

That did not occasion—nor warrant—immediate surprise. You need luck, as well as judgment, to catch wrongdoers red-handed; and one might suppose, quite feasibly, that Goddard's luck was out with Mrs. Gadda, Mrs. Meyrick, and Ribuffi. But gradually, as time went by without his bad luck changing, uneasiness in high police echelons began to grow. The "43" was raided, without Goddard's prior knowledge, by officers from outside his division; they found illegal drinking there on an extensive scale; Mrs. Meyrick admitted it, and was sent down for six months.

That substantially deepened the doubts of Goddard's probity, but still gave insufficient ground for taking drastic steps.

It was a letter to the Chief Commissioner that touched off the climax, and brought the storm raging down on the delinquent's head.

"*I am desirous*", this anonymous letter opened formally, "*of bringing a matter of great public importance to your notice. It concerns the activities of Sergeant Goddard. . . .*"

The writer then roundly denounced Goddard for taking bribes from various club and house proprietors, and declared that Goddard's capital assets and his mode of life were totally unrelated to his police remuneration.

"*I would suggest*", the nameless accuser then concluded, "*that if you caused officers to inquire into the truth of the statements contained in this communication, they would all be proved both in substance and in fact.*"

Secret inquiries were accordingly made into the second, more easily checked, assertion. The results may, not extravagantly, be termed sensational.

Goddard possessed a freehold house, a Chrysler car, two prosperous bank accounts, and three Deposit safes—one of which contained £12,000 in cash.

His wages stood at £6. 15s. 0d. a week.

Confronted with these discoveries, Goddard declared that he had been lucky on the horses and in currency speculations. He did not, at that stage, condescend to details. Hauled up before a Disciplinary Board, he pleaded guilty to Neglect of Duty (failing to account for large sums received by him from unknown sources) and Discreditable Conduct (betting, and associating with bookmakers). "I shan't say anything; I don't want to disgrace the force", he said.

When the Disciplinary Board dismissed him from the service, Goddard may well have thought that now the worst was over; that a full-scale criminal prosecution would not follow. But patient research into the previous history of the banknotes richly lining his Deposit safes successfully traced the source at least of some. They had been paid out, by their bank managers, out of their bank accounts, to Mrs. Meyrick, Mrs. Gadda, and Ribuffi.

From that moment, a graver sequel became inevitable; and in January, 1929, at the Old Bailey, alongside of Mrs. Meyrick and Ribuffi (Mrs. Gadda had prudently gone abroad), ex-Sergeant Goddard came face to face with Nemesis. . . .

Avory looked through rather than at, the prisoners as they were brought up and disposed before him. Not a particle of emotion softened the lines of that gaunt and shrivelled face. People might have supposed —people often did suppose—that no human blood flowed through those knotty veins; only the distilled water of cold intellect.

If Goddard did not feel a sinking of the heart when his eyes absorbed the little deity, he was more intrepid—or less sensitive—than most.

The Crown, naturally enough, were unable to produce direct evidence of bribes actually passing; Mrs. Meyrick and Ribuffi denied giving, as strongly as Goddard denied receiving, them. So the practical issue for the jury to decide was: *Where had Goddard got his money from?*

Did Mrs. Meyrick and Ribuffi—to say nothing of Mrs. Gadda—*give* him the banknotes that had been traced back? If so, there was room for only one construction.

Might he, though, have come into possession of them in some other way? That was the sole—the only possible—defence.

Avory sat silent and impassive while Goddard struggled to establish this defence on oath. The judge entered without comment in his note

15

the explanations tendered for that carefully hidden fortune: to successful bets with street bookies ("£7,000 or £8,000") and successful gambling in francs ("£2,000 or £3,000") Goddard now added an interest in a music business ("about £5,000"), and in the sale of rock at Wembley Exhibition ("about £4,000").

There was no documentary mark, he said, of these transactions; being a police officer he desired none. He took his gains, as they accrued, in Treasury notes, and—for easier storage—changed them into banknotes as opportunity occurred. Changed them with anyone he met who had the banknotes: club proprietors, club *habitués* (including his informers), respectable West End residents such as Mrs. Gadda (who, Goddard claimed, had been slandered and traduced).

Suddenly Avory leaned forward. Only an inch or two, but he had been so motionless that the effect was like that of a movement by a statue.

"Why didn't you tell the Disciplinary Board that you had acquired the money in the way you have told us that you did?"

The dry, slightly crackling, voice made the question an accusation also.

"I knew," said Goddard, "that in any case I should be relegated or dismissed."

"If you didn't give an account?"

"At that time I didn't anticipate criminal proceedings."

"Why didn't you give an account?"

"I didn't want to bring the names of my friends into the matter."

"Why," persisted Avory remorselessly, "were you so anxious to protect their names?"

Goddard licked his lips.

"I didn't anticipate my coming here," he said again.

It buzzed all through the building: *Avory's against him.*

Any lingering doubts that this conclusion was well-founded were totally dispelled by his lordship's summing-up. Goddard's counsel had legitimately dilated on his client's good character and excellent police record, and urged that these should count in favour of his credibility. Avory, however, would not brook that argument. "What is the use of parading his career before you," he said to the jury, in that same dry, slightly crackling voice, "when he himself had to admit that for years past he has been systematically amassing money by breach of the regulations under which he held his office?"

A just point, doubtless, but a merciless one, too.

It was, though, when the jury—after a long absence—pronounced a guilty verdict upon all three accused that the instrument of retribution reached its pinnacle. Mrs. Meyrick and Ribuffi were each sentenced to fifteen months' hard labour. Stiff, but the real flailing was reserved for Goddard.

Unlike them, of course, he had held a position of trust. But unlike them also, he had lost a reputation, a pension, and a job. Avory gave him eighteen months' hard labour. He ordered him to pay the costs of the prosecution. He imposed a fine on him of £2000.

Reeling under this shower of blows, the prisoner feebly bowed and half turned to go below. But the pitiless recital had not ended. "If," the dry, slightly crackling voice continued, "that fine has not been paid when your sentence has expired, until it *is* paid you will remain in custody."

So ex-Sergeant Goddard painfully learnt that, in defiance of traditional mythology, Nemesis had a tail—and that the tail contained a sting in it.

Mr. Justice Cassels tries Daniel Raven

WHEN I heard that Daniel Raven would be coming up for trial at the last Old Bailey sessions of 1949, my immediate—and sustained—personal reaction was: Thank goodness, Jimmy Cassels will be trying him.

It is not from presumptuousness or in disrespect that one employs that familiar designation. Mr. Justice Cassels is generally so known by those who have professional connexion with the courts; it is at once a token of genuine affection and a spontaneous tribute to his warm humanity. But equally prominent among the judge's qualities are practical sense and businesslike behaviour; they had characterized his fine performances at the criminal Bar, and it was particularly comforting to know that at Raven's trial they would function on the Bench.

The special problem presented by the Raven case derived from the peculiar ethos of its time. In 1948 capital punishment, always a provocative issue, had aroused even more controversy than usual. The House of Commons had actually voted in favour of abolition; and for several months, until the Bill was thrown out by the Lords, convicted murderers were automatically reprieved. The consequent backwash of muddled thinking and confused emotion still influenced many in 1949. And Raven's crimes were of a type that might have eluded retribution simply because, on the subject of murder and its punishment, the public mind had been unsettled and bewildered.

It was rightly described as an "unnatural" story. On the evening of 10 October Raven, with his parents-in-law, Mr. and Mrs. Goodman, called at a nursing home in Muswell Hill to visit his wife and firstborn infant son. All three visitors drove from there to the Goodmans' home in Edgware, arriving—by Raven's own account—at half past nine.

17

Exactly how long Raven stayed is a matter of conjecture. One only knows for certain that he had gone by ten. For at that hour some other members of the family called, and, obtaining no reply, got in by a window.

The sight that met their eyes was described in court by Mr. Justice Cassels as "a shambles". Mrs. Goodman lay already dead, Mr. Goodman lay deeply unconscious and on the point of dying, in positions which suggested that she had come downstairs when she heard the attack on him. The injuries to both, said Cassels, were "fiendish in the extreme"; they had been slaughtered "almost with the ferocity of a maniac". And the photographs exhibited by the Crown were so unnerving that counsel warned the jury not to look at them till necessary, and the judge proposed that one should be omitted altogether. "It is so horrible," he said.

The instrument of this butchery had not been far to seek. A television aerial, previously in the hall, was found reposing in the kitchen sink. Its heavy base was copiously splashed and smeared with blood . . .

Now I am—I admit it—what is known as "defence-minded". I have an innate tendency to weight the rules concerning proof in a prisoner's favour—to interpret that decisive phrase "reasonable doubt" as though it included any grain of doubt at all. I feel uneasy about several convictions recorded at famous English trials of the past; not only glaring and manifest bad verdicts (like those on Edith Thompson and Steinie Morrison), but also some that are generally accepted and approved (like those on Norman Thorne and even Frederick Seddon).

But I have never felt the slightest qualm about the fate of Raven; the evidence against him was, in my view, overwhelming.

The Goodmans lived alone. Raven, in the temporary absence of his wife, was also living alone—five hundred yards away. Responding to an urgent summons from the little family group which had come upon calamity unawares, he appeared as astonished and as dumbfounded as they. That he had been expecting—and *preparing* for—such a summons, that he had looked upon this dreadful spectacle before, were imputations which—had anyone made them at that stage—Raven would have totally and strenuously denied. He had left the Goodmans fit and well, he said, and knew absolutely nothing more about them until a startling message brought him post-haste from his home.

He maintained that position, through a number of separate interviews, until late next afternoon.

Meanwhile, though, the police had been following up a clue spotted early on by a keen-eyed officer. Inspector Diller, observing those assembled at the stricken house, had noted the immaculate state of Raven's clothes: crisp shirt front, spotless cuffs and collar, jacket and trousers without a single wrinkle—not a mark, not a trace, of the busy, soiling day. The inquiries thus prompted bore significant fruit.

18

A telephone call to the nursing home at Muswell Hill established that, since leaving there, Raven had changed at least his suit. An inspection of Raven's house revealed a charred suit in the boiler—a suit on which could still be seen the stains of blood. Laboratory tests fixed that blood in the rare AB group—the group to which both Mr. and Mrs. Goodman had belonged.

These successive discoveries were damning. It was in an attempt to surmount them that Raven changed his story, adopting that which, substantially, he repeated in the box.

"After I left my parents-in-law," he said, "I went round to a cousin of mine, but got no answer. On the way home I had to pass the Goodmans' house; the lights were on, so I thought I'd go in again."

"And what did you see?" asked counsel.

"I saw Mrs. Goodman first. That face—I can never forget it—I felt sick. I knelt down beside her. Then I saw Mr. Goodman, too. I couldn't bear it—I couldn't stay in the room another moment. I stepped into the hall . . . and there I saw blood on my trouser leg."

The rest—the secret flight, the burning suit, the lies—were all explained away as the result of panic . . .

Raven's defenders could take little comfort from these facts. Their one strong card was purely psychological. Although large sums of cash were in the Goodmans' house that night, no robbery had been effected or attempted. Although feeling between his parents-in-law and Raven was lukewarm, no open quarrels had been remarked. It might, therefore, be plausibly said that the prisoner had no motive—a proposition guaranteed, even in more normal years, to give any jury pause.

But when the facts point ineluctably to a prisoner's guilt, what do people really mean when they say "he had no motive"? Merely that he had no *apparent* motive; no motive that they are able to *ascertain*. Who can tell, though, all that passes in another's mind? And what murderer voluntarily lays bare the springs of murderous action? Mr. Justice Cassels made this point with telling simplicity in his summing-up. "Men kill," he said, "for many reasons. They do not kill and leave statements of motive by the body."

The defence's contention upon this theme, however, embraced a positive as well as a negative side. Not only did they seek to show that Raven had no motive; they also sought to show that some other person had. Mr. Goodman often helped the police in currency matters; many rogues, they argued, had a score to settle with him. Wasn't this appalling crime the obvious work of an intruder bent upon revenge?

"It may have been," Mr. Justice Cassels said. "It may have been. Give it all your careful consideration." For a brief instant, he halted in reflection. "It was a *strange* intruder, wasn't it, who went to carry out such a design without any arms or weapons? And it was a *fortunate* intruder, wasn't it, because in the hall of the house he found the weapon to his hand? . . ."

Never is it a judge's business to *dragoon* a jury. Always it is a judge's business to *direct* a jury. The direction of Mr. Justice Cassels was both sound and firm, at a period when hysteria was both prevalent and infectious; and the subsequent dispatch of a double murderer reflects credit equally on the jury and on him.

Mr. Justice Darling tries the Romney Picture Case

"MRS. SIDDONS had a double chin," declared the witness. "The band round her neck in Gainsborough's portrait of her is to hold it up."

"I've always wondered," said the judge, "what that band was for, but I never imagined it was a kind of truss."

For at least the twentieth time within an hour, peals of delighted laughter rocked King's Bench Court 4. Anyone standing just outside the door might have supposed himself in the foyer of a theatre where some popular comedy of the day was being performed; perhaps the Duke of York's, where Miss Renee Kelly and Mr. C. Aubrey Smith were in "Daddy Long-Legs", or the Haymarket, where Miss Titheradge and Mr. McKinnel were in "General Post".

But it was simply that, after twenty years upon the Bench, Mr. Justice Darling had at last secured his ideal case, and was at the very peak of his form as a public entertainer.

To acknowledge frankly that side of Darling's character is not to discount his value and integrity as a judge. The cries of dismay from both the profession and the Press over his appointment in 1897—"He has no serious knowledge of the Law, and has never handled any important practice at the Bar"—proved, in the event, without justification, and had now long since been silenced and forgotten.

Sensational criminal trials (like those of Kitty Byron, Steinie Morrison, and Chicago May); acrimonious civil suits (like those of Robert Sievier and Lord Alfred Douglas); the dull routine of everyday litigation (private grievances, personal injuries, business disputes)—they were handled by Darling, if not with exceptional genius, at any rate with firm grasp and cool competence. In each and all it might be said that he earned his salary.

But he did not derive from them that peculiar satisfaction which is generally experienced by men who are in perfect temperamental harmony with their work.

Darling was a witty and artistic dilettante—using that term strictly in its better sense—who relished the polished surfaces of life and re-coiled from, or felt indifferent to, the turbulent and disorderly forces operating beneath. Although he concealed it admirably, the sensational criminal trials evoked in him distaste, the acrimonious civil suits occa-sioned him discomfort, the routine litigation left him bored.

His true delight was to preside over an intellectual disputation, elegantly conducted by sophisticated counsel, in which no deep emotion or high passions were aroused, and where the subject-matter furnished ample scope for his own brand of mocking drollery.

Never before, and never after, did he find all these conditions so consummately fulfilled as when the cause of *Huntington versus Lewis and Simmons* happily and appropriately came into his list.

Darling had rejoiced inwardly over the point at issue: was a picture of two ladies in eighteenth century garb a portrait of Mrs. Siddons and her sister by George Romney? He rejoiced still more over the setting for the controversy: Society beauties cheek by jowl with Royal Aca-demicians facing him expectantly in a solid phalanx. He rejoiced even more over his colleagues in the cast: those notable leaders, Sir John Simon and Mr. Leslie Scott. He rejoiced most of all when the former, before opening for the plaintiff, asked that the suspect picture might be displayed on an easel by his lordship's chair. No comic actor could have asked for a handier prop.

Darling's eyes twinkled a little in anticipation as Simon traced the picture's history. In February, 1912 it had been sold for 361 guineas as a Reynolds. In May Mr. Lewis, of Lewis and Simmons, well-known London art dealers, esteeming it a Romney, bought it for £717. Authori-tative opinion, confirming Mr. Lewis's own, further claimed to identify the female figures, and to link the picture with entries recording sittings by "two ladies" in Romney's Appointments Book on dates in 1776 and 1777.

So Mr. Huntington, an American millionaire, was given all three guarantees—guarantees of the painter, the painted, and the painting—when he paid a hundred thousand dollars for it in November.

"Would your lordship care to examine the work," said Simon, "for characteristics?"

"Characteristics of whom—Romney or Reynolds?" replied Darling.

"Or of Mrs. Siddons," Simon suggested helpfully.

Darling submitted the canvas to a critical appraisal.

"They certainly are remarkably small feet," he finally said.

Simon's attack was double-pronged. Diligent research appeared to indicate that young Mrs. Siddons, the wife of a strolling player who went the Oxford Circuit ("Before my time, I'm afraid," said Darling, with a wistful glance sideways at her contested likeness), had been a gloomy failure on her début at Drury Lane ("Many people when they hold their first briefs are," said Darling, with a sly glance downwards at the forensic luminaries), and had been playing continuously in

Liverpool and Manchester while Romney was supposed to be painting her in London.

The weight of evidence to this effect was such that the defendants soon conceded that they could not refute it; Mrs. Siddons could not possibly have been sitting for Romney on the relevant dates in his Appointments Book. But Darling intimated he would still find in their favour if they substantiated the primary guarantees: that, whenever the picture may have been done, Mrs. Siddons was the sitter, and, above all else, Romney was the artist.

The second prong of Simon's attack—and the defendants' counter-strokes—thus became the dominant feature of the trial. "It *is* Romney"; "It's *not* Romney"; "It *is* Siddons"; "It's *not* Siddons"—the battle of experts made a lively spectacle, and Darling quickly warmed to his gratifying task of pouring Attic salt upon the troubled waters.

When Simon requested permission to bring into court what he called "some *real* Romneys" for purpose of comparison, Darling said: "You may leave them here permanently, if you like."

When a rather opinionated art agent ("The draperies hanging on the lady's arm look like bicycle tyres hanging on a peg") admitted being wrong in his attribution of another picture, and cross-examining counsel sarcastically inquired what was his strong point, Darling said: "I should say it is giving evidence."

When the Director of the Irish National Gallery, asked if he wrote the essay on Romney for the Dictionary of National Biography, responded with the oddly phrased statement "I believe so", Darling said: "That is a very cautious answer for an expert."

When, opposing charges of anatomical error, Leslie Scott proposed to clasp hands with his junior precisely as the two ladies were doing in the picture, Darling said: "If you do, I shall expect to see you appearing at a music-hall as The Boneless Barrister."

When the defendant Mr. Lewis, in the box, declared he had originally bought the picture as a "knock-out", and defined this mystical expression as "where dealers do not bid against each other", Darling said: "What exactly happens? Do they stand in front of the picture and say; 'What wretched work'?"

"They don't make it out better than it is," said Mr. Lewis. "But I'm sure they don't stop the general public from bidding."

"That consoles me very much," said Darling.

The judge would not have been distressed if this delicious trial could have pursued its civilized and elevating course for ever. The atmosphere was amiable. The parties were well-off. No one challenged anyone else's bona fides. It was an honest difference of opinion between men steeped in art history and aesthetics, which they themselves took an ardent interest in resolving, and which prompted Darling to innumerable jests.

But on the seventh day, when there seemed far more to come, the Great Romney Picture Case suddenly collapsed.

A sketch had been belatedly unearthed which at once substituted fact for speculation. It was patently the rough sketch for the finished picture which stood upon the easel at his lordship's side. But, unlike the picture, the sketch had been initialled—by Ozias Humphry, one of Romney's artist friends.

The defendants threw in their hand with generosity and grace. Without delay or quibble, they agreed to return Mr. Huntington his purchase price, with interest; to pay the (extremely heavy) taxed costs of the action; and, of course, to take the much disputed picture back. In addition Mr. Lewis offered it to the National Portrait Gallery as Ozias Humphry's last surviving work in oils.

"He has not thought whether the Law Courts have a claim," said Darling.

"Perhaps," Sir John Simon murmured, "we might have a knock-out".

The last laugh, after all, was with the Bar. The last judgment, though, was with *The Times*. "Mr. Justice Darling," that paper wrote in a leading article next morning, "deservedly enjoys a high reputation for many qualities befitting his great office. But he does not improve it by the manner in which he too often chooses to conduct certain cases. The presence of a crowd of fashionable women come to hear a constant exchange of witticisms—some of which plainly bear the mark of previous elaboration—does not increase public respect for the administration of the law."

Some of which plainly bear the mark of previous elaboration—that, one feels, rather than *The Times*'s graver strictures, must have been for Darling the unkindest cut of all.

Lord Goddard tries the Laski Case

"YOU will remember that this is not a personal matter," said the Lord Chief Justice, summing up to the jury in the most spectacular suit for libel since the War. "It is eminently a political matter."

Lord Goddard had put the situation in a nutshell. The issue was not Harold Laski's private character, but his public utterances on public affairs. The Professor—an outstanding lecturer and writer, the bright particular star of the London School of Economics, and at that time also Chairman of the British Labour party—had made a speech in the Market Place at Newark during the election campaign of 1945. The local weekly newspaper reported him as saying that, if Labour could not obtain what it needed by general consent, " *We shall have to use violence, even if it means revolution*".

23

Professor Laski at once took out a Writ against the newspaper and its editor. They retorted that their report was fair and accurate, that those were words Professor Laski might be expected to use, and that for years he had been preaching violence and revolution through the medium of his voluminous published work.

Yes, it certainly was a highly political matter. But beneath the factual dispute about what Professor Laski said at Newark, and the semantic dispute about what he meant by certain passages from books like *Democracy in Crisis* and *Liberty in the Modern State*, there ran an undercurrent of intensely personal feeling—the antagonism existing between the famous plaintiff and the famous counsel on the other side.

It might seem odd that the *Newark Advertiser*, with its necessarily limited circulation, should be able to secure the costly services of the finest jury advocate at the Bar. But the local journal did not stand alone. Other papers—including the *Daily Express* and the *Evening Standard*—had given space and publicity to that fateful speech; the Professor had accordingly served Writs upon them also, and the consequent actions were set down for trial immediately after that against the *Newark Advertiser*. The result of the first action would probably be accepted, by winner and by loser alike, as the result of all; the defendants, therefore, sensibly combined their forces for it; and the *Daily Express*, assuming conduct of the litigation, briefed Sir Patrick Hastings to appear for the defence.

Harold Laski and Patrick Hastings: I knew, admired, and cherished a great affection for them both. Never, though, in my experience were two brilliant men temperamentally more inimical and less in harmony.

Laski was a magnificent theorist, a superb logician, with an open dislike for pure flair. Hastings was a magnificent improviser, a superb empiricist, with an open dislike for pure intellect. Laski was a Socialist through deep historical study and philosophical conviction which could survive any conflicts in or with the Labour party. Hastings had joined that party, without political grounding, through a vague, instinctive, desire to be "of use"; had been badly let down, as Labour's first Attorney-General, by Ramsay MacDonald over the Campbell case; and had retired from politics, "without any great regret", to consolidate a dazzling career in the courts.

Laski and Hastings: great figures, standing poles apart. They may have respected—I believe they did respect—each other. But they also irritated each other, even at a distance, and came close to hating each other in proximity.

It was as well that their long duel, the most dramatic feature of a most dramatic case, should have been refereed—in the circumstances, a not inappropriate term—by the strongest, as well as the senior, judge of the King's Bench Division.

Hastings began by narrowing the scope for dispute, the area for manœuvre. He did it with matchless expertise. As in a polished knife-

24

throwing act, the demarcating barbs flew unerringly into their assigned positions.

"Do you believe that the use of violence to achieve your political aims is practically inevitable?"

"No."

"Have you ever believed it?"

"No."

"Do you believe that if achievement of political aims can't be arrived at without the use of violence, then violence is justifiable?"

"Not in all circumstances. When a burden is intolerable, violence may be inevitable, but not otherwise."

"When you made this speech at Newark, did you believe then that if the aims of the proletariat could not be achieved without the use of violence, then violence was justifiable?"

"No."

"Do you agree that anyone who preached that doctrine would be a a public danger?"

"Yes."

"Have you preached it for twenty years?"

"No."

"If you had, you agree you would be a public danger?"

"Yes."

"Then we shall have to see what you have been preaching."

Hour by hour they went through quotations from the Professor's books. Laski kept complaining that they were taken out of context. Hastings kept pressing for unqualified replies. The tension between them steadily built up—and presently reached breaking point.

Hastings had been inviting Laski to elucidate a phrase: "The antithesis between the governors and the multitude."

"Doesn't that mean the capitalists and the socialists?"

"It means the privileged and the unprivileged," Laski said.

"Isn't that the same thing?"

"Not quite."

"*Are* there any privileged in the Socialist party?"

The temptation was there, and Laski could not resist it.

"Why, Sir Patrick," he began, "when *you* were a member——"

"No, Mr. Laski," intervened Lord Goddard warningly.

Laski stopped at once, but the shaft had got under Hastings's skin. "Don't be rude," he snapped.

"It's the last thing I want to be."

"It may be difficult for you to be courteous, but don't be rude. You're rude to everybody, aren't you?"

"I don't think so."

Normally Hastings was the coolest man in any court. Now, for a rarity, he had lost his temper—as was clearly demonstrated by what happened next.

"*I will just ask you a question I was not proposing to ask you.* You know that some people in this country possess religious beliefs, do you not?"

"Yes," Laski said; upon which Hastings put to him a past utterance which, he suggested, meant that Wesley had blackmailed factory workers into accepting bad conditions by specious promises of eternal life. Laski called that "a fantastic rhetorical exaggeration", and maintained that he was honestly expounding "the historical problem Wesleyism presents".

"Of course, when you are rude to other people, Mr. Laski, you think that is argument; when other people say something about you, you bring actions for libel." With that verbal score, Hastings's anger passed. "I will go on with this reading. I'm sorry I was taken off it for the moment, but I thought you were unnecessarily offensive."

Lord Goddard, like an eagle poised upon the Bench, had then swooped in order to restrain the witness. When circumstances warranted, however, he swooped with equal swiftness in order to protect him.

"Isn't that a terrifying theory?" Hastings asked, when Laski had affirmed some political belief.

"It is a theory," said Laski, "that Abraham Lincoln ——"

"Never mind about him," interrupted Hastings brusquely. "He is not in court."

"I think the witness is entitled to answer in that way," Lord Goddard said.

Hastings was both generous and prudent.

"I am sorry," he said. "I apologize to Mr. Laski."

Lord Goddard, always in complete command of his own court, no matter how redoubtable the witnesses and advocates, proceeded himself to tie up the loose ends.

"What you mean is," he said to Professor Laski, "that great people have led revolutions?"

"Yes, and have been held by posterity to be justified."

I venture to assert it is certain that Lord Goddard did not share Professor Laski's political opinions. "I have no politics," he said in his summing-up, "in the sense that I take part in politics or utter a word to show what politics I hold. But that does not mean that I have no views on politics." These views, however, did not colour in the least degree his scrupulously balanced observations to the jury. Harold Laski could not blame the Lord Chief Justice because they ultimately found for the defendants.

Some people say that Laski ought to have blamed himself, that he made an exceptionally bad witness. There is no doubt that he frequently *appeared* to split academic hairs and to dodge questions. But that appearance may have been due less to the defects of Laski than to the gifts of Hastings. The latter was a superlative cross-examiner, and

I believe that, confronted with almost any other contemporary counsel, Harold Laski would probably have won.

Mr. Baron Alderson tries Wood versus Peel

I T is not necessary—it is not even possible—for any judge to be intimately acquainted with the subject matter of every case he tries. Claims against tailors are not always best resolved by fashion experts, nor claims against doctors best resolved by trained physicians. But occasionally exercise of first-hand knowledge on the Bench does prove the determining factor of a trial, as was illustrated in the celebrated action arising from the Derby of 1844.

That year, although the race itself was uneventful, the events both preceding and succeeding it seem to issue straight from the pages of Nat Gould; one sensation followed another in such rapid sequence that the sporting world got breathless trying to keep up.

First, the favourite, Ratan, who had thus far been outstandingly the best among a rather mediocre bunch of three-year-olds, was poisoned in his stable by an undetected hand just before the race.

Next, a well-backed entry named Leander had a leg broken at the start through a kick from Running Rein—which then went on to win with extraordinary ease.

Next, the owner of Orlando, which ran second, successfully sought an order from the Court prohibiting the stakeholders from paying out the stakes to the owners of the winner—which he contended was not Running Rein at all but a substitute four-year-old (and therefore, on that count alone, ineligible to run).

Finally, the remains of Leander—which had been destroyed—were dug up and examined by veterinary surgeons, who unhesitatingly pronounced them a four-year-old's remains. So, if the allegations against Running Rein were true there had been at least *two* substitutions in the race; and one, by shrewd design or by fantastic accident, had violently removed the other from its path. . . .

It was against this melodramatic background, never paralleled in the Derby's history, that Mr. Wood, the owner of Running Rein, brought a suit against Colonel Peel, the owner of Orlando, for recovery of the stake money due to the rightful winner.

Public interest in the suit as such was bound to be immense; but when it is added that the Jockey Club had declared all bets off pending investigation, and that the jury's verdict would decide whether they remained off or came on again, one may better imagine the excitement that prevailed throughout the land on the day Mr. Baron Alderson began to hear the case in a court crammed with greater and lesser gentlemen of the Turf.

Their company, though, would not cause him to feel odd man out. The judge was a distinguished example of an old tradition—still vigorous in the nineteenth century, rather faded now—that leading lawyers should be very much at home on the racecourse, or the hunting field, or both. Mr. Baron Alderson needed no instruction in the technical aspects of Wood versus Peel. He knew about horses.

He also knew his mind.

He listened while plaintiff's counsel, Alexander Cockburn—who later prosecuted the notorious murderer Palmer, and was to become a memorable Chief Justice—asserted that the winning horse was the genuine Running Rein ("a colt by Saddler out of Mab in 1841"), and that Colonel Peel was merely a respectable front for some society gamblers who had bet heavily against the horse and now wanted to get out of paying when it had won. He listened while Cockburn produced a string of witnesses, who purported to trace in detail Running Rein's career from birth and to identify it at every single stage with the horse that had so lately won the three-year-old's blue riband. He listened— and as he listened he reflected.

Presently, as yet another enters the box, he intervenes.

"Is the horse here?"

Before Cockburn can—or does—reply, defendant's counsel has jumped smartly to his feet.

"Though we obtained an order from your Lordship for inspection of the horse," he says, "we have been refused permission to inspect it."

"We refused," Cockburn explains at once, noting the judge's frown, "because the manner in which inspection was demanded was improper."

"There may be a good reason for the refusal," the judge says, "but it will only be overlooked if the horse is produced now. I should like to see it myself. I should like to look at his mouth."

"Of course, my Lord, there will be no objection," Cockburn says.

Counsel appears to give some orders to those briefing him. Then he continues to call his evidence.

The court adjourns for lunch, and reassembles with no sign of the horse. Doubtless time is needed to transport a Derby winner; you can hardly lead it through the traffic in the streets. None the less, as the afternoon wears on, Mr. Baron Alderson grows visibly impatient; and soon after William Smith, the trainer of Running Rein, is sworn, this impatience finds vent in an explosion.

"Is the horse in your possession now?" he suddenly says.

Smith looks uneasy.

"No, it's not," he says.

"Where is it?"

"It was fetched away from me last Wednesday."

"By whom?"

"I had a verbal order from Mr. Wood to deliver it over to a man who called for it."

"And so," says the judge, in formidable tones, "you gave up this horse to a man who came to claim it, without any written order from Mr. Wood?"

"I thought . . ." Smith begins.

"No, no; I see the drift of it." The judge does not dissimulate his indignation. "This was the very day before my order reached the place —an order that was contemptuously disobeyed."

"When your Lordship's order was read to me," pleads Smith, "I said that, if they required, I would go to Mr. Wood and get his authority to hand over the horse."

"When the horse had been taken away, and you had no idea where! Why did you not say you hadn't got the horse?"

Smith shuffles helplessly.

"I wasn't asked the question."

"I don't believe you, sir," the judge declares flatly. "The horse was sent away in anticipation of my order; it was a gross contempt of court for which you will have to answer."

Counsel have remained as silent during this exchange as the spell-bound gentlemen of the Turf. But now Cockburn tries to protect his witness.

"My Lord, there will surely be time enough to discuss that when . . ."

"No doubt," the judge says curtly. "It seems to me that justice demands the production of this horse."

"There will be no objection, my Lord," Cockburn says again. "But my witnesses have proved identity."

"Let us have the advantage of seeing it."

"I regret," says Cockburn, as critically as he dares, "that this has made so great an impression on your Lordship's mind; if only . . ."

"I will tell you what has made a great impression on my mind: that is your anxiety to conceal this horse."

"But my Lord . . ."

"Produce the horse!" It was an imperative decree. "Produce the horse—that is the best answer to the question."

The next day's sitting ended with Mr. Baron Alderson still insistent upon his still unsatisfied demand.

That night there was fierce activity in the plaintiff's camp. And next morning, after the judge took his seat, Cockburn remained standing.

"Yes, Mr. Cockburn?"

"My Lord, after what fell from your lordship yesterday I feel extreme difficulty in attempting to proceed without producing Running Rein for the court's inspection."

"It is the only course to pursue," the judge observed sternly.

29

"Then, my Lord, I am left without any course at all. Last night, when my client went to the stables, he found that Running Rein had been taken away, without his sanction and against his will."

One or two gentlemen of the Turf could not suppress a whistle.

"A clear case of horse-stealing," said the judge, and went on meaningly: "If I ever try the parties who have removed him I will transport them for a certainty."

Cockburn made no comment. He simply said that his position had become untenable, and that he had no option but to submit to a verdict for the defendant. . . .

Nothing more was ever seen officially of the horse that won the Derby in the name of Running Rein and was subsequently disqualified in favour of Orlando. The mystery has therefore never been completely solved. But enough was uncovered to justify the statement that a gross fraud had been practised on the public—a fraud, however, in which the horse's owner had no part—and much of the credit for frustrating it belongs to Mr. Baron Alderson's equine expertise.

Judge Jeffreys tries Lady Alice Lisle

JUDICIAL outrages are not always the work of inhuman monsters. Most often the contrary is the case; they are the result of characteristically human failings and defects. In the three worst modern miscarriages of justice for which a judge has been wholly or partially responsible, Mr. Justice Stephen (who tried Florence Maybrick) was seriously sick, Lord Guthrie (who tried Oscar Slater) was unversed in criminal practice, Mr. Justice Shearman (who tried Edith Thompson) was unimaginative and vain. None, however, could be fairly described as malevolent or evil.

One must indeed turn back across the centuries to find the really classic exception to this rule—a judge whose countless abuses of his court were occasioned, not by lack of knowledge or want of faculty, but by wilful and deliberate wickedness; a judge who used his public office to indulge his private vice; a judge whose crimes—committed under the guise of legal process—far exceeded those of the prisoners he hounded.

Such a judge was that villain of our early history books, Judge Jeffreys.

Notwithstanding the usual pendulum swing of scholarly opinion, notwithstanding one or two literary attempts to whitewash him, Jeffreys remains, in the last analysis, true to his own legend—a judge possessed and bedevilled by an insane lust for cruelty.

30

Never was this appetite more shamelessly displayed than during the trial of Lady Alice Lisle.

That trial—if such a grotesque event can be thus called—took place in August, 1685 at Winchester, where Jeffreys was beginning a tour of the Western Circuit ever afterwards to be remembered as The Bloody Assize. His principal task upon that tour—entrusted to him by the new King, James II—was to secure the conviction of, and impose fierce punishment on, all those West Country folk then standing accused of complicity in Monmouth's abortive insurrection (a task so greatly to Jeffreys' personal taste, and discharged by him with such fidelity and fervour, that within a month more than 300 had been hanged).

It was not alleged that Lady Lisle, an aged, ailing widow, had been an active rebel. It was alleged, though, that she had *harboured* a rebel, and because of this allegation she faced a charge of treason with Jeffreys as her judge and God as her sole shield.

The facts—before Jeffreys had recast and supplemented them—were few, simple and virtually undisputed. Lady Lisle was an extremely devout Christian, without sectarian prejudice, who felt a respect amounting almost to reverence for any divine of any denomination. Consequently, when she received a request, through a tradesman of a neighbouring town, to shelter a Nonconformist minister, she did so.

In that period of bitter religious persecution, dissenting clergy were often on the run, and Lady Lisle, in her charity, had sheltered them before. It so happened, though, that this particular incident occurred immediately after Monmouth's rebellion had collapsed at Sedgemoor, and that this particular minister had been at Monmouth's side.

But did Lady Lisle know this when she took him beneath her roof? There could be no *evidence* that she knew unless the intermediary tradesman, a man by the name of Dunne, would say upon oath that he had told her so himself. Dunne (as the Crown—and also the judge—were well aware) was honest, and determined that he wouldn't. Jeffreys, on the other hand, was dishonest, and determined that he should.

As Dunne enters the box, Jeffreys greets him with a scowl intended as a portent of forthcoming favours. And these are not long delayed. For prosecuting counsel, asking leave to treat Dunne as a hostile witness, craftily suggests that my lord might deign to conduct his examination "with more than the customary strictness".

My lord is nothing loath. With some reassuring references to eternal flames and bottomless lakes of fire, and a friendly promise to punish the slightest prevarication, he gathers his robes about him and begins.

What reward did Dunne receive for acting as Hicks's (the minister's) envoy? None. How far is it from Dunne's home to Lady Lisle's? Twenty-six miles. How often did Dunne make the journey? Twice: once to convey Hicks's appeal, once to direct him thither.

"You are a baker, are you not?" the judge demands, in a manner implying that baking is an acknowledged crime.

"I am, my Lord," says Dunne.

"Do you bake bread at such easy rates as those at which you lead rogues into lurking-holes?" As Dunne stands silent Jeffreys adds: "But I assure thee, thy bread is very light weight; it will not pass the balance here. Hast thou a horse?"

Dunne says that he has not; that he rode to Lady Lisle's on one lent him by a friend of Hicks's—a man he did not know.

"How came he then to trust thee with his horse?" sneered Jeffreys. "By the little I know of thee, I wouldn't trust thee with two pence."

Having thus proclaimed unmistakably, his opinion of the witness, Jeffreys now sets out to bend him to his will—so to terrorize him by fulmination and abuse and threats that in the end he will give such answers as the judge desires.

It is a macabre farce—somehow intensified as the evening wears on, and it proceeds by candlelight. Dunne is a "vile wretch"; it is "infinite mercy on the part of the Almighty not to strike him instantly into hell"; he "cants", he "snivels", he "lies", he "forswears himself"; Turks have greater title to eternal bliss than he.

The very rafters of the court ring with Jeffreys's bellowing. A stronger man than Dunne might have been confused and shaken by the time he was brought face to face with the question of what actually passed between himself and Lady Lisle.

Jeffreys's approach to this crucial matter is oblique. A man named Barter, who lives in Lady Lisle's locality, and who guided Dunne on the last few miles of his visits to her, has sworn that she asked if Barter knew anything of the business he was on, and that Dunne gave her a negative reply.

"The business"—a highly non-committal phrase; but Jeffreys saw its possibilities and prepares to exploit them now. "Did you tell my lady that Barter knew nothing of the business he was on?"

Yes; Dunne admits it.

"*What* business? Tell us *what* business?"

Dunne looks up; looks down; says he can't recall.

"Can't recall!" Jeffreys flings up his arms. "Oh, how hard the truth is to come out of a lying Presbyterian knave! I charge thee—what was that business you and my lady spoke of?"

Dunne looks up longer; looks down longer still; at last says he can give no account of it.

"Oh blessed God!" cries Jeffreys, "Was there ever such a villain on the face of the earth? Oh blessed Jesus, what a generation of vipers do we live among!" He leans over his desk like a springing beast of prey. "*What business did you speak of?*"

Dunne can apparently hold out no more. He drops his voice to a whisper—but he answers.

"She asked me . . . Lady Lisle asked me . . . whether I did not know that Hicks was a Nonconformist."

Jeffreys was enraged when he could not get an answer. Now he has got—to him—a useless one, he is quite beside himself.

"Dost thou think," he thunders, "after all these pains I have been at, that thou canst banter me with such sham stuff as this?" A pernicious inspiration seizes him. "Hold up the candle—hold it up—that we may see his brazen face."

This grisly piece of pantomime proves decisive. As the candle is held close to his cheek, Dunne gives way to despair.

"My Lord, I am so baulked," he falters, "I do not know what I say myself. I am cluttered out of my senses; *tell me what you would have me say.*"

Tell me what you would have me say. It is the signal of Dunne's complete collapse. It is also the most terrible indictment of a judge delivered by a witness in the annals of our courts. . . .

Even then the verdict was not a foregone conclusion. Although Dunne (whom Jeffreys had ordered Crown Counsel to charge with perjury) now went so far as to say that he had heard Hicks talk with Lady Lisle of the army and the fighting; although the judge persistently interrupted the prisoner's attempt to speak on her own behalf; although the jury were told from the bench that her guilt was plain as the sun at noon—none the less, on their first return to court, they declared themselves unwilling to convict. It was only after a further harangue from his lordship that, with obvious reluctance, they pronounced her guilty.

Jeffreys sentenced the old lady to be burnt alive. He did not conceal his gratification. After some uncomfortable birth pangs, the Bloody Assize had satisfactorily begun.

Mr. Justice McCardie tries
Lieutenant Malcolm

E VERYBODY wanted the prisoner to get off.
      The privileged and breathless company in court, gripping their precious seats from a sub-conscious fear of losing them; the unlucky and disappointed throng outside, unable to tear themselves away from the fortress they had failed to storm; the unseen multitude across the length and breadth of Britain devouring each edition of the papers, and then waiting in mingled hope and apprehension for the next— one and all devoutly wished Lieutenant Malcolm to go free. Even that granite prosecutor, Richard Muir, whose thankless task it was to present this murder charge, momentarily disclosed the trend of his own feelings when he warned the jury: "*Beware of sympathy*".

For what exactly had he done, this stalwart fighting soldier, to be snatched from peril of death in the Flanders trenches and placed under the selfsame peril in the Old Bailey dock?

In August, 1914, when the First World War broke out, Douglas Malcolm seemed a man more than ordinarily blessed. Thirty years old, he had means, he had good looks, he had social position, he had a beautiful young bride. There was no conscription at that stage, nor any thought of it; not even a moral obligation rested on married men. But without a day's delay Malcolm gallantly volunteered; husband and wife were thus abruptly wrenched apart, and, as the War dragged out its long and painful course, they were only to experience the briefest of reunions.

This fact precipitated an entanglement which finally exploded into violence and death.

In the July of 1917, Malcolm unexpectedly obtained a spell of leave, and hurried from France, unheralded, to London. His wife was not at home; he learnt that she was staying with a friend named Mrs. Brett at the latter's cottage in a rural part of Hampshire. Still unheralded, and entirely unsuspecting, Malcolm dashed out there as quickly as he could.

He found Mrs. Brett downstairs in a sitting-room, alone. His sudden entrance appeared to disconcert her, and his inquiries drew uninformative replies. Eventually, exploring the cottage on his own, he came upon his wife upstairs, in a bedroom. She wore a dressing-gown. With her was a man Malcolm had never seen before. He looked about his own age, and wore only underclothes.

The time was half past two or three o'clock in the afternoon. It was the kind of situation that is described as compromising.

Malcolm, however, did not believe that his wife had been unfaithful. He did believe she had been picked as prey by a seducer—and reacted in the approved style of medieval chivalry.

There and then he soundly thrashed the Count de Borch (for such was the title falsely assumed by the man in underclothes). Next he removed his wife from Mrs. Brett's over-indulgently hospitable abode. Finally ("Pistol or swords, you can take your choice") he wrote challenging the phoney noble to a duel.

This challenge, though renewed from France after Malcolm had returned, passed—not altogether surprisingly—unanswered. A crucial letter certainly arrived—but from his wife. Its purpose was to say she could not give up de Borch, and to ask her adoring husband for divorce.

Somehow or other, Malcolm got a further grant of leave, and on 11 August he was back again in London. At first he could find neither his wife nor her squalid cavalier. Even Scotland Yard could not help in this regard, though they could and did assure him that Baumberg (alias de Borch) was a thoroughgoing villain—a White Slave trafficker and possibly a spy. The notion of his beloved in such a creature's clutches fomented Malcolm's anger and hardened his resolve.

Three solid days of close investigation reaped reward. On 14 August, at quarter to eight in the morning, Malcolm rang the bell at a Bayswater lodging-house. Under his arm was skilfully concealed a hunting-crop. In one pocket of his civilian suit he carried a pistol; in another a letter addressed to his absent wife.

"My dear, very own, darling Dorothy," it said. "I simply cannot stand it any longer. I'm going to thrash him until he is unrecognizable. I may shoot him, if he's got a gun. I expect he has, as he's too much of a coward to stand a thrashing. If the inevitable has got to happen, I may get it in the neck first. I know I shall meet you in the next world."

Malcolm gave his name to the landlady as "Inspector Quinn". A moment later, she had led him to the third floor back. A moment later still, and he was inside—with de Borch.

The tenant of the adjoining room overheard a desperate struggle. Then there were four, or perhaps five, pistol shots.

Malcolm came out, and at once gave himself up. "I did it for my honour", he said when he was charged. . . .

The valiant warrior at the front; the unprotected wife at home; the vile snake in the grass that exploits their separation. Who could help bestowing all his sympathy on Malcolm? Even Crown Counsel—notwithstanding it was Muir. Even the judge—especially when it was McCardie.

In McCardie were linked a great head and a great heart. The former was already fully recognized, though he had not yet been twelve months upon the Bench; just as his speeches at the Bar, with their scholarly detachment, often bore the distinctive stamp of judgments, so his judgments, ranging wide in precedent and rooted deep in principle, often bore the distinctive stamp of ultimate analysis.

McCardie's strong humanity was at that time less well known; his advocacy had been precise rather than intense, and the years were yet to come in which his outbursts against the divorce laws and the penal system were to reveal him as more of a crusader than punctilious legal pundits deemed judicial. But the warm feelings that produced those later outbursts were always part and parcel of the man, and he could not privately have lacked commiseration for the tormented prisoner whom he had to try.

That did not, though, in the least deflect him from his public duty. The prerogative of mercy might be applied by others. Meanwhile, however, McCardie was determined that a verdict should be reached by proper process of the law.

The judge noted, as the Crown story was unfolded and the Crown witnesses were called and cross-examined, that certain evidence supported Malcolm's plea of self-defence; supported the contention of his counsel, Sir John Simon, that "the struggle in that little room became a matter of de Borch's life—or of his own".

Malcolm's expectation had been right—de Borch did have a gun; he had bought one shortly after his thrashing at the cottage; he had exhibited it to Mrs. Brett—she told Sir John—with the remark that if Malcolm laid a finger on him, he would use it.

The police had found that gun when they searched de Borch's room; in a drawer that was, significantly, open. The gun, however, still lay inside its leather case—a point which obviously exercised McCardie, but which he in some measure cleared up for himself.

"Could it have been fired," he asked, "without being taken from the case?"

"Yes," the Crown ballistics expert said, "if the case was open so that the muzzle was exposed."

Less helpful, on the other hand, to the cause of the accused were the words, recorded by an escorting officer, which he uttered before de Borch's body had grown cold. "I went to give him a good thrashing," Malcolm said. "Can you wonder what I did on the spur of the moment when I saw the man who was bringing my wife to dishonour?"

On the spur of the moment. Did that mean—could that mean—an act of self-defence?

McCardie, though, was the last man to forget that people speaking under high emotional stress seldom care about the niceties of language. Too much weight could be attached to mere semantics. The gun in the drawer—there lay the key to the whole problem. *If* de Borch had been trying to get at it; *if* he had succeeded in opening the drawer; *if* the next second would have seen it in his hand . . .

But these, so far, were matters of surmise. What light would Malcolm throw upon them in the box?

None. Malcolm did not go into the box. Whether on Sir John's advice or at his own desire, he took his stand upon the evidence tendered by the Crown—reinforced, of course, by his counsel's eloquence falling on receptive, and even eager, ears.

McCardie, whatever may have been his secret sentiments, scrupulously fulfilled his ordained function as a judge. He commented severely upon the prisoner's silence. "This man stands indicted with the gravest charge," he said, "and offers not one word of testimony. He invites you to guess things he could have proved on oath. The result is there's no evidence that the dead man tried to get the pistol; that he ever threatened to use it; that the pistol was even in the room. The whole thing is simply left open to conjecture."

The jury retired, and, presumably, conjectured. In twenty-five minutes they returned with an acquittal, and Lieutenant Malcolm stepped from the dock amid resounding cheers.

What McCardie really felt about those cheers one does not know. He contented himself with a prim expression of regret that the deliberation of the court had been disturbed by hubbub.

Mr. Justice Swift tries the
Mongoose Case

THERE may have been greater judicial *wits* than Rigby Swift, but never a judge with richer *humour*, a livelier sense of *fun*.

You could usually read it in his face—a cherubic moon with wide mischievous eyes, and lips parted as though in constant readiness to smile. You could usually hear it in his voice—in those full, warm tones, laced with a Northern accent, which conveyed an almost boyish zest for merriment. You could usually experience it, and even share it with him, whenever he tried a civil cause in which there lay one spark of potential comedy.

But there was no readiness to smile, no zest for merriment, no truck with comedy on the part of Mr. Justice Swift that November morning back in 1936. He was angry—and his anger could be frightening to behold. . . .

And yet, initially, this jury suit for slander—now in its third successive day at the Royal Courts of Justice—had seemed what the theatrical profession call a "vehicle" for the display of Swift's most familiar characteristics.

Mr. Richard Lambert, then editor of *The Listener*, complained that Sir Cecil Levita, then well known in public life, had told Mr. Gladstone Murray of the B.B.C.—significantly tapping his forehead as he did so —that Lambert was, in effect, mentally unbalanced, and that the B.B.C. should get him off the British Film Institute Council (where he and Lady Levita had come into sharp conflict).

Sir Cecil denied saying so, but pleaded that if he had done (as Mr. Gladstone Murray swore) the occasion would have been privileged and the statement justified.

All this was doubtless serious enough for Mr. Lambert—and was to prove, in the upshot, even more serious for Sir Cecil. But the allegations relied on by the latter to support and establish his justification plea could hardly have failed to provoke mirth among others— quite irrespective of their falsity or truth.

It was said that Mr. Lambert dabbled in the occult; that he had more than once changed house to escape the Evil Eye; and that he believed in the existence of a ghostly talking mongoose, which supposedly haunted a farm somewhere on the Isle of Man, and about which he had written a book, with a psychical specialist, describing their joint investigations on the spot.

Quotations from this book, put to the plaintiff in the box, made the mongoose temporarily chief figure of the action and certainly its most convenient symbol on the posters. No matter that Mr. Lambert desperately protested that he had always considered the mongoose was a fraud. "Mongoose: Latest"; "Mongoose: Speeches"; "Mongoose: Jury Out"—the variations replaced each other in an unbroken sequence on the streets.

The Mongoose was named Gef, one learnt, and was eighty-six years old. It knew Russian, Flemish, Italian, Arabic, Hebrew, Welsh, and Hindustani. It sang nursery rhymes. It practised the tonic sol-fa scale. It was interested in flying. It killed a great many rabbits, but never out of season, and could on occasion turn itself into a cat.

The recital of Gef's personal history and accomplishments naturally created a hilarious atmosphere to which Swift's contributions were eagerly awaited. At least once he obliged. "Does a Manx mongoose have a tail?" he inquired—a rather better spoken jest than cold print will allow. But the judge appeared less than customarily puckish. Some even imagined him unwell, or out of sorts. But more likely his keen forensic instinct had detected in the skein of the case a darker thread than simple defamation; a thread only first—and then but partially —uncovered when Sir Patrick Hastings, for the plaintiff, was questioning the defendant.

"Did you tell Mr. Gladstone Murray," asked Sir Patrick, "that, if Mr. Lambert were not dismissed from the Film Institute Council, you would go to see your friend Mr. Norman, the chairman of the B.B.C.?"

"No," replied Sir Cecil.

"Did you in fact go to see Mr. Norman very soon after you had seen Mr. Gladstone Murray?"

"Yes," replied Sir Cecil.

"Did you go to see him about Mr. Lambert?"

"When I appreciated," Sir Cecil Levita said, "that there had been a gross misunderstanding between Mr. Gladstone Murray and myself concerning what I had said about the plaintiff, I decided that, in the interests of both the Film Institute and the B.B.C., the truth should be made known, so I went to Mr. Norman."

"Why go to the plaintiff's employer and tell him your side of the case?"

Swift had listened with gradually lowering brows as this exchange developed. There were colleagues who excelled him in the splitting of legal hairs and the niceties of construction, but none in stalwart championship of individual freedom and individual rights. He did not like what he thought that this portended—and he liked it even less when it actually took shape.

Sir Cecil Levita completed his evidence on the second afternoon. Swift's continuing stern mood was unmistakable as he took his seat upon the Bench next morning. It brooded like a thundercloud over the court—fitting accompaniment to the forked lightning of Sir Patrick Hastings, by which the sorry business was finally exposed. . . .

Mr. Fuller—a governor of the British Film Institute—had made his bow as a very minor witness. Sir Cecil's counsel called him on one or two points of detail; most probably expecting, and quite certainly intending, his spell in the limelight to be short and uneventful.

Sir Patrick, however, determined otherwise.

"Do you know"—he began his cross-examination—"that the Writ in this action is dated March the 5th?"

"Yes," said Mr. Fuller.

"Did you ask the plaintiff for lunch on March the 24th?"

"Yes," said Mr. Fuller.

"Between those dates, did you see Sir Stephen Tallents, the head of Public Relations at the B.B.C.?"

"Yes."

"Did anyone ask you to go and see Sir Stephen Tallents?"

"Specifically, no."

"Did you go to see him about this action?"

"Yes."

"What in the world had it to do with you?"

"Nothing at all."

Swift's face had reddened slightly with his rising indignation. He glared at the witness, then glared down at the cluster in the well.

"Did Sir Stephen Tallents ask you to do your best to stop this action?" Sir Patrick went on suavely.

"No."

"What did he say?"

"That Mr. Lambert was suffering from a nervous breakdown."

"Did you understand from that that he had gone out of his mind?"

"No," said Mr. Fuller. "Just that he was run down in health."

"What in the world had it to do with you?"

"Nothing at all."

Swift snorted. He would have dearly liked to join in the questioning himself, but Sir Patrick was now in full and devastating spate.

"Did you go to see Sir Stephen Tallents with the object of persuading the B.B.C. to stop this action?"

"I went to try to get a settlement of the action," admitted Mr. Fuller.

"Did you get information from Sir Stephen Tallents which you gave to Mr. Lambert at that lunch?"

"Yes."

"Did you tell Mr. Lambert that Sir Stephen Tallents had told you, if he didn't persist in his action, the B.B.C. would treat him well?"

"No."

"Did you tell Mr. Lambert that Sir Stephen Tallents had told you that, if he persisted, the B.B.C. would turn him out?"

"Certainly not."

"What in the world has this action to do with the B.B.C.?"

"Nothing at all."

The judge was now making visible efforts to restrain himself. All his worst suspicions were confirmed as Sir Patrick dexterously dealt his *coup de grace*.

"Did you later get to know of a memorandum made by Sir Stephen Tallents about this action?"

"Yes."

"Did you discuss that memorandum with Sir Cecil Levita?"

"Yes."

"Is *this* a copy of that memorandum?"

"Yes."

Instantly defendant's counsel was upon his feet. Swift, however, firmly overruled his objection.

"Let the memorandum be read aloud," he said.

The effect of its essential part was stunning. "*I saw Mr. Lambert on 6 March*," Sir Stephen had recorded. "*I told him I was instructed to tell him that if he went on with the course which he had indicated the previous morning there was a serious danger that he might well prejudice his position with the corporation, because (1) he could make the corporation doubt his judgment, and (2) he could seem to be placing his own interests in priority to those of the corporation. . . .*"

Summing up that afternoon, the judge did not reject the chance to speak his mind. "It is a dreadful thing," he said with solemn emphasis, "that, when a man brings an action demanding redress for a wrong, his employers should be approached behind his back and asked to bring pressure to bear on him to settle."

The jury awarded punitive damages against Sir Cecil Levita; the enormous sum of £7,500. As Swift, having granted judgment accordingly, left court for the day, it was noted that he had regained much of his normal cheerfulness.

Lord Chief Justice Alverstone tries Horace Rayner

A T the time of his violent death in 1907, Mr. William Whiteley enjoyed a public esteem that bordered upon reverence.

He had personally founded and built up the great Bayswater store which remains his monument. Although seventy-six, his appetite for work had not diminished and he still exercised control over his self-made empire. He appeared the symbol, almost the incarnation, of those qualities currently most praised; individual initiative, unremitting industry, and the special aptitudes which bring success in business.

So when the British people learnt, one January afternoon, that Mr. Whiteley had been shot by a caller at his office who had contrived to secure admission through imposture, their first reaction was to treat it as a heinous crime and to call for the blood of the heinous criminal.

But when presently they discovered that the captured culprit claimed to be Mr. Whiteley's illegitimate son—a son who, having long endured extremes of poverty, had implored help in vain from his wealthy father, common feeling underwent complete revulsion. The dead titan was widely stigmatized as a stony-hearted parent and an immoral humbug; and the reflected wave of sympathy with his young assailant reached its highest peak on the day he faced his trial.

It has never been conclusively established whether Horace Rayner was or was not Whiteley's natural son—or whether he honestly believed himself to be. There was no doubt that Whiteley had had a liaison with Rayner's aunt, whom he afterwards granted an allowance. And there was equally no doubt that the relationship, if any existed, between Whiteley and Rayner could not properly affect the issue of the trial at all. Sons are not entitled to kill their fathers for refusing them money; not even if the son then turns the gun upon himself and—as Horace Rayner did—blows out one of his eyes.

No one knew that better than George Elliott, K.C., the practised defender who appeared for the accused. His tactics were the best that could have been adopted in a well-nigh hopeless situation. While making at least a show of fighting on the facts for an outright acquittal (the prisoner swore that he had only threatened to shoot as a "last card" and had never intended to carry out his threat), Elliott also raised the question of Rayner's mental state. He appreciated that a jury influenced by sympathy—whether or not that sympathy had adequate foundation—would welcome an excuse to find the prisoner insane.

Before this could become a practical possibility, however, the defence had to reckon with their judge.

Lord Alverstone—who had formerly been Sir Richard Webster—was a man who excelled in every phase of his profession. He had enjoyed one of the largest private practices at the Bar; had made an admirably efficient Law Officer of the Crown; and was now almost exactly half way through what was to be a tenure of thirteen years as Lord Chief Justice. During that time he earned a place among the very best of those who have occupied that great and honoured post.

Alverstone was a sound lawyer of strong character, who sat to dispense justice *according to the law*; he did not consider mass emotion a trustworthy guide, nor did he look with any degree of favour upon verdicts obtained by forensic sleight-of-hand. Insanity, as a criminal defence, was defined and governed by the M'Naghten rules; the onus lay squarely on an accused to prove either that he did not know what he was doing, or that he did not know that it was wrong; psychiatric pressure groups had not then made their mark on the administration of law and punishment. The M'Naghten rules were as clear as they were binding, and the Lord Chief Justice was fixedly resolved that they should not be obscured or circumvented.

He listened, courteously but warily, as George Elliott opened the prisoner's case. He noted the tendentious and emotive phrases, following one another in steadily mounting force; "Fits of depression"; "felt his position acutely"; "gradually operated on a mind never of powerful equilibrium"—the way was skilfully prepared for a bold culminating statement that "there are men and women who have mental explosions, when they are sometimes guilty of acts of impulsive insanity".

Impulsive insanity—what exactly did that mean? The Lord Chief Justice stroked his chin reflectively, and thought again about the M'Naghten rules.

He was still thinking about them when the two doctors were called for whom Elliott's semi-medical discourse had been an introduction. Both strove manfully. They referred to Rayner's poverty; to his lack of regular food; to his distress of mind occasioned by anxiety. These factors, they said, would progressively weaken his self-control, and make him an easier prey of impulse in a crisis.

It was well calculated to exploit any nebulous and arbitrary feelings of compassion. But—as Lord Alverstone instantly perceived—the doctors only tendered one single piece of evidence that mattered in court, as distinct from a consulting-room. And even that single material piece of evidence did not emerge until their cross-examination.

"Do you say the prisoner was, or is, insane?" prosecuting counsel bluntly asked of each in turn.

"No, I do not," each honestly replied.

That was that—twice neatly underlined. Even according to Harley Street, always less exacting in these matters than the Temple, Rayner did not qualify for deliverance by derangement. When the prosecutor submitted that there was no evidence to support a plea of insanity, Alverstone agreed. "You can dismiss that question from your minds," he told the jury. "There is no loophole for supposing that the prisoner didn't know perfectly well what he was doing."

The ensuing verdict was quite inevitable—and so, it then appeared to one exceptional authority, was the penalty that Rayner would be required to pay. Passing sentence of death, the Lord Chief Justice warned him not to entertain "the slightest hope" that this sentence might later be commuted.

It is indeed difficult, even after more than half a century has passed, to think of any valid reason why it was. The nature of Rayner's crime stands out in sharp outline. He went to Whiteley with the idea of blackmail, assuming that a man so rich and so respected would pay up handsomely rather than run the risk of scandal. He took a pistol with him to reinforce, if necessary, more orthodox persuasion. When he found Whiteley unyielding to every form of pressure, the infuriated Rayner wreaked summary vengeance; and then tried to anticipate—a pity he failed—the hangman.

There were no grounds whatsoever to justify a reprieve.

And yet—unlike Mr. Bridgeman who remained adamant (wrongly) in the case of Edith Thompson, and unlike Sir David Maxwell Fyfe who remained adamant (rightly) in the case of Derek Bentley—the Home Secretary concerned with Rayner (Mr. Herbert Gladstone) gave a decision which, coincidentally or not, satisfied vociferous popular demand.

Comment on that is best left to Alverstone himself, writing, years later, with judicial detachment. "The crime was a deliberate one," he said, "but, for some reason which I was never able to fathom, the then Home Secretary advised remission of the sentence."

Lord Braxfield tries Deacon Brodie and George Smith

LORD BRAXFIELD was a sound lawyer, a clear logician, a shrewd judge. He was also a rough talker, an impatient listener, a conceited egotist.

This combination of characteristics made him, during his tenure of the Scottish Bench, an intolerant and intimidating despot who mercilessly crushed opposition to his will. And it was in the full blaze of this alarming reputation, at the full height of these formidable powers, firmly installed as Lord Justice-Clerk (the second highest office in the Scottish judiciary) strongly buttressed by four of his most learned colleagues, that Braxfield took his seat at Edinburgh in August, 1788 to preside over the trial of Deacon Brodie and George Smith.

No doubt Braxfield was right in thinking that both prisoners (Brodie a distinguished figure of the city, Smith merely an obscure confederate in the other's hitherto unsuspected double life) were guilty, and ought to be convicted, of the house-breaking and robbery with which they were jointly charged.

No doubt he was right to reject a defence submission that testimony by two turn-coat members of their criminal gang—testimony without which the Crown could not succeed—should be excluded, for technical reasons, as inadmissible.

No doubt he was right to condemn certain comments on that ruling subsequently made by counsel to the jury. From a purely legal stand-point, no complaint of substance can be fairly laid against him.

It was not the matter but the manner of Braxfield's interventions, not what he did but the way in which he did it, that earns for his conduct of this trial the adjective outrageous—and that in court gave rise to an unprecedented scene as the dreaded tyrant was openly defied by a youthful, but intrepid, advocate. . . .

John Clerk, representing the prisoner Smith, had been less than three years in professional practice. Upon an advocate so relatively inexperienced, the defence of any contested charge must impose a nervous strain. The strain greatly increases when the charge is capital (as housebreaking then was), and he knows himself to be entrusted with his client's life.

The strain reaches an uncomfortable peak if the proceedings are a focus of public interest and excitement—and to such a degree had the split personality of Brodie gripped the imagination of his fellow citizens that troops had to protect the courthouse from the milling crowds.

Even in the harsh forensic ethos of the eighteenth century, an unknown junior shouldering such a burden might reasonably have expected consideration from a judge.

But not from Braxfield. It is doubtful whether the latter, bestowing his usual preliminary glare upon the ranks of counsel—adorned on this occasion by the Lord Advocate and the Solicitor-General for the Crown, and the Dean of Faculty (doyen of the Scottish Bar) for Brodie —consciously noted that, among these luminaries, somewhere Clerk was inconspicuously squeezed. If he did, and gave him a passing thought, it could only have been to resolve that—in the unlikely event of necessity arising—this novice should be swiftly taught his place.

The first growl of the lion in Clerk's direction, presaging the volley of roars that were to come, occurred when Smith's defender—opening his mouth for the first time—attempted to pursue an objection to the indictment which the Dean of Faculty had made on behalf of Brodie, and which their lordships had pronounced against.

"What!" Braxfield ejaculated, his rising tone a compound of astonishment and anger. "What! After the Court have delivered their opinions, it is not decent in you to propose to say anything." And then, as Clerk remained on his feet, he added, "I apprehend the prisoners are in no danger of suffering anything by *your* not being allowed to supply the defects of the Dean of Faculty."

The wounding sarcasm cracked like a whiplash. But Clerk, contrary to the onlookers' expectations, did not crumple.

"My lord," he said boldly, "the Dean of Faculty has no authority to plead for *my* client."

Braxfield, face like thunder, waved an arbitrary hand, and Clerk reluctantly sat down. Perhaps he realized he was, procedurally, in error.

Perhaps he recognized the argument was not vital to his cause. One can confidently affirm, at any rate, that he had not been overawed.

For presently the engagement was resumed—on a not dissimilar issue, but one in which Clerk stood on rather better ground.

He had objected to the Crown tendering Smith's wife as a witness because a woman could not, in law, give evidence against her husband; the Lord Advocate immediately declared that his questions to Mrs. Smith would concern Brodie only; Braxfield had decided that she should be sworn. "If anything should drop to her husband's prejudice," he said, "the jury are to give no attention to it."

"My lord——" Clerk began.

The spectacle of this audacious nobody again addressing him—as it appeared—out of turn excited the judge's wrath more sharply than before.

"What! What! Would you *insist* on being heard after the Court have spoken?"

"My lord," Clerk did insist. "I was only heard on the general point of the admissibility of this witness, but not on the special objections which I have to put."

"Mr. Clerk," Braxfield stormed, "this is really intolerable."

But his second castigation did not find Clerk without allies. The Dean of Faculty—interfering, he said, as holder of that office—thought that, even if Clerk were not strictly in order, "some indulgence ought to be shown to a young gentleman"; Lord Hailes from his exalted place at Braxfield's side, thought that counsel should be allowed to put the particulars he mentioned.

Braxfield controlled himself with an effort.

"Mr. Clerk, we will hear what you have to say."

Clerk's qualified triumph—the decision stood unaltered—left Braxfield in a continuous smoulder of concealed resentment which, at the slightest opportunity, flamed into overt rage. "That is not an answer to my question." Clerk remarked to one witness. "It is enough," Braxfield snapped, "to satisfy any *sensible* man." Similar sour pleasantries henceforward flavoured the trial's course.

The great explosion, though, did not take place until the court, with the object of concluding the case in one single session, had sat on without any real break far into the night. It is indeed already two o'clock in the morning when Clerk, having fortified himself in the robing-room with claret, faces the jury to make his speech for Smith.

He has barely had time to say that "as his most imperfect counsel" he will "do his best" when Braxfield interrupts.

"Be short and concise, sir, at this time of the morning."

"Pray let me proceed, my lord."

Clerk proceeds—and presently is telling the jury that the Bench was wrong to admit the evidence of the accuseds' accomplices. Braxfield can hardly believe his ears.

"That is a most improper observation." The other judges indicate assent. "Have a care, sir, what you say."

"What I say," says Clerk, "is that your lordships should not have admitted those witnesses, and of that the jury will judge."

"I tell you, sir, the jury take the law from me."

"Gentlemen," Clerk continues, turning towards the jury box, "*I* tell *you* that you are the judges of the law as well as of the facts."

"You are talking nonsense, sir," shouts Braxfield.

"My lord, you had better not snub me in this way."

The whole court is now seething with commotion, and Braxfield looks on the verge of apoplexy.

"We cannot tolerate this. It is a gross indignity."

But Clerk is now riding high; the suppressed plaudits of the crowd have joined the claret in his head.

"Unless I am allowed to speak to the jury in this manner," he declares, "I am determined not to speak another word. I am willing to sit down if your lordships command me."

As proof of this assertion, he does sit down forthwith. There is a sudden and absolute silence until Braxfield, almost literally breathing fury, speaks.

"Go on, sir. Go on—to the length of your tether."

Slowly Clerk gets up again—and again assures the transfixed jurymen that they are the judges of law as well as facts.

"Beware what you're about," shouts Braxfield, still more loudly than before.

Clerk immediately sits down again, and folds his arms.

"Have you done with your speech, sir?"

"No, my lord, I am not."

"Then go on," says Braxfield, "at your peril."

"This has been too often repeated," Clerk retorts. "Unless I'm allowed to speak in my own way, I'm resolved to proceed no further."

"Very well," says Braxfield, "I shall charge the jury."

But as he prepares to do so, Clerk leaps to his feet, and shakes his upraised fist at the Lord Justice-Clerk.

"Hang my client if you dare," he cries, "without hearing me in his defence . . ."

What happened in the judges' private room, whither they retired to discuss what they should do, can only be a matter of intelligent conjecture. But when they returned, Braxfield asked Clerk to go on with his speech—which that doughty fighter did without further interruption.

Clerk's exertions could not save Smith's neck (any more than Brodie's could be saved by the Dean of Faculty). But he was first set along the road to fame and fortune by his plucky stand against browbeating from the Bench—that same Bench on which John Clerk himself, years later, sat under the designation of Lord Eldin.

Lord Justice Lawrence tries the Nazi Leaders

NOT only the Nazi leaders were on trial at Nuremberg. At the International Tribunal, which opened in November, 1945 and did not finally close till October, 1946, four great countries—Britain, France, the Soviet Union and the United States—were represented on the Bench, each by a team of two. It was a tremendous test, made with the whole world watching, of four legal systems and their administrators.

One need not be a rabid patriot to assert that Britain passed through this test with flying colours. And one need not disregard the institutions and traditions which partly fashioned them to believe that this may be ascribed to the British delegates—the men who are now respectively Lord Oaksey and Lord Birkett.

Mr. Justice Birkett had long been a household name. Among the very greatest advocates who have ever lived, his dazzling career while still at the Bar had won him continuous notice and imperishable renown. Lord Justice Lawrence—he became Lord Oaksey in 1947—had pursued a distinguished but less conspicuous course. Deeply respected within his own profession for his learning, wisdom, and integrity, he had not made a comparable impact on the general public.

That impact he was to make at Nuremberg where, as permanent President of the court, he bore supreme responsibility.

The International Tribunal had to grapple with many difficulties. It was without any precedent—a lawyer's nightmare in itself. It was without a common source of doctrine and procedure. And—most serious—it was expressly constituted to deal with events that had torn the world asunder, and had aroused hatred, pity, fear, and detestation to a degree and on a scale never previously known.

That fact generated its own Scylla and Charybdis. On the one side, the danger that generous emotion might make the court a mere instrument of vengeance; on the other side, the danger that despairing virulence might lead to the proceedings getting out of hand.

It is easy to perceive, in retrospect, how Lord Justice Lawrence safely piloted the Nuremberg Tribunal through these perils. He dealt with the trial of those cosmic criminals in exactly the same manner as, for a dozen years, he had dealt with hundreds of ordinary trials in England. He brought to his task the qualities of his training—and his temperament: an open mind, an attentive ear, calm courtesy—and firmness. . . .

47

The half-anticipated challenge to discipline and order was made at the very outset by the strongest challenger.

Lord Justice Lawrence had quietly intimated that he would begin by calling on each of the prisoners to plead either guilty or not guilty of the charges laid against them. That was all, he stressed, they were then required to do; they would have full opportunity to put forward their defences at a later stage.

With a mildness of expression they may have misinterpreted, the President surveyed the twenty men inside the dock, who were to face him thus at such innumerable sessions, and eleven of whom he was to sentence to be hanged.

"I will now call on the defendants," he said, and carefully repeated "to plead guilty or not guilty. . . . Hermann Wilhelm Goering."

The former Reichsmarschall rose from his place with his familiar swagger. This courageous bully—the terms are not, as is sometimes supposed, mutually exclusive—showed every sign of bidding for dominion of the court by exercise of his formidable personality. Goering's whole demeanour stirred uneasy memories of his performance at the Reichstag Trial in 1933.

"Before I answer the question," he said arrogantly, "whether or not I am guilty——"

"I informed the court," the President interposed, "that defendants are not entitled to make a statement now. You must plead guilty or not guilty."

The accent was polite. The expression remained mild. But the eyes that Goering looked into defiantly conveyed a message that he understood.

"I declare myself not guilty," he said, and sullenly sat down.

"Rudolf Hess," said the President, as tranquil and unruffled as if a crucial clash of wills had not just been decided.

Hess, who was deranged, or pretending to be so, stupidly answered "No", which prompted a burst of inappropriate laughter.

"If there is any disturbance," said the President, unchanged in voice and manner, "those who make it will have to leave the court. The plea of Hess will be entered as Not Guilty . . . Joachim von Ribbentrop."

"Not guilty."

"Wilhelm Keitel."

"Not guilty."

"Alfred Rosenberg."

"Not guilty" . . .

The note had been struck, the tone set, authority established right away. Everyone knew henceforward that it was to be a trial, not a political meeting or a circus.

And indeed, from those first decisive moments, justice reigned at the Nuremberg Tribunal as completely and securely as it does at the Old Bailey. The prisoners, conscious who was master, all behaved themselves. The President, conscious of his professional duty, protected the prisoners beside controlling them. Though they might be the wickedest band of fiends since the Creation, he was continuously watchful of their legal rights.

"Have you got copies of these for defendants' counsel?" he asked an American prosecutor who proffered certain documents.

"In room 54, sir," said the prosecutor.

"They will be wanting to follow them *now*," said the President.

The prosecutor sought to meet this clear hint by stating that six copies were available for the defendants' use.

"Defence counsel should *each* have a copy," the President said pointedly.

He returned to the subject, in somewhat sharper terms, a few days later, when he asked how many copies of another set of documents had been given to the Press.

The U.S. prosecutor accountable thought about 250.

"Defendants' counsel," said the President, "should have these copies in preference to the Press."

The prosecutor protested that defendants' counsel had received five copies twenty-four hours ago.

"What I am pointing out to you is," replied the President, "that if two hundred and fifty copies can be given to the Press, defendants' counsel should not be limited to five."

"I have a receipt to show," the prosecutor persisted, "that those copies were delivered twenty-four hours in advance."

The President patiently spelt out his patent meaning.

"You don't seem to understand what I am putting to you, which is this: That if you can afford to give two hundred and fifty copies to the Press, you can afford to give defendants' counsel more than five. One each, in fact." Without wig or formal robes, without pomp or ceremonial, Lord Justice Lawrence embodied the majesty of law. "Well, there is no need to discuss it further. *In the future, that will be done.*"

Throughout the President held the ring impartially; his decisions were influenced by principles, not persons. He kept defendants' counsel in line, when necessary, with the same sure grasp as he directed their opponents. One of them—possibly encouraged by the foregoing—raised a dust about alleged faults in translation, and moved for a German shorthand note by German shorthand writers. When he had finished, it transpired that one was already being taken.

"Then I withdraw my motion," said defending counsel, like a man making some magnanimous gesture.

"I think we shall get on faster," said the President dryly, "if the defendants' counsel, before making motions, inquire into the matters about which they are making them. . . ."

The wonder of the Nuremberg Tribunal was not its drama, but its studied lack of drama; not its tempestuous scenes, but its freedom from

THE JUDGES AND THE JUDGED

such scenes; not its blazing passions, but its cool inquiry. Notwithstanding the extraordinary circumstances, despite the unprecedented pressure of mass feeling, the Nazis were tried, fundamentally, by English methods—the best, I do not hesitate to say, so far devised on this imperfect globe.

As a result, the great assize at Nuremberg will occupy an honourable niche in history. There are some, of course, who question the legitimacy of trials for war guilt, and for crimes against peace and humanity. There are others—far more numerous—who consider this particular trial a sheer waste of time; who hold that the principal prisoners, at least, should have been shot without ado on capture.

None, though, can reasonably refrain from admiration for the even-handed conduct of that unique tribunal presided over by an English judge with such unaffected dignity and strength.

Craigie Aitchison tries Jeannie Donald

THE Scots for judges, the Irish for advocates.

That generalization holds good ninety-nine times in a hundred, firmly based as it is on national characteristics: Irish imagination, flair, and partisanship; Scots logic, realism, and impartiality.

But there have been occasional exceptions on the part of both.

The Scots, particularly, looking back over the years, can point with justifiable pride to at least two Scottish advocates who cannot be denied their place in the very highest rank—that exclusive rank attained by barely a score of counsel throughout the long and often glorious history of the Bar.

In the last century there was John Inglis, Madeleine Smith's defender, who fully bears comparison with his great English coevals, Cockburn, Hawkins, and Serjeant Ballantine. And in our own century there was Craigie Aitchison, who similarly could hold his own with contemporary giants across the border—towering giants like Patrick Hastings and like Norman Birkett.

Aitchison is now perhaps best remembered for two outstanding feats of dazzling advocacy; the acquittal of John Donald Merrett on a charge of matricide in 1927, and the great speech he made on behalf of Oscar Slater, when that unhappy man, after eighteen years in jail, obtained belated justice in 1928 from the recently constituted Scottish Court of Criminal Appeal.

These, though, were merely the twin peaks of a massive mountain range; a rich experience and a royal achievement lay behind Craigie Aitchison when he was appointed, in 1933, Lord Justice-Clerk.

Craigie Aitchison, the judge, did not altogether discard and leave to rust the gifts that had made him so superlative a pleader. But he canalized these gifts—of relevance, of exposition, of incisive questioning —into the service of his new position.

This was abundantly apparent in the most remarkable murder case he ever tried—that of the Aberdeen housewife, Jeannie Donald. . . .

Mrs. Donald, her husband, and her nine-year-old daughter (who, with Church activities, was her principal interest) occupied a two-roomed flat on the ground floor of a four-storied tenement house containing seven others. Between her and Mrs. Priestley, immediately above, a coolness existed ("We had no row, but did not speak."), and the latter's eight-year-old daughter, Helen, sometimes reported that Mrs. Donald (whom, for no obvious cause, she had nicknamed 'Coconut') eyed her and watched her as she made her way upstairs.

There is no sworn evidence on the record to indicate whether little Helen Priestley was disrespectful or disparaging before Mrs. Donald's face as well as behind her back. It can, however, safely be said—without apportioning blame—that a somewhat unfriendly atmosphere prevailed whenever the woman on the ground floor encountered the small girl who was bound to pass her door a dozen times a day.

On 20 April, 1934, shortly after they had had their midday meal, Mrs. Priestley sent Helen to buy a loaf of bread at a shop only a hundred yards away. She reached the shop, bought the loaf, and walked back towards her home. It was some time between half past one and two o'clock when a schoolmate on the other side of the road saw her, alone, within a few steps of the tenement.

Never again was Helen Priestley seen alive by anyone—man, woman, or child—who wished her well.

They searched all afternoon, all evening, and far into the night. The police, informed by Helen's family, scoured the city. The public, informed by the police and word of mouth, turned themselves into auxiliary detectives, and kept a sharp look-out for tokens of kidnapping or abduction. Inside the tenement, activity was continuous; some comforting the stricken mother while her husband ceaselessly patrolled the neighbouring streets, others partly appeasing their desire to help by exploring what had been explored a dozen times before.

The final discovery, though, was accidental.

At five next morning, a friend of Mr. Priestley's called with a car to accompany him on a resumption of the search. As he passed through the entrance lobby, something caught his eye; something lying in a recess beneath the stairs—the stairs that began their rise by Mrs. Donald's door. This recess, which led to the ground-floor lavatory, had been traversed several times since Helen's disappearance; it was known for certain that no object had been there even as recently as 1.30 a.m. But now . . . a sack, with the feet of a child protruding.

The search for Helen Priestley was over.

She had died—a simple pathologist's calculation from the stomach contents and the time of her last meal—about half past one or two o'clock on the previous afternoon. Gross injury to the genital organs and blood upon the thighs naturally led to an initial presumption that death had occurred during a savage act of rape. That meant that the killer must have been a man.

Closer examination at the autopsy, however, replaced this presumption by a definite conclusion even more horrible in its implications. The injuries had been caused by hand, or by an instrument. That meant that the killer *might* have been a man—but, equally, *might* have been a woman.

And whereas a man could only perpetrate such an outrage at the instigation of perverted lust, a woman who had attacked the child might have a colder motive. *She might try to counterfeit the appearances of rape in the hope of excluding herself from all suspicion. . . .*

It was primarily the scientific evidence that brought the matter home to Jeannie Donald. But it was evidence not easy for the jury to assimilate. The comparison of hairs in the sack with hairs from Mrs. Donald's hairbrush (both "rather uniquely" distinguished by "an irregular bulge of lumen"); of fibres in the sack with fibres from Mrs. Donald's rugs (glass slides, microscopical observations); of germs found on Helen's undergarments with germs on Mrs. Donald's washing cloths ("an unusual variety of coliform bacillus")—these tests were doubtless categorical to specialists, but ordinary folk, dizzy at such heights, would feel the need of reassurance from ordinary "facts".

This they received in plenty, as the trial developed, through the interventions of the Lord Justice-Clerk.

"When you last saw Helen," he said to the schoolmate who had noticed her from across the road, "she was near the door of her own house?"

"Yes," the girl replied.

"And going on as if she were going home?"

"Yes."

"Carrying a parcel?"

"Yes."

To Mrs. Priestley he addressed a cognate question.

"You say you warned Helen not to go away with anyone. Did she understand that clearly?"

"Yes."

"Do you think she would be likely to go away with any person she did not know?"

"No."

"You are quite satisfied of that?"

"Oh yes," said the weeping mother. "Oh, yes; I'm quite sure."

The Lord Justice-Clerk again reinforced his underlying theme when he wound up the interrogation of another witness.

"Did you go forward to the sack?"

"Yes."

"Did you touch it?"

"I touched Helen's feet," the witness said.

"Were they dry?"

"Yes."

"Was the sack dry?"

"Yes."

The Lord Justice-Clerk spoke with great deliberation.

"*Had it been raining heavily for hours?*"

"Yes, it had."

The whole sequence of inquiries raises the same inference—that Helen Priestley had been murdered in the house. And this raises a further inference in turn.

She never reached the first floor, where her mother waited. Not a shadow of suspicion—far less a grain of proof—lay against anyone in any flat but Mrs. Donald's. Her husband and child could establish that, at the material time, they were not there. Mrs. Donald *said* she was not there, but could not establish it.

In what direction did this point? That if Helen Priestley was killed in the house, Mrs. Donald was the killer.

This would not have been enough—as the Lord Justice-Clerk made plain—to found an adverse verdict in itself. "If the case had ended there," he told the jury, "I would have directed you that, in a matter of this gravity, it would not be safe to infer that the accused committed the crime by a process of exclusion *only*."

The process of exclusion, though, enabled them to see that the "facts" fitted in with the scientific theses. . . .

Mrs. Donald (who did not give evidence, relying on a denial in her statement to the police) was convicted, sentenced to death, but subsequently reprieved.

An application for leave to appeal that had been lodged was then abandoned. It had never commanded much prospect of success. The great advocate on the Bench had re-employed, but not misused, his former mastery.

53

Lord Chief Justice Hewart and the case of William Cooper Hobbs

T HE qualities that make an attractive personality or a persuasive advocate do not necessarily make a good trial judge. Some of the best judges have been totally insignificant at the Bar and in ordinary life. Some of the worst have excelled as counsel and fascinated as men.

A comparatively recent Lord Chief Justice—Lord Hewart, who held that office from 1922 to 1940—must be included in this latter category. As a personality, Hewart radiated charm. It was my privilege to be acquainted with him, and I can testify to the effortless ascendancy he established over social gatherings, large and small, by his agreeable manners, erudition, fluency and wit.

As an advocate, he allied great technical skill to these natural advantages. His merit was reflected in a lucrative private practice, and in the distinction he achieved as a Law Officer of the Crown.

But, ironically enough, with his elevation to the Bench, Hewart's stature started to diminish—and continued to diminish as time passed. He could not accomplish the transformation of himself from a competitive player into an impartial referee.

He adopted a side early—often in the opening minutes of a case— and thereafter could seldom resist taking a kick at the ball whenever it came near enough for him to do so. This highly unjudicial trait was rendered more injurious by those very gifts—of speech, of style, of colour—that served him so well in non-judicial spheres.

A specially glaring instance occurred in 1928 during a libel action brought by William Cooper Hobbs.

Hobbs was a professional villain of the deepest dye (his own counsel that sturdy Irish character, Serjeant Sullivan, later described him— variously but consistently—as "this brute", "this beast", "this horrible character", "that loathsome and repellent individual", and "the greatest scoundrel with whom I have come in contact in my life").

Naturally, as a cheat and crook, Hobbs preferred to work in the obscure shadows, but his dominating role in the biggest blackmailing coup for generations—the fleecing of a rajah, pseudonymously known as "Mr. A."—had given him widespread notoriety, and within the Law Courts made his name a household word. It is a fair assumption that, when his suit came up for trial before the Lord Chief Justice and a jury, the former at least knew Hobbs's record with precision.

That, however, cannot excuse what followed.

The libel of which Hobbs complained was, in my opinion, glaring. During the aftermath of the Mr. A. sensation, a provincial newspaper had published a "biography" which purported to present a truthful picture of the numerous criminal episodes in Hobbs's life.

It might have been thought almost an impossibility to say anything bad about Hobbs that wasn't true, but this newspaper triumphantly succeeded. It imputed to him a murder and an attempt at murder; neither imputation could be substantiated, and Hobbs's claim to redress was therefore irresistible—save upon the premise that such an evildoer had forfeited his common law rights as a subject of the Crown.

That, in effect, was what the defendant newspaper contended. It did not—dare not—say: We are going to prove that the charges we made against you are true. It said: We are going to prove you are so infamous a character that even defamatory lies cannot cause you any damage. The formidable talents of Norman Birkett were engaged to conduct this defence and—particularly—to cross-examine Hobbs.

From the very first moment Hewart took pains to make it clear that he wanted—and was resolved to get—a verdict for the defendants. He displayed a pronounced restiveness during Sullivan's opening. He greeted the plaintiff with a hostile scowl when he took the oath. He commented acidly on Hobbs's replies to his own counsel; and, when it was Norman Birkett's turn to question him, the judge assisted—if that be the aptest word—with a whole series of snarling indications that he didn't believe a single word the witness said.

On the third day, matters suddenly came to a head.

The court assembled as usual at ten-thirty. Hobbs—still under cross-examination—waited to be called back once again into the box. But when Hewart took his seat, he unexpectedly addressed Serjeant Sullivan.

"Do you intend to offer any evidence other than that of Mr. Hobbs himself?" he said.

"I was proposing," Sullivan replied, with complete propriety, "to consider that at the end of the cross-examination."

"I am asking you," said Hewart, "to consider it now."

Sullivan betrayed astonishment—as well he might—and the Lord Chief Justice rather belatedly condescended to explain: "I have received an intimation from the jury that they are unanimously agreed they have heard enough."

If a judge acts upon an "intimation" from a jury, that intimation should be disclosed to counsel. Hewart did not disclose it. He merely asked the jury whether they were prepared to find for the defendants.

"Yes," the foreman said.

"Before that result is arrived at," Sullivan observed, "I should insist, my lord, upon addressing the jury."

The Serjeant was entirely within his rights; he could insist on completing his case before the court could take a verdict. But the Lord Chief Justice reddened angrily.

"You would insist? That is a strange phrase to use."

"My lord, I conceive I am *entitled* to address the jury."

"Please do not use the word 'insist'," growled Hewart, and he sat openly fuming with impatience while Sullivan exercised his right and made his speech.

That speech lasted three-quarters of an hour. In the special circumstances, it should have been followed by a summing-up from the judge making quite clear what the issues were the jury had to decide.

Nothing of the kind.

As Sullivan sat down, Hewart, with the air of a man whose tolerance and self-restraint have been tested to the limits, turned to those he treated as his fellow-sufferers.

"At ten-thirty you intimated you were prepared to find a verdict for the defendants. It is now nearly eleven-thirty. Are you still of the same opinion?"

It was left to the Court of Appeal (where Sullivan promptly took his undeniable grievance) to restore the deserved reputation of our courts for giving everyone—even the devil—his due. This they did, however, handsomely.

"The worst of criminals," said Lord Justice Scrutton who presided, "is entitled to a fair hearing. Without expressing any opinion whether Hobbs would ultimately be proved to be of such a character, I say he is entitled to be presumed innocent till proved guilty by a trial *according to the rules of law*. I regret to say I do not think Hobbs has had such a trial. He is entitled to justice. I hope he will get it."

Some may think that Hobbs got rather more than justice. The action was finally settled for a substantial sum. But while one may deplore the enrichment of a rogue, one can only rejoice in the power of the English law to protect the lowest against injustice from the highest.

Mr. Justice Horridge and the Condover Case

FOR more than an hour the jury have been out in this suit for defamation against a newspaper. Now they are reassembling in their box, but with a curious air of men frustrated rather than resolved.

Mr. Justice Horridge surveys them stonily. "You have sent a message to me," he said, "saying there is very little chance of your agreement. First, is there anything I can do to help?"

The judge waits. There is no sign of response.

"Very well. If there is not, I want to say this to you before sending you back." He leans forward and speaks with utmost emphasis. "If any of you have in your minds a lurking feeling that this libel is in any way true, you have no business to harbour such a feeling. It is admitted that the libel is untrue. It is admitted that the plaintiffs were perfectly straight and honest." The judge's tone becomes peremptory. "You have sworn to administer justice between the parties. Go and do so."

Before anyone else can move, Sir Edward Marshall Hall, representing the newspaper, rises in his place.

"Will your lordship allow me to say——"

The judge breaks in angrily.

"I will not allow you to interfere between the jury and me. Sit down."

"I will, my lord," replies Marshall Hall, not doing so. "But I wish to submit that is clearly misdirection."

"Then you have your remedy," snaps the judge, and, with this oblique allusion to the Court of Appeal, the exchange concludes and the jury once again retire.

Marshall Hall's quick temper and impetuous tongue sometimes lead him into clashes with the Bench which can be neither justified nor excused. But it is easy to understand his intervention here, and his grounds for a complaint of misdirection.

By explicitly referring to "this libel" and "the libel", Mr. Justice Horridge was—no doubt unconsciously—pre-judging the only issue in the trial. The defendants admit that the plaintiffs were straight and honest; what they deny is that any words of theirs suggested otherwise.

Libel or no libel?—that is the very question that has been constantly argued back and forth these last three days, before a crowd of onlookers who might have felt more at home if each had had a pair of binoculars and a card to mark.

For this action is as sporting in its content as the back page of this evening's newspaper. It revolves round the form of a horse called Condover, and, more especially, its disappointing showing in the Lincolnshire Handicap of 1924.

That year the Lincoln was run on 26 March Condover finished twelfth and had never been in the race. On 12 April, however, Condover won the Newbury Cup with consummate ease, beating a field which included several of the horses which had passed the post before it in the Lincoln.

These unequal performances attracted some attention, and when, on 15 April Condover was scratched from the City and Suburban, a London daily took the opportunity to comment.

"In the ordinary way," it said, "the victory of Condover in the Newbury Cup would have gained it many more admirers for the Epsom race. But the public would have none of it. Condover is the only winner of a big race which has not been seized on at once by backers for its next engagement."

The paper then proffered an explanation why Condover ("good and honest horse as it is") had been so ignored and cold-shouldered in the betting. "When the backer is *palpably outwitted*, he is inclined to think that the game is not so nice as it ought to be."

It was those two words "palpably outwitted" that really touched off the present litigation and which have been the main bone of contention ever since.

Condover's owner and trainer and jockey (the same on both occasions), together with the owner's racing manager, interpreted the newspaper's phrase as a suggestion that the horse had not been run to win at Lincoln so that they all might profit more if it won at Newbury; and that the public, having been thus deceived, had lost belief in the honesty of Condover's management.

To which they replied that Condover was a moody horse; that in the Lincoln it carried top weight; that the going was heavy, which it disliked; that it drew a low number, which worked to its detriment over the two furlongs where the Carholme narrows; that it got shut in and mud was kicked up in its face; and finally—a clinching point for the most sceptical—that, while the stable connexions won £7,000 on Condover at Newbury, they had stood to win more than £30,000 on Condover at Lincoln.

The honest management of the horse was established so completely that, if "palpably outwitted" implied dishonesty, there could be no defence. But the newspaper said that all it had meant—and should be taken to mean—was that Condover's form and condition were kept secret before Newbury in order that the S.P. should not be affected.

Marshall Hall cross-examined accordingly.

"Supposing," he asked Condover's trainer, "that the owner, trainer or manager of a horse entered for a particular race took every possible step to prevent any intimation to the public that the horse was fancied, that would be outwitting the public, would it not?"

"No," said the trainer, "that would be outwitting the bookmakers."

"But it would also be outwitting the public," went on counsel, as the laugh died down, "because they would have no lead to follow, would they?"

"I don't see that."

"Don't you? If a stable begins to back a horse some time before a race, won't the public probably back that horse as well?"

"They can please themselves," the trainer said.

"But it's probable, isn't it?"

"Yes."

"And if stable and public back the horse, the price shortens?"

"Yes."

Marshall Hall, familiar with racing, was enjoying himself.

"You have trials on your beautiful downs in Wiltshire?"

"Yes."

"Do you take every possible precaution to keep off touts?"
"Yes."
"Isn't the object of a trial to enable the stable to get a line on the running of a horse?"
"Yes."
"And isn't the object of keeping off the touts to prevent the public from getting to know what that line is?"
"Yes."
Marshall Hall had almost reached his limited objective.
"There is nothing dishonest in that, is there?"
"No," agreed the trainer.
"Isn't every SP coup dependent on how far the stable can keep the public in ignorance of the fact that a particular horse is fancied?"
"Yes."
"There is nothing dishonest in that, is there?"
"No," agreed the trainer.
This may have shown that an SP coup is not in itself dishonest. Did it show, though, that the newspaper merely meant an SP coup?

That is the vital question. And as the jury return into court a second time, the difference in their bearing indicates they bring their answer.
"Are you agreed?"
"We are."
"Do you find for the plaintiffs or for the defendants?"
"The plaintiffs."
"For what damages?"
The foreman lifts his voice.
"A farthing each," he says.
There is a moment of silence. Then counsel for the plaintiffs asks for judgment, and—as is usual for successful parties—costs.
Mr. Justice Horridge slowly shakes his head.
"No," he says. "The jury have found a verdict for a farthing damages, and I accept that verdict loyally, *whatever I may think of it myself. . . .*"

It is not surprising that the judge felt deep dissatisfaction; the verdict did not coincide with common sense. If it was not libel, the defendants should have won. If it was a libel at all, it was a grievous libel, and the plaintiffs—whose characters had in no way been assailed—were entitled to substantial damages as their vindication.

Possibly it represented a kind of compromise between some who thought the words a libel and others who did not—a compromise arrived at without sufficient regard being paid to its effect. In the event, they achieved a paradox: a case where, all in all, the plaintiffs would have been better served if the jury had found for the defendants.

Mr. Justice Singleton tries Peter Barnes

"Have you ever made any attempt to find MacMahon?"
"No."
"So far as you know, have any of the other prisoners ever seen MacMahon?"
"No."
"I suggest that MacMahon has no existence?"
"Yes, he has."

With a barely perceptible shrug of scepticism, Crown Counsel closed his cross-examination and sat down. The witness, supposing his ordeal at an end, prepared to leave the box and resume his place inside the dock. He was checked, however, by a restraining gesture from the Bench.

"I would like to ask you one or two questions, Barnes."

The Irish labourer, who was on trial for his life, and the English judge, who was engaged in trying him, came now into immediate contact, face to face. . . .

Thirty-two-year-old Peter Barnes, from Banagher, Co. Offally, had only set foot on English soil a bare three weeks before his arrest upon a charge of wilful murder. This is less surprising when one knows that he had come with hatred as his spur and violence as his mission.

Barnes was, in fact, an active member of the I.R.A.—that fanatical brotherhood of Irish patriots whose methods were derived from the nineteenth-century Fenians and whose grievances were rooted deep in past misrule. From its inception, the I.R.A. aimed at a single goal: a completely separate republic of an undivided Ireland.

Action, of course, had to be governed by expedience; often it was merely local, often there were protracted lulls. But in 1939 the rising German menace and the increasing likelihood of general hostilities convinced the I.R.A. commanders that the time was ripe for a series of stealthy blows at the homeland of their enemy—England.

From 16 January, when the series opened, until 18 March in the following year, when it finally subsided, the I.R.A. time-bomb and incendiary incidents all over the country totalled several hundreds. Injury and damage were frequent and extensive, but loss of life was relatively—and fortunately—small. The worst in this regard—and, indeed, the true and dreadful climax of the entire campaign—was that at Coventry on 25 August, just seven days before Hitler started his world war.

The explosion of a bomb in the carrier of a bicycle left by the kerb in crowded Broadgate on a market day resulted in the death of five, the mutilation or the wounding of some fifty more, and the subsequent appearance of Peter Barnes and others before Mr. Justice Singleton at Birmingham Assizes.

Singleton was a handsome man with a striking personality, curiously compounded of suavity and steel. Had he been an actor, managements would constantly have cast him as a successful and fashionable advocate—which accurately describes John Singleton at the Bar. The polished grace of manner irresistibly attracted; the relentlessness of purpose inevitably impressed. A stylish and sophisticated counsel, he commanded stylish and sophisticated clients.

Many barristers undergo a metamorphosis—some for the better, some distinctly for the worse—upon being transplanted to the Bench. Not so with Singleton; his characteristics were unchanged, merely re-adapted. He was a strong judge (at times a stubborn one), but always urbane even when—as he could be—severe. His purely legal merits ultimately made him a Lord Justice of Appeal, and his gift for clear analysis of complicated facts is familiar to every student who has ever read his admirable summing-up in the Ruxton Case.

"I would like to ask you one or two questions, Barnes."

The intervention which these words presaged was perfectly proper both in substance and in form. It is a matter of record, not of criticism, that its effect was absolutely deadly. . . .

Barnes's job—it is evident on retrospect—was to carry explosives from secret depots to I.R.A. men in the areas selected for explosions. Throughout his short-lived English assignment, he had lodged in Westbourne Terrace and spent his spare time with his Irish fiancée in Warwick Avenue. Ostensibly he was looking for a job.

The great Coventry explosion happened on a Friday. The Crown could prove that on the previous Monday Barnes had travelled from London to Coventry, and had visited a house in Clara Street where, beyond doubt, the bomb was afterwards assembled; that on the Thursday he had travelled from London to Coventry again, and again had visited the house in Clara Street; that on this second occasion he took with him a suitcase; that on the Friday night, five hours after the explosion, police searching Barnes's room in Westbourne Terrace discovered packets of potassium chlorate and, searching Barnes himself, found in his jacket pocket an unposted letter which was as packed with dynamite as any bomb.

This scrawled document, signed with the name of "Dixon" but—as Barnes did not deny—written in his hand, was aptly termed by Crown Counsel The Letter of Prophecy. "I go from one place to the other and brings the S" it said. "I am after coming back from Coventry tonight so by the time you get this the Paper should have some news." It was dated 24-8-39—the day before the Coventry explosion.

In the witness box, Barnes tendered explanations.

A casual acquaintance called MacMahon had suggested there were better prospects of work at Coventry, and had told him to ask for "Norman" at the Clara Street address. No one on his first visit seemed to know of Norman, but, at MacMahon's prompting, he tried a second time, with the same abortive outcome as before. The packets of potassium chlorate had been sold to him as shampoo powders by a girl in Oxford Street. The letter was one he had copied for MacMahon, whom he had met by appointment after returning from Coventry on Thursday, and who had asked him to deliver the letter personally to Dublin.

As for the suitcase which he carried on that Thursday, it had contained merely his hat and overcoat and pyjamas; for he had always intended spending Thursday night, not at Westbourne Terrace, but at Warwick Avenue.

It was these two last statements in particular which Mr. Justice Singleton began to probe.

"Can you tell me where your suitcase is now?" he quietly asked.

"The police have it," said Barnes.

"Is it the one that's been produced?"

"No, I haven't seen it in court. It is a small suitcase."

"Still, big enough to take a hat, an overcoat, and pyjamas?"

"Yes."

The judge's eyes never strayed from the prisoner's.

"When you went from Westbourne Terrace to Warwick Avenue, how did you go?"

"By bus."

"Is it five or six hundred yards?"

"Somewhere about that."

"When you went from Coventry Station to Clara Street, how did you go?"

"I walked."

"How far is that?"

"It took me about half an hour."

"You carried the suitcase all that way round," said the judge deliberatively, "and then brought it back to Coventry Station and then from Coventry to London?"

"Yes."

"Rather than pack it up in the evening to take it from Westbourne Terrace to Warwick Avenue?"

"It was handy to take what I wanted with me," Barnes replied.

"It would have been as handy, perhaps, to take your hat on your head. . . . What time did you get back to London from Coventry that Thursday?"

"About ten."

"What was your arrangement as to meeting MacMahon?"

"He told me that he would meet me at Euston Station when the train came in."

"What time?" inquired the judge.

"He must have known the time the train would come in, for he was there."

His lordship allowed that curious gloss to pass. He saw a point arising here which was more important.

"MacMahon hadn't been to Coventry, had he?"

"I don't know."

"But you were friendly with him. If he was going to Coventry that day, was there any reason why you shouldn't go together?"

"No."

"He told you to go, you say, and he would meet you when you came back?"

"Yes."

"So you knew he was not at Coventry?"

"Yes, so far as my knowledge went."

The judge relaxed slightly, and leaned back.

"And, according to you, that was MacMahon's letter, saying 'I am after coming back from Coventry tonight'" . . .

The whole episode, from start to finish, did not last three minutes. But during those three minutes there fell on Peter Barnes the shadow of the scaffold on which he was to die.

Judge William Callahan tries The Scottsboro Boys

THERE was great rejoicing among the white population of Alabama and her neighbour States when the news broke that Judge William Callahan would preside at the second re-trial arising from the notorious case of those nine young Negroes known as The Scottsboro Boys.

Because—although the nine were charged with raping two white girls—the Deep South had begun to despair of hanging them. The record—viewed from Nashville or Atlanta—was depressing.

Twice had an all-white Alabama jury—one at Scottsboro in 1931, one at Decatur in 1933—pronounced a verdict of guilty, and (as sentence lay with them) a penalty of death. And twice had the expressed will of Alabama been defied.

The original verdict (against all nine accused) was set aside by the United States Supreme Court, whose niggling legalisms ("Fair Trial", "Presumption of Innocence", and the like) so often cut across the Deep South's simpler ideas of equity.

The verdict at the first re-trial (of one youth only, Haywood Patterson —used as a stalking-horse and try-out for the rest) was actually set aside by the trial judge himself—who, in contrast to his predecessor and successor, happened to be a conscientious and impartial man. "The prosecution testimony," Judge Horton had declared, "is not only uncorroborated; it also bears on its face indications of improbability, and is contradicted by other evidence."

The Deep South by then had had enough of both the Supreme Court and Judge Horton. They wanted someone to conduct Trial Number Three who would be fly enough to forestall interference from the former, and tough enough to be immune from the scruples of the latter.

In the second respect especially, Callahan seemed to be their man— and in that respect it cannot be said that he let the Deep South down.

He struck his first sharp blow for white supremacy even before the main proceedings had begun. Seated in a court which required protection from armed guards, facing a prisoner sickeningly accustomed to the baying of lynch mobs at his prison wall, Callahan rejected the defence's application to transfer the venue of the trial to a region less inflamed. "You have failed to prove charges of local prejudice," he drawled; and so once again in that tense and baleful atmosphere the prosecution furnished their recital of The Facts.

It was a pure formality; at this stage nobody needed to be told The Facts—neither Eskimoes nor Hottentots nor South Sea Islanders, never mind those lantern-jawed, tobacco-chewing jurors who had brooded darkly over The Facts for several years. How the two white girls— Victoria Price and Ruby Bates—after spending a night at an open-air hobo haunt near Chattanooga with some male companions jumped a slow-moving freight train. How a number of Negroes scrambled on to the same train just after it had crossed the Alabama border.

How a fight broke out between the Negroes and the whites. How the train was stopped by a sheriff's posse and the hoboes rounded up. How Victoria Price, on being questioned, suddenly asserted that she and Ruby Bates had been raped in their truck by each of the nine Negroes at that time still remaining on the train. How Ruby Bates acquiesced.

Oh yes, the jury knew The Facts by heart. They had brooded less deeply—and much less willingly—on what may be called the facts behind The Facts: the fact that the State's examining doctors found no signs—mental or physical—of rape, only of intercourse (that might have occurred twenty-four hours before); the fact that after the first trial Ruby had recanted, saying she was only induced to support Victoria's story so that they might both avoid being jailed and charged as vagrants.

And, of course, this telling combination of events is now by-passed and glossed over by the prosecution—but it makes Victoria Price a highly vulnerable witness when she takes her place for the third time on the stand.

Certainly Leibowitz, the famous New York advocate who has given his services to the Scottsboro Boys, knows that—if accorded the scope properly due to counsel—he can demolish her utterly in cross-examination.

Callahan knows it, too. And intends, in consequence, to deprive Leibowitz of that scope.

The extremes to which he will go first become fully apparent when Leibowitz is questioning Victoria about the garments she was wearing on the train. The defender suggests that her overalls—supposedly *torn* off by the Negroes—had been voluntarily *taken* off by herself.

Callahan lifts his voice in uninhibited anger at the implication that he sees—or thinks he sees.

"Treat the lady with more respect," he orders, and—when Leibowitz attempts to insist upon his obvious rights—clamps down on any argument or discussion. "I won't allow such questions in *my* court," he says peremptorily.

A little later, when the female hobo is being asked whether she has not sustained convictions for fornication and vagrancy—she has— Callahan steps in again and forbids her to reply.

"Are you trying to impugn the witness's chastity?" he demands.

That is exactly Leibowitz's object, and it constitutes an essential element in his case. For the defence seeks to illuminate and explain the medical evidence by reference to the conduct of Victoria (and Ruby) at the Chattanooga hobo haunt on the night before their train ride.

But Callahan continually blocks this entirely legitimate and justifiable course.

He forbids Leibowitz to press Victoria Price for the names of the hoboes who were there on that occasion. He forbids Victoria Price to answer when Leibowitz himself puts forward names. When counsel vehemently protests, he says: "The more I shut you off, the better shape you're in" (which must be presumed an endeavour after humour). When the State calls one of the male hoboes Leibowitz has named, Callahan prevents the advocate from ascertaining whether he went anywhere that night with the girls.

"Will your Honour excuse the jury," Leibowitz pleads in desperation, "so that I can tell your Honour what I'm trying to prove?"

"I can imagine," replies Callahan. "Get on to something else."

Just as the judge shielded and extolled all those concerned with the prosecution, so he insulted and harassed all those concerned with the defence. He refused to wait for a medical expert they were bringing. He conspicuously dozed during Leibowitz's speech. And in his own charge to the jury—delivered with a liberal use of sinister inflections and venomous glances directed at the prisoner—he failed to warn them that they must be satisfied of guilt beyond reasonable doubt.

"Oh yes, I forgot," he casually remarked, when Leibowitz pointed out this monstrous omission. He also forgot, in the last scene of the trial, to utter the words, "May God have mercy on your soul. . . ."

I cherish no romantic concept of the Scottsboro case, which aroused such violent racial and political emotions that millions lost all contact with its foul reality. There were no Robesons, no Booker Washingtons, among these Negroes; no noble martyrs, no crucified *élite*. They were tramps, illiterates, some of them defectives, all of them floating denizens of a sub-human jungle; belonging to the lowest order of their race (as their white accusers belonged to the lowest order of theirs).

But even the lowest orders, whatever their kind or colour, are entitled to justice through processes of law. And if, for reasons of ignorance or hate or prejudice, they cannot get it at the hands of their ordinary fellow citizens, it should be the satisfying privilege of a judge to exert his power in redress of their weakness.

Callahan deliberately declined this privilege, and for that—though in the distant end all the Scottsboro Boys went free—lawyers, proud of their great profession, never will forgive him.

Mr Justice Ridley hears Smith versus The Winning Post

WOULD you, sir, as a sedately married man of fifty, feel desperately aggrieved if you found reports circulated that you had won the favours of a famous actress when you were a carefree bachelor of twenty-eight?

Would you, sir? Would you? Honestly?

Yet this is the complaint of the man now occupying the witness box and facing the jury in Mr. Justice Ridley's court. This is the "disgraceful conduct" which his counsel says was imputed to him by a "serious libel" in *The Winning Post*.

The Winning Post—a saucy and characteristically Edwardian publication, dedicated to racing but not uninterested in sex—has been printing extracts from the memoirs of Helena Odilon, one of the best-known Austro-German actresses of her day.

In these she describes how her liaison with a certain Herr Oehlschaeger was ruptured through his jealousy of a gentleman rider named Smith who came over from England to ride for Oehlschaeger in 1888.

Smith stayed at their house, and one day, when he had been hurt in an accident, the actress visited his room to see how he was progressing.

"I was on the point of leaving," Miss Odilon wrote, "when Herr Oehlschaeger appeared. He stormed at me in rage. Not a word would he allow me to say in self-defence. I left the house without obtaining a chance of proving my innocence."

Later on, however—by her own account—Miss Odilon caught up

with Herr Oehlschaeger's premature suspicions. The innocent pair consoled each other for the injustice done them, and she became in truth the mistress of the gentleman rider named Smith.

Now the man in the witness box bears the name of Smith. He is, or has been, a gentleman rider ("One of the best known on the Turf", according to his counsel). He did go out to Germany in 1888—and 1887, and 1889—to ride Oehlschaeger's horses. He did there meet Helena Odilon.

These facts, it is argued on Mr. Smith's behalf, would identify him in the eyes of anyone knowing him well as the English lover of whom Miss Odilon wrote. So now he seeks damages for a slur upon his chastity.

Because, as he repeatedly and indignantly insists, he has never been the lover of Miss Odilon at all.

It is no part of *The Winning Post*'s defence to contradict him. Quite the reverse. They say that Smith was not even the lover's real name; that they deliberately conferred it on him as a pseudonym, just as they might have chosen Jones or Robinson or Brown; and that use of our commonest surname could not reasonably be held to single out the plaintiff from all the other Smiths.

This argument acquires piquancy through counsel for *The Winning Post* being a Smith himself—the redoubtable F.E., afterwards Lord Chancellor, and at present reaping the harvest of his brilliance at the Bar. It has almost the savour of a family dispute when the two Smiths confront one another.

"You don't suggest, do you," asks F.E., "that you have suffered any pecuniary damage?"

"I do," says the plaintiff.

"How?"

"When a copy of the paper was posted to me by a friend I thought the safest thing to do would be to show it to my wife. When she read it she got extremely angry."

"Of course you assured her that there was nothing in it?"

"Oh yes." The plaintiff nods. "But my wife said it wouldn't be in the paper if it were not true."

There is a laugh. The plaintiff shows no disposition to join in.

"How long have you been married?"

"Since 1891."

"Nearly twenty years," observes F.E. "No doubt your wife has learned by experience to rely upon your word?"

"On this occasion," says the plaintiff, "I could not convince her."

"That is regrettable. But I am still waiting to hear how you have suffered pecuniary damage."

The plaintiff looks embarrassed and takes time before replying.

"You see, it's my wife who has most of the money," he explains.

"Did she cut down your allowance?" asks F.E., sarcastically.

67

"It's nothing to do with an allowance. She was going to buy me a new farm. Because of this, she wouldn't."

Such a loss is not ingratiating, though it may be real. But the issue of damages will be academic if the plaintiff fails to establish a recognizable likeness between himself and the picture drawn by Miss Odilon.

"After all," F.E. says, "I'm sure you've found out, as I have, that our name is often taken simply to label types?"

"Yes," agrees the plaintiff.

"Miss Odilon's story is that of a gentleman rider who spent several months in Germany during 1888?"

"Yes."

"She says it was some time before the love affair began?"

"Yes."

"And the gentleman rider remained in Germany till the affair concluded?"

"I suggest," says F.E., with sudden menace, "that you were not so well known as a gentleman rider as has been made out?"

"I was well known."

"Many were better known?"

"Some."

"Many?"

"Perhaps."

"A *great* many?"

The plaintiff concedes the point.

"Possibly," he says.

"I suggest, too," says F.E., pressing his advantage, "that during 1888 the amount of time you spent in Germany was very small indeed?"

"I rode there for Herr Oehlschaeger."

"Staying only a few days?"

"I didn't stay long."

"Staying only a few days?"

The plaintiff concedes the point.

"Possibly," he says.

So far the action has proceeded on a highly moral basis. It has been tacitly assumed that the allegation is defamatory, and that the plaintiff need only prove it points in his direction. No one has asked whether a pre-marital affair would be treated with profound concern outside a monastery.

The first intrusion of more realistic values is effected by a witness called to testify that when he read the story in *The Winning Post* he believed that Mr. Smith, the gentleman rider, was the plaintiff.

"Have you a good opinion of the plaintiff's character?" F.E. asks.

"Very good," says the witness.

"You would find great difficulty, then, in believing that he would get involved in an immoral intrigue with an actress?"

It is an ingenious move by counsel, but doesn't work out exactly as intended.

"Well," says the witness, with cheerful amorality, "we were all younger once than we are now."

Prim Mr. Justice Ridley gives him a disapproving glare. The judge and *The Winning Post* look on life from different angles. If he is out of sympathy with its readers he is even more out of sympathy with its writers, as becomes manifest with startling clarity when the principal witness is called for the defence.

Yes, that witness translated Miss Odilon's memoirs. Yes, he edited them for *The Winning Post*. Yes, he had changed the gentleman rider's name to Smith. Yes, he took it for granted that what Miss Odilon said was true.

"Did you not think," asks the plaintiff's counsel, "that it would interest a certain section of the public to know of a gentleman rider who had had such an intrigue?"

"That was certainly the most interesting part of it."

"Don't you think," counsel goes on, "that people would think the worse of the gentleman rider referred to?"

"Oh, well," says the witness, with a cynical shrug, "everybody has had adventures of that sort."

The sentiment might pass muster at the offices of *The Winning Post*. It is altogether too much, though, for Mr. Justice Ridley.

He turns upon the witness.

"I am sorry to hear you say such things. It rouses my wrath." The judge does indeed appear ablaze with fury. "I don't believe the whole of mankind is as bad as you say. If we are all to be classed in the same condemnation, I won't stand it."

The storm of applause that followed this outburst demonstrated how closely it echoed *public* thought—not *private* thought, maybe, but the thought men suppose it is their duty to think when they think *en masse*.

It could not affect the verdict, but it could affect the damages. And the jury, finding there was a libel on the plaintiff, awarded him no less than £550 to compensate him for the shame and odium of being credited with a prize he really hadn't won.

Mr. Justice Stable
tries The Philanderer *Case*

JUST as there are horses for courses, so there are judges for cases. The occupants of the Bench justly command respect and admiration, but, being human, no one of them is omniscient, nor is his experience—of law or life—exhaustive. Cases in court, civil and criminal alike, thus usually embrace one element of chance; an unescapable gamble on the men assigned to try them.

Sometimes the luck of the draw works out badly; as when a cloistered commercial lawyer, sitting for the first time as a Red Judge on assize, gravely called the jury's special attention to the fact that an illiterate navvy, charged with a sanguinary murder, had next day been heard inquiring: "Where's my bloody shirt?"

Sometimes, though, the luck of the draw works out very well. And never more so than when, in 1954, Mr. Justice Stable took the Old Bailey summer session, and was thereby automatically appointed to preside over the proceedings arising out of *The Philanderer*. . . .

The Philanderer was the title of a novel that had gained some critical acclaim. Its theme—the career and character of a man wholly obsessed by his desire for women—might be considered unsavoury by some, but then so might the theme of Balzac's *Cousin Bette* or Zola's *Germinal*. The appropriate authorities, however, doubtless after careful scrutiny, decided that *The Philanderer* furnished grounds for prosecution, and its highly reputable publishers were indicted for issuing an obscene publication.

Now everybody knows there is a trade in dirty books, just as there is a trade in filthy pictures. But one does not equate the female nudes of Rubens with the female nudes depicted on the postcards of olive-skinned touts outside the Madeleine. It is treatment, and not subject, that creates pornography—in the literary arts as well as the pictorial.

That had been generally recognized by those with common sense even in the far-off days of 1954. But the law—which ought to consist of organized common sense, and of contemporary common sense at that—had failed to keep abreast with the majority.

The trouble lay partly in the test of obscenity laid down by Lord Chief Justice Cockburn the best part of a hundred years before, and partly in subsequent interpretations of it.

Cockburn defined obscenity as matter tending "to deprave and corrupt those whose minds are open to such immoral influences and into whose hands a publication of this sort may fall"—a definition begotten in an epoch when piano legs were draped for decency and authors were constrained by public squeamishness to refer to men's trousers as "unmentionables". It could be construed, and was so construed, even by some of Cockburn's more remote successors, to brand as obscene any work—at least, any work of fiction—that was likely to exert an unwholesome influence upon any child old enough to read.

Such a conception had become utterly out-moded. Its practical effect was to inhibit serious writing, frighten honest publishers, and induce adult readers who wanted a great book like Joyce's *Ulysses* to smuggle copies in their baggage from the continent. Both English law and English literature were injured; the latter by repression, the former by ridicule.

Historians of the future, looking back upon the social fabric of our age, will accord high credit to Mr. Justice Stable for his share in the removal of this anomaly, and in bringing about a closer accord between law and opinion.

That will not cause surprise to anyone who has ever encountered Mr. Justice Stable at close quarters.

I well remember him going the Northern Circuit as a newly elevated judge just before the War. He was chiefly known to us youngsters by his reputation at the Bar as a specialist in bankruptcy. It sounded rather technical and dull, and we were prepared for someone rather dull and technical.

Our expectations could not have been more agreeably belied.

Instead of a dusty, desiccated pedant, a conspicuously warm and vital character appeared—I had almost said, exploded—in our provincial courts. Quick to smile, quick to frown, quick to indicate dissent; quick, even quicker, to indicate agreement; temperamentally dynamic, intellectually alert—one did not seek then to assess his stature as a jurist, being gratefully content with his stature as a man.

I understand from those who are supposed to know these things that Mr. Justice Stable isn't really a Great Lawyer; not as Lord Blackburn or Lord Atkin or Lord Porter were. Whether or no, he certainly possesses other qualities equally exceptional—and perhaps more valuable in the everyday employments of a puisne judge. He is a natural humanist, with a quenchless zest for life, a keen interest in the way that other people live it, and a manifest belief that law, so far from being inflexible, ultimately depends on the community's support.

These qualities determined his approach to *The Philanderer*.

Upon a trial for obscene publication, the work, in itself, constituted the evidence of fact. Five years were to pass before the enactment of the Obscene Publications Act, 1959, which made it a defence that the work was for the public good by reason of its literary merit and so paved the way for the spate of oral evidence that intrigued and titillated the public for days on end in the case of *Lady Chatterley's Lover* a year later. Assisted by such guidance as they might receive, it was on the work alone that the jury must decide.

Accordingly, Mr. Justice Stable, after all the necessary preliminaries were completed, adjourned *The Philanderer* case for a couple of days so that the jury might peruse the challenged book at leisure.

At that stage, he only advised them to consider it as a whole rather than to pounce on single passages out of context. It was after they had returned to court, their homework done, that he discussed the requisite criteria more fully, in the course of a summing-up which has acquired —and will retain—a fame extending far beyond purely legal confines.

The judge early impressed on the jury—three women and nine men —that their verdict would be of the utmost consequence. "It will have a great bearing," he said, "upon where the line is drawn between liberty, that freedom to read and think as the spirit moves us, and licence, which is an affront to the society of which we all are members."

Then he quoted Lord Chief Justice Cockburn's definition—and violently wrestled against its stranglehold.

"Because that is the test laid down in 1868, that does not mean that what you have to consider is: Supposing this book had been *published* in 1868, and the publishers had been *prosecuted* in 1868, would the court or the jury, nearly a century ago, have reached the conclusion that it was obscene? Your task"—Mr. Justice Stable spoke with emphasis—"is to decide whether you think that the tendency of the book is to deprave those whose minds *today* are open to such immoral influences, and into whose hands the book may fall *this year*."

His first major point was thus luminously stated—that the Cockburn definition had not been fossilized, that a book must be judged by the standards operating *now*.

Next came an instructive and acute appraisal of the different attitudes adopted towards sex.

"At the one extreme, you get the line of thought that sex is sin; that the whole thing is dirty; that it was a mistake from beginning to end; that the less said on that distasteful topic the better."

And the other extreme?

"The line of thought that nothing but mischief results from a policy of covering up; that the whole thing is just as much part of God's universe as anything else; that the proper policy is one of frankness and plain speaking, and the avoidance of any sort of pretence. . . . Somewhere between these two poles," the judge suggested, "the average, decent, well-meaning man or woman takes his or her stand."

There followed his second major point: an elucidation, in conformity with modern trends, of the canonical words, "Those whose minds are open to such immoral influences and into whose hands a publication of this sort may fall."

"What exactly does that mean?" Mr. Justice Stable said. "Are we to say our literature should be measured by what is suitable for a schoolgirl aged fourteen? Or do we go even further back, and are we to be reduced to the sort of books one reads as a child in the nursery?"

The crucial question had been asked. Cultural emancipation waited on the answer.

"*Of course not*." At his lordship's robust and forthright disavowal, a score of master writers, from Geoffrey Chaucer to David Herbert Lawrence, must have joined their countless admirers in a ghostly cheer. "Of course not. A mass of literature—*great* literature—is, from many angles, wholly unsuitable for reading by the adolescent, but that does not mean a publisher is guilty of a criminal offence for making these works available to the public."

The publishers of *The Philanderer* were acquitted. But matters of deeper significance had been settled than the legal status of one particular book. A wind of change had started blowing through the courts; it dispersed stale smoke-screens, revived half-stifled victims, and did much to clear a passage for the reforming Obscene Publications Act of 1959 which Mr. Roy Jenkins, with notable skill and patience, piloted through the House of Commons.

PART TWO

THE JUDGED

Alma Rattenbury

IN the domain of sexual partnerships, there is an accepted code of seemliness as well as of morality. It has been shaped and settled by a collective instinct which operates with a force superior to law.

One requirement of this code applies to relative age. The man may be considerably older than the woman—fifteen, twenty even thirty years —without offending society's delicate sense of fitness. But there is immediate dislike of an alliance where the woman is considerably older than the man. The collective instinct rejects it as unwholesome.

No use asking whether instinct here is buttressed by mere reason. The prejudice exists and it cannot be ignored—a prejudice based on the surmise that, in these circumstances, the man has been seduced; that Innocent Lad has fallen prey to Sophisticated Siren.

This attitude of mind breeds a dangerous by-product. If any external mischief should ensue from the association of young man with older woman, there is a tendency—irrespective of, or even despite, the evidence—to assume that the latter must be principal delinquent. That assumption is greatly reinforced if the former is also beneath her socially.

The cards were thus stacked against Alma Rattenbury when she stood trial for murder in 1935.

Beside her in the Old Bailey dock, and similarly charged, was her chauffeur, whose mistress she had been in more respects than one. The pair were accused of murdering Mrs. Rattenbury's husband, who had died as a result of savage injuries to his head.

Mr. Rattenbury, at the time of his death, was sixty-seven. Mrs. Rattenbury was thirty-eight. The chauffeur—by name George Stoner— was eighteen.

The British public noted these ages and compressed its lips. . . .

At first sight, it was a wholly squalid tale, without even a saving glimpse of human dignity. The intrigue, which they hardly took the trouble to conceal, between the mature woman and the callow youth; the gifts and the money which she lavished on him; their unedifying quarrels and hardly less unedifying reconciliations—these formed a most appropriate background to a crime that in itself achieved the nadir of replusiveness.

Late one night the doctor was called to the Rattenburys' home; Mr. Rattenbury lay bleeding and unconscious in a chair; Mrs. Rattenbury was manifestly drunk and when police officers arrived, made amorous advances. "I did it," she said. "I hit him with a mallet, which I hid outside. I did it deliberately and I would do it again."

77

It all added up, didn't it? A nymphomaniac drunkard, equally unrestrained with sex and alcohol. Just the sort to throw in a murder for good measure.

Such, at any rate, was the swift snap judgment of the time, barely modified by Stoner's insistence that Mrs. Rattenbury's spectacular confession was untrue, that it was he who had done all that Mrs. Rattenbury said she did, only telling her afterwards, when the crime had been accomplished; nor did opinion materially alter when close investigation bore Stoner's statement out. All right, all right, grant that his hand struck the blow. She must have put him up to it; hers must have been the dominant will, the master mind.

Quite right then that, when Mr. Rattenbury died, the Crown alleged conspiracy to murder, and put her as well as Stoner in the shadow of the rope. She's not to get away with it because she used a catspaw; especially a woman of her degraded type.

The profound significance of her effort to shield Stoner was at this stage entirely overlooked. . . .

The crowd in court were puzzled about Mrs. Rattenbury, even while she sat in the dock, silent and withdrawn, her face almost hidden by the hand against her cheek. The whole aspect and aura of the woman, poised, controlled, tastefully attired—it didn't suggest the coarse Hogarthian slut who drank herself stupid and was ravenous for men.

The shock really exploded when she went into the box.

Who was this refined and sensitive woman with the wide grey eyes and the modulated voice and the frank, open, courteous replies?

Not, surely, Mrs. Rattenbury of the bestial orgies?

It was one of those rare occasions in the courts when a witness has overturned a case just by appearing; when a preconceived notion of the truth was set aside by a personality who defied that version to be true.

She made no attempt whatever to gloss over her failings or offer excuses for them. Yes, she said, she had been Stoner's mistress; relations had taken place frequently between them; Stoner was jealous and there were several scenes—notably on the afternoon before the murder, when she had talked of going away on a visit with her husband. But she had pacified her angry lover, so she thought, and that evening when she returned to her own separate bedroom, she expected him to come to her and was not disappointed.

"What happened?" counsel asked. "What did Stoner look like?"

"I noticed he looked a little bit strange," Mrs. Rattenbury said.

"How was he dressed?"

"In his pyjamas."

"What did he do?"

"Got into bed."

"And then?"

"Well." Mrs. Rattenbury steeled herself. "Well, he seemed agitated, and he said he was in trouble and couldn't tell me what it was, and I said 'Oh, you must tell me', and we went back and forth like that for two or three minutes."

"Yes?"

"And then he told me."

"Yes?"

"He told me I wasn't going away because he had hurt my husband. It didn't penetrate my head until I heard a groan, and then I jumped out of bed and ran downstairs." She described the spectacle that met her eyes: the battered husband; the blood upon the floor. "Then I trod on his false teeth and that made me hysterical. I took a drink of neat whisky to stop myself being sick. I was sick, all the same, and I poured out another one. I tried to become insensible, to blot out the picture."

"Have you at other times," said counsel, "given way to drink?"

Again Mrs. Rattenbury did not spare herself.

"Well, my life was so monotonous that at times I used to take too much to liven myself up—cocktails, it would be, or wine—but not spirits, like that night."

Nor did she seek to take refuge in evasion when questioned about the nature of her feelings for young Stoner.

"It was just an infatuation, wasn't it?" suggested counsel.

"It was more than that," she answered. "I fell in love with him."

And in that answer is the key to the whole case.

Stoner was not merely the hireling of a nymphomaniac. Strange as it may seem, Mrs. Rattenbury was in love with him, and hers was a romantic love of most familiar pattern. Romantic love has its evils and absurdities—not least, perhaps, in the case under review—but it is far removed from the crude debauch of nymphomania. And it can inspire—it had inspired Mrs. Rattenbury—to dramatic sacrifice for the protection of the loved one.

None has the right to say that hers had been an empty gesture, that she wasn't ready to go through with it even though it cost her life. She did not prize life highly without Stoner. Four days after his conviction and her own acquittal, Alma Rattenbury stabbed herself to death. She had no desire to wait for his inevitable reprieve. What would that mean but fifteen years in jail? And then . . .

He'd be a young man still. She would be fifty-three.

John Alexander Dickman

JOHN ALEXANDER DICKMAN is universally regarded as a brutal murderer. A jury thus pronounced. History has handed it down. Posterity accepts it.

But all this may have happened through the accident of date. Had he been tried before, instead of after, the legally momentous year of 1898, Dickman might have been triumphantly acquitted.

For in that year an Act of Parliament revolutionized every prisoner's position. It permitted him—as formerly he had not been permitted—to give sworn evidence on his own behalf.

In theory, this confers on him the unqualified advantage of electing whether to go into the box. In practice, it also imposes on him the serious disadvantage that, if he does not, his guilt is likely to be assumed. A person accused is thus virtually compelled—unless the prosecution make out no case at all—to take the oath and submit himself to cross-examination. Dickman, like countless other persons less notorious, yielded to this pressure with disastrous results.

The Newcastle train murder, with which Dickman was charged, occurred on 18 March, 1910.

That morning, a colliery book-keeper named Nisbet, in accordance with his practice each alternate Friday, travelled by the 10.27 stopping train to Alnwick, taking with him wages from head office to the pit. The train possessed no corridor. Nisbet's bag contained £370 in cash.

At Stannington, an intermediate station on the route, a friend saw and exchanged nods with Nisbet from the platform, as the latter sat in a compartment with one other man.

At Morpeth, the next station along the line from Stannington, the same compartment appeared to be unoccupied when a passenger leisurely choosing his seat, glanced casually inside.

At Alnwick, where the compartments were examined, Nisbet's dead body was discovered pushed right back under the seat. He had been shot five times. His bag was missing, but was later come upon by chance—empty of course—at the bottom of a colliery airshaft, less than two miles from Morpeth Station and close to the high road.

Now it is as clear as anything can be in this world that Nisbet was murdered by his travelling companion while the train was between Stannington and Morpeth; and that the murderer, having stowed his victim out of immediate sight, alighted instantly the train pulled up at Morpeth and forthwith sought out the most convenient spot for disposing of the bag and pocketing the loot.

The whole case, therefore, hinged upon a single point: Who was

Nisbet's travelling companion? He and the murderer inevitably were one.

The Crown alleged that this double role had been fulfilled by Dickman.

On a simple count of heads, they had abundant evidence. One man said that he saw Dickman and Nisbet (both of whom he knew) walking together towards the departure platform at Newcastle. Another said that he saw Dickman (whom he knew) and a man of slight build (which Nisbet undoubtedly was) actually about to board the train together.

Another said that he saw Nisbet (whom he knew) getting into his compartment with a man whom Dickman "very much resembled". Yet another (the friend of Nisbet previously mentioned) saw him at Stannington sharing a compartment with a man who "resembled Dickman" though he "could not swear to him".

And, as sensational and unexpected witness, there was Mrs. Nisbet, the wife of the dead man. They had lived near Heaton Station, between Newcastle and Stannington, and it had been her habit to meet her husband there as he passed through. She also claimed to recognize in Dickman the other occupant of Nisbet's compartment, though "he had his collar turned up" and "a shadow from the tunnel fell upon him".

Five of them; but counting heads does not amount to much, especially where something so intangible as identification is at stake. The deponents varied in their degree of certainty, and it became painfully apparent as the trial progressed that there had been some jiggery-pokery at the identification parade.

Moreover, no weapon was ever traced to the prisoner's possession. Moreover, the contents of the bag were never found. Moreover, Dickman did not deny his presence on the train, but at the very outset had given the police a statement that might be reconciled with inaccurate observation by some, at least, of those called for the Crown.

He booked a return ticket to Stannington, Dickman said, where he intended—though he had no appointment—to visit a Mr. Hogg. He saw Nisbet at the booking office but never again thereafter. He sat in the rear of the train (Nisbet's compartment was at the front), closely reading a racing paper, and consequently did not notice when the train reached Stannington.

He therefore got out at Morpeth; paid the excess fare; set off to walk the two or three miles back to Stannington; felt ill on the way, returned to Morpeth, and caught a Newcastle train.

Enough, surely, to make an impartial jury waver if the case had perforce terminated there. But this is the twentieth century, and Dickman had no practicable alternative to facing the questions of Tindal Atkinson, leading for the Crown.

"You have been connected with a colliery company?" asks that very expert cross-examiner.

"Yes," says Dickman, "as the secretary."

"Do you know that wages are paid fortnightly?"

"I do."

"And they are usually paid on a Friday?"

"They are."

"You know that the wages must be carried by someone to the colliery from the bank?"

"Yes," says Dickman, "I've done that myself."

"Did you go from Newcastle to Stannington exactly a fortnight before 18 March?"

"Yes."

"You had no appointment with Mr. Hogg on that date, either?"

"No."

"Why did you select a Friday?"

The quicker-witted jurymen get the drift of this at once. The earlier journey takes shape in their minds as a possible trial trip to study the line and the routine—or even as an endeavour at murder that misfired.

"Mr. Hogg paid his men's wages on Friday," Dickman says.

"What had you to do with his wages?"

"Nothing particular."

"Did they concern you at all?"

"In this respect, they did. I wanted to know whether he was receiving part of his fortnightly pay from a man I know called Christie."

"Why should you care?"

"I wanted to know whether Christie was bluffing me saying he had no money."

"Supposing he hadn't?" asks Tindal Atkinson. "What had that to do with you?"

Dickman does not answer. Even if what he says is true—and he and Christie certainly had had financial dealings—he may feel that it does not sound a plausible excuse.

The prosecutor has made his point. He quickly scores another.

"Did anybody travel with you in your compartment?"

"I think some people did."

"Did you know who they were?"

"No."

"This occurrence has caused widespread interest?"

"Yes."

"Have you heard of any of these people since?"

"No."

Tindal Atkinson moves forward a stage.

"Having passed Stannington Station you set out to walk back there from Morpeth?"

"Yes."

"Did you know that a train for Stannington was leaving Morpeth in a few minutes?"

"Yes," Dickman agrees, "but besides seeing Mr. Hogg, I wanted to inspect some sinking operations half-way between Stannington and Morpeth."

"What had these sinking operations to do with you?"

"A friend of mine had asked me what they were worth."

"What was his name?"

"Is it necessary to disclose it?"

"Why not?" asks Tindal Atkinson. "It can't do him any harm."

"Mr. Houldsworth," Dickman then says, reluctantly.

"Had you arranged with him to see it?"

"No."

"Did he know you were going to see it?"

"No."

Two puncturing blows that destroy any faith the jury have in the story of Mr. Houldsworth. There is nothing now that obscures their vivid picture of an airshaft, a falling bag, and Dickman peering down.

Only one question troubles them still; *why* should he murder for the comparatively modest sum in a colliery wages bag?

"Were you borrowing from a moneylender in October?"

"Yes."

"Were you pledging jewellery in February?"

"Yes."

"At the time of the murder, had you anything in the bank?"

"A few odd shillings," Dickman says.

"And you had no job?"

"No."

"And none in prospect?"

"No."

Thus Dickman is compelled to qualify for inclusion in the category of brutal murderers. For me, perhaps, even now not without slight misgivings—but they are better crushed; that verdict cannot be reversed. Dickman's life fell forfeit in the witness box—forfeit to the Act of 1898.

Alfred Arthur Rouse

ALFRED ARTHUR ROUSE had conceived a highly original plan for ridding himself of his financial and domestic troubles.

It involved picking up acquaintance with a tramp possessing neither roots nor family ties nor friends; inducing him to accept a lift on a night drive which Rouse was ostensibly undertaking alone; making a plausible excuse for stopping in the early hours of the morning on a deserted country road; seizing his sleepy companion by the throat and choking him to death or, at least, into unconsciousness; and then—having removed the top of the carburettor, loosened the petrol union joint, and poured petrol on the ground—striking a match and setting the car alight.

Rouse, a commercial traveller by calling but by inclination an amateur engineer, knew that the resultant blaze would be instantaneous and fierce. The trapped passenger should be swiftly consumed beyond all recognition. Thereupon Rouse could conveniently vanish and somewhere begin life afresh with a new identity, while the fire was attributed to accident and the charred carcase assumed to be his own.

No more complications with what he called his harem; the wife in Friern Barnet, the girl friend in Birmingham, the girl friend in Southampton, the girl friend in Hendon, the girl friend in South Wales. No more expenditure on his growing array of bastards (in the autumn of 1930, when that criminal plan first took shape in Rouse's mind, Hendon had just added one and South Wales had given unmistakable presage of another).

No more jealousies, suspicions, recriminations, quarrels.

The more Rouse dwelt on this enticing prospect, the more resolved he grew to put his plan into effect. But he did not move without careful preparation. It was typical of his thoroughness as well as his sharp wits that he finally selected for the venture Guy Fawkes Night, when the glare of a fire would attract the least attention.

Rouse went nine-tenths of the way towards success, as is disclosed in his confession published after he was hanged.

He discovered an extremely suitable victim for his purpose ("A down and out . . . He did not tell me his name, but he did say that he had no relations and was looking for work"). He provided him with a whole bottle of whisky, to drink from as he pleased on their journey north from London, so that when Rouse turned off the main road a few miles from Northampton his companion was virtually without means of self-defence ("Quite fuzzled, half dozing . . . He did not resist").

He contrived the fire with expertness and speed ("The whole thing was a mass of flames in a few seconds").

But on the very last lap Rouse's cleverness recoiled upon his head.

Just because it *was* Guy Fawkes Night, with its attendant celebrations, two young men returning from Northampton to a neighbouring village, walked into that quiet road at the unprecedented hour of 2 a.m. They saw the raging furnace that had lately been a car. They also saw Rouse hurriedly departing.

Rouse, on his part, saw them—and his heart stopped. He knew the instant they turned their eyes upon him that his design had irretrievably miscarried. When the police came to make inquiries they would now have a *second* person to account for—a person alive and apparently uninjured. There could thus be no presumption that the perished remains in the car were those of Rouse.

Had Rouse made advance provision against failure? I think probably not; smart murderers—and he ranks among the smartest—frequently suffer from over-confidence. But he gained time for subsequent improvisation.

Dropping his original project of total disappearance but keeping a wary distance from the police, he travelled from the scene of his crime to London in a lorry, and then dashed off by coach to his girl friend in South Wales. When at last they picked him up on his arrival back in London Rouse had had two whole days in which to think.

Oh, yes, it was his car, he said, that had got burned out. (After all, they knew that from the registration number.) I don't know what happened exactly, Rouse went on. I'd given this chap a lift—he signalled me on the Great North Road. Later on I had to get out of the car, and I asked him to pour a can of petrol into the tank meanwhile. He said something about a smoke as I went a little way down the road. Then suddenly I saw the car on fire. I ran to it, but couldn't get near because of the flames. I lost my head and I didn't know what to do, and I really don't know what I have done since.

It was not a bad story, as lawyers sometimes say with unintended cynicism. Rouse doubtless thought it would pass muster. He would now be none the better off for all his pains, but at least he expected to be none the worse.

What he did not expect was to be charged with wilful murder. What he did not expect was expert evidence tending to show that his car had been deliberately set on fire. What he did not expect were his present circumstances—as chief witness in his own defence, under cross-examination by Norman Birkett for the Crown.

He gives his early answers in a tone of confidence which contrasts strangely with his explanation that he did not seek help for the hapless tramp because he "got panicky".

"But you had nothing to do with the fire, had you?" Birkett says.

"It was my car," says Rouse.

"Did you think you would be blamed?"

"No."

"Then what were you panicky about?"

"The blaze."

"Do you mean that the mere blaze frightened you?"

Rouse hesitates.

"Yes," he says, "and I thought the man was inside."

"Was that not all the more reason why you should try to help or get help?"

Rouse hesitates longer.

"Yes," he finally admits.

"But even when those two young men passed you on the road,

85

while your companion was being burned, you did not ask them for help?"

"I was in a panic," Rouse doggedly repeats.

But it sounds considerably less convincing now, and Birkett points out that his panic did not prevent him making his way back to the main road and boarding a lorry going in the right direction.

"Did you tell the lorryman that you had been waiting for a mate with a car that had not turned up?"

"Quite possibly I did."

"It was not the truth?"

"No."

"You were sufficiently out of your panic to invent a lie?"

"Put it that way."

"But that is right, is it not?"

Rouse shrugs his shoulders.

"Yes."

"Did you tell the lorryman it was a good idea to have the floorboards up because it made the lorry warm?"

"Yes."

"Does that look like panic?"

"I do not know."

"Does that look like panic?" Birkett asks again.

Very reluctantly Rouse replies.

"It does not, perhaps," he says.

The excuse of panic has indeed worn thin. And what other reason can there be for failing to ask help?

"When you got back to London did it not occur to you that the thing to do, being innocent, was to go to the police?"

"I wanted to visit my girl friend in Wales first."

"Did you tell an official at the coach station in London that your car had been stolen during the night while you were at a coffee stall?"

"Yes."

"That was a lie?"

"Yes."

"A lie from a man who was going to the police next day to tell the truth?"

"Yes."

"I put it to you"—Birkett speaks with particular gravity—"that you never intended going to the police at all?"

"Yes, I did," Rouse maintains, but his confidence has given place to a stubborn desperation.

"Did you tell the coach driver your car had been stolen at St. Albans?"

"Yes."

"Did you tell the father of your woman friend that it had been stolen at Northampton?"

"Yes."

"Did you tell a publican on the route that it had been stolen in London?"

"Yes."

"All those two days you invented lies, until you were met by the police?"

"Yes."

"What was your purpose?"

Rouse has no option left. To all intents and purposes, he throws in his hand.

"*I did not want to give a long explanation to everyone,*" he says.

In retrospect the guilt of Rouse is absolutely clear, even without his own belated confirmation. And yet, at the conclusion of the prosecution case, when he walked from the dock to the box and took the oath, his chances of acquittal seemed not unfavourable. Juries are rightly loth to convict in a capital trial on technical opinion, however knowledgeable, and the Crown's main evidence was necessarily such.

It was only after his cross-examination—as acute and deadly as it was courteous and fair—that Rouse's crime stood nakedly revealed, and society could without misgiving exact retribution for the murder of a being forever nameless and unknown.

Louise Masset

S OMEHOW she looks an even sadder figure in the box than she has done these last days in the dock. Slighter, frailer, considerably more than her thirty-six quiet and inoffensive years.

"Your name is Louise Masset?"

"Yes."

The cultivated voice rises just above a whisper.

"You are a spinster?"

"Yes."

"Four years ago, did you give birth to a child?"

The mousy little woman flinches, hesitates, and then begins to weep.

None can be absolutely positive for whom: whether for that child, who has now been murdered; or for his mother, who is charged with murdering him.

Sometimes compelling motives prompt an unmarried mother to contemplate ridding herself of an illegitimate child. Its mere existence may involve her in continuous shame. It needs may place an insupportable strain upon her purse. It may frustrate her matrimonial ambitions. It may even—for the child can become an unwitting symbol—excite her animosity instead of her affection.

But none of these motives affected Louise Masset.

Her offence against the moral code—so far as it was ever known—had long since been forgiven and forgotten. Her earnings as a teacher of French, regular if modest, were supplemented by an allowance from the child's father. Her present lover, in whom she had unreservedly confided, was hardly more than a boy, and never broached—nor seemed likely to broach—the theme of marriage.

Above all, Louise was a fond, attentive, and solicitous mother; visiting her small son on every opportunity at the home of a kindly woman, named Miss Gentle, with whom he had been "boarded out".

The Crown, indeed, did not suggest any convincing motive for the crime they sought to lay at Louise Masset's door. Of course—though juries can't be prevented from asking themselves "Why?"—no rule of necessity required the Crown to do so. They took their stand, as they were entitled, upon what appeared the grim logic of events. . . .

It was in October, 1899, that Louise told Miss Gentle of new plans which had been made for the future of her boy. His French father, she said, wanted him to be educated in France; and so, with many regrets and deepest gratitude, she found herself forced to take him out of Miss Gentle's tender care. The ladies embraced each other sympathetically (the boy had been with Miss Gentle since he was three weeks old), and Louise arranged to call for him on Friday the 27th in good time to catch the boat train at London Bridge. She would take him across to France herself, and see him safely settled.

Louise had given exactly the same account of her intentions at her married sister's house in Stoke Newington, where she lived; the journey abroad and back, with perhaps a night or two in France, meant she would be away for the whole of that week-end. Her young lover, though, heard rather differently. She was going away for the week-end, yes—but instead of to France with the child, by herself to Brighton; and he agreed to follow her there on the Saturday.

Louise punctually kept her Friday appointment with Miss Gentle. The latter, as a final token of devotion to him, had arrayed the little boy in his distinctive best: a blue coat, with bright gilt buttons, over a blue frock, ornamented with white braid.

The next—and last—authenticated sight of them occurred inside a passengers' waiting-room at London Bridge (a departure station, incidentally, both for Brighton and the Continent). They remained some time, so that the child grew fretful, and Louise volunteered to the attendant that she had come to meet someone who was late. But nobody appeared, and, shortly before three o'clock, mother and son went out hand in hand.

What happened to them, where did they go, what did they do, during the rest of that autumn afternoon? In court, and upon oath, Louise declared she could answer only for herself.

"You see, immediately after we left the waiting-room, I found the two ladies I had been looking for."

"Which ladies?"

"The ladies I had met at Tottenham Green. You know—three or four weeks earlier." Louise spoke—witnesses often do—as if everybody knew her story without her telling it. "The ladies with the little girl who knew my little boy. 'Hallo, Manfred,' she said. 'Hallo, Millie', he said. And the ladies and me, naturally, while the children were playing we got talking."

Naturally enough. And, just as naturally, they talked about themselves: Louise, of her growing concern for Manfred's education: the two ladies (who gave their name as Browning) of their residential kindergarten school in the King's Road.

Their interests patently converged and, after much discussion, an offer made by one side was accepted by the other.

London Bridge station was fixed as a mutually convenient point for transfer of the boy and for payment, in advance, of the annual fee.

"Twelve pounds," Louise said, almost musingly. "It was really more than I could afford. But they seemed such nice people."

"Had you inspected their school?"

"I meant to go with them that Friday, but they arrived so late it would have meant missing my train. I said I was off to Brighton for a day or two, and to expect me up some time during the following week."

If those two "nice people" ever existed at all, then assuredly they were baby farmers, and they coldly murdered that little boy for profit. If, though, they did not exist, then, no less assuredly, Louise murdered him herself and invented them as a blind. For at twenty past six on that same afternoon, Manfred's body, stripped of all his clothing, was discovered in the ladies' toilet at Dalston Junction, on the other side of the river and some three miles away.

The Brownings of King's Road were never traced. But there were much doubtful features in Louise's narrative that counsel now called upon her to explain.

You lied to Miss Gentle about your plans for Manfred. Why?

"My relations with Miss Gentle were of the friendliest possible character." No conscious affectation prompted her meticulous teacher's English. "She would have been heartbroken if she knew the child was going to be placed with anyone else in England."

But you told the same lies to your sister. Why?

"So that I could snatch a little while with . . . him." She couldn't, or wouldn't, utter the young man's name. "So that I could be away without creating any trouble."

Why didn't you ask these women for proper references?

"They were such nice people," Louise repeated. "Such perfect ladies."

And get their exact address?

"I didn't think there'd be many other schools in King's Road," Louise said.

The white lie to spare the feelings of a friend, the grey lie to conceal a sexual peccadillo, the naïve trust in external respectability—all these might have passed as feasible, if not as conclusive, explanations.

There was, however, a far worse hurdle to negotiate, a hurdle that Louise had been dreading long enough.

You have listened to the evidence called before my lord and the jury?

Yes. Louise had listened, with fast-beating heart.

You know from that that on Sunday, 29 October a parcel containing clothes was found on Brighton Station?

Yes, heaven help her, Louis knew.

And that Miss Gentle has identified those clothes as Manfred's?

Yes—and she also knew Miss Gentle had been right.

You were at Brighton that week-end?

Yes, she had been at Brighton.

Did you take Manfred's clothes to Brighton?

Never, never, never.

Can you suggest how otherwise they got there?

Could she suggest how otherwise they got there? No, she couldn't. Rack her brains as she might, it wasn't any good, she couldn't.

In that moment of trembling helplessness, Louise Masset's fate upon the scaffold was foretold by a child's blue coat with bright gilt buttons, by a child's blue frock ornamented with white braid.

And yet . . . And yet . . .

If you can imagine yourself a baby farmer—that is, an utterly ruthless and stony-hearted criminal, who for £12 will murder a small child— what would you do, under similar circumstances, in order to shift suspicion and divert the blame?

You have got the dead child's clothes. You know that his mother has gone off for a day or two at Brighton. You know that unclaimed parcels left on railway premises are likely to be opened and officially examined.

Think carefully over those three factors once again. *What would you do?*

Yes. So would I.

Lord Haw Haw

ON that hot June morning in 1945 when they put him up before the chief magistrate at Bow Street, we certainly were an unusually large crowd. Unusually large—and unusually mixed. Scotland Yard moguls as well as traffic cops. Best-selling novelists as well as crime reporters. Social celebrities as well as anonymous plebs. All drawn together by a common interest—whether occupational or otherwise—in the accused.

He made his entrance on the dot. As he first came into view, under the lee of a gigantic jailer, most of us blinked, then gave vent to an incredulous gasp.

Could this possibly be he? Could this possibly be the masterful and supercilious foe of whom we had formed an appropriate mental image? For—even discounting the contrast with the giant beside him—this was, to all intents, *a dwarf*.

But a malevolent and determined and unflinching dwarf. You had only to glance at that mask-like countenance; that bitter and ruthless mouth; those cold pale eyes in which trained observers might occasionally detect the characteristic intermittent glint of paranoia.

He stepped forward in brisk fashion, and smartly turned to face the Bench. He brought his hands, palms inward, to his sides, squared his slight shoulders, and stood there motionless. His impeccable military bearing clashed incongruously with his diminutive stature and his civilian clothes.

Silently, he heard that the charge against him was high treason; that the Crown did not propose to open their case today; that they would only tender formal evidence of arrest.

Silently, he listened while that evidence was given by a chief inspector from the Special Branch. Silently, and without apparent awareness, he held the intense and ceaseless gaze of all the onlookers—many of whom, still rocking from that initial shock, remained half convinced that we had captured the wrong man.

The chief inspector finished his short testimony, and waited. The magistrate addressed the rigid figure of the prisoner with a remote and stately courtesy.

"William Joyce, are you legally represented?"

Now was the real test, surely. We leaned forward, all ears.

"No, sir."

Two words only—not enough.

"Do you wish to put any questions to the witness on what he has said?"

"No, sir."

Two words only—not enough.

"It is proposed," went on the magistrate, "to remand you for a week. Have you any objection?"

"I have no objection sir, but I would like to apply for legal aid."

That was more than enough. Then, and only then, we knew for certain. All of us had heard those distinctive, metallic, menacing tones too often for any doubt or misgiving to linger.

Lord Haw Haw, who throughout the war in his broadcasts from the Reich had nightly threatened Britain with destruction and defeat, was now evoking the protection of the British law from the relative haven of a British police court dock.

I myself had gone that day to Bow Street both for professional and for personal reasons. Professional, because I was subsequently to broadcast an account of the proceedings. Personal, because, in an impersonal conflict of masses and machines, Haw Haw and I had joined battle on the radio as directly and intimately as medieval knights.

Indeed, I felt overwhelming thankfulness that it was I now reporting his scrupulous impeachment rather than he reporting my summary execution. For I cannot seriously doubt that he would have gained—and grasped—that opportunity had the Germans won.

There was, though, a vital distinction between us to be noted. My crime —accountable to Nazi demonology—was to broadcast for my own side against the Germans. Haw Haw's crime—subject to British legal proof —was to broadcast for the German side against his own.

Haw Haw had slipped quietly out of Britain immediately before, and in anticipation of, the war. A militant Fascist, fiercely anti-democratic by inborn temperament and acquired conviction, his goal was Germany and his fixed intention to play some active part in her forthcoming bid for the domination and enslavement of the world.

"I was not actuated," he afterwards asserted, "by desire for gain, material or otherwise"—and, without reservation, I accept that statement. His purposes were *evil*, but they were not *selfish*; Haw Haw was not a calculating opportunist, but an ideological fanatic.

The Germans—or, at any rate, their shrewd and highly efficient propaganda organization—were quick to realize Haw Haw's potentialities.

He began broadcasting to Britain in September, 1939; during that first cold, dreary, and blacked-out winter more than half our population grew familiar with his voice, and burlesques of his idiosyncratic accent ("Jairmany Calling") formed a welcome addition to many an English comic's stock-in-trade.

As the war spread, so did the range of his activities, and the United States was included in his scope; ultimately, he became chief commentator of Germany's English service with an augmented salary of 1,200 marks a month. His record reflects the value Goebbels placed upon him.

Not without good reason. Haw Haw had excellent claims to be considered the enemy's ablest full-time broadcaster of the war. His precise diction and sinister timbre were compelling; no nickname could have been less suitable for him than "Lord Haw Haw", for no man could have sounded less effete and la-de-dah. His talks were ingeniously conceived and skilfully composed; by their blend of fact and dialectic, of half truths and downright lies, they were well designed to weaken Britain's backing for her leaders, confidence in victory, and consequent will to struggle on.

"The people of England will curse themselves for having preferred ruin from Churchill to peace from Hitler." "British soldiers find themselves utterly at a loss to cope with the German dive bombers and other modern engines of scientific warfare. German forces are destroying Britain's armament works, crippling her railways, closing her harbours, smashing her convoys, and invasion is expected to come to her soil at any moment."

Even after the strategic situation was transformed, and Haw Haw could no longer draw the same assistance from events, he still exploited human apprehension to the full. "After the collapse of the Second Front," he would say in the early months of 1944, "the whole of the British people will want to know what compensation they can expect on the score of their sacrifices."

And, "If Churchill responds to the Kremlin's demands for an invasion of Europe, the result will be a catastrophic defeat for the British forces."

A nation with less steady nerves might have fallen prey to Haw Haw —especially during the dark days of isolation, when there was little to sustain us except faith. But the British sturdily upheld their great traditions. They paid Haw Haw the compliment of listening to his broadcasts—but, in general, out of curiosity or for sheer amusement. A few hearts may have beaten faster at his dire predictions ("Tomorrow night strong units of the German air force will attack an important south coast port"); a few minds, preoccupied with distant dear ones, may have taken alarm at his unverifiable "news" ("Yesterday German submarines in the Atlantic wiped out ten British merchant craft and their escort vessels").

These, however, were occasional exceptions. Haw Haw utterly failed in his attempt to lower British morale and undermine British resolve. But, though he failed, the British public did not forget that he had tried, and they nourished for Haw Haw a peculiar detestation—greater than any they ever felt for Hitler and his gang. These, however aggressive and brutal, had not been *disloyal*; it was simply that their loyalty lay to a wicked cause. Haw Haw—in the popular British view—*had* been disloyal; he had fouled his own nest, he had bitten the hand that fed him, he had perfidiously changed his colours before the match.

There was widespread satisfaction when our occupying troops picked him up in Germany three weeks after the war, and widespread expectation—and desire and hope— that he would suffer the traitor's ordained punishment.

Nevertheless—to the eternal credit of our system—the safeguarding rules were punctiliously observed. Legal aid was granted, and Haw Haw was most ably and painstakingly defended through three patient hearings by separate tribunals—the Old Bailey, the Court of Criminal Appeal, the House of Lords.

These hearings offered scanty drama to the layman. There was no real dispute that Haw Haw had broadcast for the Germans, and the prisoner did not go into the witness box. The successive courts were entirely concerned with an issue of pure law: Did Haw Haw actually owe allegiance to the King? For unless you owe allegiance, you cannot commit treason.

The defence brought overwhelming evidence to prove that, despite his Lancashire mother and his Irish father and his own long continuous residence in England, Haw Haw was technically an American citizen (being born in New York after his father's naturalization there). Everything thus turned upon a British passport, which he had obtained by falsely representing himself as British and which had remained valid till the July of 1940. By that passport did the British Sovereign confer on him protection for which allegiance was owing in return?

Many days and much learning were expended on this question before the Law Lords finally and irrevocably confirmed the affirmative answer of the lower courts, and—with the same breath—sealed the prisoner's doom.

Haw Haw was hanged. The British are far from being a bloodthirsty or intolerant people, but that day they rejoiced to see theoretical law and natural justice coincide.

Mary Blandy

AN invitation to Lord Mark's. No honour, no privilege, was more highly prized among the local gentry of Henley-upon-Thames. The Town Clerk's wife showed it to him proudly as soon as he returned from his day's work.

"Good, good."

He penned the reply with real, as well as formal, pleasure. "The thirtieth of July, 1746. Mr., Mrs., and Miss Blandy are happy to accept . . ."

With that acceptance, however, the Town Clerk simultaneously assured for himself a premature death and for his only child a dubious immortality . . .

At Lord Mark's dinner-table they all noticed the attention paid Miss Blandy by a guest from other parts, the Honourable William Cranstoun. The pair had never met before.

Cranstoun was ugly, undersized, impoverished—but he was also the fifth son of a Scottish peer.

Miss Blandy was past first youth, and her fine eyes and shapely figure were somewhat offset by the residual scars of smallpox—but she was also reputedly backed by a dowry of £10,000.

Miss Blandy may have fallen in love with the Honourable William's rank. The Honourable William certainly fell in love with Miss Blandy's fortune. During the month that followed he pursued a zealous courtship,

Miss Blandy herself offering discreet encouragement, and Mrs. Blandy —until she unexpectedly died—manifested unalloyed delight.

Mr. Blandy, though, was less enthusiastic than his womenfolk.

The Town Clerk had previously heard indeterminate gossip reflecting adversely on Cranstoun's character. This gossip sharply crystallized when Lord Mark, hearing what was afoot and feeling some responsibility, informed Mr. Blandy that his daughter's current suitor had already got a wife in Scotland.

Although Mrs. and Miss Blandy willingly accepted Cranstoun's explanation—that the so-called wife had actually been his mistress, and had been termed otherwise only "to save her honour"—Mr. Blandy emphatically did not; and presently his disbelief obtained full confirmation from a decree issued by the Commissary Court at Edinburgh that Cranstoun's "mistress" was indeed his lawful spouse.

Once again mother and daughter swallowed Cranstoun's protestations—that the Commissary Court was wrong, that it would be upset on appeal—but from that moment Mr. Blandy wanted no more of the Scottish peer's fifth son, and could hardly tolerate his presence in the house.

A crisis was somehow averted while Mrs. Blandy lived; when, however, that staunch ally had departed, Cranstoun deemed it prudent to return to Scotland and maintain the siege from there by correspondence.

Correspondence—laced with occasional packages. . . .

Cranstoun had often impressed upon Miss Blandy the virtues and powers of a Scottish sorceress whose magical compounds included a certain powder which could change dislike or even hatred to affection.

"If I had one of these powders," he used to say at Henley, "I would put it into something Mr. Blandy should drink."

Back in Scotland, of course, the sorceress was more nearly at hand. So when Miss Blandy received by post a quantity of powder, marked— in Cranstoun's hand—"to clean Scotch pebbles" (the name of an adornment fashionable that year), she drew two immediate conclusions: first, this must be that wonder-working stuff which her gallant believed would make her father better disposed towards him; second, Cranstoun had falsely described its purpose lest it be seen by other eyes than hers and he be ridiculed for superstition.

Those, at any rate, are the conclusions Miss Blandy said she drew. Did she speak the truth?

At her subsequent trial for murdering by poison, that constituted the one point on which the whole case turned.

All else had become clear as day. That the powder was in fact white arsenic; that Cranstoun (who, when the scandal broke, escaped abroad) intended it to be the means of killing Mr. Blandy; that Miss Blandy administered the arsenic to her father; that Mr. Blandy died as a direct result—none of this, eventually, lay in the smallest doubt, and in court could not be seriously contested.

"But," declared Miss Blandy, "I really thought the powder an innocent, inoffensive thing, and I gave it to him to procure his love . . ."

Normal people living a normal life do not readily attribute bodily ills to poison, and suspicions only gradually formed in the Blandy home. It was a little *odd* that Mr. Blandy—previously always in reasonably good health—should now be seized so often by stomach convulsions and acute internal pains.

It was a little *more* odd when one day the parlourmaid finished off her master's discarded cup of tea, and a similar attack prostrated her.

It was *extremely* odd when a hungry charwoman gratefully ate some gruel he had left, and a similar attack prostrated her.

If by then Mr. Blandy had not begun to put two and two together, the servants had, and they talked among themselves. They remarked that his attacks invariably occurred as soon as he had taken either tea or gruel; that Miss Blandy concerned herself with the preparation of both; that—since the illnesses among the domestic staff—she had gone out of her way to prevent anyone else taking tea or gruel originally meant for him.

Finally, one of them spotted some white powder in the gruel pan— and Mr. Blandy's doctors knew the nature of his malady . . .

Too late.

While Miss Blandy desperately tried, without success, to burn all remaining tell-tale traces (the watchful servants rescued Cranstoun's package from the fire with his familiar writing still plainly legible), her father was slowly but obviously dying—dying, perhaps, a thousand deaths that we shall never know. For in response to his repeated demands for his dear daughter—now, not unnaturally, barred from his sick-room—he learned the circumstances that deprived him of her presence.

No father, though, has ever risen, or could ever rise, to nobler heights of protectiveness and love. The terrific anguish that he felt at this disclosure was not at all upon his own account—but hers.

"I have put powder into your food," Miss Blandy admitted, weeping bitterly, at their last reunion, "but if you are injured, sir, I am entirely innocent. It was given me with another intent." Mr. Blandy's face, half eaten away by poison, grew more soft; the faces of his relatives, standing by like sentries, grew more hard. "I beg you will not curse me, sir."

"I curse thee?" The selfless old man struggled to rise. "My dear, how couldst thou think that I could curse thee? No, I bless thee, and hope God will bless thee, but"—the most miraculous touch of all, seasoning saintliness with sense—"do, my dear, go out of my room and say no more, lest thou shouldst say anything to thy own prejudice."

Not by a single word or look or gesture did Mr. Blandy, in those ebbing hours, convey any hint of reproach towards his daughter. It was

Cranstoun alone he railed and raged against—during his spells of consciousness—as the evil spirit and destroyer of them both. The servants, anxiously hovering round, could not fail to note this firm expression of belief—however greatly it might conflict with their own.

"Did he not treat her," Miss Blandy's counsel asked one of them in the box, "as if she herself was innocent?"

"He did."

"Did he think her wholly unacquainted with the effect of the powder?"

"So it seemed."

"You have told us he said, 'Poor, unfortunate girl! That she should ever be led away by such a villain.' What do you imagine he meant?"

"Giving him," the witness replied, "that which she did not know what it was. . . ."

The jury, however, took a harsher view. So must posterity. Whatever she may have supposed upon receipt of the powder, the correlation and sequence of the events that supervened could only have been misinterpreted by an imbecile.

And Mary Blandy was not an imbecile. Sheltering behind her mild words and her gentlewoman's guise was a cold-blooded parricide whom the gallows justly claimed.

Patrick Mahon

"DID you desire or intend the death of Emily Kaye?"
"Never. Never."

His appearance lends additional force to the witness's reply. Absurd to think of him desiring or intending anyone's death, this agreeable-looking, nicely spoken chap with the wavy hair and the ready smile and the wide, candid eyes. Difficult to keep in mind that he is standing trial for a peculiarly shocking and repulsive murder. Impossible to deduce—and, in accordance with British legal practice, the jury trying him have not been informed—that he has earlier served a five-year sentence imposed for violent crime.

Even the most unfriendly and cynical observer would not be likely, at first glance, to discern any greater springs of wickedness in Patrick Mahon than those which normally characterize a tennis club Lothario.

This latter description certainly does Mahon no injustice. He is strongly attracted by, as he strongly attracts, women, and has always liberally indulged his sexual fancies among those he has encountered through his job as salesman or in the sportier social circles of a London suburb.

D
97

He has, however, never left, nor wished to leave, his wife. To Mahon, an affair is a temporary frolic, enjoyable only as one of a succession, to be terminated just as lightly as it was begun.

That policy, long successfully pursued, met its first grave crisis in the spring of 1924 with Emily Kaye.

Emily Kaye differed in several respects from most of Patrick Mahon's previous mistresses. She was thirty-eight—four years his senior. She was strong-minded and strong-willed. She was not promiscuous. After twenty years of earning her own living as a secretary she wanted to marry and to settle down. Add that she genuinely fell in love with Mahon, add that presently she found herself with child, and the situation may easily be guessed. So far from being prepared to call it a day when Mahon pleased, she began to insist in unequivocal terms that he should permanently break with his wife on her account.

Mahon played for time, and continued as her lover. But by 12 April, when they went down to Eastbourne to stay together at a rented bungalow, he undoubtedly regarded Emily Kaye, not only as a nuisance and a bore, but also as a menace to his chosen way of life.

Emily Kaye did not return alive from Eastbourne. Exactly how she came to die now forms part and parcel of this court's inquiry. But it is not disputed—Mahon himself admits it—that after her death he dismembered her body with horrifying minuteness. When the police—put on his track by the deposit at Waterloo Station of a gladstone bag which he had used in an attempt to scatter some of the grisly relics—made their way into the bungalow, they came upon a shambles of boiled flesh and smashed bone.

The head, though, was missing—Mahon said that he had burned it on the sitting-room fire—and the immediate cause of death could not be ascertained.

This leaves the way open for Mahon's explanation (in which the dismemberment is attributed not to a guilty, but to a panic-stricken, mind).

Eastbourne was Miss Kaye's idea, he tells the jury. She thought that if they were on their own, sharing the same house, she could convince him that he would be entirely happy with her. It was, so to speak, a sort of love experiment. But on their fourth night at the bungalow—the 15th of April—they quarrelled over his unwillingness to leave his wife; beside herself with anger, Emily Kaye first threw an axe and then leaped at him, clawing at his face.

"We struggled backwards and forwards," Mahon said. "She was beginning to get the better of me, when, with almost a last despairing throw, I pushed her off. We both fell; she was underneath; her head hit the coal cauldron, and she never moved again."

On this basis—in the teeth of Bernard Spilsbury's opinion that rapid death could not be occasioned by the fall described—Mahon's defender even flies the kite of "accident". But his highest hope really rests in a verdict of manslaughter—or, in other words, a decision by the jury that Mahon, while responsible for the death of Emily Kaye, neither desired nor intended it.

Hence his vehement cry of "Never. Never." when the question is broached by his own counsel. Hence the course to be followed in the most vital passages of his cross-examination by Sir Henry Curtis Bennett for the Crown.

"Did you say," the latter asks him, "that Miss Kaye's intention in going to Eastbourne was to convince you that you could be happy with her?"

"Yes," Mahon replies.

"What was *your* intention?"

For a moment Mahon considers.

"To convince her that I did not love her sufficiently. I thought she would discover it."

"If that was so, why did you not say to her: 'This relationship between us must now stop?"

"I did."

"You did?" Sir Henry lifts his eyebrows. "Is it your case that this unmarried lady was seducing you—seducing you away from your wife?"

"It might be so put."

"Is it the fact?"

"Yes," said Mahon boldly.

"How long did you think it was going to take to finish this love experiment with Miss Kaye?"

"I meant to stay there only three or four days."

"And then?"

"I intended to make a clean breast of the whole thing to my wife."

"Then why go with Miss Kaye at all?" says Sir Henry swiftly.

"Because I promised", is the best Mahon can think of.

May any further light be thrown on the reason for his going? Sir Henry, still engaged with this same theme, refers to the employees of a London store who have sworn that, on 12 April, Mahon bought there a cook's knife and a saw.

"Do you agree that is the correct date of your purchase?"

"Yes."

"Two days before Miss Kaye died?"

"Yes."

"Did you only decide to say that you had bought the knife and saw on 12 April when you knew about the evidence forthcoming from the shop?"

"I don't quite follow," Mahon says.

"Do you not? You made a statement to the police on your arrest?"

"Yes."

"Did you say in that statement you had bought the knife and saw on 17 April?"

"I believe I did."

"Two days *after* the death of Miss Kaye?"

"Yes. There were mistakes regarding dates which could only have been made by someone in mental agony."

It fends off the threatening thrust, but not for long.

"That statement was read over by you, was it not?"

"Yes."

"And signed?"

"Yes."

"And initialled on each page?"

"Yes."

"And it contains a clear assertion, does it not, that the knife and saw were bought after the death of Miss Kaye, for the purpose of disposing of her body?"

"On the face of it, yes," Mahon concedes.

"But the fact is," says Sir Henry, in an almost meditative tone, "that you went down to Eastbourne on the 12th with a cook's knife and a saw?"

"Never. Never. I never intended nor desired the death of Emily Kaye." Those words remotely echoing, are now subjected to a final acid test.

"You say," goes on Sir Henry, "that it was an unfortunate accident which caused her death?"

"That is so."

"There were people living in near-by bungalows?"

"Yes."

"There was a telephone in your bungalow?"

"Yes."

"In working order?"

"Yes."

"As you had made up your mind to tell your wife, you need not have feared its becoming known that you were at the bungalow with this young woman?"

"No."

"Why, then, when you saw Miss Kaye had received such injuries, didn't you communicate with somebody at once?"

Every route of escape for Mahon has been closed.

"It is such an easy question," he says, "and yet such a hard one."

"I know," says Sir Henry, "and I want to know what the answer is."

Mahon stammers something, stops, and gives up the hopeless struggle.

"I cannot answer", he says despairingly, and in that instant abandons himself to the hangman's tender mercies.

Harry Pollitt and Others

MEN sometimes acquire immortality for odd reasons, unconnected with their merit or achievement.

It is unlikely that Charles Bradlaugh, energetic Victorian politician though he was, would have been, as such, a familiar name to future generations. His enduring renown rests upon the fact that Parliament, disliking his atheistic views, refused to let him take his seat after election, thus starting off the famous Bradlaugh Argument.

It is unlikely that Captain Jenkins—worthy 18th-century mariner though he was—would have been, as such, required reading in 20th-century schools. His enduring renown rests upon the fact that a Spanish Customs officer, disputing his claims to trade, subjected him to a savage act of mutilation, thus starting off the famous War of Jenkins's Ear.

It seems unlikely also that Mr. J. R. Campbell—able and expert journalist though he was—would have attained the status of a legend in his lifetime had not the first British Labour Government fallen as a direct consequence of the famous Campbell case.

The whole point, though, of the famous Campbell case—which arose out of an article printed in the *Workers' Weekly*—was that, in the forensic sense, it didn't happen; that a prosecution, at first approved by high authority, was subsequently, by the same authority, withdrawn; that Mr. Campbell never actually stood trial.

A year later, however, with the Conservatives back, he proved less fortunate . . .

There were twelve of them altogether in the Old Bailey dock; twelve men described by the Attorney-General as "the heads of an illegal organization calling itself the Communist Party of Great Britain."

To the general public Campbell was easily best known, but he was not allowed the role of solitary star. He shared the limelight with two others who had chosen, like himself, to conduct their own defences—Harry Pollitt, boilermaker, and William Gallacher, brass finisher.

They were to become, respectively, during the next decade, Secretary of the Party and M.P. for West Fife.

The charge—that of conspiring to publish seditious libels—was based on various printed documents distributed as Communist propaganda.

The Crown said that these incited the armed forces to disloyalty, mutiny and revolutionary war. The Defence said they did not; and the resultant clash of interpretation and construction occupied many hours of controversy between counsel. It did, in fact, consitute the only relevant issue.

But the three unrepresented prisoners—taking full advantage of the discretionary latitude that judges usually allow persons appearing for themselves—concentrated in massed force upon a different question, which, while not perhaps entirely germane, might serve to generate some useful prejudice. They strove to show that, by comparison with others, the Communist Party had been victimized.

Each, when he came to cross-examine the police witnesses, manfully did his share towards that end.

The chance of dealing the first blow fell to Pollitt, and highly profitable use he made of it. Only thirty years old, he exhibited a charm and an astuteness that might have secured him a successful career at the Bar had he not earlier got involved with politics and boilers.

He was cool and confident, poised and alert, as he got up to face that Scotland Yard detective—a detective who had been telling the jury that he kept a watch on the headquarters of the Communist Party at King Street "on instructions".

"Have you ever had instructions," Pollitt asked, "to keep a watch on the headquarters of the *Conservative* Party?"

"No."

"Or of the *Liberal* Party?"

"No."

"Just the Communist Party?'

Had he worn a wig and put his questions from another place, solicitors would have been asking this promising junior's name.

"Just the Communist Party?"

"Yes."

"While you were keeping watch," Pollitt went on, "did the people you saw go in and out *just like human beings*?"

The question was subtly related to the questioner; humorous, chubby, full of rich humanity, Pollitt did not correspond in any respect to the popular conception of a typical Marxist-Leninist.

"Just like human beings?" he reiterated.

"Yes."

The experienced detective was now eyeing his opponent watchfully.

"Was there an official Communist sign outside the King Street office?"

"Yes."

"During the period of your watch, did you see Fascists tear it down?"

"No."

"Do you know that they did?"

"I only know," said the detective, guardedly, "that one day, when I came on duty, I saw the sign had gone."

"The sign had gone," Pollitt ironically echoed. "Were any arrests made in connexion with that incident?"

"I am not aware of any."

"No arrests," said Pollitt, with the same meaningful inflection.

"Isn't it rather peculiar that while you were closely watching us you failed to observe the Fascists forcibly taking down our sign?"

Campbell neatly followed up with this same witness who, in addition to his King Street vigilance, had bought Communist literature "on behalf of the Special Branch".

"How often," Campbell inquired, "have you bought Communist literature on behalf of the Special Branch?"

"Frequently."

"Have you bought literature from any other political organization?"

"No."

"Has *any* member of the Special Branch," said Campbell, "been sent to buy literature from any other political organization?"

The detective again was circumspect, but his answer served the defence as well as a straight negative.

"I am not myself aware of any," he said.

Gallacher launched his attack from a slightly different angle, but it still formed part and parcel of their collective theme—that the Communists were an object of police persecution. In breezy style and a rolling Scottish accent, he tackled another member of the force about his conduct during a Communist conference.

"Did you and other policemen hide beneath the platform?"

This drew a prim correction from the officer.

"We engaged a room beneath that in which the meeting was held." And then, apparently anticipating the next thrust, he added, "To obtain access to us, you and your colleagues wrenched a trapdoor open."

"And your ear was to the trap-door?" Gallacher said.

"Yes."

"Isn't the truth that *you* and *your* colleagues wrenched the trap-door open, and that we gave you in charge?"

"Quite incorrect," the officer said.

"You were taken to Bow Street, weren't you—and in custody?"

"Quite incorrect," the officer said again. "A young constable was called who did not quite understand the position, and we offered to go with him."

A trio of professional counsel, fighting a case in concert, would be entitled to congratulate themselves if they had displayed such skill in dovetailing their efforts and creating sympathy. But it did not—could not—touch the heart of the matter, which lay in the documents, and the documents alone.

Assume, if you like, that the Communists were hounded; assume, if you like, that police methods were dubious and sly. Still awaiting answer —as the judge reminded the jury with due stress—is the only question that ultimately counts.

Was the Communist "literature" seditious, or was it not?

The jury thought it was, and Mr. Justice Swift undertook his task of dispensing punishment.

Pollitt and Gallacher, together with three others, had previous convictions for similar offences. A sentence of twelve months was passed on each. When they had gone below, the judge addressed those that remained.

"I am not anxious, if I can avoid it, to send you to prison," he said. "Those of you who will promise that you will have nothing more to do with that association, or with the doctrines that it preaches, I shall bind you over to be of good behaviour. Those who do not so promise will go to prison."

He paused impassively. In the dock, the seven prisoners hurriedly conferred. In a few moments they had finished, with much nodding of heads, and they turned to face the Clerk of the Court who had risen from his seat.

He spoke to each of them, individually, in turn.

"Will you be bound over?"

"No, I will not."

Seven times this formula was repeated without variant. The judge, impassive as before, stood by his word, and the prisoners self-sacrificed to a shadow revolution, proudly went down to join their comrades in the cells.

Buck Ruxton

BUCK RUXTON is the classic example of a physician who could not heal himself. It might have been—almost certainly would have been —quite different had his distemper been entirely physical. A fever, a chill, an incapacitated limb—doubtless for these he could have administered self-treatment with the same skill and success as he so often treated others. But Ruxton's infirmity was psychological, and it utterly defeated his own remedial powers.

He had contracted the disease of sexual jealousy.

In theory, he knew perfectly well just how this should be dealt with, and often in practice he had proved that theory right. When patients similarly stricken divulged the fact to him—for the Parsee doctor was popular in Lancaster, and popular doctors fulfil the role of father confessors too—he handled them intelligently and gave them wise advice: don't make mountains out of molehills, don't brood over suspicions, don't view the loved one through a distorting glass.

Many people profited greatly from his common sense. He was incapable, though, of applying it to himself and Isabella.

Isabella Ruxton fell a good way short of beautiful, although she possessed a certain magnetism for men. This was made more conspicuous by a rather coquettish manner; a superficial flirtatiousness without any real significance, but which perhaps did not always seem appropriate for a middle-class housewife with three children to bring up. Isabella never missed a chance of having fun; a characteristic not unendearing in itself, but which in her case led to disastrous results.

Ruxton, in the colloquial phrase, was off his head about her—a condition that does not guarantee domestic harmony. The possessive element in his passion blazed with a fierce fury, and Isabella's innocently provocative behaviour constantly added fresh fuel to the flames.

The ecstasies of passion were offset by the agonies, and as time went on the ecstasies were outnumbered and outstripped. There was a long succession of tempestuous scenes in which Ruxton raved and wept, charged her with unfaithfulness, darkly threatened violence and sometimes carried out his threats. These scenes became progressively more painful, and twice Isabella felt constrained to call the police.

By the summer of 1935, when the Ruxtons' chequered union had existed for eight years, some sort of climax seemed inevitable and imminent. *He* would leave *her*. *She* would leave *him*. At any rate, matters could not go on like that.

Someone, or something, would touch off the explosion. . . .

Jealousy is not confined by evidence or by facts; it readily accepts imagination as a guide. Ruxton had lately focused his misgivings upon a young solicitor with whom they were acquainted. These misgivings were quite without foundation; but when Isabella drove to Edinburgh —where her sisters lived—and stayed there overnight as a member of a party composed of this young man and his sister and his parents, Ruxton felt abundantly confirmed in his opinion. He awaited her return in a state bordering on frenzy.

The week that followed in the Ruxton household was one of incessant quarrelling and recrimination. It may be, though, that Isabella had become so inured to Ruxton's jealousy that she did not perceive how dangerous a pitch it had now reached. For the very next week-end she airily announced her intention of driving to Blackpool for the evening, so as to meet her sisters, now holidaying there.

She must have realized that Ruxton would assume that this was a blind, and that the young solicitor was lurking in the background. What she apparently failed to realize was the way his frantic mind would now react to this assumption.

Isabella drove to Blackpool; she had supper with her sisters; she arrived back, for next day the car was in the garage. But after that night nobody set eyes on her alive. Both she and the little nursemaid who helped her with the children were in due course reported missing to the police.

There never has been, never will be, a trustworthy account of what happened in the house that night when Isabella got home. All those involved have long since died a violent death. But there is no need to doubt the broad essentials of the picture presented to the jury by the Crown at Ruxton's trial.

Ruxton had lashed his brain with jealous images during Isabella's absence till he was beside himself. His ferment clamoured for release through the exercise of force. He struck her over and over again with all his strength; he rained blows on her face and head in demoniac repetition; and as she collapsed under the weight of this attack, he strangled the breath out of her resistless body. Then when the nurse-maid, drawn by the uproar, caught him in the act, she made her own destruction necessary and certain.

Thus far the jealous husband had been dominant. Now, frenzy spent and fear supervening, the expert professional doctor took command.

Systematically he removed from each body any features which would help to establish identity.

The nursemaid had a birthmark—that birthmark was cut off; an operation scar on one hand—that hand was severed.

Isabella's nose had a prominent bridge—her nose was cut off.

A number of teeth were extracted from each corpse so that it would cease to correspond with dentists' records.

This grisly feat accomplished—and I have not detailed in full these operations—Ruxton carved up the remains, wrapped them in several bundles, drove out by night, and pitched them into a ravine a hundred miles away. . . .

So skilfully did Ruxton do his work that when the remains were come upon by chance, some two weeks later, at first even the sex of the bodies was in doubt. But a *tour de force* of scientific reconstruction ultimately established the identity of each—a reconstruction dramatically buttressed and confirmed when it was ascertained that a national newspaper used as wrapping in one bundle formed part of a limited edition reserved for Lancaster.

From that moment Ruxton's plight was desperate indeed. Trails of blood were discovered in his house; partly burned and bloodstained carpets were discovered in his yard; patches of blood were discovered on a suit that he had requested a daily help to burn.

He was formally charged with murdering both women, though it was actually for Isabella's death that he stood trial.

To my mind, his defence was hopeless from the start, and none but that incomparable defender, Norman Birkett, could have given it even such a semblance of a fight. The interest of the case lies not in *whether*, but in *why*, he did it; in its anatomizing of the jealous psyche.

"Did you not once call your wife a prostitute?" he was asked.

"No," he answered, "but I did once use the words 'You have the mind of a prostitute'. *That was because she was always thinking of men.*"

And again:

"Did you complain to her sisters of her infidelity?"

"I didn't mean misconduct. *One can be unfaithful even in thought.*"

And again:

"What do you say about your relationship in general?"

Ruxton, already in the shadows, took a long look back.

"We were the kind of people," he said, "*who could not live with each other, and could not live without each other. . . .*"

It may be a true epitaph on both. It is certainly a true epitaph on him. For so strange is the synthesis of love and hate in jealousy that Ruxton went to the scaffold still nourishing his passion for the woman whose corpse he had dismembered.

Charles I

THE Van Dyck portraits of him—unlined face, youthful demeanour, jet black glossy hair—have largely ceased to correspond with the reality. The man now led by custodian guards to the Great Hall at Westminster is deeply furrowed, care-laden, prematurely grey.

One element, however, does survive from those happier Van Dyck days—that distinctive arrogance, that unsuppressible pride. No prisoner ever gazed upon his judges with more open disfavour and disdain.

And no judges ever gazed upon a prisoner with more open prejudice. There are more than sixty of them on their scarlet benches, and every face is grim and set relentlessly as the President formally addresses the lonely figure waiting at the Bar.

"Charles Stuart, King of England," he solemnly intones. "The Commons of England, assembled in Parliament, being sensible of the evils and calamities that have been brought upon this nation and of the innocent blood that has been shed in it, which is fixed upon you as the principal author, have resolved to make inquisition for this blood."

The President pauses, as though to give that last word greater emphasis. "And according to the debt they owe to God, justice, the kingdom and themselves they have resolved to bring you to trial and judgment, and have therefore constituted this high court of justice where you are to hear your charge."

It is an extravagant claim that the President makes for his tribunal. "This high court of justice"; "Constituted by the Commons of England"—poppycock.

This is no more a judicial proceeding than any of the military engagements—Edgehill, Marston Moor, Naseby, Preston—during the recently concluded Civil War. It is merely a last, and phoney battle, rigged by the victorious in that war against the vanquished.

Less than fifty members were present in the Commons that passed an Act—by a majority of six—providing for the trial of the King, and this mere rump, under protection from the Army, appointed these so-called "Commissioners" who now, muttering hostility and vengeance, claim to sit as impartial arbiters. Appearance, at least, might have been maintained if an eminent judge had consented to preside. None, however, did, and this most responsible of tasks has been assigned to an insignificant lawyer named John Bradshawe, whose sole qualification for fulfilling it rests in his unbridled antagonism to the King.

At Bradshawe's order the charge against Charles I is read—a charge of treason, but of treason curiously inverted. Traitors are commonly charged with levying war against their king. Here the King is charged with levying war against his subjects, in furtherance of a plan to acquire despotic power. The details simply comprise a list of the battles he has fought: Edgehill, Marston Moor, Naseby, Preston.

As they are recited, Charles laughs scornfully. Bradshawe says nothing, but purses his lips tightly, and keeps them pursed until the reading ends.

Then, on an unmistakably threatening note, he speaks.

"Sir, the court expects your answer."

Charles, who has been seated, stands—to enhance his own dignity, not out of deference to the court.

"I am your lawful king," he says, in words of cold command. "Think well upon it before you go from one sin to a greater. I know no authority you have."

The murmuring on the scarlet benches is louder than before. Bradshawe fidgets angrily.

"You come here, Sir, by authority of the Commons, acting on behalf of the people of England, by which people you are elected king."

Charles seizes on this ill-considered phrase as might have done the professional counsel who—by the custom of the time—is not allowed him.

"I do tell you, Sir, England was never yet an elective kingdom; it was an hereditary kingdom for near this thousand years."

Enjoying Bradshawe's temporary check and the sharp frowns of his colleagues, Charles raises his voice in imperious demand. "Show by what lawful authority I am here.

"You will do well," retorts Bradshawe, raising his voice also, "to consider whether this be all the answer that you offer."

"I ask for your lawful authority," Charles stubbornly repeats. "Satisfy God and me and the world in that, and you shall receive my answer."

The crowds in the galleries have so far maintained silence. But now there are scattered rumbles of approval and even audible cries of "God save Your Majesty!"

Charles calmly folds his arms. There is a hasty conference on the scarlet benches, which are exhibiting signs of considerable disarray.

Finally Bradshawe announces the conference's decision.

"The court," he says, "will adjourn until the day after tomorrow. The guards are accordingly bidden to withdraw the prisoner."

"The prisoner?" echoes Charles majestically. "*The King.*"

The day after tomorrow—and the day after that—follows a similar, though more protracted, course. "Confess or deny," reiterates Bradshawe. "I will answer as soon as I know by what authority you sit," reiterates Charles. "Sir, 'tis not for prisoners to *require*", Bradshawe asserts. "Sir, I am not an ordinary prisoner," asserts Charles. And once again the guards are told to take away their captive—this time, though, a captive branded in default and in contempt.

Before they again met their dauntless monarch face to face, the Commissioners tried to procure a bit of cover. They held, *in private*, an examination of sundry witnesses. And what exactly—if anything—did these witnesses prove? That Charles had been on the losing side in the Civil War.

The Commissioners then felt able to agree upon the verdict they had agreed on before the trial commenced.

"This court doth adjudge that the said Charles Stuart, as a tyrant, traitor, murderer, and public enemy to the good people of this nation shall be put to death"—Bradshawe licks his lips—"by the severing of his head from his body."

Charles shows no trace of fear or dread, but speaks direct to Bradshawe in even, level tones.

"Will you hear me a word, sir?"

"Sir," snaps Bradshawe, "you are not to be heard after the sentence."

"No, sir?" says Charles, with an air of incredulity.

"No, sir. Guards, withdraw your prisoner."

This ultimate rebuff does what the sentence could not do. It breaks Charles's composure.

"I may speak after the sentence," he insists, as the soldiers close around him. "By your favour, sir—hold—the sentence, sir—sir, I do——"

"Guards" says the implacable Bradshawe. "Withdraw your prisoner."

"I am not suffered to speak," Charles calls out bitterly as they hustle him away. "Expect what justice others will have."

His shrift was short. Three days after that last encounter with his massed opponents, Charles was publicly beheaded on a charge to which he had never pleaded, either yea or nay. Whether *morally* he deserved that fate historians must decide. But the *legal* process by which he reached it calls for a different judgment; and that judgment, whenever invoked, is likely to consider the royal prisoner less guilty than the court.

Herbert Armstrong

YOU may have the most balanced legal system in the world, but human temperament and ability varying as they do, each individual's case must be in some degree affected by what in other spheres is called the luck of the draw. Luck with counsel. Luck with the jury. Luck with the judge. Herbert Armstrong is an example very much in point.

I do not doubt for a moment that Armstrong poisoned his wife early in 1921; nor that, later in the same year, encouraged by several months of immunity from suspicion, he over-reached himself by trying to poison a fellow solicitor practising right opposite him in the Brecon town of Hay—a crime that led to the exhumation of Mrs. Armstrong's body and thus to the disclosure of his previous crime as well. In both instances, Armstrong's guilt is a moral certainty.

None the less the capital charge, upon which he was tried, presented difficulties in the way of legal proof—no one still alive could swear that he had actually given his wife either food or drink or medicine which would have served to carry the arsenic afterwards found in her corpse —and Armstrong might have saved his neck had he been before a judge cast in a different judicial mould from Mr. Justice Darling.

In an appropriate civil case Darling—as has been seen—preferred the role of wit, but in a serious Criminal Case he could be extremely penetrating; and—as he deemed the role of a judge more than that of a silent umpire—he sometimes exerted this quality with profound effect in court.

He did so when Armstrong, up at Hereford Assizes, had just completed his testimony in the witness-box.

Up to that point, matters had gone fairly well for the defence—despite Darling's ruling that evidence of Armstrong's attempt to poison the solicitor could be admitted on the present charge of murdering his wife "as showing what he had got in the way of poison, and what he was prepared to do with it" (a ruling later endorsed by the Court of Criminal Appeal).

That nasty setback early on had been largely overcome, and—with the Crown's continuing inability to show, except by inference, any act of administering poison to the wife—the verdict seemed to depend on whether Armstrong could satisfactorily explain why considerable quantities of poison had undoubtedly been in his possession. Had they any credible purpose which was not criminal?

The police had traced several purchases of arsenic by Armstrong and told him so, with a formal caution, before his arrest. Oh, yes, Armstrong had said, it wasn't any secret. He'd first bought arsenic seven years ago when he'd read a recipe for a weed-killer composed of arsenic and caustic soda, which was cheaper than the weed-killer his gardener then used. The chemist he'd bought it from told him that the arsenic had to be mixed with charcoal; accordingly it was so mixed, and the charcoal coloured it. Oh, yes, two years ago he'd bought more arsenic, and again he'd bought some early on this year; always mixed with charcoal and consequently coloured.

"This arsenic I speak of," Armstrong said, "is the only poison in my possession anywhere," and when they wrote this down, he read it carefully before signing.

Thus Armstrong fairly reasonably accounted for his possession of coloured arsenic. But when they searched him after his arrest, they found in his pocket a little packet containing some white powder. It turned out to be in exact measure, a fatal dose of arsenic—*white* arsenic, without any charcoal mixed with it at all.

That makes a much more awkward hurdle to surmount. Armstrong, though, is a highly intelligent and resourceful man, and he now offers the jury an explanation of this also. It was all through his being served by the chemist's assistant, he tells them, instead of by the chemist himself; didn't see the arsenic before it was wrapped up, didn't know it was white arsenic till he'd got it home; made it up into twenty packets or so to use on dandelions; stuffed them in his jacket pocket; thought he'd used them all, but was obviously mistaken.

A simple and commonplace occurrence. One of the packets gets squashed away among a lot of other things—easy enough if you're the sort whose pockets are always crammed; and there it can stay until there's some reason for turning the pocket out—as the police made Armstrong turn it out when he was in custody.

Plausible, isn't it, on the surface? Certainly Sir Ernest Pollock, the Attorney-General—a fine legal brain, but not a first-class cross-examiner—does little or nothing to destroy that impression. But as Armstrong proposes to regain the shelter of the dock, Mr. Justice Darling makes a sign to him to stay.

"In your statement to the police," he says, "the only arsenic you mention purchasing was arsenic coloured with charcoal, was it not?"

"Yes."

"And you were particular to tell them that you had mentioned all the arsenic you had had?"

"Yes."

"How can you account for having forgotten all that *white* arsenic?" There's quite a long wait. Armstrong doesn't attempt to answer.

"How do you account for it?"

"I can't account for it," he says.

"You made it up into twenty little packets?"

"Yes, my lord."

"And with regard to nineteen of them, you gave separate doses to nineteen dandelions?"

"Yes." Armstrong replies, "and I noticed that those dandelions died afterwards."

"Yes." The judge presses his fingers together, palms spread, and taps his chin reflectively. "That was very interesting, was it not?"

"It was at the time," says Armstrong, "but it had passed from my mind."

"Do you tell the jury that you absolutely forgot about that white arsenic?"

"I do."

"And the dandelions?"

"I do."

"You are a solicitor," says the judge. "Does it not occur to you that it would have been a very bad case for you if you had had to tell the police that you had got not only weed-killing arsenic but white arsenic in your possession?"

Armstrong does the best with it he can.

"It would have had to be explained," he says.

"If you were simply dosing dandelions, why did you make up that arsenic into twenty little packets?"

"Because it was convenient, to put it in the ground."

"But you did it all on one day?"

"Yes."

"At the same time?"

"Yes."

"Why go to the trouble of making twenty little packets, one packet for each dandelion, instead of taking out the arsenic you'd got and giving something from it to each of the dandelions?"

Now Armstrong has his back right against the wall.

"I don't really know," he says.

"Why make up twenty little packets, each a fatal dose for a human being, and put them in your pocket?"

"I can only say, my lord, that at the time it seemed to me the most convenient way of doing it."

The judge nods slightly, as if he had confirmed something in his mind.

"And there is no other explanation you can give?"

Armstrong looks round the court, then brushes his forehead with his hand.

"No, my lord," he says.

Not every judge would have thought it part of his duty to put those questions. Not every judge could have framed them with such devastating skill. It is hard to suppose their consequence was other than decisive, or that Armstrong, in the hours remaining before his execution, did not bitterly lament his luck in the draw.

Julius and Ethel Rosenberg

I REMEMBER one June evening in 1953 impatiently waiting to cross over Regent Street. In front of me, appearing almost to fill the roadway, marched an irregular but closely formed procession—youths in mackintoshes, girls in head scarves, middle-aged and elderly folk in heterogeneous garb—uttering the most mournful cries that I had ever heard. Above their heads, thrust aloft by aching arms, improvised banners blazoned: *The Rosenbergs Must Not Die.*

And that was in England; that was on the periphery of it all; that was merely a dim reflection, a faint echo, of the tremendous social and political upheaval which the Rosenberg couple—plump nondescript young housewife Ethel, pale nondescript young husband Julius—created throughout the entire United States during their slow progress towards the electric chair.

Were they—as Mr. Eisenhower affirmed—guilty of deliberately betraying a whole nation? Or was theirs—as M. Jean-Paul Sartre wrote—a legal lynching that smeared a whole nation with blood?

It is not easy, even after this lapse of time, to approach the Rosenberg case with an uncommitted mind, disentangled from the power groups of the Cold War and from the abstract ethics of the atom bomb. It is not easy to approach it with unengaged emotions, for, even upon the assumption of their guilt, they were treated with a medieval harshness that prompted clergy and statesmen everywhere to intervene—unavailingly—on their behalf. But no attempt at answering those questions posed above can be of real value unless it is based on a detached and unbiased examination of the Rosenbergs' trial *as a trial.*

There is—and has been from the start—an almost universal belief that the charge against the Rosenbergs was treason. Not surprisingly, as phrases like "treasonable acts", "betraying their country" and even "these traitors" were freely employed at every stage in the proceedings by a prosecuting team which the appellate court severely condemned for its methods and its tactics.

The actual charge was that of conspiring to commit espionage—a very different thing, as it need not involve violation of allegiance.

The story advanced to support this accusation is as familiar as any of our time. The Rosenbergs, alleged the prosecution, were spies and agents in the service of the Soviet Union out of sheer devotion to the Communist cause and creed. In 1944 a providential opportunity offered itself to them when Ethel Rosenberg's younger brother, an army mechanic named Greenglass, was assigned to the secluded plant at Los Alamos, in New Mexico, where crack scientists were working on the atom bomb. The Rosenbergs persuaded him to procure and furnish secret information: precise location, names of personnel, form of security measures, type of experiments, and—most important of all—a cross-section sketch and 12-page explanation of the bomb used at Nagasaki in 1945.

So, at any rate, Greenglass testified in court, obtaining partial confirmation from his wife, who—swore he and she—had sometimes been his messenger.

The Rosenbergs repudiated every word of it; they had sought nothing, they had got nothing, they were not spies, they were not agents, they were not even Communists. The issue was therefore sharp and quite narrowly confined. A head-on clash, Rosenbergs versus Greenglasses, with the onus by settled law resting on the latter. As the Court of Appeals said of the Greenglass testimony: "If it were disregarded, the conviction could not stand."

Very well. Let us—under such high judicial guidance—start from there.

Greenglass is on the stand—has been for some hours. We are sitting, with our fellow members of the jury, closely attentive to his fluent narrative. How his sister Ethel—seven years older than himself—had always been a focal point of his affections. How his brother-in-law Julius—four years older than himself—had always been an object of his hero-worship. How as a G.I., accidentally placed in a post of highest trust, he had yielded—after much misgiving—to their joint pressure. How he drew for them the sketch, with its alphabetical symbols (A = light source, B = detonator, C = high-explosive lens). How he interpreted for them the formula of the lens's curve. How he expounded to them the means of detonation.

Detailed, plausible—and, if accepted, damning. It is, however, for us, the jury, to assess its value by the just criterion of "reasonable doubt".

We ignore—of course—the war against "The Reds" now raging in Korea; *that* might prompt irrational sympathy with the witness. We ignore—of course—the fate he invokes for his own sister; *that* might prompt irrational antipathy against him. We rely—it's what juries are summoned for, is it not?—upon the aseptic test of common sense.

The first sharp blow to our confidence in Greenglass comes when he is cross-examined by defender Bloch about his capacity to grasp, and to impart, the occult technicalities marking nuclear physics.

"Did you ever get a degree in science?"

"I did not," says Greenglass.

"Did you ever get a degree in engineering?"

"I did not," says Greenglass.

"Did you ever take a course in calculus?"

"No."

"Differential calculus?"

"No."

114

"Thermodynamics?"

"No."

"Atomic physics?"

"No."

"Quantum mechanics?"

"No."

"Have you read any basic works," asks Bloch, "on any of these subjects?"

"*No*," Greenglass is forced to acknowledge, "*I have not.*"

A second sharp blow lands just as squarely on its target when Bloch inquires how Greenglass won the confidence, or pierced the defences of qualified savants pledged to absolute reserve.

"Give an instance of how you picked up information," counsel says.

"Well," Greenglass says, "once I came into a room; there was a piece of material on the table; I picked it up, and remarked 'It's an interesting piece of material, and interestingly machined'."

"Yes?"

Bloch pressingly invites him to go on.

"Well," Greenglass says, "the man I spoke to answered me 'That is neutron source'."

"Yes?"

"Well," Greenglass says, as if it were the most natural occurrence in the world, "*we had a conversation, and he explained to me how it was used.*"

These two peculiar features of Greenglass's *exposé*—the apparent ability of the scientifically untrained to cope with abstruse scientific formulae, the apparent inability of the scientifically trained to fulfil a bare minimum of security demands—would by themselves make a detached observer pause.

But they acquire additional weight from a collateral factor, affecting not only Greenglass but his wife.

Both—on their own showing and by their own assertion—were the accomplices of those they now denounce. And that it is dangerous to act on such uncorroborated evidence—not least when hopes of clemency or immunity rest on it—has long been a firm maxim of British and American law.

No, I would not have convicted Julius and Ethel—nor, I conjecture, would a typical British jury directed by a typical British judge in the typical temperate atmosphere of a British court. I would not have been —I am not today—satisfied of their guilt.

That does not mean, however, that I am satisfied of their innocence.

Did they—as Mr. Eisenhower affirmed—betray a nation? Or was theirs—as M. Sartre wrote—a legal lynching?

The statements, odd as it may seem, are not mutually exclusive. There is at least a lively possibility that both Mr. Eisenhower and M. Sartre were right.

115

Thomas Henry Allaway

T HE Bournemouth police had suspected him for weeks. And when at last they charged Thomas Henry Allaway, a professional chauffeur locally employed, with the wilful murder of Miss Irene Wilkins, they were completely satisfied that they had got their man.

But a case that satisfies the prosecuting police is one thing; a case that satisfies a judge and jury is another. When Allaway's trial opened at the Winchester summer assize of 1922, the Crown were none the less upon their mettle for any inward assurance that they felt. . . .

The instrument that had enticed Miss Wilkins to her violent death was a telegram sent in response to her announcement in a national paper that she required a situation as a lady cook. This telegram struck a curious note of tension, which, in hind-sight, seems highly ominous.

"Come immediately," it said. "4.30 train Waterloo. Bournemouth Central. Car will meet train. Expense no object. Urgent. Wood, Beech House." Only the sender seemingly could not spell "Bournemouth" or "expense", and both "Wood" and "Beech House" proved the purest fantasies.

The misspellings were self-evident, but not, of course, the fantasies, and Miss Wilkins, having pushed some essentials into a small valise, left her Streatham home at three o'clock for Waterloo. From that moment onward, she is virtually lost to sight until, as a bleak December dawn broke on the next day, an early labourer found her battered body by the fence of a field in Bournemouth's eastern outskirts.

The advance of rigor mortis and the condition of her clothes showed she had been lying dead since the evening before.

Cannot one vividly imagine, even now, that brief and terrible dialogue, spoken in the half light outside Bournemouth Central station, between the well-bred, well-educated woman of thirty-one (she had expressly stated her age in the advertisement), and the scheming, semi-literate criminal who had decoyed her there to serve his own dark ends?

"Excuse me, are you . . .?"

"Miss Wilkins, is it?"

"Yes." A sigh of relief; the telegram honoured; the newcomer spotted. "You're from Beech House? The Woodses?"

"That's right." The valise carried to the waiting car. "Jump in. We'll be there in no time."

"Thank you."

Thank you. The car doors close; the engine revs; the ride starts to the slaughter . . .

Was it, though, initially *meant* to be a slaughter (in which case the

116

culprit, seeking a victim indiscriminately, could only have been a psychopathic killer)?

Or was it meant to be a carnal gratification, in the outcome literally resisted to the death (in which case the culprit, making a blind date, could only have been a sexual maniac)?

Or was it, perhaps, meant to be a simple robbery (in which case the culprit, staking so much for so little, could only have been an insensate gambler)?

These represented the feasible alternatives. Choose which you like; you will in any event be left with a criminal of unusual, if perverted ingenuity. Trying to picture him, you might recall the features of familiar and established cunning felons—the subtle mouth of Sidney Fox, the crafty nose of Neill Cream, the sharp sea-lawyer's eye of Peter Manuel . . .

But cunning such as theirs does occasionally lie hid behind the stolid, blunt exterior of an Allaway. . . .

The case against Allaway, although superficially strong, was not without weaknesses just below the surface.

First Crown point—the sole motor tracks leaving an impression on the unfrequented road that ran nearest to the body had a wheel base and tyres identical with those on the car which Allaway drove. But more than one car has a 4 ft. 6 in. wheel base, and Dunlop is not an unfamiliar name in tyres.

Second—one witness positively swore that it was Allaway whom he had seen, clad in chauffeur's uniform, meeting the designated train at Bournemouth Central, and driving away a lady, dressed exactly like Miss Wilkins, in a very distinctive and uncommon-looking car.

Now it is true that the car in Allaway's charge was a Mercedes, then as now exceptional in this country, but the witness, although styling himself a consultant engineer, did not forthwith recognize as such the car he saw. And all evidence retrospectively "identifying" persons lay, as it lies now, under the warning shadow cast by the heart-chilling case of Adolf Beck—that case in which ten witnesses wrongly "identified" one who was, long afterwards, conclusively proved guiltless.

Third—a handwriting expert tendered his opinion that Allaway had written the decoy telegram. But the notorious and repeated blunders of handwriting experts even rival those pertaining to "identification"; one need only think of the young naval cadet, George Archer-Shee, to run a mile from their comparisons and charts and diagrams.

Finally—the dead woman's valise had been found behind some bushes directly opposite a house where Allaway had waited a full hour and a half for his employer's wife on the afternoon immediately following the murder.

It was a fair and reasonable conjecture that the valise, missing from the locus of the crime, remained in the murder car, unnoticed and forgotten, till the murderer realized he must get rid of it. But everyone in

Bournemouth had access to those bushes. Supposing the valise had turned up in East Cliff Road; would it have told in any substantial measure against Allaway that he had been obliged to wait outside the Russell-Coates museum?

These weaknesses, barely concealed in the Crown strength, would have been forcefully exploited by a great defender, with the constructive effect of building up a counter-strength that could have been cemented by a credible defendant. But in the event no great defender was forthcoming, and the prisoner's credibility failed to survive the formidable test of his appearance in the box.

His was a blanket denial, absolute, unqualified: never sent any telegram, never was near the station, never knew or saw or even heard of this Miss Wilkins, save what he read in the papers during subsequent days. As he pledged his oath to these negative assertions, he wore an air of injured innocence, consonant with that of a simple, harmless man caught in the paralyzing web of circumstances.

Allaway's life reposing in their hands, the jurors anxiously sought some definite sign which would denote how far they could rely on his sworn word.

That sign was not delayed unduly, and when it came left none in further doubt. . . .

Thomas Inskip, K.C. (afterwards Lord Chief Justice Caldecote) had been questioning Allaway, in rather pedestrian fashion, for the Crown. Whom he saw that night; the time he put the car away; the keys to the garage.

Allaway stonewalled steadily. Inskip made small progress.

But now counsel turned to the fatal telegraph form, and to certain postcards, found at Allaway's home, with which it had been meticulously compared.

He handed one of these up to Allaway.

"Is that in your handwriting?"

Allaway paused—to make quite certain, or to calculate?

"No," he said. "I don't think that is mine."

"Do you swear it?" Mr. Justice Avory interposed.

"It's too good for my writing," Allaway said doggedly.

"It is addressed," the judge said, reading, "to Miss Gladys Allaway?"

"Yes."

"That is your daughter?"

"Yes."

"And it is signed 'Daddy'?"

"Yes."

"And you will swear that is not your handwriting?"

"Yes," said Allaway.

The judge wrote gravely. Inskip handed up another postcard.

"Is that in your handwriting?"

"No," replied Allaway. "That's the same as the other."

118

Mr. Justice Avory examined this card also.

"It is addressed to your wife?"

"Yes, to Mrs. Allaway."

"Signed 'Tom with kisses'?"

"Yes."

"Is there any other Tom who would be writing to your wife?"

Allaway seemed to reflect.

"No, I don't think so."

"But you swear," said the judge, "that this is not in your handwriting?"

"Yes."

Again the judge wrote gravely. Inskip, still holding the postcard, tried a third.

"Is *that* in your handwriting?"

Allaway—if the metaphor may be used—was now beginning to see the writing on the wall.

"If this one is mine, they are all mine," he said ambiguously.

"But is it yours?" Inskip persisted.

What was going on in Allaway's mind, what protective mechanisms conflicted and collided, nobody to the end of time will ever surely know.

"I will say it is in my handwriting," he answered finally, "because it's very much like it."

"And so the others also are," said Inskip quickly.

"Yes."

The judge, with great deliberation, laid down his pen.

"You say they are all in your handwriting?"

"Yes."

"*Having just said they are not?*"

There was utter silence. Allaway flushed to the roots of his hair, glancing from side to side, as if searching for escape . . .

There remained two days to go, but the trial was virtually over.

The liar had betrayed himself and, in so doing, had also betrayed the murderer as well—as clearly as if he had then and there confessed in open court, instead of in prison upon execution eve.

Mary Queen of Scots

MILLIONS who are quite unmoved by greater names in history. nevertheless respond with curiosity and interest to any casual mention of Mary Queen of Scots. For hers is that perennial and boundless fascination attaching to a tragic blend of opposite extremes.

On the one hand, no woman has ever lived a life more royal. She became—through the death of her father, James V—sovereign of Scotland when she was one week old. She became—through the death of her cousin, Mary Tudor—heir to the English monarchy when she was sixteen. At seventeen—through the accession of her spouse, the Dauphin —she doubled her regality by becoming Queen of France.

On the other hand, no woman has ever lived a life more wretched. She spent some childhood years on a remote and lonely island as a safeguard against kidnapping by the hostile English. At eighteen she was prematurely widowed, and constrained to return from Paris to her northern realm, where she felt a stranger—as she was felt to be. At twenty-four she witnessed with horror-stricken eyes the brutal murder of her most devoted aide upon the instigation of her jealous second husband. At twenty-five she learned—with less distress, say cynics—that the latter had been violently done to death in turn. At twenty-six she herself was overthrown by a conspiracy of rebellious Scottish lords, and immured in the dour fastness of Lochleven Castle—first in the series of real or quasi-prisons within whose walls this young and cultured and attractive woman henceforth was to spend virtually all her life, until its termination in a cruel and bloody death.

Not, however, at the fiat of the Scottish lords. Inside a year, she had escaped from Lochleven, and sought refuge, not in the Highlands, nor in France nor Spain, but with her kinswoman, Elizabeth of England.

History, rather than personal antipathy, had decreed that these two women should be deadly rivals. It was not only that they symbolized the Protestant and Roman Catholic camps, whose mutual hatred at that time split Great Britain. It was not only that genealogists of any creed acknowledged Mary's title to succeed a virgin queen already approaching middle age.

It was not only that the English Papists had always queried Elizabeth's own title.

There still remained a culminating factor. Shortly after Mary's appeal for succour, Elizabeth was formally excommunicated; the Pope pronounced that she was not the lawful Queen of England—thereby obviously implying that Mary was.

Mary thus constituted a focus of, and a spur to, disaffection, and it would have taken a more quixotic character than Elizabeth to refrain from exploiting her unexpected trustfulness.

Mary had asked for Elizabeth's protection; she received it—as a mildly privileged but closely guarded captive, shifted from one house of detention to another as the requirements of security might suggest. Nor did general opinion consider this treatment harsh; on the contrary, there were constant demands for sterner measures—demands that reached an extra strident pitch each time a plot against Elizabeth was exposed. Even if Mary did not actively participate in any—so ran popular argument—she was the primary inspiration of most, and the prospective beneficiary of all.

What long restrained Elizabeth from complying with these demands was neither scruple nor compassion. It was simply a shrewd and selfish fear of boomerang effects if she violated the divinity of an anointed queen.

The extent to which this weighed with her may be measured by the fact that when at last she did decide to strike, Mary had been under her "protection" eighteen years. The good looks which had graced her earlier had gone; age and frustration and stale air had taken toll; at forty-four the legendary Queen of Scotts was round-shouldered, fat, and distinctly double-chinned.

It hardly mattered. Enhanced by her maturing years, her innate dignity—of spirit as well as presence—exercised a spell against which mere good looks could not compete.

That dignity was conspicuously manifest from the first moment of her ultimate ordeal—from the moment she received formal intimation that Commissioners, specially appointed for the task, were foregathering at her current jail, Castle Fotheringay, to try her for conspiracy against Elizabeth's life.

Having briefly declared herself clear of any crime, she gazed, unflinching, at the Commission's envoys.

"It seemeth strange to me," she said, "that I should be commanded to appear in judgment. I am an absolute Queen."

The envoys, taken aback, claimed for their Commission an authority by patent.

"An authority by patent!" she repeated scornfully. "But I am not a subject, and would rather die a thousand deaths than acknowledge myself one."

The envoys respectfully urged her to reconsider, for the Commission both could and would proceed despite her absence. "Lay aside bootless privilege," they pleaded, "and show your innocence, lest, by avoiding trial, you draw upon yourself suspicions."

"I will not offend," she resolutely persisted, "against my progenitors, the Kings of Scots, by acknowledging myself a subject to the Crown of England."

None the less, she pondered that argument overnight, and next day, when the full Commission of twenty-four assembled, the Queen of Scots reluctantly appeared to stand her trial.

A strange trial, in which the accused was allowed no advocate, no notes, no documents; in which the judges were her handpicked adversaries; in which the ordinary courts were by-passed and ignored.

A strange trial, in which the evidence rested on alleged copies of letters, whose authenticity—even as such—was not attested.

One of these letters—if the copy merited reliance—had been addressed to the Queen of Scots and signed by Anthony Babington himself beheaded for treason less than a month before.

Its language did not offer scope for misinterpretation; it referred to "invasions", and "the deliverance of your majesty", and—most sinister

121

of all—to "the dispatch of the usurper. There be six noble gentlemen," it added, "who, for the zeal they bear the Catholic cause and your majesty's service, will undertake the tragical execution."

Mary firmly denied any knowledge of that letter.

"It was confessed by Babington," the prosecutor said.

"It may be Babington wrote it," she retorted, "but let it be proved that I received it. Other men's crimes are not to be cast on me."

It was a shrewd thrust, but instantly met by counter-thrust.

"Listen now to this," the prosecutor said.

The second letter—if the copy merited reliance—had been addressed by the Queen of Scots to Babington and was patently in answer to the first. It also referred to invasions; it also canvassed methods of escape; and—most sinister of all—the writer anxiously inquired "By what means do the six gentlemen deliberate to proceed?"

When those words were read, the Queen burst into tears—whether from conscious guilt or outraged innocence we shall never know.

"I would not so make shipwreck of my soul," she cried.

"Your secretaries have vouched it," the prosecutor said.

"Then they are men forsworn," Mary declared. "Might they not have inserted in my letters things I had not dictated? The safety of all princes falleth to the ground if they depend upon the testimony of secretaries."

It was again a shrewd thrust, by an unpractised defender—but this time the counter-thrust accomplished infamy. Adjourning their session from Fotheringay to London the Commissioners called the Queen's secretaries before them.

She was not present, nor even represented; there was no cross-examination—there was no cross-examiner. And yet, upon hearing this untested evidence—the only evidence that skirted the fringe of legal proof—the Commissioners felt able to pronounce Mary's guilt and to presage its expiation on the headsman's block.

Frederick Nodder

WHEN the River Idle yields up the body of little Mona Tinsley, and an examining pathologist observes she has been strangled, the police do not have to go far to find the man they want. He is in jail, serving a sentence of penal servitude. For Mona has been missing five whole months, and Frederick Nodder has already been convicted of abducting her.

The circumstances of that abduction were so mysterious that they excited nation-wide attention—an attention stimulated rather than diminished by an outcome that left the mystery unsolved.

It was on 5 January, 1937, that Mona, an intelligent and vivacious child of ten, failed to return from afternoon school to her modest home in Newark. At first her family assumed that, upon impulse, she had gone to one or other of her relatives in the town. But as the evening passed and she still did not appear, and the relatives were severally visited in vain, her continued absence was officially reported.

Investigations began at once, and continued all next day. These unhappily did not succeed in discovering the child, but at least indicated the direction in which she should be sought. They disclosed that shortly after school hours on the 5th, Mona had been seen in company with a man who was a friend of her married aunt in Sheffield, and who—upon the introduction of this aunt—had once lodged at the Tinsleys' house for a few weeks.

He had there passed by the name of Hudson. Mona and the other children called him Uncle Fred.

His real name was Nodder.

The phoney name rightly suggests a shady past. Nodder, indeed, was a shady character; one can only suppose he successfully concealed the fact during his brief stay with the respectable Tinsleys.

He was dishonest. He was drunken. His sexual habits were promiscuous and crude. He had no apparent regular means of livelihood, and frequently found himself in sore financial straits (a warrant for non-payment under a bastardy order had been hanging over his head for a considerable time). But somehow or other he usually contrived to get along and, at the time of Mona's disappearance, he was living by himself in a small, semi-detached house at a village near East Retford.

Only by persistent and methodical inquiry did the police finally track him down to this secluded spot. But at seven o'clock on the night of the 6th—a wild and windy night—their car drew up outside the front door of his house. No lights were visible, and no answer met their heavy knock. They had to wait in patient vigil till eleven o'clock before Nodder loomed dimly into view through the prevailing darkness.

Mona Tinsley? Yes, certainly he knew her. Disappeared, had she? Well, he was sorry about that. Thought he could help them, did they? No; he knew nothing about it at all. Account for his movements yesterday? Went into Newark in the morning; saw a chap who works on a barge about a possible job; caught the 3.45 p.m. bus from Newark home. Oh, no, never set eyes on Mona Tinsley; hadn't set eyes on her, come to that, for the past fifteen months.

They searched Nodder's house; the result was negative. The evidence so far implicating him hardly justified them in preferring an immediate charge. But the police felt in their bones that presently more would be unearthed, and they feared that if they let him out of their sight he would abscond.

So they astutely held him—as was their right—under the bastardy warrant while the search for Mona and for witnesses went on.

123

The case steadily built up. A bus conductor identified Nodder as a man who had travelled on his bus, *accompanied by a little girl*, from Newark to Retford on 5 January; the bus had left Newark at 4.45—not 3.45 p.m. A passenger on this bus corroborated the conductor and picked out Nodder likewise.

Two acquaintances of Nodder came forward to say that they had seen him in Retford later that evening, *with a little girl*. A neighbour declared that she had caught a fleeting glimpse of *a little girl* in Nodder's house next day.

Faced with this mass of testimony, Nodder changed his tale.

Yes, it was true he *had* met Mona, accidentally, in Newark. She'd asked after his friend, her aunt, in Sheffield; Nodder had said he'd expected her to call on him next day; Mona had wanted to come with him in order to see Auntie, and Nodder had "foolishly" agreed.

Then, on getting a note next day from the Aunt to say she wasn't coming, he took Mona on the bus as far as Worksop, leaving the child to travel alone on it to Sheffield, armed with a letter of explanation from Nodder to her aunt.

But nobody could be found who had seen Mona Tinsley on a Sheffield-bound bus that night. And at his trial for abduction Nodder did not go into the box to repeat his tale on oath. He was most properly convicted and given seven years—a sentence mirroring general belief that the full enormity of his crime had yet to be laid bare. "It may be," said the judge to Nodder when he sentenced him, "that time will reveal the dreadful secret you carry in your breast."

Has Nodder's secret been revealed now by the river? Were his the strangling hands? One thing is sure; he dare not stay out of the box in this, his second trial, when the charge he faces is punishable by death.

So he takes the oath and swears to the truthfulness of his second statement—that when he last saw Mona she was on the bus to Sheffield.

"Why did you not take her back to her mother in Newark?" asks Norman Birkett, cross-examining.

"Because I thought her aunt would be the one to put things right."

"Then why not tell the police the truth when they came next night?"

"For one thing," says Nodder shiftily, "I was upset."

"Why not say 'I have sent her to Sheffield' if it was true?"

Nodder seems wholly at a loss. Birkett deliberately waits.

"I don't know," Nodder says eventually.

"When did you decide to send Mona to Sheffield?"

"In the morning, when I got her aunt's letter to say she wasn't coming."

"Why not start at once for Sheffield, in the daylight?"

"Because of this warrant. I did not want to go to Sheffield in the daylight."

"You yourself never went to Sheffield. Why could you not go to Worksop in the daylight, and send Mona on to Sheffield in the daylight?"

Again Nodder seems wholly at a loss. Again Birkett deliberately waits.

"I can't say," Nodder says eventually.

"You knew that Sheffield was a great city?"

"Yes."

"And you knew that a girl of ten arriving in a great city would be a lost little soul?"

"She wouldn't have far to go from the bus terminus to her aunt's."

"A tram ride, wasn't it, if she could find where the tram went from?"

"Yes."

"Did it occur to you that the aunt might be out?"

The impact of this simple question is altogether shattering.

"Did it occur to you that the aunt might be out?"

"Well," says Nodder, moistening his lips. "I had a good idea she wouldn't be."

"Did it occur to you that you might send her a telegram?"

"No."

"'Please meet Mona, bus terminus, Sheffield, 8.30.'?"

"No."

"It never occurred to you?"

"No."

Great cross-examiners are the least verbose, and Nodder was exposed with maximum economy. But when Norman Birkett sat down, not a shred of doubt remained. Mona Tinsley never started off that night to Sheffield. She was then already dead, pathetic victim of a crime—almost certainly originating from a sexual source—for which Nodder's full payment had only been deferred.

Patrick O'Donnell

"A VILER thing never assumed human form. He left the country un-pardoned by his Queen, unrepentent to his God, against every man, and every man against him."

The speaker was Charles Russell, foremost counsel of his day, defending at a capital trial unique in history. And the "vile thing" he spoke of was no other than the man that his client in the dock stood charged with murdering.

It is, as a rule, risky for a defender to attack—especially in such opprobrious terms—the character of that individual, voiceless in his grave, who has been cast for the pity-rousing role of prisoner's victim. But Russell, on this occasion ran no risk at all. On the contrary, by such tactics he had everything to gain. James Carey, dead no less than when he was alive, could forge an instant unity of hatred among adversaries who agreed on nothing else. Long-standing battles were momentarily halted, immemorial feuds were temporarily healed, for the warring ranks to form a common front against the cut-throat Judas of Dublin's Phoenix Park.

The Phoenix Park murders of 1882 stand out even in the bloody record of Irish revolt against British rule. Not only for barbarity. Not only for audacity. Above all, for the grave set-back they administered to hopes that a more peaceful era was about to dawn.

Lord Frederick Cavendish had just been appointed Chief Secretary in Ireland. His reputation for liberal thought and conciliatory action were deliberately intended by the British Government as a symbol and a pledge of milder policies. When he strolled with the Under Secretary along the paths of Phoenix Park on the day of his arrival, the fair summer sky above their heads seemed to reflect the brighter prospect for the tortured land beneath.

Within minutes, though, that prospect was plunged into wintry darkness.

Whatever average Irishmen might feel, whatever their responsible leaders like Parnell might say, there still remained extremists irrevocably opposed to any accommodation or compromise with England. It was a bunch of these fanatical assassins that suddenly surrounded Lord Frederick and his colleague, stabbed and hacked them to death upon the spot, and made good their escape in horse-cars standing by.

They might never have been caught—for many months they passed immune—had not at last suspicion fallen on their ringleader, who, discarding loyalty and grasping at survival, purchased his own safety by betrayal of the rest.

As a result, five of his accomplices were hanged; a number of others received life sentences; and James Carey himself acquired an indivisible and enduring infamy.

The English despised him as a cowardly killer. The Irish hated him as a traitor and informer. Neither grieved on learning he had met a violent death aboard a British ship while sailing to Natal under a false name.

Patrick O'Donnell, who admittedly had shot him, became a hero in Ireland overnight; nor did he lack sympathy in England, where his guilt or innocence by law must be determined.

O'Donnell needed all the sympathy he could get, as well as his famous advocate's formidable gifts. At the Old Bailey the Crown called evidence to prove that Carey and O'Donnell had made the voyage from England; that Carey's identity, until then unknown, was disclosed by the local papers at Cape Town; that O'Donnell, there shown a published sketch of Carey, slipped it in his pocket with the remark: "I'll shoot him''; that next day, on the trip between Cape Town and Port Elizabeth, the two men met and conversed in the saloon; that while they were thus

126

facing each other at close range, O'Donnell fatally wounded Carey by firing three revolver bullets in succession.

This bare outline of events was not substantially in dispute. Unless, therefore, it could be modified or supplemented, a finding of murder was a virtual certainty.

Only one possible line of defence existed—that marked out by a formal statement which the accused had made. "What I did was in self-defence," he said. "Carey pulled a revolver out of his pocket."

Under the rules of procedure then existing, O'Donnell could not amplify that statement upon oath. It was for Russell alone to build on it as best he could. He laid the bricks, one by one, in cross-examination, working mostly with the minimum of straw.

Russell first established that none of those (and the Crown called several) who had actually seen O'Donnell shoot had also seen what had occurred immediately before. "Nothing caused me to look," said one; "Nothing drew my attention", said another; "I turned round when I heard a shot", declared a third.

Next, Russell put a fresh and more innocuous gloss upon the dangerously pointed words "I'll shoot him"; the only witness to hear O'Donnell use them agreed that they were spoken "pleasantly", and that he did not take them literally even for a moment.

Last—and perhaps most dexterously of all—O'Donnell's counsel dealt with the assertion in his statement that Carey had produced a revolver and had threatened him.

O'Donnell did not use such a revolver to shoot Carey; he had shot Carey with a revolver of his own. No revolver was found in Carey's hand; nor on his person; nor anywhere nearby.

At first glance, that seemed to smash O'Donnell's story. Yet Carey did possess a revolver, none the less—a revolver which, curiously enough, was subsequently taken from his fifteen-year-old son. "I ran and got it from my father's berth," he said in explanation. "He was past using it, so I put it in my pocket." But Russell had ascertained that not a single soul had seen this lad go near his father's berth.

"What made you think the boy had a revolver?" Russell asked the ship's officer who took it from him.

"A passenger informed me," said the officer.

"Did you challenge the boy?"

"I did."

"Did he admit having it?"

"No."

"Did you have to search him?"

"Yes."

"And then did you find it?" Russell said.

"Only on a second attempt," the officer replied.

So the way was cleared for the reconstruction Russell so forcefully offered to the jury. They had Carey, with his utter disregard for human

127

life, knowing now he had been identified. They had O'Donnell, knowing now who Carey was, and filled with the loathing any decent man would feel. Supposing—and what could be more natural?—that O'Donnell had stigmatized Carey to his face? That he had called him by his name; that he had called him an informer?

Would not Carey, in the circumstances, carry the pistol on him, and would he not respond with at least a show of force? And when O'Donnell turned out quicker on the draw, might not Carey's son try to conceal that tell-tale dropped revolver in revenge?

Could they not see it all before their eyes? Was it not consistent with the prosecution's evidence? And did it not exactly fit with all they knew of Carey—that most desperate, most ruthless, and most villainous of men? . . .

The jury were out considering their verdict for two hours. Twice during that time they came back into court, asking the judge for further direction on the law.

The nature of their questions clearly indicated that they were hesitant and reluctant to convict.

O'Donnell stood defiant as the death sentence was passed. Then, as the warders moved to accompany him downstairs, he startled the crowded court by roaring out "Stand back", and adopting an unmistakably oratorical pose.

Only a few words of his intended speech were heard, but doubtless they conveyed the substance of its theme. "Three cheers for Ireland", he cried, while they pushed and pulled him, struggling below. "To hell with the Britishers and with the British Crown."

His shouts, his oaths, and the dragging of his feet echoed weirdly in the subterranean passage that led from the Old Bailey dock to Newgate Jail.

That O'Donnell committed the crime of murder there is little doubt. That he deserved to suffer—as he did—the utmost penalty is a question much more debatable.

When one recalls reprieves distributed in more recent years by so-called progressive sociological thinkers, O'Donnell would seem to qualify for a probation order, and possibly for a sum out of the poor box as well.

Certainly few murderers can have mounted the scaffold and dropped into eternity with a clearer conscience.

Sidney Fox

TIMING was vital in the case of Sidney Fox. After midnight there would have been no point in his doing what he did—and, almost certainly, had he done it after midnight he would not have been found out.

But it was still twenty minutes short of midnight on 23 October, 1929, when Sidney, half-dressed, dashed down the stairs of that hotel at Margate, frantically shouting: "There's a fire! There's a fire!"

From the lounge and billiards room men hurried to assist. Sidney led them to the corridor where he and his elderly mother had for several days been sleeping in communicating rooms. "She's in there", he said imploringly, and pointed.

Someone opened the door. Out billowed a dense, black, acrid cloud, and those who tried to enter were at first forced back, choking. Flames glimmered dimly through the murk—it subsequently proved that an armchair was ablaze—and the resulting smoke had been imprisoned till that moment, as both the window and communicating door were closed.

Suffocation clearly threatened an immediate rescuer. Sidney himself expressed anguish, but remained outside. One courageous member of the party, though, on hands and knees and with handkerchief over mouth, resolutely fought his way into this inferno and re-emerged triumphant, carrying the woman. His gallant act, however, turned out to be fruitless, for Mrs. Fox already was beyond a doctor's aid.

As soon as he had recovered sufficiently from his distress and shock, Sidney gave them his account of the occurrence. Shortly after ten, he said, he had kissed his mother good-night and left her reading a paper in front of her gas fire. She told him that very shortly she would be going to bed. He went downstairs, had a couple of glasses of beer, returned to his own room and soon fell fast asleep.

He was presently disturbed by the rattling of a window, and on waking at once noticed a strong smell of fire. He opened the door communicating with his mother's room, met this tremendous mass of smoke that beat him back, and ran for the help that came too late to save his mother's life. Here Sidney wept, and could not be consoled.

The genuineness of his grief acquired apparent confirmation from the fact that his tender devotion to his mother had been noted during their short stay by all in the hotel. The genuineness of his story acquired apparent confirmation—in one important particular, at least—from the fact that a chambermaid earlier that evening had herself seen Mrs. Fox reading a paper in front of her gas fire.

It seemed pretty obvious, didn't it? Old lady dozes off; newspaper or piece of clothing falls against the fire; fumes would snuff her out without giving her a chance. Sidney might not have shown himself the pluckiest of sons, but lack of pluck does not constitute ground for worse suspicions.

Verdict at the inquest: accidental death.

So far, so good, for Sidney Fox; his plan was working well. Of course, the coroner and the local police might have been less easily satisfied if they had known about those two insurance policies; policies worth £3,000 in all if Mrs. Fox should die from accident; short-term policies taken out by Sidney, on which he had been buying extensions almost from day to day—the last of these extensions, costing a few shillings, having been bought by him on 21 October to expire *at midnight on the 23rd*. But nobody knew—except the insurance companies concerned, and as he was nicely in the clear with everybody else, Sidney did not anticipate any difficulties with them.

But there he had made a bad miscalculation. Mrs. Fox dies, by accident, with the beneficiary at hand, when both of those short extensions have twenty minutes to run? It was too great a coincidence for the insurers to accept. They nosed around a bit themselves and picked up sufficient scent to enlist the even more perceptive nose of Scotland Yard.

Interesting data rapidly accumulated about the civil and well-spoken Sidney Fox. He had long been a small-time professional crook and had served several prison sentences for forgery, theft and fraud. His latest racket—in which his mother had been his accomplice—was to live virtually free by bilking a succession of hotels.

And on 23 October, when Providence intervened with a bonus of £3,000, his bill at Margate had grown pressing and he could not even pay the railway fare to somewhere else. His last reserves of cash had gone on the policy extensions.

Sidney Fox, then, was a man of criminal tendencies with an overwhelming motive to commit a crime. The matter seemed to warrant meticulous review. Mrs. Fox's room at the hotel was thoroughly re-examined, and Mrs. Fox's lately buried body was exhumed.

Much now came to light that—in actuality or in significance—had been oddly overlooked. It appeared that the armchair had caught fire from *underneath*. A stretch of carpet between the armchair and the gas-fire was *unburned*. Another chair, found by the rescuers some distance from the fire, had none the less been badly scorched along one leg—which could only mean that someone had been in the room and moved it *after the fire began*.

Add to all this that in Sir Bernard Spilsbury's weighty judgment—though admittedly it brought him into dispute with other experts—Mrs. Fox did not die as a result of the fire. She had previously been *strangled*. . . .

At the trial of Sidney Fox that automatically followed one intangible element worked on his behalf. Imagination boggles at the notion of a man murdering his mother for financial gain. A common human instinct makes it so improbable—and, as records demonstrate, it does occur so seldom—that whatever the force of circumstantial evidence, there is an unconscious presumption against it in the mind.

That presumption still existed when Sidney Fox affirmed his innocence on oath. It still exists when Sir William Jowitt, Attorney-General and future Lord Chancellor, rises to open his cross-examination. But a cross-examiner so formidable and acute does not long leave this presumption without challenge.

"Did you realize," he asked, "that night when you opened the communicating door that the atmosphere in your mother's room would probably suffocate anyone inside?"

The answer is dictated by Sidney Fox's own description of his own behaviour.

"If I had stayed in there I should have been suffocated," he says.

"So that you must have felt greatly apprehensive for your mother?"

"Yes, I did."

"Fox," says Sir William, "you closed that door."

This statement is a terrible question in itself. Fox gropes vainly for a plausible reply.

"Why did you close the door instead of flinging it wide open?"

Fox's mental struggle is almost visible.

"My explanation for that now is that the smoke should not spread into the hotel."

The exclamations of horror in court are understandable. Whether Fox speaks false or true, it matters little; in that single flash what looked like a man stands revealed as a monster.

"Rather that your mother should suffocate than that smoke should get about in the hotel?"

"Certainly not."

But it is now too late—and, anyway what other construction can it bear?

"On your way downstairs," goes on Sir William, "you passed the other door—the landing door—of your mother's room?"

"Yes."

"Did you open that door?"

"No."

"So you left your mother in that room with both doors closed?"

"I rushed downstairs to get some help," says Fox.

"Don't you think that before rushing down for help you might have flung the doors open as wide as possible?"

"No."

"I suggest that if you had wanted to preserve your mother's life you would have flung open the doors?"

"I tried to get in," says Fox, "and when I could not I rushed downstairs."

131

"There was one thing in between," says Sir William sombrely. "You closed the door."

He closed the door. His mother lay in a smoke-filled room, and . . . Fox closed the door. It was a complete reversal of that common human instinct on which the mind's presumption against matricide depends. After Sir William's terse and telling questions, such a presumption ceased to operate for Fox; he was recognized as one who could—and hanged as one who did—coldbloodedly destroy the life to which he owed his own.

Aleck Bourne

THERE are few more pitiful and more repellent spectacles than that of a doctor making confession in a criminal court that he has been performing abortions on demand and for reward. At least one member of a noble calling is then seen reduced to the moral level of those backstreet harpies who extract for themselves a monetary profit from the lapses of working girls and the worries of working wives.

Nor are the ethics—only the hygiene—of the matter improved by recourse to a nursing-home instead of a frowzy kitchen, and a fee of 250 guineas instead of 30s.

The degradation of a professional man remains.

Greatly different, however, were the circumstances, greatly different was the atmosphere induced, when at the Old Bailey in 1939 a doctor confessed—or, more accurately, proclaimed—that he had, in the words of the indictment laid against him, "used an instrument with intent to procure a miscarriage".

In every respect, his case contrasted with the usual pattern. He had not operated merely on demand, but on the honest prompting of his judgment. He had not done it for reward, but as an act of charity. So far from appearing pitiful and repellent, he excited widespread admiration and respect. He symbolized the honourable dignity of a professional man dedicated to his work.

For, in fact, Mr. Aleck Bourne, one of London's foremost gynaecologists and obstetric surgeons, stepped into the dock of his own deliberate choice.

A girl of fourteen had been raped most shockingly by soldiers. Pregnancy resulted, and all concerned with the care of her thought it should be terminated, for the sake of both her physical and mental health. But, having regard to the law governing abortion, this did not seem to be a very likely prospect, "unless"—as the girl's physician wrote to Mr. Bourne—"someone of your standing is prepared to undertake the operation".

Mr. Bourne wrote back asking to see the girl, so that he could form an opinion at first hand. If he decided that the pregnancy endangered the girl's health, he would perform the operation willingly. "I have done this before, and have not the slightest hesitation in doing it again." And he added; "I have said that the next time I have an opportunity, I will write to the Attorney-General and invite him to take action."

For Mr. Bourne knew that abortion only ceased to be an offence against the law—with a maximum punishment of imprisonment for life—if it was performed to *preserve the life of the mother*. And no authority had laid down exactly what that meant. . . .

Mr. Bourne saw the girl. He performed the operation. Then he did what his letter had foreshadowed.

"I decided to get a ruling," he says in the witness-box, answering his counsel, Mr. Roland Oliver. "That is why we are here."

And now they are there, with his plea of Not Guilty duly entered on the record, the issue really turns upon the correct interpretation of that liberating phrase, "preserving the mother's life".

The Attorney-General, Sir Donald Somerville, maintains that the words should be construed literally and strictly. The judge says, non-committally, that everything must depend on the evidence adduced and the circumstances of the case.

Mr. Bourne contends strongly for a progressive attitude.

"My interpretation of the law," he says, "based on everyday prac-tice by men of repute in my profession, is that it is justifiable to perform the operation when there is danger to health. I can't distinguish between danger to health and danger to life. If we wait for danger to life, the woman is past assistance."

Thus Mr. Bourne throws the gauntlet down, and in effect challenges the law to prove itself consistent with humanity and sense.

"What mischief to this girl's health," Mr. Oliver asks, "did you fear when you did this operation?"

"There was a possibility of physical injury, but that was less impor-tant. Being the type of girl she is, I felt that the mental injury would last a long time; it would be a sort of psycho-neurotic trouble that might easily continue all her life."

"It was to avoid that, was it, that you operated as you did?"

"Yes."

The Attorney-General, whatever his secret feelings—and these still offer scope for speculation—cross-examines with his customary vigour.

"You say in your letter, 'I have done this before and have not the slightest hesitation in doing it again'. What," asks Mr. Attorney pointedly, "is 'this'?"

"The operation of abortion". Mr. Bourne does not mince words. "My record of abortion is such that it would stand any examination. But where there is a case definitely indicated, I will do it."

133

Where *what* is definitely indicated? *What* exactly renders the act of abortion lawful? That the court sits to determine at this moment.

"I suggest," the Attorney-General says, "that there is a perfectly clear distinction between danger to life and danger to health."

Mr. Bourne seizes the chance.

"There is a large group whose health may be damaged, but whose life almost certainly will not be sacrificed. There is another group whose life will definitely be in great danger. There is also a large group between those extremes"—he pauses a moment, carefully picking his words—"in which it is not possible to say how far life will be *in danger*, but we find health depressed to such a degree that life is *threatened*."

The Attorney-General abruptly changes course.

"You didn't take any second opinion?"

"I did not."

"At therapeutic abortions, isn't a second opinion generally taken?"

"I should think always," says Mr. Bourne.

"But in this case," the Attorney-General repeats emphatically, "you did not take any second opinion?"

"I am usually appealed to as a consultant," Mr. Bourne says, "and in this case I considered myself as the second opinion."

It is accurate—and flattering. Mr. Attorney, asks no more.

Other distinguished doctors confirm Mr. Bourne's view that the developing pregnancy endangered the girl's health. But that is virtually undisputed; the Crown calls no evidence to the contrary. The problem the jury are asked to solve is this: Does preserving health constitute preserving life?

It takes them only forty minutes to agree it does, and the voluntary prisoner is triumphantly acquitted. . . .

At no time had it been Mr. Bourne's intention—as was plain from his advocate's notable defence—to obtain a verdict based upon mere sympathy, and arrived at in defiance of the existing law.

His object was rather to get that law *declared*; to run his case in such a clear-cut fashion that the verdict would put an end to vexatious doubts and wearisome disputes about the extent of a doctor's legal right to perform an abortion where he deems it beneficial.

The verdict has had precisely that effect.

Since Rex. v. Bourne, the standard books on criminal law have revised their chapters dealing with abortion. Operations done, they say, in the course of proper medical treatment are not unlawful if in the interest of the life *or health* of the mother.

Ambiguity has thus been swept away. Today doctors know where they are; and for this knowledge they can thank one distinguished surgeon's self-sacrificing act.

PART THREE

WITNESSES—EXPERT AND OTHERWISE

Lord Rosebery

IN 1930 Don Pat, trained by Charles Chapman, won the Bedfont High Weight Handicap at Kempton Park. Subsequently a statement concerning this event was issued by the Stewards of the Jockey Club. It reported that, after the race, the acting Stewards of the Kempton meeting had given orders for an examination of the horse. On receiving the result of the examination they had referred the case to the Stewards of the Jockey Club.

"After further investigation," this statement continued, "the Stewards of the Jockey Club satisfied themselves that a drug had been administered to the horse for the purpose of the race in question. They disqualified the horse for this race and all future races under their rules, and they warned C. Chapman, the trainer of the horse, off Newmarket Heath."

You are an ordinary member of the public. You are interested in racing, bet once or twice a week, study the Press tipsters, have theories about form. But you do not know a thing about the racing hierarchy, or how it operates, or its self-appointed rules.

What, then, would you have inferred from that official statement, published not only in the Racing Calendar, but also in a number of national newspapers? Could it mean anything other than that Mr. Chapman had been warned off for administering dope to the horse Don Pat himself? Or, at the very least, for being mixed up in the business?

I confess that would certainly have been my own conclusion. But it would have got me nowhere near the truth.

That Don Pat was doped lay established beyond question by the usual veterinary tests. No one, though, ever suggested for a moment that Mr. Chapman, a young man of highest character, doped the horse or had prior knowledge of the doping. He—in the outcome, more than anybody else—was the hapless victim of another's roguery.

But among the rules, or practices, of the Jockey Club—by which all who seek a living out of racehorses are constrained, willy-nilly, to abide —there is one, affecting trainers, which the Stewards applied rigorously to the doping of Don Pat. Because it is difficult to detect the perpetrators of doping, and because an essential element in it is access to the horse, the Stewards hold the trainer absolutely liable unless he can *prove* that he is not to blame.

This rule reverses the general rule of law that a person's *guilt* must be proved, and not his innocence. It may be expedient; it may even be necessary; but the effects of it on innocent parties are bound to be severe, and one might expect every measure to be taken by the Stewards which would at least reduce this to a minimum.

But if Mr. Chapman entertained such expectations, they were shattered.

Not only was he warned off; not only was he refused an adjournment of the Stewards' Inquiry so that he might further pursue inquiries of his own; not only was that elliptical and misleading statement published, but the Stewards flatly declined to explain or qualify it even when Mr. Chapman, finding the statement widely construed to mean he was a rogue, begged them to make clear to the world what they had really meant.

No appeal lies against a decision of the Stewards to warn a trainer off. But even the Jockey Club is not above the laws of defamation, and therefore—lacking any other means to clear his name—Mr. Chapman brought an action in the High Court, alleging that their statement constituted libel.

It was an action studded with famous and distinguished names. Among the defendants were my lords Harewood, Rosebery and Ellesmere (sued as Stewards of the Jockey Club), and no less notable a journal than *The Times* (unluckily involved through automatically printing the statement in good faith). Among counsel engaged were Patrick Hastings (for the plaintiff) and Norman Birkett (for the Jockey Club), the two brightest stars of the Special Jury courts and old opponents, truly worthy of each other's steel.

The major battle of the trial centred round one question: What did the words of the statement mean in their *ordinary, natural sense?*

Did they mean, as the plaintiff said, that he had been a party to the doping of Don Pat? Or did they merely mean, as the Stewards still maintained, that he was warned off because he had failed to *prevent* Don Pat being doped?

It devolved upon the Earl of Rosebery, as the senior Steward, to act as chief witness in support of this contention and to bear the main brunt of Hastings's cross-examination.

"Do you realize," it began, "that the decisions of the Stewards of the Jockey Club may bear the gravest consequences?"

"Yes," Lord Rosebery said.

"A trainer who is warned off will be ruined, socially and professionally?"

"Yes," Lord Rosebery said.

"In a case like this," said Hastings, "where a trainer has had nothing to do with the doping of a horse, you convict him of carelessness?"

Lord Rosebery demurred.

"I think it is more than carelessness. I should call it a grave dereliction of duty."

Hastings accepted the amendment.

"Do you realize that, in the eyes of fair-minded persons, there must be all the difference in the world between a man who has doped a horse and a young trainer at the beginning of his career who is guilty of dereliction of duty?"

"Yes," Lord Rosebery said.

"If the wording of the notice sent out by the Stewards conveyed to ordinary people that Mr. Chapman had been warned off the Turf for doping, a grave injustice would have been done him, would it not?"

"It would be an injustice."

Hastings did not take kindly to the omission of his adjective.

"The answer is Yes?" he said sharply.

"The answer is Yes."

"It would have been a simple matter for the Stewards of the Jockey Club to have stated in the notice that Mr. Chapman had been found guilty, not of doping, but of dereliction of duty as a trainer?"

"Yes."

"Why did they not do it?"

"I think we did."

Hastings flourished the document that was the cause of all the trouble.

"Is there a word in this notice that would convey to a man of ordinary intelligence that the only thing Mr. Chapman had been found guilty of was not taking care of the horse?"

"Yes."

"Where?"

Lord Rosebery could only repeat the hotly disputed words.

"You say that conveys his sole fault was not taking care?"

"Yes."

Hastings let the statement drop with manifest derision.

"Were you informed last summer by the Duke of Richmond that Mr. Chapman was anxious that it should be made public that he'd been warned off, not for doping, but for negligence?"

"Yes."

"Why didn't you make it public?"

"*I did not think it necessary,*" Lord Rosebery said, "*as the Stewards had never said that Mr. Chapman doped the horse.*"

This is the attitude I find so hard to fathom—why the Stewards so stubbornly resisted the addition to their statement of a dozen words which, without remitting Mr. Chapman's punishment, would have defined in plain terms what he was punished for. I fancy the jury found it equally hard to fathom, and that they expressed their disapproval in the damages—£13,000 against the Jockey Club, £3,000 against the morally unoffending *Times*.

This sensational verdict, however, was not held.

The Court of Appeal pronounced that the Stewards were protected on the legal ground of privilege (a plea that had been rejected by the trial judge), and they were dismissed completely from the suit. *The Times*, ironically, could not claim privilege, but the Court of Appeal, considering the damages excessive, ordered a new trial—a trial that never came to pass, though Mr. Chapman received a sum in settlement of his claim.

Nevertheless one is bound to think that Mr. Chapman suffered a raw deal. The Stewards may have correctly interpreted *their* law, the Court of Appeal may have correctly interpreted *theirs*; but one is left with the uneasy feeling that this was a case where both private law and public law did something less than justice.

Evelyn Thaw

THE twenty-fifth of June, 1906. Evelyn Thaw, some months short of her twenty-second birthday, sits at a favoured table in a celebrated night haunt—Madison Square Roof Gardens in New York. Beside her is her husband, Harry Thaw, the millionaire. Around her are all the trappings of luxury and high living.

But Evelyn's lot has not always been cast in such society. She has come up, if not the hardest, at least the steepest way.

She has known what it is to go hungry and go homeless; to spend a childhood shifting from town to town in the wake of a widowed mother, who was at a loss how to provide for her children and herself; to endure, at a tender and impressionable age, the ugly consequences of defalcation and distraint.

Evelyn's escape was made by a well-trodden route. Her rare beauty attracted artists, for whom she gladly modelled. It attracted Press photographers, for whom she gladly posed. The resulting pictures attracted theatre managements, who detected a potential showgirl of the strongest pulling power.

At seventeen, in the full flower of her youth, Evelyn joined the chorus of a Broadway musical—in an epoch when, traditionally, men of means and fashion sought beautiful companions from this source of supply.

Among her earliest admirers was a man of international eminence. Stanford White ranked high among great architects. He also ranked high among great voluptuaries; though married with a grown-up son, and far into middle age, he found his relaxation in erotic drinking parties at which he entertained young ladies of the stage.

Harry Thaw had come somewhat later on the scene. He, too, though a younger man than Stanford White, was also a well-established libertine. But at least he did fall genuinely in love with Evelyn. He courted her with violent and unremitting zeal, cosseted her when she was ill, took her—and her mother—abroad when she recovered, and finally married her in April, 1905.

In so doing, as one writer has put it, he plucked her from the very arms of Stanford White. . . .

The Roof Gardens show is rather boring, Evelyn thinks. Though she still conveys the innocent freshness of a child, she is an experienced woman now, even a trifle jaded. Let's go, she says.

She and Harry Thaw get up. She walks ahead of him towards the exit. She turns to say something but finds he is not there.

At the same moment three shots are fired in quick succession. Harry Thaw, pistol in hand, is standing a few yards away, looking down at a dying and disfigured Stanford White.

"My God, Harry, what have you done?" she cries.

"I have saved your life," he says.

What he had done, in fact, was to make the Broadway butterfly principal witness in one of this century's greatest trials.

Principal witness, yes. For what was the defence?

That Thaw was born with a psychopathic temperament; that when first he asked Evelyn to marry him, she refused for reasons concerning Stanford White; that the story she told him about White and herself preyed upon Thaw's mind till eventually he believed he was divinely charged with Stanford White's destruction.

So the defence is temporary insanity. The doctors can do no more than furnish scientific evidence. All else depends on this story that Evelyn is supposed to have told Thaw, and that she now ascends the witness-stand to tell to a jury who are trying him for his life.

Very quietly she unfolds the momentous narrative. How she had first fallen in with Stanford White right at the start of her theatrical career. How he had asked her out, made the acquaintance of her mother, sent Evelyn presents of finery and of clothes. How at his insistence she had supped with him at his house alone; how afterwards he had begged leave to "show her round the place"; how they went into a bedroom; how he had made her drink down a goblet of champagne; how—here the soft voice fades to a mere whisper—her ears had begun to pound and she became unconscious.

All of this, says Evelyn, she disclosed to Harry Thaw in explaining why she did not think it right for them to marry.

"What effect," defending counsel asks, "did this statement of yours produce on Mr. Thaw?"

"He would get up," answers Evelyn, "and walk up and down the room, and then bite his nails and say: 'Oh God, oh God,' and he kept sobbing. It was not like crying; it was a deep, deep sob."

Was it any wonder that Thaw's insecurely balanced reason had been overthrown when he heard this pitiful tale five years ago? This is the direction in which the jury's thoughts are tending when the District Attorney, Mr. Jerome, gets up to cross-examine.

His is a difficult and thankless task. But there is only one course open —to try to expose that air of simple innocence as a sham.

141

First blow is struck in silence. Jerome hands a sheet of paper over to the witness. As she recognizes it, Evelyn's face falls in dismay.

"Did you write that letter?"

"I . . . er . . . yes."

"Is it addressed to the Mercantile Trust Company?"

"Yes."

"Does it relate to a weekly sum of 25 dollars that was being paid to you by Mr. Stanford White?"

"Yes."

"Was that being paid to you in 1902?"

"Yes."

"Thank you. Please hand the letter back . . . Do you remember the Lederer divorce case?"

"Yes."

"Were you cited in it as a co-respondent?"

"Yes."

"Do you know a Mr. James A. Garland?"

"Yes."

"When you were playing with the Floradora Company was this gentleman awaiting a divorce?"

"I believe so."

"Did you spend most of your Sundays on his yacht?"

"With my mother."

"Didn't you and your mother quarrel about your relations with this man?"

"No."

Jerome eyes her coldly. He is not without some compassion for the girl herself. All the same, he is not pulling any punches. He regards this as a clear case of murder which the Thaw millions are being expended to obscure.

"Your suggestion is that you were betrayed after being drugged by Mr. Stanford White?"

"Yes."

"After that occasion didn't you go with him again?"

"Yes."

"Time after time?"

"Often."

"Didn't you frequently get drunk together?"

Evelyn's hands are trembling.

"We . . . have done so."

Still lovely, still large eyed—and yet the picture changing fast.

Jerome squares his shoulders. "This story about Stanford White— you say you told it to the prisoner while you were in Europe?"

"Yes."

"On that trip to Europe, did you have a letter of credit from Mr. Stanford White?"

"I did."

"And did you repeatedly receive sums of money from him?"

"I did."

"And when you got back to America, did you receive more?"

"Oh yes, oh yes," she moans.

The transformation has been mercilessly drastic. "Drugged and despoiled!" Jerome is to comment later. "Why, what nonsense to come here and tell twelve men! She of the Floradora chorus! She dragged into this den of vice and drugged! Because she has a childish face, is she to tell a tissue of lies like this? If acquittal is to be the result. . . ." He throws wide his arms.

But the last word was not to be with Jerome.

The jury did not acquit, but nor did they convict. After two days' retirement, they were unable to agree. A second time Thaw was placed upon his trial. A second time his wife sustained her public crucifixion. A second time a jury stayed out many, many hours.

But on this occasion, at long last finality was reached. They found that the prisoner was insane when he committed the crime.

And even then the Broadway butterfly's final triumph remained. For as they filed out of their box, each member of that jury respectfully and solemnly shook hands with Evelyn Thaw.

Sir Bernard Spilsbury

IT is not till late on the fifth day of the tensest murder trial that Scotland has experienced for nearly twenty years that at long last counsel calls the magic name, and the five-star expert moves from the wings to the centre of the stage.

Attention focuses upon him absolutely. Everyone gazes fascinated at that handsome head, everyone listens fascinated to that level voice—as people are, and always will be, fascinated by those who manifestly wield the power of life and death.

A power, it should be stressed, in this particular instance unsought by its possessor. Sir Bernard Spilsbury—in 1927 at the peak of his international fame—remains the same modest medico-legal scientist who once was a young resident assistant at St. Mary's. But, as Home Office pathologist for a generation, he has acquired a dominion over the public mind far beyond any of his distinguished predecessors, and could cite—if he chose—an impressive list of names which his findings and conclusions have engraved upon the gallows.

Repeatedly, throughout the length and breadth of England, Spilsbury has been a key figure in court battles for the liberation or the forfeiture of human life. This afternoon he is again fulfilling this familiar role.

But with one vital and momentous difference.

Here in Edinburgh—outside the scope of his Government retainer—for the first time in his life Spilsbury appears on behalf of not the Crown but the defence.

It is possible to feel some little regret, in retrospect, that Donald Merrett should have been the prisoner accorded this unprecedented and incomparable advantage . . .

What can you deduce about this eighteen-year-old lad—broad-shouldered, heavy-featured, over six foot tall—simply by studying him as he sits there in the dock?

That he is a public schoolboy? Possibly, from the deferential arrogance of his bearing. That he is a profligate? Possibly, from the coarse lines of his mouth. That he is a dissembler? Probably, from the calculated and self-conscious candour of his eyes.

But can you deduce that he is capable of cold-bloodedly murdering his mother, who had devoted her whole life to her only child; who had brought him up and educated him out of her own resources (his father having deserted them both many years before); and whose sole object was to secure him a happy future? Can you deduce *that*?

For if the case presented by the prosecution is well founded, you are indeed looking directly on the face of matricide . . .

Whatever the subsequent obscurities and contentions, this initial fact at least is clear and undisputed: *Mrs. Merrett was fatally shot one morning, after breakfast, while alone with Donald in the sitting-room of their Edinburgh flat—shot with a pistol Donald had purchased a few weeks before* ("to use on holiday abroad," he had declared to get his licence).

The daily maid, making the kitchen fire, heard a crack, a scream, a thud. She stood still for several seconds, paralysed by shock. Then Donald ("very much upset") came to her in the kitchen. "My mother has shot herself," he said.

On the sitting-room floor Mrs. Merrett lay insensible, bleeding profusely from a wound in the right ear.

An accident, for practical purposes, could be excluded. It was either a case of suicide, or else a case of murder. . . .

No credible motive furnished a clue why Mrs. Merrett, in the middle of writing a chatty letter to a woman friend—the police found that letter, unfinished, on the table—should, suddenly and without the slightest warning, commit suicide in the presence of her son. For murder, however—and no one, of course, except Donald could have murdered her—a credible motive was not far to seek.

Donald Merrett had been leading a double life. By day his supposed attendance at university classes, by night a locked bedroom door and a rope from the bedroom window, had enabled him to spend nearly all his waking hours with the gay sparks—male and female—of Edinburgh's raffish life. His occupational outgoings—payments at the *palais de danse*, gifts to sweeten the hostesses, motor-cycles to impress them and transport them—far exceeded the weekly ten shillings he received as pocket money.

So he had drawn forged cheques on his mother's bank account. During the seven weeks before the shooting there were no fewer than twenty-three, which resulted in Donald pocketing more than £200. By various strategems with pass sheets and with cheque books he had, up till then, kept Mrs. Merrett in the dark. But it could not go on for ever, and that morning unescapable exposure loomed ahead. The current loot, moreover, was exhausted. But there was still potential plunder in the bank—and Donald was sole beneficiary under his mother's will.

The suspicions aroused when all this came to light were strongly reinforced by his conduct during the fortnight that Mrs. Merrett lingered (the forged cheques mutiplied more rapidly than ever, and his *palais* friends had no cause to complain of his neglect); and still further by the dying woman's assertion in hospital—frequently reiterated—that she had been simply sitting writing when "a bang went off in her head."

But motive does not prove murder. Nor does callousness. And Mrs. Merrett might—on the evidence it is a big Might, but big Mights count in court—have been mentally unhinged through the effects of her injury and of hospital drugs.

Suicide or murder? The answer is going to depend upon the opinion of the experts.

The Crown heavyweights have already given theirs. They have pointed out—as is apparent even to a layman—that in suicide by shooting there must be a near discharge. They have declared that a near discharge produces blackening round the wound (blackening which will survive even thorough cleansing). They have recalled that the house surgeon who first treated Mrs. Merrett, though carefully looking for it, saw no blackening at all.

Therefore—they say—it was not a close discharge; therefore it was not Mrs. Merrett's hand that fired the gun.

It is this simple and cogent argument—inevitably fatal, if sustained, to the defence—that Spilsbury now prepares himself to challenge.

Has he made experiments by firing at skin with a similar pistol? Yes. And with similar cartridges? Yes. Did it cause blackening round the aperture? At short range, yes.

The Lord Advocate, William Watson, for the Crown, looks satisfied. But so does Craigie Aitchison, defence counsel, for the sting is in the tail.

"Did you afterwards wipe the skin?" Craigie Aitchison asks.

"Yes, with damp cottonwool."

"Did you bring much pressure to bear?"

"As much," Spilsbury replies, "as I'd use to remove coagulated blood around a wound."

"What was the result?"

"To remove the blackening—except for a little trace that could only be made out with a lens."

The assembly follows him as eager students follow a popular lecturer.

"If there was considerable bleeding, would it be easy to miss any blackening there might be?"

"Very easy. The blood would certainly flow all over that part of the ear."

There you are, says Aitchison's expression as he resumes his seat. The Lord Advocate, rising, picks his way with circumspection.

"The *side* of the head is not one of the more normal points for suicide?"

"Not one of the more *usual* points," Spilsbury concedes.

"And a suicide would naturally hold the weapon *against* the head?"

"Yes," says Spilsbury, "or very close to it. But the head may be turned instinctively as the trigger is pulled."

Encouraged nevertheless, the Lord Advocate elaborates his theme.

"You know there was little destruction of tissue round the wound?"

"Yes."

"Doesn't that suggest that the muzzle wasn't up against the skin?"

"I'm sure of that." Spilsbury knows the art of giving generously. "In this case it's impossible that the muzzle could have been pressed up against the skin."

The Lord Advocate has at least obtained an ancillary benefit. But Spilsbury's fairness here buttresses him on the issue that is paramount. *Blackening can be removed in cleansing*—Spilsbury has said so, and the judge need hardly have bothered to tell the jury that he imagines they will be disposed "to attach the very greatest weight to Sir Bernard's evidence."

They do, and, even though the accused does not go in the box, return a majority verdict of Not Proven—that verdict which enables Scottish juries in effect, to say: We *think* he did it, but the evidence falls short of legal proof.

Others who also think he did it may be forgiven for feeling that their belief was belatedly confirmed by the Chesney case in February 1952. You may recall it—a case of a swashbuckling desperado who murdered his wife and mother-in-law at their home in Ealing, and afterwards ended his own life in a park outside Cologne. Chesney, he called himself, but that was a pseudonym adopted to cloak a string of prison sentences served under another name.

Under his real name. Donald Merrett.

Mr. Douglas

AN early morning labourer, walking over the Yarmouth sandhills on his way to work, came across her lying face upwards in a hollow.

Young. Pretty. Hair loose over her shoulders. Skirt pulled high above her knees. A knotted bootlace sunk deep into her throat . . .

The doctor, who made his examination just after 6 a.m., formed the opinion that she had been dead seven hours.

For what purpose does a woman go at night to such a spot? In that year of 1900 as to-day, only, one would suppose, for some illicit commerce—whether with secret lover or with casual companion.

Yet, as inquiries progressed and—after many difficulties—the murdered girl was identified as a Mrs. Mary Bennett, the police found themselves drawn to the conclusion that she had repaired to those sandhills with her husband. If so, however, the intentions of this married couple did not coincide.

Herbert Bennett had left his wife several months before she went with their baby to spend a few days at Yarmouth near the summer season's end. He had gone to live at Woolwich, leaving her at Bexleyheath. His earnings—her sole source of maintenance—were modest, and the Yarmouth trip must have strained them to the utmost. For Herbert Bennett now had *three* parties to consider.

Not only himself, and his wife, but also the respectable girl in Woolwich to whom he had lately become "engaged", and whom he was about to "marry". If he went through with it, and was found out, he would be faced with a charge of bigamy. If he went through with it, and was not found out, he would be faced with a threat of bankruptcy. If he didn't go through with it . . . But that was an alternative the enamoured Bennett did not care to contemplate.

Motive for removing the wife could hardly have been stronger. *Opportunity* had offered itself through her holiday; what better plan than to slip down for a few hours to Yarmouth, and, under the pretence of reconciliation, tempt her to go with him in the dark on to the beach?

Thus the detectives reasoned. The only element lacking to make an overwhelming case was *evidence*—evidence that Bennett had seized the opportunity and acted on the motive.

Laboriously, items of evidence were assembled. Bennett's Woolwich landlady declared that he did not sleep in his lodgings on 22 September, the night Mary Bennett died. A local licensee claimed to recognize Bennett as a man he had seen in Yarmouth on that evening. So did a newsagent. So did a hotel boots.

The most damning single point against Bennett, however, only

147

emerged *after* the police had chanced an arm and put him under arrest. While searching his room, they discovered in a suitcase a gold link chain of unusual design which appeared identical in every respect with one that Mary Bennett had inherited—a chain she took with her to Yarmouth; a chain clearly visible on a snapshot taken there; *a chain that was round her neck on that last night when she went out, but was no longer round her neck when she lay dead next day*. . . .

The chain in his possession looked very like conclusive proof of Bennett's guilt, and the Crown at the Old Bailey presented it as such. But Bennett's defenders vigorously countered with what they termed conclusive proof of Bennett's innocence.

This consisted of two interdependent propositions. One: that on 22 September, the last train from London to Yarmouth left at 5 p.m. Two: that—notwithstanding the licensee and the newsagent and the boots—Bennett *could not possibly* have been in Yarmouth on that evening because he was somewhere else more than 100 miles away.

Proposition One stood undisputed. For establishing Proposition Two —to be disputed strongly—they rely on the testimony of a gentleman named Douglas, whom they call immediately on opening the defence.

That Mr. Douglas's words will carry weight becomes apparent almost as soon as he steps into the box. He is a middle-aged business man of substance, with no conceivable axe of any sort to grind. He has no interest, direct or indirect, in Bennett, whom before today he has seen only on one occasion.

But about that one occasion, Mr. Douglas is quite certain.

Certain of the face; can swear the prisoner is a man he fell in with during a walk through the South East London outskirts, who told him his name was Bennett and that he worked as a draughtsman in Woolwich, and with whom he had a drink in a public house at Lee.

Certain of the date—22 September; can fix it by the new account he'd gained that very morning, and recorded in his Order Book which he's brought with him to court. Certain of the time; close on 6 p.m. at their first encounter, and they were together approximately an hour. . . .

If, of course, the jury are convinced that Bennett really was with this witness in Lee as late as 7 p.m. on 22 September, then an acquittal will be automatic. An alibi *successfully* pleaded is unanswerable. But an alibi plea is always double-edged; if it *fails*, it is apt to drag the whole defence down in its wake, and actually make a conviction much more likely than before.

So when Charles Gill, leading for the Crown, gets up to cross-examine Douglas, both sides have ample cause to hold their breath.

"Are you quite sure," the prosecutor asks, "that you didn't learn Bennett was a draughtsman from the papers?"

"Quite sure," Douglas says.

"It was *in* the papers?"

"Not saying it wasn't, but he'd already told me."

148

"Are you sure you didn't learn he worked at Woolwich from the papers?"

"Quite sure."

"It was *in* the papers?"

Gill cannot impute dishonesty. He can impute faulty recollection or mistake.

"Not saying it wasn't in the papers," repeats Douglas. "But he'd already told me."

"You say this meeting took place in September," Gill continues. "Now we are in March." Counsel suddenly leans forward. "When did you first get in touch with the defence?"

Douglas ponders.

"Oh, some time in January; five or six weeks ago."

"By then the police court hearings of this case were long since over?"

"Yes."

"They had been widely reported?"

"Yes."

"You had seen those reports?"

"Yes."

"There were photographs of Bennett?"

"Yes."

"You had seen them?"

"Yes."

"And recognized the man you had met?"

"Yes."

Gill straightens up in a movement fraught with menace.

"Why did you not come forward till so long afterwards?"

For the first time Douglas shows signs of awkwardness.

"I had business reasons."

"Tell us what they were," Gill snaps.

Douglas hesitates in the way of honest men when they are conscious that the truth is not going to ring true.

"I was negotiating a partnership."

"How would this have interfered with it?"

"I didn't want any publicity," says Douglas, "at that time."

It was a forensic score for Gill, but not in essence deadly.

Bennett's alibi still trembled in the balance. If he himself had followed Douglas into the witness box, and corroborated the latter's story of their walk and drink at Lee, the scales might easily have been tipped in his favour.

But Bennett—at his own choice—did not go into the box.

He undoubtedly had much to fear from cross-examination. He had behaved badly to his wife; he had made untruthful statements; Gill's expert questioning was bound to show him up as a person who should not readily be trusted. But this would not necessarily have branded him a murderer in the jury's eyes.

His dock-bound silence did.

Whether rightly so, it is not easy to pronounce. Personally I would be inclined to answer Yes. But one cannot altogether dismiss the possibility—with all its grim and terrifying implications—that a sexual killer was on the prowl in Yarmouth while Bennett was walking quietly with Mr. Douglas into Lee.

Maud Sands

"DO you say you have been living a respectable life?" asks counsel. "No, I do not say that," replies the woman in the box.

But make no mistake about the meaning of this answer, given frankly and fearlessly on oath, in a crowded court that has long been waiting for it. Not respectable; very well, be that so; it does not indicate that the speaker is a gum-chewing fly-by-night in slacks; that she bashes around drinking clubs or pin-table saloons, that she is a stranger to elegant manners or good taste.

Mrs. Maud Sands, the woman who makes this straightforward admission, is a creature of classical and superbly moulded beauty; cultured, refined, and above all dignified; clad one day in sables, another day in ermine; escorted only by the very smartest escorts to the very smartest operas, plays, race-courses, restaurants. Her deportment is exemplary, her demeanour is perfection.

She lacks respectability in one regard alone: her private relations with her escorts. As counsel on the other side has already told the jury, with the delicate indirectness customary in 1902, she is known to be accessible to gentlemen prepared to pay somewhat heavily for her favours.

A prostitute? According to the dictionary, perhaps; but not in the popular acceptance of that word. Such a label is as out of place on Mrs. Sands as on Madame Pompadour or Lady Castlemaine. Indeed, she takes rank with their historical successors: she is an exquisite and glamorous and fashionable cocotte . . .

Mrs. Sands is unhappily placed in this prolonged divorce suit even though—while it cannot justly be described as exquisite—it is every bit as fashionable and glamorous as she. Day after day, the pick of the Bar and the pick of Debrett foregather at the Royal Courts of Justice in the Strand, while a titled wife and a titled husband seek to terminate their marriage, each upon the basis of the other's guilty conduct.

Sir Charles Hartopp, baronet, was accusing Lady Hartopp of adultery with Lord Cowley; Lady Hartopp was accusing Sir Charles of adultery with Mrs. Sands. Everyone denied everything, and everyone was cross-examined at great length, but for Mrs. Sands especial torment was reserved.

The ammunition lay ready; it had only to be fired: and Mr. Inderwick, K.C., who was Lady Hartopp's leading counsel, proceeded to fire it.

"You are living apart from your husband, are you not?"

"I am."

"Are you an actress by profession?"

"Yes."

"When was your last engagement?"

The lovely head is set at a proud and resolute tilt.

"I have not worked in the theatre for some time."

"I see." Counsel gives those simple words a significant inflection. "I see . . . Do you have many friends who visit you at home?"

"Yes."

"Gentlemen?"

"Some of them."

"I see . . ." Counsel pauses; then suddenly leans forward. "Is your association with these visitors always innocent?"

Mrs. Sands lowers her voice, but her answer can still clearly be heard in the remotest corner.

"Not always," she says.

"There are those who come for immoral purposes?"

Mrs. Sands, with melancholy grace, bows her assent.

Immoral purposes—the phrase evokes a picture of some mean back room in Bloomsbury or Paddington where sexual intimacies are traded for spot cash.

But these immoral purposes enjoyed a different setting; one of Chinese carpets and handsome satin curtains, deferential butlers and well-trained parlour-maids; a setting in which finances are delicately adjusted through the medium of cheque-books and current bank accounts. You do not leave the money on an Adam mantelpiece. . . .

"Was there a formal deed of separation from your husband under which periodical payments were to be made to you?"

"There was."

"Last year did the payments cease?"

"Yes."

"And did you bring proceedings to enforce them?"

"Yes."

Counsel takes his time. He knows that he can't miss.

"Do you remember the defence your husband raised?"

"Yes."

"Was it that you had committed adultery with three named men?"

Mrs. Sands is very pale, but unflinching and erect.

"That is so," she says.

"Were those three charges correct?"

Somehow she contrives to be frank without being brazen.

"They were correct," she says.

"And, as a result, the proceedings you had brought were discontinued?"

"That is so," she says.

The disclosures are complete. Now, surely, is the moment to dispatch her.

"Mrs. Sands," counsel wears his gravest frown. "Mrs. Sands, coming back to the facts of this particular case, do you still deny committing misconduct with Sir Charles?"

Mrs. Sands completely changes. Her eyes flash, her voice is lifted, the colour sweeps back into her cheeks.

"I do deny it," she declares with ringing emphasis. "I have kept back nothing; I have confessed to all that I have done. But I will not confess to what I have not done, and there has never been anything between Sir Charles and me."

Counsel gives a shrug. Can one believe that from a woman with her past, it implies.

One can—twelve did. The jury accepted her disclaimer in relation to Sir Charles (as they accepted Lady Hartopp's in relation to Lord Cowley).

And it was precisely this past of Mrs. Sands—a past honestly admitted by herself—that made the particular denial so convincing. A woman might well lie in one specific instance to save a reputation hitherto unblemished. But Mrs. Sands could not hope to recapture lost esteem by deleting one from the tally of her lovers.

In the light of this fact she is entitled to be judged. By going into the box, she had nothing to gain and everything to lose. She did so, none the less, because otherwise an inference would clearly have been drawn highly detrimental to the innocent Sir Charles.

The ordeal of Mrs. Sands thus offers something more than the mere exposure and disgrace of a cocotte. It presents the spectacle of a gallant woman who, whatsoever her sins and frailties, selflessly surrendered to pain and punishment rather than cause injustice to another.

Lord Plender

IF you were writing a novel about a man endowed with *glamour*—that magical fascination which defies analysis—what would you make him by profession so that his daily work contributed some little extra glamour of its own?

A surgeon, maybe. Or a top-rank politician. Or a popular advocate. Or a racing motorist. Or even—if you have never encountered one—an actor.

But an accountant? No.

Accountancy demands great skill, and—in this modern age—often confers great power. Glamour, however, is not within its ambit. And accountants themselves—except, of course, for you, sir, and that very special exception, madam, whom you know so well—do not as a rule possess the type of personality that makes every heart beat faster by its presence.

One associates the accountant, not with glamour, but with diligence and worth. . . .

Mr. Harold Morland, one of Britain's most respected and ablest accountants during the period between the two world wars, might well, have stood as his profession's prototype. He was quietly efficient, undemonstratively solid, perhaps a trifle fussily correct. He represented perfectly—though at the topmost level—that vast army of anonymous automata which pours into the City at nine o'clock each morning, adds up and subtracts, and at five o'clock departs.

And yet Mr. Morland's trial in 1931—for aiding and abetting the publication of false company reports—surpassed in glamour any other ever held at the Old Bailey, whether one looks to the background, to the Bar or to the dock.

The dock? Side by side with self-contained and modest Mr. Morland sat a more striking and majestic figure—Baron Kylsant, Lord Lieutenant of Carmarthen, former M.P. for Chester, and a pillar of British commercial life for more than 30 years.

The Bar? A glittering cluster of forensic glory included, with one solitary absentee, all the most fashionable leaders of the day; Sir John Simon, Sir Patrick Hastings and Sir William Jowitt rubbed shoulders with Mr. Pritt and Mr. Stuart Bevan in the nine-day marathon of evidence and argument.

And the background? In the background lay that national institution of which Lord Kylsant was chief and Mr. Morland auditor—the Royal Mail Steam Packet Company, which with its considerable fleet, numerous subsidiaries, large capitalization and century-old connexions, had long been considered by Stock Exchange investors as a blue chip closely verging on gilt-edged.

The true state, however, of the Company's finances—so Attorney-General Jowitt has been telling the jury—does not justify this public confidence, and has not justified it for several years past.

Why not? Because, asserts the Crown, the annual balance sheets have been artificially fortified and the annual dividends artificially inflated by undisclosed transfers from "hidden" or "secret" reserves, accumulated in earlier and more prosperous times. The effect of this continuing practice, Mr. Attorney says, was to present "an absolutely untrue picture," in which the Royal Mail group appeared as making heavy profits when it should have appeared as incurring heavy losses.

Lord Kylsant is charged as the emperor of the Royal Mail empire, and the man responsible for Royal Mail policy. Mr. Morland is charged as watchdog for Royal Mail shareholders—existing and potential—and the man responsible for certifying, by his signature, that each balance sheet gave a true view of the company's affairs.

It is not suggested—it could not be suggested—that the auditor paid *no* regard to this use of the reserves. As far back as 1925 he personally insisted upon introducing the words "Adjustment of taxation reserves" in describing the company's balance for that year. But the Crown, so far from accepting this phrase as exoneration, are turning it into the very spearhead of their case against him. Had it been "*Taken* from reserves," or "*Transferred* from reserves," they might have looked on Mr. Morland with a more benevolent eye. But "*Adjustment* of taxation reserves" —it was deliberately chosen, Mr. Attorney claims, because it would convey nothing to an ordinary person, but would furnish cover if necessity arose. "It betrays an uneasy conscience and a guilty mind."

The fate of Mr. Morland—reputation, livelihood, even liberty—thus hinges upon the jury's answer to a single question: Did he employ that form of words with intention to deceive? And the jury's answer in its turn, will largely hinge upon the exchanges that are just beginning between Sir Patrick Hastings—Morland's counsel—and Lord Plender.

"Have you known Mr. Morland many years?"

"I have," Lord Plender says.

"And had close contacts with him?"

"Yes."

"Do you know any member of your profession," Hastings asks, "who enjoys a higher reputation for integrity?"

"No," Lord Plender says without hesitation. "I do not."

The reciprocal suavity does not mask—as in court it so often masks— reciprocal hostility. This is a cross-examination with a difference; cross-examination minus its traditional characteristics. No attack looms upon the witness's *evidence*; that would be pointless, as his evidence is formal. No attack looms upon the witness's *credit*; that would be not only pointless but virtually impossible—Lord Plender is the acknowledged doyen of accountants.

The beckoning prize for Hastings—if only he can get it—is Lord Plender's endorsement of Mr. Morland's conduct.

"Lord Plender, I would like to ask some questions about what the Attorney-General has referred to as 'secret reserves', *I* would like to refer to them," Hastings casually adds, "as '*inner* reserves'."

"Why?" the judge interpolates.

"Because it sounds rather better," Hastings replies, with disarming frankness. "But whatever we call them, Lord Plender, it is the practice, is it not, of many large commercial enterprises to have secret, or inner, or internal, reserves?"

"Yes."

154

"And to set aside sums of such reserves out of an unusually prosperous year or years?"

"Yes."

"Isn't it—or rather, wasn't it—quite usual for companies to set aside large sums against their liability for excess profits duty?"

"Yes."

"And if it was later discovered that these sums were not required, they would be properly brought back into the profits for subsequent years?"

"Yes," Lord Plender agrees once more. "Quite a regular credit."

"Often without disclosing in a profit and loss account that they have been brought back from secret or inner reserves?"

For the first time Lord Plender qualifies.

"That has been done," he says.

"And by firms of the highest repute?"

"Yes." The answer comes after a pause. "But, generally speaking, you will find an indication."

Lord Plender, whatever his personal sympathies and feelings, is primarily governed by jealous regard for the ethics of his calling. He will not pledge his famous name one inch beyond their scope, and every question needs to be framed with exquisite art and tact.

"Where reserves have been called on without indication, might there come a time when the auditor would say that if the reserves are to be used again, *some* indication must be given?"

"Yes," Lord Plender says.

"Are there certain phrases commonly used by auditors as an indication?"

"Yes."

"Is one of them 'Adjustment of taxation reserves'?"

"Yes."

Step by tiny step the advance continues.

"That expression indicates that there have been transfers from reserves?"

"Yes."

"Those transfers might be either large or small?"

"Yes."

Hastings can now compress the whole of Mr. Morland's case into a single question—with complete assurance of a favourable answer.

"*If you saw such words in a profit and loss account, would you understand from that that there had been a transfer, which might be small or large, from excess profits duty or other reserves?*"

Lord Plender gives his verdict.

"Certainly," he says. . . .

Certainly. It was the appropriate word. Mr. Morland's defenders heaved a huge sigh of relief. Only a jury perverse beyond normal calculation could, upon an issue so highly technical, run counter to the

155

clearly expressed judgment of one so knowledgeable—and so conscientious.

Mr. Morland was acquitted. In my opinion, he should not have been charged. Lord Kylsant, on a separate accusation (that of publishing a fraudulent prospectus) received a sentence of 12 months' imprisonment. In my opinion, he should not have been convicted.

I hold both men victims, in differing degree, of a national near-panic following on the Hatry slump of 1929.

Edith Pegler

IN a great murder trial, one of this century's most notorious, she stands aloft under the unwelcome glare that beats upon the box. A quiet, respectable, unassuming individual.

"Do you know the prisoner?" counsel asks.

"Yes," she says, "I do."

"When did you first meet him?"

"Seven years ago, when I answered an advertisement."

"An advertisement for what?"

"A housekeeper."

"Did he employ you in that capacity?"

"He did."

"And did you live at his house alone with him?"

"I did."

There is a gasp in court; a gasp of wonder and of dread.

Counsel continues in unemotional tones.

"Did he later propose marriage?"

"Yes."

"You accepted him?"

"Yes."

"And were you wed in 1908, on the 30th of July?"

"Yes."

As she is handed and identifies her certificate of marriage—tainted, because her partner was committing bigamy—another, deeper gasp conveys the audience's horror.

What is there about this inoffensive woman that chills the spine and takes away the breath? What makes them stare at her in frightened fascination?

Nothing in her personality or conduct. Nothing active or direct. Something indirect and passive.

She has lived with a monster—and survived . . .

The monster—no other word will do—was the prisoner on trial; a wholesale killer brought to his account. One need not be too scrupulous and wait upon the verdict; his guilt had been painfully evident for weeks. In the result, after a hearing spread over eight days, the jury will require but twenty minutes to decide. For this, the accused, is the neutrally named George Joseph Smith, soon to be immortalized as "Brides-in-the-Bath" Smith.

The criminal history of this sub-human creature has passed into British folklore like a nursery rhyme. None but could recount, in greater or less detail, the nature and repetitious method of his crimes; how he exploited his attribute of sexual magnetism to attract the interest of unattached young women, how he took each victim through a marriage ceremony (there were no less than seven during his last six years), how he systematically robbed and swindled them, how—where it was necessary to gain the maximum profit—he systematically murdered them as well. Three of these poor ladies died in precisely similar fashion —died, as the world knows, from drowning in a bath.

What is less well known than this grim chronicle of evil is the one anomaly in Smith's pseudo-matrimonial life; the one "marriage" that contains no mercenary motive; the one association that he sought to make enduring. It is his partner in this isolated union, extraordinary in its ord-inariness, who draws and holds the awe-struck gaze of everyone in court.

Edith Pegler was the third "wife" of Smith's eight. At the time of his trial they had been "married" seven years. He may initially have marked her out as a prospective victim, and upon closer acquaintance changed his mind; certainly she alone among his numerous spouses never suffered positive ill-treatment at his hands.

This does not mean that, by accepted standards, George Joseph Smith was anything like an ideal husband. His temper was sharp, his suspicions quick, his meanness pathological; he spent less of the year at home than he did away "on business"; and he never disclosed his whereabouts on these protracted absences, nor did he give her any notion when he would return.

Still, he *did* return, sooner or later, every time, and Edith Pegler could suppose herself Edith Smith and her lot that of the average woman harassed by the shortcomings of the average man.

Life was not idyllic. But nor was it insupportable.

Until that catastrophic day when the detectives called.

For quite a long time she hadn't believed a word. There had been a mistake, they'd mixed it up, they meant somebody else. And then, when the full hideousness of the accusation dawned, and the fact that her dear George was the accused became established, the world rocked and trembled and dissolved beneath her feet. . . .

And now, at the Old Bailey, with dear George in the dock and herself talking to strangers about their life together, she must pretend as best she can that everything is normal; put on a normal expression, speak in a normal voice.

The Crown have finished with her; it is the defender's turn.

"Just take your mind back to before you knew anything about this." If only she could; if only she could. "You were fond of the prisoner, weren't you?"

"Yes," she says, "I was."

"And he had been kind to you?"

"Yes."

"He had *always* treated you kindly?"

"Yes."

"And *you* were kindly disposed towards *him*?"

"Yes."

She cannot refrain from a glance towards the dock, at the professional murderer of whom she had been fond, and her mind reels in bewilderment and retrospective terror . . .

More than thirty years later, in that self-same court, this scene is re-enacted with a slightly different twist.

The sadistic Neville Heath, who murdered not for gold but to indulge his lust for cruelty, sits in the place where Smith once sat, doomed to the same fate. He does not deny the charge the prosecution lay against him—that he induced a girl to sleep with him at a Notting Hill hotel, and there in his bedroom slashed and killed and mutilated her. The mere recital of the story makes the toughest-minded shudder.

A pretty young girl is called into the box. The court is tense and silent as she gives her evidence—evidence that *she* had been induced to sleep with Heath *at the same hotel, and in the same bedroom, four nights before the murder was committed.*

"Did he treat you kindly?" the defender asks—it echoes down the years.

"Yes," she whispers.

And she, too, cannot refrain from a glance towards the dock, and her mind also reels as she starts back from the depths, and the spectators gape at her as they had gaped at Edith Pegler, filled with the fearful wonder of miraculous escape.

Professor Ames

IT is a commonplace in our courts of law that there is hardly any evidence so unreliable as that of handwriting experts. This class of witness can usually be got to testify on either side, in equal numbers, and with equal confidence. Experts of all classes give evidence only as to opinion, but those who decide on handwriting believe in their infallibility.

I make haste to add that none of the foregoing statements is my own.

The first was made by Craigie Aitchison (afterwards Lord Aitchison), finest Scottish advocate within living memory; the second by Mr. Dickson, author of a classical text book upon evidence; the third by Lord Brampton (formerly Henry Hawkins), an outstandingly illustrious figure of English Bench and Bar.

I do not say that I agree with them. But I certainly would not venture directly to disagree with three such legal luminaries—practical and scholastic—whose wealth of experience so far outstrips mine.

Certainly the record does not, upon examination, appear to confute Lord Aitchison, at least. On the contrary, his stamp of "unreliable"—interpreting that word in its non-pejorative sense—gains confirmation at the very highest level of honesty and skill in handwriting expertise.

No greater name—I was tempted to say no name so great—has flourished in this field than that of Thomas Henry Gurrin. In the last years of the nineteenth century and the first years of the twentieth Mr. Gurrin sat as securely on the throne of handwriting as did the reigning monarch on the throne of England. Yet how did Mr. Gurrin, from his exalted eminence, make a lasting impact on forensic history?

Once when, upon oath in court, he proclaimed himself "perfectly satisfied" that certain incriminating documents were written by Adolf Beck—who afterwards served a long term of penal servitude before his unquestionable innocence was signalised by a Free Pardon and a compensation grant.

And once when he advised my Lords Commissioners of the Admiralty that young Archer-Shee had forged the endorsement to a postal order—an allegation that only ended, under the nation's eyes, with the Crown case lying in irreparable ruin, and an abject, unreserved, exculpatory withdrawal.

It may be said that both instances are British, and therefore possibly not of universal application. But such errors of judgment by handwriting experts are not indigenous to these islands, but endemic to their craft. They could be duplicated, in varying form and degree, the whole world over, wherever reading, writing, and organized courts exist.

One notable example—and one where the expert also stood at the top of his profession—occurred, three or four generations back, at the trial of Frank Ellison in the United States.

Trials for simple assault seldom quicken the fashionable pulse; seldom set tongues wagging under modish hats; seldom penetrate the gossip of exclusive clubs. The assault, however, with which Ellison was charged arose in unusual circumstances and from an unusual source.

It was no climax to a navvy's shindy; no part of a backstreet brawl or a bar-room Saturday night. Some of the parties involved were considered Society by the world; others were at least considered Society by themselves. And the moral and emotional issue underlying the case conferred on it a semblance of conventional Romance: A father (Mr.

Henriques) had forbidden his house to a younger man (Mr. Ellison, the defendant) because of the latter's attentions to his daughter (Mrs. Noeme).

Society found itself a place in court; Romance did not. The trial—almost a private battle—was contested tooth and nail. Mrs. Noeme, as well as Mr. Henriques, gave evidence for the State—evidence that in no way spared her over-eager suitor. The defence countered—gloves off equally—by producing letters purporting to be from her to Ellison; letters which, to say no more, cast doubt upon her sworn verbal account of their relationship.

But Mrs. Noeme flatly denies that she wrote those letters; denies knowledge of their contents; denies the signature.

The defence, however—singularly prescient—has come amply prepared for this eventuality. Professor Ames is present; Professor Ames —the expert, the *authority*, on handwriting; Professor Ames, who has closely studied the disputed letters and compared them with an admitted specimen of the lady's writing. The professor's conclusion? They are by one and the same hand.

Professor Ames—who is really very widely known and whose appearance creates a considerable sensation—duly repeats that last assertion on the witness stand. An experienced performer, he does it in high style. "The obliquity of the upstroke"; "the perpendicularity of the downstroke"; "a peculiar formation—your Honour will observe that *there* the pen, surprisingly, has been raised"—a good many such remarks garnish his opinion, and a good many charts and gestures garnish his remarks.

When the demonstration ends, the defender is smiling sunnily and fingering his bundle of letters with fresh zeal. Professor Ames has surely *proved* that they were written by Mrs. Noeme, and now he can hardly wait to unload their dynamite.

He is compelled, though, temporarily to possess himself in patience while the District Attorney asks a few questions. Just a few.

"Professor Ames, as I understood you, you were given only one sample of the lady's genuine handwriting, and you base your opinion upon that?"

"Yes, sir." The professor is unfailingly courteous. "But it was quite a long letter and afforded me great opportunity for comparison."

"Wouldn't it assist if you were given a *number* of her letters with which to make a comparison?"

"Oh, yes," comes the professor's inevitable reply.

Looking back subsequently over the whole picture, some may feel that this last question of the District Attorney's contains an element of unfair deception. I cannot concur. The question may be self-contained as well as introductory, and will trap no one of independent and dependable judgment.

On the other hand it may conduce to reveal the want of both. . . .

"Would you mind taking this?" The District Attorney passes the witness a letter—with the signature folded back and fastened down. "Compare it with the others and tell us—is it the same writing?"

For several minutes—literally minutes—Professor Ames inspects the letter closely; doubtless paying particular attention to obliquity, perpendicularity, and places where the pen has surprisingly been raised.

At last he issues his decree.

"It is the same," he says.

The District Attorney bows acknowledgment.

"Is it not a fact, Professor, that the same individual may write a variety of hands upon different occasions and with different pens?"

"Oh, yes, sir," Professor Ames agrees.

The District Attorney passes him a second letter, folded and fastened exactly like the first.

"Would you kindly compare that with the others that you have?"

As easy and calm as if at home in his own study, the professor carries out another meticulous inspection.

"Yes, sir, it is a variety of the same penmanship."

The District Attorney bows a little lower.

"I don't want to weary you—but just one more—if you would be good enough."

A third letter, similarly fixed; similar question, similar interval, similar reply.

"Is it then your honest opinion," the District Attorney asks, "that those three letters are all in the same writing?"

"Yes, sir, it is."

The District Attorney steps back, relaxed, rather as conjurers do when the trick—though the audience doesn't know it—has already been performed, and they can afford a mild indulgence in panache.

"Would you please unfold the first letter and read the signature aloud."

The professor does so—with a quiet air of triumph.

"*Lila Noeme*," he solemnly intones.

"And now the second?"

The professor's air of triumph fades. He stares at the second signature, puzzled, hesitant.

"Yes?" says the District Attorney in an encouraging tone.

"*William Henriques*," the professor reads.

"And the third?"

The third must be a knock-out, for the professor takes the count. He is metaphorically helped up, sponged, and dusted down, before he can bring himself to utter what he sees.

"*Frank Ellison*," he feebly gives forth.

And that is the last we ever hear about the letters—and, for all I know, about Professor Ames.

All because the District Attorney, noticing some similarity in the hands, shrewdly used it to expose the overblown pretensions of one who may well have ranked, in good faith, among his own biggest dupes.

Dr. Thomas Stevenson

"I HOPE," said Dr. Lamson when they arrested him, "that this matter will be kept as *quiet* as possible for the *sake of my relatives*." Such tender concern for family connexions was especially touching from a man who had just poisoned his crippled brother-in-law. But the hope he expressed, however nobly prompted, proved illusory.

Nobody could have kept "quiet" the "matter" then beginning. Even in an epoch seasoned to sensation by the trials of the Stauntons, Kate Webster and Charles Peace, that of George Henry Lamson excited a commotion which has not altogether subsided even now.

The roots of the "matter" were both deep and twisted.

All through that year of 1881, young Dr. Lamson had been desperately hard up. Writs, distress warrants, unrequited loans—his situation uninterruptedly moved from bad to worse until by November he was pawning his surgical instruments and issuing phoney cheques on bank accounts that had been closed. With a wife and small child as well as himself to keep, Dr. Lamson must have felt at his wits' end.

It was against this sombre background that two events occurred whose juxtaposition lends them a grave significance.

On 24 November, Lamson bought two grains of aconitine from one chemist after an unsuccessful attempt to buy some from another. Aconitine is a poison so deadly in its effects that the fraction of a grain constitutes a fatal dose.

On 3 December, although apparently pressed for time and about to go abroad, Lamson dashed out to a boarding school at Wimbledon to visit Percy, eighteen-year-old brother of his wife. This boy—with a curvature of the spine that had paralysed his legs—stood to inherit £3,000 when he reached 21; if, however, he should die before (although then in good general health) that sum was to be equally shared by his two surviving sisters—which meant in those days before the Married Woman's Property Act, that £1,500 would pass straight into Lamson's hands.

The penniless doctor arrived in the evening shortly before seven. He was received by the proprietor of the school, Mr. Bedbrook, who forthwith sent for Percy, and a chum carried up the latter from a lower floor. Percy's spirits were excellent; the day had been a holiday and the pupils had amused themselves by playing charades.

Mr. Bedbrook poured his guest some sherry and for a few minutes there was general talk between the three. Then Lamson opened a black leather bag he had brought in with him and took out of it a Dundee cake and some sweets.

"Have some," he said.

Percy had some of each. So had Mr. Bedbrook. So had Lamson. As they munched they went on chatting socially. It appeared like a casual thought, suddenly remembered, when Lamson once again plunged into his bag.

"Oh, by the way, Mr. Bedbrook," he remarked, rummaging, "I didn't forget you when I was in America last September. I bought"— producing two similar boxes—"these capsules for you. You'll find them very useful for giving medicine to the boys."

Lamson put one of the boxes immediately in front of him and pushed the other towards the schoolmaster.

"Try one and see."

Mr. Bedbrook obliged. Meanwhile Lamson had been pouring into another capsule caster sugar from a basin on the table—sugar, incidentally, that he himself had asked for, and had put into his sherry "to destroy the alcoholic effects."

"Now, Percy," he said, "you're a champion pill-taker. Take this and show us how easily it can be swallowed."

Percy demonstrated as he had been bidden. One gulp, and it was down.

Within five minutes Lamson, pleading great hurry, had left. Within ten, Percy's last illness had begun.

Its progress was swift and dreadful. The first bout of sickness and stomach pains had mounted by mid-evening to such a pitch of violence and convulsion that several people were required to hold him down upon his bed. One doctor was summoned to his side, and then another, while the hapless boy continually cried out that his throat was burning and his skin felt "all drawn up". Minute by minute his agony increased. Nothing availed—neither brandy nor white of egg nor linseed poultices —and, at twenty past eleven Percy died.

The two doctors were not only shocked, but puzzled; this was something altogether off the track normally trodden by family practitioners; it needed a post-mortem—at which they were joined by a specialist in autopsies, Dr. Bond—to determine their opinion about the cause of death.

There, when they saw no sign of any natural fatal disease, but did see tell-tale yellowish-grey patches in the stomach, they felt competent to concur in Dr. Bond's pronouncement of death by poisoning.

This pronouncement—as far as it went—could not seriously be challenged. And if the poison was once established as *aconitine*, the evidence against Lamson—who so recently had it in his possession— would be overwhelming.

But whatever one may believe at heart, one's head must be convinced before convicting.

163

Certainly Lamson had both opportunity and motive. Had he also got the means—control of the *particular* poison from which Percy died? Therein lay the one great difficulty of the prosecution's case.

Aconitine was a poison hardly known. It had never before been used —or at any rate traced—as an instrument of murder. It was not discoverable by chemical tests. The family doctors (they did not conceal the fact) knew nothing at all about it, and even the well-versed Dr. Bond knew little more. The post-mortem appearances were consistent with aconitine poisoning, he said; but—questioned in court—"any other poison would produce the same local condition of the stomach."

All thus stood poised—the trial, the verdict, and the life of Lamson —when Dr. Thomas Stevenson, self-assurance hanging about him like a mantle, paced out those few familiar steps to the Old Bailey box. . . .

As actors match Irving against Garrick, as cricketers match Hobbs or Bradman against Grace, so connoisseurs of the courtroom still dispute whether Stevenson or Bernard Spilsbury was the outstanding expert witness of all time.

The impressive list of Stevenson's attainments and appointments (he was Home Office analyst, Professor of Medical Jurisprudence at Guy's Hospital, and famous internationally as a toxicologist) did not in itself explain his singular power in court. That power resided rather in the agility of his mind, the conviction of his manner—and the fact that he always knew his subject inside out.

The Lamson jury listened to him with absorbed attention as he described his scientific tests on certain organs and contents of the body—tests that resulted in his detecting the presence of aconitine by *taste*. "There was a sensation of burning, of tingling," he said, "of numbness, of swelling at the back of the throat, followed by a seared sensation at the back of the tongue. The total effect was peculiar to aconitine."

Moreover, Stevenson had injected mice with extracts from the body and the mice had promptly died after exhibiting the same symptoms as would result from injections of pure aconitine.

The oracle had spoken. The jury took notes. For Montagu Williams, defending, the crisis had arrived.

"Have you been *present* at any case of aconitine poisoning?" he began.

"No," said Stevenson coolly. "There has never been one in this country."

"Or at a post-mortem?"

"There has only been one abroad."

It really only scored half a point for Williams, but even half a point was precious against Stevenson.

"Is aconitine used externally in the form of ointment to relieve pain?"

"Yes."

"For neuralgia?"

"Yes."

"And for rheumatism?"

"Yes."

As witnesses had testified that Lamson suffered from both, that counted a full point. One point and a half to the defence—but at this early stage their scoring virtually ceased.

No exertion, no deployment of forensic skill, by Williams—primed by a distinguished scientific expert of his own—could shake Stevenson's credibility on the essential matters. Had he not found the *normal* residue of the stomach frequently fatal to lower animals? No—and he had made many experiments. Wasn't the taste he had described characteristic of other things—veratria, for instance? No, he had tried veratria on his tongue—there was a difference. Delphinia, perhaps? He had tried that, too; it is more bitter. Pepperine? You get the burning sensation *at once*.

Consistently baulked by this effortless omniscience, Montagu Williams made his supreme attempt to break it down—to discover *some* gap in that solid wall of knowledge.

"You say there is no chemical test for aconitine?"

"I do."

"Isn't phosphoric acid a test?"

"No."

"Has it not been used as one?"

"Yes," said Stevenson, and without a hint of sarcasm, "but not by those who have studied aconitine recently."

"Do you know this book?" asked Williams.

"Yes." Stevenson instantly recognized the volume at a distance. "It is by Flückner."

"Doesn't *he* give the reaction?" Williams demanded, on a note of triumph.

"Yes," Stevenson agreed. "But he is referring to *German* aconitine. That is very different from *English*," he added helpfully. . . .

Lamson was hanged and to Stevenson goes the credit. For credit it was without a shadow of doubt. Between trial and execution, this vicious poisoner, who had strenuously protested innocence, confessed.

Whittaker Chambers

TODAY is a generation after and, though the story remains vividly alive, the emotional dust has settled—as far as it ever will. This may well be, then, the most appropriate moment to examine afresh the extraordinary case of Alger Hiss.

First, however, let me state my angle of approach.

I disregard deliberately the political implications: party debits and credits resulting from the fact that a distinguished New Deal Democrat was convicted—albeit by a circuitous legal process—of actively operating as a Communist spy.

I disregard deliberately the melodramatic trimmings; vanishing cars, mysterious foreigners, microfilms in pumpkins—trimmings that made some more certain, some more sceptical.

I disregard deliberately the tragic overtones; a fine career cut short and prematurely ending—whether justly or unjustly—in a prison cell.

Above all, I shall not attempt to choose between the formidable absolutes of guilt and innocence.

I am concerned only to make what may fairly be called the lawyer's occupational inquiry. Was the case against Hiss satisfactorily *proved*?

The two trials of Hiss—at the first the jury disagreed—between them lasted literally for months. And yet that question does not require complex investigation. It simply requires concentration on essentials. . . .

Hiss was confronted by a solitary accuser. His name—which he sometimes masked by an alias—was Whittaker Chambers. Chambers was, on his own volunteered admission, a former member of the Communist underground.

Back in the 30's, so Chambers on oath alleged, Hiss had been his fellow-Communist and his intimate friend; had repeatedly smuggled out to him State Department papers, which, after photographing or typing, he returned; and had resisted, when Chambers finally severed his Communist ties, all appeals by him to follow suit.

Hiss's reply was icily contemptuous. He identified Chambers as a past acquaintance—an obscure journalist apparently seeking legitimate copy—who had then used (Hiss emphasized) an entirely different name. But the charges made by Chambers, Hiss totally denied—and he totally denies them to this day.

It was a straight fight. No one but Chambers said that Hiss had been a Communist. No one but Chambers said that Hiss had smuggled out papers. Others—wives, friends, servants, partisans—might make encouraging noises at the ringside. But the two men, Hiss and Chambers, were in the ring alone.

Everything, therefore, turned on the credibility of Chambers; on his capacity to inspire belief. That was granted by the prosecution in plain terms. "*If you don't believe Chambers,*" their principal counsel said, "*we have no case.*"

This remark should be quite literally construed. And belief, in such a context, must be positive and active. It is not enough to be unconvinced that what he says is false; one has to be convinced that what he says is true.

Was Chambers entitled to that mark of confidence, which, once bestowed, would seal another's ruin?

In the course of a long trial that seeks to penetrate the dark and undisclosed recesses of men's minds, a single dazzling flash of light may be decisive. For me that comes with Chambers on the stand at the first hearing and Hiss's defender, Mr. Lloyd Paul Stryker, advancing upon him from his chair to cross-examine.

"Do you know what an oath is, Mr. Chambers?" Stryker asked.

"Yes," Chambers answers, "I suppose I do."

"What is your definition?"

"It is a declaration a man makes when he promises to tell the truth."

The defender is holding in his hand some sort of Photostat, which Chambers regards with disinterested calm.

"Right up to October 1937," goes on Stryker, "you were an underhand enemy of your country, doing what you could against it in favour of a foreign power." He pauses a moment, to give those words full force. "Is that right?"

It summarizes evidence Chambers has already given; a denial would be ridiculous and is not forthcoming.

"Do you recognize *this*?" demands Stryker sharply, holding out the Photostat in cinematic close-up. "Is it an oath of office that you took when, during that period, you got a government job?"

A glance at the Photostat and Chambers has agreed.

"Signed by you?"

"Yes."

Stryker reads it aloud in all its weighty connotation. "Solemnly swear . . . will support and defend the Constitution of the United States against all enemies . . . bear true faith and allegiance . . . without any mental reservation. . . ."

Chambers nods serene agreement with each clause. Stryker tosses the Photostat aside. The gesture is theatrical, but sometimes life intrudes upon the province of the theatre.

"False from beginning to end, wasn't it, Mr. Chambers?"

"Of course," says Chambers coolly.

"What?" cries Stryker, as though doubting his own ears.

"Of course," Chambers repeats, coolly as before.

"And it was perjury, wasn't it?"

"If you like," Chambers says indifferently.

"And you did it in order to cheat and deceive the United States Government." Stryker peremptorily folds his arms. "Is not that true?"

"Perfectly true," Chambers instantly concedes.

Now there is more illumination in that brief passage of arms than a casual spectator may immediately detect. Chambers has not only admitted former lies. He has not only admitted former perjury. More important still are the particular circumstances in which these lies were told, this perjury committed, and the indication given ("Of course . . . Of course") that, *in such circumstances*, lies and perjury are natural.

What exactly were the circumstances that produced such a dangerous effect?

167

It is not disputed that Chambers had once been a perfectly sincere and genuine Communist; that he had entered the party without thought of personal gain; that he had cherished an idealistic faith in Communism as the sole hope of cure for a sick world.

He was a brooding and earnest and dedicated man; a born crusader, perhaps a born fanatic; a thinker in cosmic rather than in specific terms.

And, as he revealed upon the witness stand—whether consciously or not is a matter for speculation—in pursuit of a crusade for what he deemed the ultimate good, "of course" he had been prepared, if necessary, to lie; "of course" he had been prepared to play the role of perjurer.

Anything and everything lost individual value when the object was a panacea for mankind. . . .

Yes, this was the single dazzling flash of light. It didn't establish that Chambers was lying on this occasion too. But it did establish—out of his own mouth—how prone he had been to lying, even on oath, in the past, *not to benefit himself but to promote a "Cause"*.

How could a juryman feel reasonably assured that, since his disillusion and abandonment of Communism, some other "cause" had not possessed his troubled soul?

Some other cause—social, religious, or political—which made Alger Hiss appear to him as anti-Christ?

Some other cause in which, following that precedent, Chambers considered the end justified the means?

I still cannot feel that reasonable assurance. Had I been on the jury I might not have known whether Whittaker Chambers spoke the truth or not. But at least I would have known where my own sworn duty lay.

Mrs. Watson

THE lady's tones are hushed, almost as if in church. Her hands are clasped, almost as if in prayer. Her lids are lowered, almost as if her female modesty could not survive an encounter with male eyes.

The Divorce Court has surely seldom seen a woman of such manifest piety and virtue.

"Yes," she is murmuring, as judge and Bar—and spectators—strain to hear, "yes, a close friendship developed between the four of us— Admiral Codrington and his wife, and my husband and I."

"Were you and Mrs. Codrington specially intimate?"

"Yes."

"Did she confide in you?"

"Yes."

"Did she ever mention one Lieutenant Mildmay?"

"Yes."

The Admiral's counsel, examining this final witness in support of his distinguished client's petition, pauses impressively before continuing.

"Tell us Mrs. Watson; what did she say about Lieutenant Mildmay?"

So gently, so delicately, does Mrs. Watson start to tell them, you could almost mistake it for the cooing of a dove. But it were better characterized as the hissing of a viper. . . .

It had all begun with a chance acquaintance that ripened into rottenness under Mediterranean skies.

In 1858 Admiral Codrington was appointed to the Malta station as its naval chief. He had then been married for nine years to a wife considerably younger than himself.

They occupied his official Malta residence, lying across the harbour from Valetta.

The Admiral, a serious man with an appetite for work, soon became absorbed in his many professional tasks. Mrs. Codrington, a frivolous woman with an appetite for pleasure, soon became absorbed in her many social sprees.

Unlike her husband, who dodged as many social functions as possible, Mrs. Codrington would not miss a minute of the fun. She had eager and admiring escorts at her beck and call. A private gondola always waited on her bidding, and often it would be two or three or even four a.m. before Mrs. Codrington, with some favoured officer to keep her company in the gondola's unlighted wooden cabin, prepared to embark upon the water towards home.

The Admiral enjoyed his job, Mrs. Codrington enjoyed herself, and a moderate degree of harmony prevailed. That is not to say that he approved her flightiness, nor that he always refrained from comment on it. But it was merely a grievance, not a burning issue, until, in 1861, the Watsons came to Malta, and Mrs. Watson swiftly got to work.

Long afterwards, trying to find reason for Mrs. Watson's artfully masked vindictiveness towards her, Mrs. Codrington believed she must have got what would nowadays be called a crush on the Admiral.

I think, myself, that Mrs. Watson hadn't anything so healthy as a crush; she had a canker—a canker that infected and consumed her heart.

Fanatically puritan, she considered feminine attractiveness a sin, and any woman who frankly made the most of hers a sinner beyond either mercy or redemption. Mrs. Codrington unquestionably fell into this category, and Mrs. Watson secretly resolved on her undoing.

It is uncertain how far she loosened Mrs. Codrington's tongue. It is certain that she completely acquired Admiral Codrington's ear. For two years she wove a web Iago might have envied, and by 1863, when the Admiral was recalled to England, his thoughts were constantly dwelling on divorce.

What had been so successfully begun, Mrs. Watson now intended to complete. Uprooting her shadowy and dominated husband, within two months she had followed the Codringtons to London. There she galvanized the undecided Admiral into action.

She induced him to have his wife spied on (and found him suitable spies); to break open his wife's desk (and helped him read her papers); to consult his lawyers (and went with him to the consultation); and, finally, to institute these proceedings (crowned by her present performance in the box).

Mrs. Watson, however, feels uncomfortably aware that the ultimate outcome is still conjectural. Some evidence by which she set great store has not entirely stood the test of open court.

There was the boatman from Malta who gravely testified that whenever Lieutenant Mildmay happened to be with Mrs. Codrington in the cabin the gondola—contrary to its wont—"got out of trim." That drew a laugh in which several jurors joined.

There was the draft of a letter in Mrs. Codrington's hand (principal trophy from the violated desk); to Mrs. Watson it had signified adultery, to the jury it appeared only to signify imprudence.

There was the hired sleuth who swore that he had seen Mrs. Codrington enter a London hotel one evening with an officer; but he had also seen them leave later that same evening, and could not deny that they might have done nothing more infamous than dine.

There is great suspicion; there is equally great doubt. Mrs. Watson has thus become key witness as well as prime conspirator—and no one realizes it better than herself.

Behind that guileless face, her sly brain carefully calculates.

"Tell us, Mrs. Watson; what did Mrs. Codrington say about Lieutenant Mildmay?"

Oh yes, she can answer that question from the Admiral's counsel; answer it in precise conformity with the statement that she gave months ago to the Admiral's solicitors. Mrs. Watson can repeat that statement almost word for word, so that counsel can tick off the points in the margin of his brief.

"Mrs. Codrington told me that the lieutenant had formed an attachment for her." Tick. "She told me that he had attempted to make love to her." Tick. "She told me she awoke one night and found him in her bedroom." Tick. "She told me he remained there until the small hours." Tick. "She told me she had still not severed the association." Tick.

The ticks have all been marked. The witness—to the best of counsel's belief—has said her piece. He is about to sit down, when Mrs. Watson, unprompted, speaks again.

"One moment," she says. The downcast eyes are raised, and momentarily glitter. "Mrs. Codrington did make a further communication to me."

170

Counsel checks himself, stands erect again, and stoutly tries to dissemble his surprise.

"One night she arrived at our house very late for dinner." Mrs. Watson, in her eagerness, forgets to be subdued. "She was highly agitated, and put me under promise never to repeat what she was about to disclose."

The Admiral's counsel is as much in the dark as anyone as his unpredictable witness rapidly goes on.

"Mrs. Codrington told me that the *climax of evil* had been reached." (This, one may presume, was Mrs. Watson's paraphase.) "Lieutenant Mildmay had just walked with her to our house. They had gone together into a secluded lane. And there"—Mrs. Watson excels at sexual ellipsis —"there, in that secluded lane, *the deed was done.*"

"Do you recall the date of that?"

"Yes," says Mrs. Watson confidently. "13 November, 1861."

The Admiral's counsel, with an imperceptible shrug, resumes his seat. There is something as close to hubbub as ushers will permit. Mrs. Codrington's counsel, justifiably protesting that no such act of adultery was alleged in the petition, asks for and obtains an adjournment of the court. . . .

On its resumption, his questions are penetrating and barbed.

"Have you ever spoken before of that confession?"—"No."

"It passed your lips for the first time in that box, did it?"—"Yes."

"Weren't you interrogated on the Admiral's behalf before the trial?" —"Yes."

"Did you see the Admiral immediately you returned to England?"— "Yes."

"But you never mentioned her confession of adultery till you were examined in this court?"

And yet, notwithstanding, Mrs. Codrington lost her case. *For Lieutenant Mildmay would not give evidence, as she beseeched him, and as he was free to do.*

Why? We are left to speculate. Because he abhorred the limelight in a sensational divorce? Because she had *not* surrendered to him, and he harboured spite? Or because—the easy inference which the jury drew— she *had*?

Even on this last—and far from sure—assumption, Mrs. Watson remains unchallenged villain of this suit. A distinction must be drawn between frailty and wickedness. Mary Magdalene is a less dishonoured name than Judas.

171

Dr. Hubert

O N holiday by the sea you may dispense with the conventions that normally govern the acquirement of new friends. What is strictly taboo for the respectable citizens of London or Birmingham when they are at home is perfectly good form for those same respectable citizens when they are at Brighton or Weston-super-Mare.

Especially does this operate among the younger folk. The retrieval of a beach ball, adjacent deckchairs on the pier, an involuntary smile at a third encounter on the front—these will sometimes fulfil the same purpose as the most formal introductions do elsewhere.

So nobody need be shocked because Miss Doreen Marshall—a charming girl of good family and irreproachable background—struck up chance acquaintance with a smooth-mannered young man while staying at Bournemouth in the July of 1946. Nobody need be shocked because she—who had served in the WRNS during the war—accepted from him—who plausibly styled himself an RAF Group Captain—a proposal that they should dine at his hotel. Nobody need be shocked even though he escorted her when, at midnight, she departed.

Not shocked at all; just perhaps surprised. Unless—like me—you have ceased to be surprised at women's woeful, often catastrophic, lack of judgment in reading the pointers to a character from a face.

Neville Heath—for such in reality was the man known to Doreen Marshall as Group Captain Brooke—has been described by some as "handsome" or "good looking". Perhaps I do not correctly understand these terms. His low forehead, his gelatinous eyes, the ugly and sinister curtailment of the skull, his anomalous dimpled chin, his anomalous cupid's bow, above all the parted mouth with its hint of uncontained saliva—these would always suggest to me without profit of hindsight, some form of depravity or perversion.

In that respect, however, through age and sex and—unsought—experience, I should have had what is called the edge on Doreen Marshall.

She did not guess that her new friend was a cheap crook and show-off, with a criminal record overshadowing all his adult life. Still less did she guess that, at the very moment they were exchanging dinner-table banter, he was wanted—urgently wanted—by the Yard.

Still less did she guess the reason why: that they suspected him (and rightly) of murdering a woman two weeks ago in London—a murder accompanied by mutilations so sadistic and obscene that it is agony to read the pathologist's report.

Doreen Marshall guessed nothing. She was as naïve as she was pretty.

Untroubled, she walked with him through the pine-scented Bourne-mouth night.

Five days later her corpse was found in Branksome Chine—torn and outraged even more than that of her London predecessor. . . .

Heath met police questioning with a complete denial. He had left Doreen Marshall at the pier, he said; while still in his view she had crossed the road and gone into the gardens; what happened to her after that was not within his knowledge. (He gave this lie some colour by adding that he had been half expecting her to phone.)

Thus Heath bluffed it out in the station-house at Bournemouth. But it was—literally—a different story at his trial.

Though Heath had also been *charged* with murdering Doreen Marshall, that trial concerned his earlier victim, Margery Gardner. And under the rules that protect a prisoner in our British courts, during that trial the prosecution were debarred from making any reference to his second crime. It was the *defence* that deliberately intro-duced it, admitting—or rather, insisting on—Heath's guilt, in an attempt to buttress their plea of insanity without which there would have been no defence at all.

The two murders in succession—so ran the argument—indicated "progressive mania"; especially as the injuries in the second murder achieved the grisly feat of being worse than in the first. J. D. Casswell, Heath's highly skilled defender, made great play with this in opening his case. This progressive mania, he said, formed the foundation for the evidence to be given by Dr. Hubert—the latter being the psychiatrist on whom rested the success or otherwise of Heath's insanity plea.

"In having Doctor Hubert as a witness," Casswell told the jury, "you are extremely fortunate." Considered in perspective, these words have an ironic ring. Certainly Doctor Hubert boasted a long and resounding list of psychiatric qualifications. But the jury's good fortune —if it were such—in having him as a witness resided less in these than in his enlightening if unwilling demonstration of the arrant rubbish that may be talked upon occasion by a highly qualified person in the box.

The keen mind that enforced and controlled this demonstration was that of Anthony Hawke, leading counsel for the Crown.

His cross-examination vied in its economy with its effectiveness.

"Doctor Hubert, may I take it from your evidence that at the time Heath murdered Margery Gardner he knew that he was doing some-thing that was wrong?"

"No," said the psychiatric expert flatly.

"May I take it that he knew what he was doing?"

"Yes," conceded the psychiatric expert.

"So he knew when he inflicted seventeen lashes on her with a thong that he was inflicting seventeen lashes on her with a thong?"

"Yes."

"But he did not know that that was wrong?"

"No."

Hawke neatly inverted his previous question.

"Then at the time he was inflicting those injuries he thought that it was right?"

"Yes," said Doctor Hubert, after a short pause.

"Because he is a sadist?"

"Yes," said Doctor Hubert.

"A person who acquires satisfaction by inflicting cruelty?"

"Yes," said Doctor Hubert.

"Because he could only obtain satisfaction by inflicting cruelty, you say that he thought he was *right* to inflict it, do you?"

"Yes," said Doctor Hubert.

Hawke, with infinite restraint, never raised his voice.

"Are you saying that a person in that frame of mind is free from criminal responsibility if what he does causes bodily harm or death?"

Doctor Hubert—rather late—began to feel the skids beneath him. He answered affirmatively, but without enthusiasm.

Hawke played his ace.

"Would it be your view that a person who finds it convenient to forge a cheque in order to free himself from financial responsibility is entitled to say that he thought it was right?"

Doctor Hubert temporized and argued; but in the end there was no escape.

"Would such a man be entitled to claim exemption from responsibility on the grounds of insanity?"

"Yes," Doctor Hubert ludicrously said.

More followed, but the Crown was already home. Heath's insanity defence rightly met rejection and his conviction for the murder of Margery Gardner brought upon him the appropriate penalty.

So it has never been formally and officially proved that he murdered Doreen Marshall. That would have been superfluous. It is impossible to hang even a monster twice.

Margaret Hare

THAT is she, in the box, instead of in her rightful place, the dock; there, peering craftily round the court as she grips the Bible; a sullen, mean, vindictive-looking hag; that is she, the legendary and barbarous Mrs. Hare.

The judge's face and tone alike are stern as he addresses her.

"Margaret Hare." The woman jerks her head suspiciously, dimly

174

aware that her very name now sounds like an indictment. "You are at present a prisoner involved in a murder charge. It is my duty to tell you that, in respect of that murder, you can never be brought to trial if you speak the truth today."

She jerks her head again, this time with a trifle more assurance. So it's all right, what they promised when she turned King's Evidence; as long as she tells her dreadful story, *she* shall go scot-free.

Comforted and fortified by His Lordship's declaration, Mrs. Hare wheels relentlessly on those of her fellow-prisoners who have not been permitted her own method of escape. . . .

There had been four of them altogether in that hideous gang: William Burke, William Hare, and their respective trollops ("Mrs." Hare was only designated thus by courtesy). The two couples dwelt, within a few yards of each other, in one of the vilest slums that disfigured ancient Edinburgh.

Burke and his companion, Helen M'Dougall, occupied one room; it was sixteen feet by seven; its furniture consisted of a chair, two wooden stools and a wooden bed made up of old straw and filthy rags. The Hares had a rather more commodious abode, but practically filled it with cheap and wretched pallets which they let to casual lodgers for a penny or two a night.

One can readily picture those who would endure such lodging. None but the down-and-outs, society's cast-offs; the unattached and unknown and unwanted of this world.

It was indeed the continuous flow of these to Hare's establishment that first set the entire quartet upon their villainous course.

An old pensioner had died upon the premises; died where he lay, unattended, on his couch. Burke and Hare, ears always to the ground, had heard it rumoured you could get good money for a corpse from lecturers on anatomy in need of specimens. They offered the pensioner's remains to one Dr. Robert Knox, from whom they received, with much delight, a suitable reward.

From then on the Burkes and Hares, female as well as male, became inseparable. Their community of interests, always strong, had been made absolute. Their main object was gain. Their main pleasure was drink. And as the pensioner had shown an easy way to achieve both, and as mortality unaided would not furnish enough corpses, their main business—a wholesale business—was concerted murder.

Occasionally the lodging-house provided fresh material; a sick or drunken inmate would be quietly dispatched and inconspicuously removed to Dr. Knox's in a cart. But mostly more enterprising measures were required; subjects had to be sought and spotted and enticed; and in this respect the women, especially Mrs. Hare—now enjoying sanctuary in the witness-box—played a prominent and enthusiastic part.

The technique of extermination seldom varied. One or other of the four would mark down likely prey—a tramp, a prostitute, or other rootless person; liquor would be used as bait to tempt that person in—sometimes to Burke's, other times to Hare's; everyone concerned would engage in a carousal, until the unsuspecting visitor was tipsy; the women conspirators would then temporarily withdraw while Burke and Hare brought the matter to completion.

Subsequently, at the trial, the Crown was to suggest that this withdrawal in itself was an act of criminal cunning—that the women were simply keeping a look-out.

Possibly, but there is another feasible explanation—that they may have been repelled by the actual kill.

Between February and October, 1828, at least sixteen persons were sent to their account by this unholy and infamous alliance. The toll might have passed to scores, it might have passed to hundreds, had long immunity not induced a mood of carelessness. The body of their last victim was discovered, hidden but unguarded, in a corner of Burke's room; the police were summoned to institute inquiries; and, bit by bit, the whole grisly traffic came to light.

Ideally all four should have been tried and been convicted, but the Crown were confronted by difficulties of proof. Whichever case they elected to proceed on, they could not establish which of the four was the first-hand perpetrator without calling one or more of them to depose against the others.

After much thought they decided to use the Hares against the Burkes. That is how this female ogre, following on the heels of her consort, appears in the role of retributive accuser.

Burke and his woman, from the dock, scan her anxiously. They know her too well to hope for anything but the worst.

"You remember last Hallowe'en?" the prosecutor asks.

"Yes," Mrs. Hare replies in her cracked virago's voice.

"Did you go to Burke's room?"

"Yes."

"Was Hare with you?"

"He was."

"Was Burke in?"

"Yes."

"And Helen M'Dougall?"

"Yes."

"Did you see an old woman there?"

"Yes."

"Say now what happened to her."

The glances shoot like serpents' tongues between witness-box and dock.

"She got a push," said Mrs. Hare, "and fell upon the ground."

"Who pushed her?"

"I don't know. But it was Burke who fell upon her."

"Did she make a noise?"

"I couldn't say; Mrs. M'Dougall and me flew out into the passage."

"How long did you stay in the passage?"

"Maybe quarter of an hour."

"When you went back into the room, did you see the old woman?"

"No."

"What did you suppose?"

"I supposed she had been murdered." Mrs. Hare draws breath, then grimly adds: "I had seen such tricks before."

"Had you any *particular* reason to suspect that mischief?"

"Yes." Mrs. Hare is keeping her contract; she is telling it all. "Mrs. M'Dougall had said there was a shot in the house that her husband had brought in."

"A shot? What did that mean?"

"A person to be done away with."

"You had heard the word used on former occasions with that meaning?"

"Yes."

She has said her say—in self-preservation—against her old associates; in doing so she has rendered the solitary service of her wicked life; she has been a vital instrument in the processes of judgment.

But what of the instrument herself, this blood-stained murderess? She may well indulge in a grimace of satisfaction as, snapping her fingers at the law's impotence, she steps out of court together with the grinning Hare.

It is a sight to make the gods laugh—and the blind goddess weep.

Dr. East

AFTER her death, during the trial of the man who murdered her, Gertie Yates was described by a kindly witness as a Lady With Friends.

Such Ladies are, in general, dubious murder risks. They tend to form their friendships without discrimination, and every so often a Friend turns out a sexual maniac. Then the unfortunate Lady's career may abruptly end with a pathologist's report which the papers cannot print.

Gertie Yates, however—in this respect, at least, unrepresentative of her kind—brought to bear upon the exercise of her affairs strong qualities of prudence and of caution. In so far as this led her—as it did —to be choosey over clients, it made her safer than most prostitutes from sexual maniacs.

But in so far as it led her—as it also did—to accumulate her earnings, keep her purse well-stocked, and invest in good jewellery which she loved to wear, it made her *less* safe than most from a rogue like Ronald True. . . .

Thirty years old in 1922, True had consistently displayed from early childhood a cynical and egocentric amorality. He was a liar, an idler, and a braggart, sporadically dishonest and indifferently cruel. Possessing easy manners and a sleek exterior—sole asset salvaged from a gentle upbringing—he had recently achieved his destined terrain, the West End, where his exploits as a playboy were spurred by morphia and financed out of subventions from an indulgent mother.

Mother's means, though, while considerable, were not unlimited, and during February it became clear to True that this source of supply had temporarily dried up. No other lay in immediate prospect, and with March's advent the extravagant roisterer, accustomed to gay night clubs and chauffered limousines, found himself without the loose coins for a cup of tea.

With pawning, with borrowing, with some minor forgery, by bilking a rapid succession of hotels, for a time True contrived to keep himself afloat. But as his situation grew progressively more desperate, more desperately he cast around for fresh expedients—and more desperate the expedients over which he brooded.

At this crucial period he encountered—as she was looking out for business—Gertie Yates.

True noted her comparative affluence, realized her professional accessibility, ascertained that she lived in a basement flat alone.

The cold-blooded and mercenary plan was promptly born.

Gertie Yates rejected all his early overtures. She instinctively disliked True and, I think, almost certainly suspected his intention was to cheat, if not actually to rob. But in the end—it was on a Sunday, and trade may have been slack—she named her price, and True (of course) agreed. She believed, poor girl, that she could look after herself. It did not cross her mind—why should it have crossed her mind?—that, in pursuance of his crookedness, this particular crook would stop at nothing. Nothing at all. . . .

True killed Gertie Yates on Monday morning while she was still half asleep.

As a physical act of murder it was commonplace. Five heavy blows with a rolling-pin on the head. A towel stuffed into the mouth, doubling back the tongue. The girdle of her dressing-gown tied tightly round her neck. The dead body moved from the bed into the bathroom, and the pillows instead placed lengthwise beneath the coverlet.

Delaying tactics with the daily maid, whose early appearance took him by surprise ("Don't disturb her; we were rather late last night").

Then the pocketing of the jewels and the loose cash, and away. . . .

From the moment the detectives tracked down and arrested True a straight verdict of Not Guilty was virtually excluded. He had been recognized by the maid, contrary to his hopes. He was proved to have passed from indigence to prosperity overnight, redeeming pawned articles and paying off pressing debts. Furthermore, on the day of the murder he pledged some jewellery identified as stolen from Gertie Yates's flat. "I can explain how I got possession of it," he assured the police—but it is an explanation for which the world still waits.

Not surprising then that Sir Henry Curtis Bennett, his defender, told the jury he assumed they would "find the hand that had killed this woman to be the prisoner's hand," and that he went all out for a verdict of Guilty but Insane.

Whether a person ranked as a lunatic under the criminal law—i.e., whether he was deranged so as to be exempt from responsibility for his act—had been determined for almost eighty years in the light of what are commonly known as the M'Naghten Rules. These are simple, concise and, to my mind, entirely adequate for their purpose. They say that, *to acquire immunity* on the grounds of madness, you must either not have known what you were doing, or not have known that what you were doing was wrong.

Doctors have usually disliked the M'Naghten rules, judges and juries have usually approved them. That is due to a fundamental difference of approach. Doctors exist to cure mental and physical illness, and regard madness primarily as something to be treated; judges—and their attendant juries—in the criminal courts exist to protect society as a whole, and regard madness primarily as something to be guarded against and kept under control. Each approach can be fully justified—*in its place*. Judges and juries do not issue orders in Harley Street consulting rooms, and doctors might impose on themselves the same restraint in court.

Far too often, however, medical experts try to replace the law's definition of madness by their own.

That, fortunately, did not occur at the trial of Ronald True. The defence's principal witness, Dr. East, certainly sustained a vocational bias against the M'Naghten rules ("I think they ought to be relaxed," he candidly admitted, in response to a prosecution challenge). But this outstanding prison medical officer (currently at Brixton, where True had been confined) scorned verbal subterfuge or psychiatric claptrap as a means of frustrating the Rules' operation. "I think," he said simply, "that True is incapable of distinguishing moral right from moral wrong."

When Sir Richard Muir for the Crown rises to cross-examine, it is this statement, with its M'Naghten overtones, upon which his powerful guns are trained.

"He arranged the pillows to look as if the person was in the bed," Muir says. "Isn't the obvious reason that he desired to conceal what he had done?"

"Yes," Dr. East straightforwardly replies.

"Then he removed the body from the bedroom into the bathroom?"

"Quite so," Dr. East agrees.

"Wasn't that obviously to conceal from anyone looking into the bedroom that he had committed the act?"

"I should think so," Dr. East agrees again.

"Then he told the maid not to disturb her mistress?"

"Yes."

"Was that for the purpose of giving him time to get away?"

"Probably."

Muir lifts his massive head until he and Dr. East are eye to eye.

"All those acts, *committed on the spot and immediately after the crime*, were consistent with a desire to conceal the fact of murder?"

"Yes."

"And his connexion with it?"

"Yes."

Muir, a practised artist in timing, allows himself to pause.

"Does it not show," he presently goes on, beating out each word with separate emphasis, "that he knew what he had done was punishable by law?"

"Yes," Dr. East says. "I think it does."

But Dr. East's opinion about True's mental state at the material time has only been constricted in scope, not totally dislodged. The M'Naghten Rules, it will be remembered, classify as insane anyone who did not know that what he was doing was *wrong*.

Ronald True, Dr. East concedes, knew that what he was doing was wrong *according to the law*. But the word "wrong" in the Rules has been generally interpreted so that a prisoner may still secure their dispensation if he did not know that what he was doing was wrong *according to the standard of his normal fellow citizens*.

Did True?

Under the strongest pressure from Sir Richard Muir, Dr. East honestly maintains that he did not. In the end, it is the judge who exposes the utter superfluity of this double interpretation in a democratic state.

"If he knows it is punishable by law," Mr. Justice McCardie says, "he must know it is wrong in *some* sense?"

Impossible to dispute *that*, and Dr. East does not.

"And if he knows it is a crime, wouldn't you think that he must know it is a moral wrong *according to the community's existing moral code*?"

It might be possible to dispute *that*—casuistically. But Dr. East is not a casuist, but an honourable physician.

"Yes, I would think so, my lord," he says. . . .

There is a footnote to be added to the verdict—unconditional and unqualified—of Guilty that the jury most properly returned. True was subsequently granted a reprieve—on the grounds that he had since been certified insane by a Commission of medical practitioners, and that it had long been a principle of British law that no insane person should go to execution.

This decision, the Home Secretary took pains to point out, did not in any way conflict with the finding of the jury which was solely concerned with criminal responsibility, not with insanity at ordinary law.

There is also a footnote to be added concerning the Commission of medical practitioners. It is by John Allen—better known as The Mad Parson—who was with True at Broadmoor, where the latter managed the canteen. "In every way he was a model inmate," Allen says; and when Superintendent Hopwood was looking for men to help him run the institute, "he found the greatest of them all in Ronald True."

William Hay

THROUGHOUT a week of mounting fear, the riots wrought havoc upon London. Notabilities were brutally attacked, great mansions were pitilessly plundered, and the red glare encircling the sky had not been matched since the days of the Great Fire and was not to be matched again until the German Blitz.

It had all begun—as appeared, at any rate, on the surface—with a perfectly lawful petition addressed to Parliament.

In 1780 religious differences still roused high passions among many Englishmen, and a recent Act lightening the burden upon Catholics had outraged and affronted fervent Protestants.

A strong association of those Protestants was formed; a strong plea for repeal of that Act was drafted and subscribed; a fanatical young Scotsman, Lord George Gordon, as leader of the former was entrusted with the latter; and on the appointed day, accompanied by adherents, he delivered it personally to the House of Commons.

Lord George Gordon's accompanying adherents numbered approximately 60,000 men, disposed in vast groups resembling military formations, and all wearing the same distinguishing cockade.

The Commons' refusal to deal with the petition there and then acted like a lighted match on a stick of dynamite. For six successive days London lay at the mercy of a mob continuously whetting its taste for violence with its own excesses.

Members of Parliament were seized in the streets or from their carriages, threatened, insulted, manhandled, beaten up. The Parliament building was besieged and the nation's representatives helplessly imprisoned within its hallowed walls.

Houses of Catholic citizens—and Catholic foreign envoys—were demolished, and their contents looted or destroyed. Newgate jail was stormed and a horde of desperate felons released to swell the ranks of their despoiling rescuers.

Finally, wholesale incendiarism supervened; the fire engines were swamped, obstructed, sometimes set on fire themselves; Bloomsbury, Holborn, Fleet Street, Blackfriars—at point after point the flames shot up unhindered, amid the wild prevailing cries: "No Popery! Repeal!"

When at last a dilatory and enfeebled government succeeded in suppressing tumult and restoring order, the toll of death ran into many hundreds and the wreck of property spilt over many miles.

The jury called to the Court of King's Bench a few months later hardly required formal proof of these enormities. They were all inhabitants of London; they had heard with their own ears, seen with their own eyes.

Of course—everyone knew—there had been an insurrection; the entire city could have testified to that. But was the insurrection prompted by the man accused?

They took another long, hard look at Lord George Gordon, now standing trial before them for high treason, charged with levying war against the King.

Had his own intentions been legitimate and peaceable—as defending counsel so strenuously maintain—and were the crimes really committed by an extraneous rabble exploiting the situation for their wicked ends?

Or had his own intentions been culpable and bellicose—as prosecuting counsel so strenuously allege—and were the crimes committed under his influence and management by followers whom he had gathered for that purpose under pretext of petitioning Parliament?

A man's thoughts must be read through his deeds and words. But even the deliberate summoning of so huge a crowd does not, of itself, establish Lord George Gordon's guilt; who can altogether discount his explanation that signatures upon petitions are generally suspect, and that physical presence best confirms their authenticity?

So the issue boils down to what Lord George Gordon *said*—and to the bona fides of those who swear he said it.

The crown is more than willing to cross swords upon this basis. For they have an ace of trumps to play, and immediately after Mr. Attorney's opening speech, they play it. As their first and star witness they put up William Hay.

Hay has in him material for half a dozen trials, every one of them resulting in conviction. Not only did he attend most of Lord George Gordon's meetings during the weeks immediately prior to the riots; not only did he stand by, an interested spectator, when his lordship gave verbal orders for the mass assembly; not only did he spend three hours in the parliamentary lobby and hear his lordship's speeches to the mass when they assembled.

More important, he preserves a detailed recollection of phrases and expressions that his lordship used. "The King has broken his coronation oath"; "By assenting to the Act for tolerating Catholics, the King has brought himself to the same pass as James II after his abdication"; "Stick steadfastly to your good and glorious cause." In conjunction, their tone is sinister.

If Hay remains unshaken, the prisoner will already be more than half-way to the gallows—as nobody appreciates better than Mr. Kennyon when, on Lord George Gordon's behalf, he starts to cross-examine.

"Pray, Mr. Hay, what are you?" he asks simply.

"I am by trade a printer," replies Hay.

"I think you've had some misfortunes?"

"Yes."

"You have been a bankrupt?"

"Yes."

Bankruptcy is rightly described as a misfortune. The admission, nevertheless, reduces the status of the witness—and his impecuniosity provides a feasible motive for conduct Mr. Kennyon will be probing later on.

"When did you first resort to these Protestant meetings?"

"On the 10th of the December before the riots," says Hay precisely.

"And then you attended others, at some of which Lord George was present, at some of which he was not?"

"Yes, he was not present at all the meetings," Hay agrees.

"Just now you told my learned friend that Lord George was present at a meeting on 21 January?"

"Yes."

"Reflect carefully," says counsel. "Did you see him there or not?"

Hay hesitated.

"I *think* I saw him there."

"Be on your guard," says counsel. "Did you see him there or not?"

Hay hesitates again.

"I could speak with more certainty," he says, "if I might look at my notes."

A harmless-sounding ordinary remark—but actually the turning point of Lord George Gordon's case. It furnishes occasion for a line of questioning that ends in both Hay and his notes being blown sky-high.

"Notes?" Mr. Kennyon repeats incredulously. "Notes? How came you to take notes?"

"I will tell you very freely." Hay suddenly feels uncomfortable. "Originally, my curiosity led me to those meetings, but in time I came to dread and foresee the consequences of them."

"When did you first foresee the consequences?"

Hay plunges.

"At a meeting on the 20th of February," he says.

"If that was the first time you were moved to take notes," says Mr. Kennyon, "how would your notes help you with the 21st of January?"

Hay fully realizes the trouble he is in and the sweat begins to run down his face as he tries to extricate himself.

"I took notes at *all* the meetings," he says, "right from the 10th of December."

"Why did you take notes before you foresaw the consequences?"

"Whenever I go to public meetings, I take notes."

"Give me an instance, ot her than these," says Mr. Kennyon. "Tell me where and when you have taken notes before."

Seconds pass while he stands in gloomy silence.

"Tell me where and when."

More seconds go by.

"Tell me where and when."

At Hay's belated answer, there is a wave of mirth that might be held to symbolize the lifting of a shadow.

"At the General Assembly of the Church of Scotland," he says wretchedly. "When I was much younger—twenty-two years ago."

Lord George Gordon was acquitted. There were other witnesses to follow William Hay, but their effect had been blunted in advance. British juries seldom look with favour on a prosecution whose ace of trumps turns out to be a spy.

"*Helen of Troy*"

THE Helen of Troy case is interesting to lawyers because it revived an ancient form of legal suit. To others it provides a social study and a problem: what constitutes evidence, at a given place and time, of guilty conduct between one man's wife and another woman's husband? . . .

The place, Cambridge; the time, 1932. Helen of Troy (the tag affixed for ever by a quip of counsel's) was the attractive mate of a grocer's young assistant. She was also the close chum of an eminent local doctor, and had been so for something like six years.

In a town the size of Cambridge, and with its corporate character, eminent doctors do not make close chums of married ladies without due attention being accorded to that fact. For long enough, the grocer's assistant seemed alone in unawareness.

When, though, he became aware, he kicked up a very great and angry fuss. He challenged the eminent doctor to a fight, and the challenge was unreservedly accepted. This childish bout of fisticuffs had twofold consequence: the challenger got much the worse of it, and the challenger's wife immediately left home.

After weeks had passed and still she did not return, the grocer's assistant went to lawyers for advice, and there was then launched his celebrated action for enticement—an action in which he claimed damages from the doctor for enticing his wife away from his society and service.

Underlying this claim, of course, was the implication that between Helen of Troy and her chum, the eminent doctor, there had been something more—or would a wit say, less?—than friendship; that, although she had not fled to the protection of the doctor—who was indeed with his own wife at his own home—none the less, the latter had successfully campaigned to win her as his mistress, and that therein lay the substantial cause of their disrupted marriage.

The doctor's defence was a direct denial. There had been no enticement; Helen of Troy had walked out of her own accord, not because of him, but because she did not get on well with her husband.

Immense public interest was focused on the trial, and most of all upon the female subject of dispute. She must be the vital witness on the doctor's side; more essential even than the doctor. . . .

The modern Helen steps into the box and disclaims any parallel with her classical forerunner. It has been perfectly innocent, this relationship with the doctor; so far from trying to take her away, he tried to patch things up; but she could stand no more and would not be dissuaded.

All this in answer to the doctor's advocate. That was the easy part. Now begins the crucial cross-examination.

"Did the doctor, in your presence, tell your husband that he loved you?"

"Love was never mentioned," answers Helen flatly. "What he did say was that we were great friends."

"What are your feelings towards the doctor?"

"I like him very much, as a friend."

"No passionate love?"

"None."

The next question is an extremely shrewd one.

"What used you to talk about?"

"The weather mostly," Helen says.

The judge later interpreted this as a humorous retort. If so, it was a pity; one would have liked to hear her serious reply. What used they to talk about?—surely it goes to the root of the whole matter.

Where sexual passion is involved you do not ask what the partners have in common; it is enough that they share passion, which can temporarily unite the most disparate individuals. But friendship depends on exchange of minds through the instrument of talk, and rarely exists without some clear community of interest.

What exchange of minds took place between Helen and the doctor? We shall never know; it is lost in a mediocre joke; we are already passing on to other themes.

"Did you often go out with the doctor in his car?"

"About two afternoons a week," is Helen's reckoning.

"Did you have tea together?"

"Yes."

"Did you go out shooting with him?"

"Yes."

"Did you go out riding with him?"

"Yes."

Counsel's voice hardens.

"Was there anything you gave him in return for all this?"

The meaning appears plain, but Helen somehow doesn't get it.

"I have only given him handkerchiefs," she observes demurely.

Counsel underlines his point.

"The only things you did for him," he says ironically, "were to talk about the weather and to give him the pure love of a good woman?"

Helen understands him now, and shies at once.

"I've told you," she insists, "it was not love at all."

Simply two pals who happened to be of opposite sexes; two pals revelling in each other's company. Is that a feasible construction to place upon the admitted facts?

Hardly, perhaps, if it were 1832. But in 1932 the social climate is transformed; there are innumerable harmless and rewarding friendships, in outward appearance indistinguishable from theirs, founded upon mutual sympathy of outlook.

More than ever one would have liked to know what they talked about. . . .

"Have you and the doctor, from the day you left your husband, gone on exactly as before?"

"We have," says Helen frankly.

"You mean to go on doing so?"

"Yes."

The arrow flies.

"Would you stay anywhere except at a place where the doctor could come to see you?"

Helen falters.

"I haven't thought about it."

"Think about it now. Would you? Would you?"

We have to wait for her answer, but it is engagingly straightforward when it comes.

"No," she says, "I wouldn't."

Does attachment to a friend go as far as that? In general, maybe not, but it might in special instances—where, for example, a woman has no other friend to lean on in a period of acute emotional distress.

Let the jury decide. . . .

The jury, however, decide precisely nothing, because they find it impossible to agree. The court adjourns with the issues unresolved and the position of the parties undefined.

A somewhat tardy epilogue tidied up the loose ends.

Nearly six years later, in the Divorce Division, an undefended petition came before the President. The grocer's assistant was seeking to dissolve his marriage on the ground of Helen of Troy's adultery with the doctor. They had been living together abroad, it was stated, since 1932.

Decree nisi with costs against the co-respondent. Helen of Troy could settle down domestically at last.

Jeremiah Smith

WHICH trade or pursuit can claim the dubious distinction of contributing to British crime its most atrocious villain? Painters could make a strong bid with Patrick Staunton. So could antique dealers with Brides-in-the-Bath Smith. So could makers of artificial fingernails with Haigh.

But, on the whole, in such a competition the medical profession are likely to start favourites. Theirs is the privilege of nominating Palmer.

Up to a point, William Palmer's career as a physician closely resembled that of countless other family doctors. He was a student at Bart's. He qualified satisfactorily. Then he set up in practice in his native town of Rugeley—a name he was later to invest with a sinister connotation which still exists today.

Palmer possessed considerable aptitude for his chosen work, and for several years Rugeley kept him busily employed. He did not, however, permit himself to fulfil this initial promise.

Palmer's true passion was not medicine, but racing. An idle gambler by nature, he greatly preferred backing horses to attending patients. Gradually he rejected the demands made by his calling, spending more and more time on the racecourse, in the surgery less and less.

It is obvious that neither this unhappy weakness—nor another, for women, which he liberally indulged—would have justified Palmer's classification as a villain, far less his title to pre-eminence as such. What constitutes him a monster of iniquity, at whom successive generations shudder, is the fact that among his various other occupations—prescribing tonics and soothing syrups, betting, making love—he was engaged upon a lengthy course of wholesale murder.

The number of his victims will never be known with anything like certainty, but eleven is a modest estimate. Bookmakers whom he owed, bastards who cost him money to maintain, relatives from whose death he might derive some profit—Palmer used poison on them all as an everyday device for relieving the financial strain which his extravagance and gambling losses rendered semi-chronic.

No one except a doctor—whose profession can be used both as a weapon and a shield—could have hoped to carry out unnoticed such a massacre within his own immediate circle of acquaintance. And even Palmer, who had more than an average share of luck, was unable to preserve his immunity for ever.

Some of the shrewder citizens of Rugeley had already begun to look at him askance, some of the more deeply involved insurance companies had already begun to investigate his activities in secret, when the death of a young man named John Parsons Cook suddenly stripped Palmer bare of all pretence and made him the talk of every club and pub in England.

Cook was one of Palmer's racing cronies; an owner of horses, who usually laid substantial sums upon them. He had followed his custom in the November of 1855 when, accompanied by Palmer, he saw his entry win the Shrewsbury Handicap.

Cook returned from Shrewsbury Races with the best part of £1,000 literally in his pocket. Palmer returned a loser—at a moment when he had seldom been more heavily in debt.

During the week that followed, Cook was unaccountably stricken. He sustained a series of mysterious and convulsive bouts of illness, which caused him agony almost beyond bearing, and which terminated only with his death.

Expert opinion pronounced he had been poisoned.

The pointers to Palmer could not be overlooked. He had been in constant attendance on Cook, both as friend and doctor; ordering— and giving him—his medicine, food and drink. He had been buying poisons from different chemists in the neighbourhood. He had ordered a coffin with indecent haste, and without reference to the dead man's relatives.

And while Cook's money had vanished with his death, Palmer forthwith paid his most immediately pressing debts. . . .

The charge of murder against Palmer in respect of Cook was supported—after exhumations—by two others; to be held in reserve, as it were, in case the Cook charge failed.

But could the Cook charge fail?

Certainly not if the jury at the trial's close felt as the population of Rugeley did before it opened. Palmer narrowly escaped a lynching as the police tried to smuggle him into the safety of a jail; and a special Act of Parliament was passed for his protection, permitting the transfer of a prisoner's trial where local prejudice appears inordinate.

Prejudice, however, is not evidence, and moral certainty falls short of legal proof. Despite the heavy weight of the cards already stacked against them, Palmer's defenders struggled hard to produce some of their own.

Palmer himself had special hopes of Jeremiah Smith.

Smith possessed a most respectable façade. He was a solicitor, and thus, as lawyers say, "an officer of the court"; one whose words might be expected to carry extra weight.

Called into the witness-box by the defence, Smith purported to give Palmer a form of alibi. He maintained that Palmer had been with him, and not with Cook, at vital periods preceding Cook's recurrent spasms; and that Cook—whom he had visited both with Palmer and alone—admitted taking medicines, in Palmer's absence, obtained from another source.

This might just implant sufficient seeds of doubt to make an Old Bailey jury, remote from Rugeley gossip, flinch from despatching Palmer to his death.

Such is the defence's aim, such the possibility, when the Attorney-General gets up to cross-examine.

Sir Alexander Cockburn treats the solicitor witness to an unfriendly glare.

"Have you known Palmer long?"

"Yes."

"Intimately?"

"Yes."

"Has he employed you a good deal professionally?"

"Yes."

"Do you remember Palmer's brother dying in the August of last year?"

"Yes."

The Attorney-General's glare grows more malevolent.

"In the previous December, did Palmer ask you to attest a proposal to the Solicitors and General Insurance Company for an assurance of £13,000 upon his brother's life?"

The witness is clearly taken aback.

"I cannot recollect," he says.

"In the previous January did Palmer ask you to attest a proposal to the Prince of Wales Insurance Company for an assurance of £13,000 upon his brother's life?"

"I cannot recollect," Jeremiah Smith says again.

"Cannot recollect! Wasn't £13,000 a large sum for a man like Palmer's brother who hadn't a shilling in the world?"

Jeremiah Smith is exquisitely uncomfortable. He does not like the look of those well-ordered documents which are lying to the Attorney-General's hand, but have not so far been used.

"Did Palmer ask you to attest another such proposal to the Universal Company?"

"I cannot recollect."

"Do you recollect getting a five pound note for attesting an assignment of such a policy by Palmer's brother to Palmer himself?"

"Well," says Jeremiah Smith, "well, perhaps I might."

Now the Attorney-General brings his documents into play.

189

"Look at that. Tell me, is it in your handwriting?"

Jeremiah Smith holds the paper gingerly, as if it were capable of inflicting physical hurt.

"Is that your handwriting?"

"It is."

"Then I put the question again: Were you not asked by Palmer to attest a proposal to the Solicitors and General Insurance Company for an assurance of £13,000 upon his brother's life?"

"I might have been."

"Were you or were you not, sir?"

He really cannot dodge it.

"I have no doubt I was," he says.

The Attorney-General flourishes the documents remaining.

"Have you any doubt that you were asked to attest similar proposals to other companies?"

It is useless to struggle further.

"Yes; I was asked," he says.

So swiftly was cut short the pose of Jeremiah Smith as an impartial and disinterested witness. His evidence did less than nothing to help Palmer escape his merited fate upon the gallows. It is certain that he took part in some of Palmer's frauds, and likely that he at least connived at some of Palmer's murders.

This equalizes matters between two great professions. If doctors feel constrained to blush for William Palmer, lawyers must do likewise for Jeremiah Smith.

Dr. Alfred Swaine Taylor

A DOCTOR who is in the dock upon a poisoning charge holds a great advantage over a layman similarly placed.

Any layman must expect to be fairly flummoxed by the evidence of the medical witnesses. While these experts learnedly discourse about Marsh's test or metabolic change or hyperaemia, the bewildered prisoner feels like a man being tried in a foreign language without the benefit of an interpreter. His life may depend on what is said, but he cannot fathom it.

A doctor upon trial, though, is himself an expert, who, under different circumstances, might have entered the witness-box in that capacity. He knows the jargon, grasps its meaning, gauges its effect.

Its effect? Such technical stuff is above the jurors' heads, no doubt, but not above the head of an experienced criminal judge upon whom they rely for explanation and for guidance.

Small wonder, then, that Dr. Thomas Smethurst, flanked as he now is by Old Bailey warders, listens with painful interest and attention while his professional colleagues testify before Chief Baron Pollock.

His Lordship's view of what they say can be a decisive factor in determining whether the jury will pronounce that Dr. Smethurst poisoned Miss Isabella Bankes.

Dr. Smethurst's association with that lady had been brief but exceedingly eventful.

It began during the autumn of 1858, when Miss Bankes, in her forties and possessing private means, went to stay at a London boarding-house where Dr. Smethurst, in his fifties and married 30 years, was already living in semi-retirement with his wife.

Mutual attraction seems to have been immediate. Within a few weeks, Dr. Smethurst and Miss Bankes had run away, and gone through a form of a wedding in a church. The doctor, however, remained on strangely cordial terms with the lawful Mrs. Smethurst, and even wrote her letters that might be construed as signifying that their separation would not be permanent.

Certainly the prime cause of it did not long survive. Shortly after her "marriage" Miss Bankes fell gravely ill. She had always suffered from a bilious tendency, but the symptoms were now much more violent and sustained than anything that she had experienced before.

For a time Dr. Smethurst attended her himself. Later he called in a local practitioner, who at first treated Miss Bankes as an ordinary case of sickness and diarrhœa. But as she grew steadily worse, his suspicions were aroused, especially by her constant complaint of a parched throat and a burning sensation in the mouth.

The local practitioner changed his mind. He thought she was being poisoned.

The practitioner's partner examined Miss Bankes, and thought so, too. A leading specialist, brought for consultation, thought so, too. They forthwith despatched specimens for chemical analysis, and reported their grave misgivings to the police.

When, almost immediately afterwards, the lady died—having signed a will drafted by her "husband," in which she bequeathed all her property to him—Dr. Smethurst was at once accused of murder. . . .

The issue now being fought out at his trial is not whether Dr. Smethurst did it, or some other. There has never been any real dispute over the fact that no one could have poisoned Isabella Bankes but he. The battle rages over an entirely different problem: Did she die from poisoning at all?

The verdict on the Doctor depends upon the doctors.

Well aware of this, the prisoner in the dock, shrewdly weighing every word, watches the experts come and go with mounting satisfaction.

Examining Physician No. 1 turns out to possess rather meagre qualifications. Examining Physician No. 2 admits that the idea of

191

poisoning was put into his head by No. 1. The leading specialist agrees that dysentery might have accounted for Miss Bankes's symptoms—and the defence has several doctors waiting to pledge themselves that dysentery is indeed what those symptoms indicate.

Above all, no poison was found in the body on post-mortem, except for an amount of antimony so small that it could have resulted from absorbing medicines.

Altogether, Dr. Smethurst feels, it is going rather well—especially as he has an extraneous card to play: no poison of any sort has been traced to his possession.

None the less, he cannot look forward with any confidence while the evidence of the analyst has yet to be surmounted—the analyst to whom the specimens were sent. And when that analyst's name is called —"Alfred Swaine Taylor," counsel intonates with pride—Dr. Smethurst knows, better perhaps than most of those in court, that the supreme crisis of his trial is at hand.

Dr. Taylor is a man of outstanding eminence; in medical jurisprudence, the greatest living name. Even Chief Baron Pollock seems impressed as he takes the oath and calmly waits for the prosecutor's questions.

Yes, he is professor of chemistry at Guy's; yes, he is a Fellow of the Royal College of Physicians; yes, he has had great experience in cases of this kind.

Yes, he analysed the specimens submitted. He used Reinsch's process. He detected arsenic.

Now this may be double Dutch to others; it is not by any means double Dutch to Dr. Smethurst, and he can tell from the judge's comprehending nod that it is not double Dutch to Chief Baron Pollock.

Reinsch's is the standard test for arsenic; employed by skilled and practised hands, it is deemed unerring. And were ever hands more skilled and more practised in the performance of such tests than those of Dr. Taylor?

Unless—and when did such a miracle occur?—Dr. Taylor is discredited, Dr. Smethurst may regard himself as doomed.

He grips the dock ledge as if holding on for life when his counsel, Serjeant Parry, begins to cross-examine.

"I think you have also analyzed the contents of some bottles taken from the prisoner's lodgings after his arrest?"

"Yes."

"Was there one that contained a clear liquid of a saline taste?"

"Yes."

"Did you tell both the coroner and the magistrate that you had discovered arsenic in that?"

"Yes."

"Was that correct?"

"No. I was mistaken."

"There was in fact no arsenic in that bottle?"

192

"No." Dr. Taylor speaks into a court aghast at this sudden disclosure of his fallibility. "I discovered subsequently that the arsenic produced came from the copper gauze that I was using."

"From an impurity in one of your implements?"

"That is so."

Serjeant Parry slowly enunciates each word at this key point in his interrogation.

"Was this gauze, the gauze that produced arsenic," he asks, "was it the same as the gauze you used in the tests you have been describing?"

"Yes," Dr. Taylor answers. . . .

Seldom has an expert witness of such standing been so swiftly and completely overthrown. The case against Dr. Smethurst was smashed to smithereens. Serjeant Parry had not established his client's innocence, of course—that will for ever be the subject of debate—but he had surely deprived the prosecution of their sole instrument for establishing his guilt.

Everybody seems to have recognized this fact—save for Chief Baron Pollock and the jury. The former summed up for a conviction, and the latter obliged.

A miscarriage of justice, however, was averted. Memorials from the medical profession and the Bar, petitions from the public, philippics from the Press—all these impelled the Home Secretary to act. Dr. Smethurst, en route for the scaffold, was granted a free pardon.

The Crown utilized this extension of his life to run him in for bigamy and get him twelve months' hard. Dr. Smethurst utilized it to propound Miss Bankes's will in court, and, despite her relatives, carry off the loot.

PART FOUR

CASES: (1) SENSATIONAL

Jimmy Thomas

O N 9 April, 1936, the Chancellor of the Exchequer disclosed in secret to his Ministerial colleagues what proposals were contained in his forthcoming Budget, due for presentation within a fortnight's time. On 10, 11, 12 and 13 April—being Easter week-end—the Colonial Secretary, Mr. J. H. Thomas, spent a golfing and social holiday with a certain Mr. Bates, one of his closest friends. As soon as the City resumed business on 14 April, Mr. Bates insured against a rise in income-tax.

On 21 April—Budget Day itself—Mr. Thomas received a morning call in his private room from Sir Alfred Butt, M.P., another intimate friend. As soon as Sir Alfred returned to his own office, he, too, insured against a rise in income-tax, and also against a rise in the duty upon tea.

A few hours later the Budget became public property. Threepence more on income-tax, twopence more on tea.

Now there is an extremely common form of faulty reasoning which professional logicians, in their slangy style, refer to as the fallacy of *post hoc propter hoc*.

It means, though, nothing more abstruse than this: the elementary error of assuming that, if one occurrence follows upon another, the earlier is cause and the latter is effect. I had strawberries for lunch, I had stomach-ache this afternoon; *therefore* it was the strawberries that gave me stomach-ache. The Conservatives (or Socialists) rule, and unemployment rises; *therefore* Conservative (or Socialist) policy produces unemployment.

Mind, these inferences are far from being excluded. The strawberries *may* have given you stomach-ache. Conservative (or Socialist) policy *may* have produced unemployment. But evidence in support of these conclusions must be sought; to rely upon the mere sequence of events is to invite derisive scorn from the logicians by committing the fallacy of *post hoc propter hoc*.

The *post hoc propter hoc* brigade swiftly got to work when gossip flew around about those successful pre-Budget operations. The proud detectives call it putting two and two together, being unable to distinguish between two and one-and-a-half. Bates had *first* seen the Colonial Secretary; *then* had correctly forecast a major Budget change. Butt had *first* seen the Colonial Secretary; *then* had correctly forecast two major Budget changes. *Therefore. . . .*

The imputations of a leakage hourly grew in volume, and ultimately reached the ears of the Minister himself.

Jimmy Thomas—known thus affectionately to millions—was an

outstanding figure in British public life. Starting his career as an ordinary worker on the railways, he had come up into politics through a hard trade-union school and achieved for himself popularity and esteem that transcended party and sectional divisions.

You could disagree with Jimmy: you could fight his ideas tooth and nail; but you could hardly fail to like and admire the man himself. Not just because he was humorous. Not just because he was genial. Not just because of his shrewdness and tact and common sense. But above all, because beneath a slightly flippant surface, one could discern a deep integrity.

That is not to say that Jimmy Thomas had no weaknesses. Gambling was with him a dominant passion: whether it took the form of betting on a horse, or buying and selling shares upon the Stock Exchange. Gambling is no crime, and the English, gamblers born, are the last to reprobate it. Had Jimmy Thomas been a private citizen, his proclivity would have been looked upon as amiable and endearing—and, indeed, his personal gambling transactions never created trouble and never inflicted harm. But the practice threw him into the company of men more acquisitive than himself—and therein lay the seeds of his political undoing. . . .

When Thomas learned of the rumours that were current, he was deeply shocked, and at once asked the Premier for an impartial inquiry. Simultaneously the Chairman of Lloyd's informed the Government that the amount of insurance taken out in the days before the Budget seemed disproportionately large compared with other years.

So three eminent lawyers Lord Porter, Lord Simonds, Mr. Justice Oliver—sat as a special tribunal to inquire whether there had been any disclosure of the Budget secrets, and if so, whether such disclosure had been used for private gain.

This inquiry lasted many days. The activities of Bates and Butt were closely scrutinized, and each in the witness-box explained what prompted him to anticipate the Budget as he did.

"I considered the general outlook serious," said Bates. "Hundreds of millions were required for rearmament; it was obvious to me that income-tax would rise."

"I thought a rise in income-tax was probable," said Butt. "As for tea, I felt convinced the Chancellor would also try to tax that part of the community that does not pay income-tax." They took their cue, they claimed, from personal judgment, not from private information.

Jimmy Thomas's own evidence of necessity was negative. Detaching himself for a few hours from the continuous flurry of Cabinet meetings, departmental decisions and major public speeches that are the ordinary lot of a senior Minister, he appeared at the tribunal and asserted earnestly that he had spoken about the Budget to nobody at all. More than that he manifestly could not say. "I simply did not do it," he repeated. "No advance knowledge of the Budget came from me."

"You saw Bates, though, constantly during Easter," said the chairman."

"Certainly."

"Whatever the fact may be, you had ample opportunity to tell him about the Budget?"

"I could have told anyone," came the justifiable answer.

"Was there any discussion of financial matters of any kind during Easter?"

Jimmy Thomas slowly shook his head.

"I don't remember any."

"Financial questions at that time were of considerable importance?"

"Obviously."

"And Bates's insurance transaction," observed the chairman, "followed immediately after that holiday at Easter."

Which was merely *post hoc propter hoc* translated into English. The juxtaposition of dates did not solve the basic problem: was it all, as Bates and Butt averred, sheer coincidence?

There were factors of conduct, however, that weighed more heavily; not factors in Jimmy Thomas's conduct, but in that of Bates and Butt. They had taken unusual pains to mask their own identities in their several transactions. They had worked—contrary to their custom—through nominees. And Butt, after his visit to Thomas, had reversed his previous trend; till that moment, he had been laying *against* a rise in income-tax.

The tribunal deemed it a case of not only *post* but *propter*; and they reported their opinion that, in both instances, Mr. Thomas had made an unauthorized disclosure.

The inquiry itself had already impelled his resignation; "the way in which my private affairs have been bandied about," he said, "renders my continuance as a member of the Government impossible." The findings rendered impossible any thought of his return, and thus, in this unhappy manner, ended a most honourable and valuable career.

It would be foolish to challenge the unanimous conclusion—formed after noting every witness's demeanour—reached by three of the most acute and experienced and responsible legal minds in England. One must accept the disclosures as a fact. But in what circumstances exactly were they made?

That remains ever open to conjecture. Disclosures may be made deliberately—or by inadvertence. A bantering retort to a semi-bantering question, a statement intended to be wholly non-committal but which gives something away that the speaker does not realize, even a miscalculated gesture or grimace—any and all may serve as a clue for those on the look out.

Whether the truth in this case may be found in these alternatives I would not presume even to suggest. But that Jimmy Thomas wilfully and wickedly betrayed the secrets of the Budget I do not believe.

W. T. Stead

"**P**UT up Jarrett," barked a court official.

Jarrett—a blowsy, nibbled woman in early middle-age—was what is technically described as "known to the police." Known as a drunkard; known as a prostitute; known best of all as a back-street procuress.

So that morning, when she was formally charged with abducting thirteen-year-old Eliza Armstrong ("out of the possession and against the will of her father and mother"), the regular patrons of Bow Street's half-filled gallery could not work up even a flicker of interest.

Just another o' them cases—pickin' some pore little brat from 'op-scotch and makin' 'er into a whore—bet she chucks 'er 'and in and arsts for leaningsy.

Rebecca Jarrett, however, did not chuck her hand in—a circumstance that in itself caught the gallery's attention. Mere attention passed into barely restrained excitement on their finding that, instead of some obscure solicitor, Treasury counsel was appearing for the Crown.

And excitement culminated in an audible thrill when Treasury counsel, applying for a remand, spoke of a conspiracy involving other persons, and nonchalantly asked for summonses against—among several less distinguished individuals—Mr. Bramwell Booth, chief of the Salvation Army, and Mr. W. T. Stead, the famous journalist and editor of the influential Pall Mall Gazette.

Theirs were household names. The effect could hardly have been more sensational if counsel had inculpated Cardinal Manning and Mr. Gladstone. All London buzzed with this extraordinary news, and on the day appointed for the adjourned hearing Bow Street's gallery was crammed to bursting point and Bow Street itself was blocked with sightseers. . . .

The prime mover, the heart and centre, of the conspiracy—for a conspiracy, in the strict sense, there had been—was Stead. He proclaimed it—proudly. "I bear the whole moral responsibility," he said. "Mine was the guiding brain and the directing hand."

This statement embodied not rhetoric but truth. A crusader by temperament as well as by conviction, during the 'eighties Stead pursued a vehement campaign against the traffic in women—and, especially, in young girls.

In 1885 a Parliamentary Bill—which had owed much to his stimulus and support—ran into heavy weather on its Second Reading and looked like being lost amid public apathy.

Stead concluded that only desperate measures could arouse opinion. He had satisfied his own mind that, in numerous instances, parents under the dual spur of drink and poverty pocketed a cash payment for delivering their half-grown daughters into a stranger's hands.

To satisfy others equally—and in the most vivid fashion—that this shameful commerce did actually exist, Stead resolved on a daring step: to engage in it himself, and subsequently report to the world what he had done.

He could not, of course, carry such a project through alone. For propriety's sake, he could not personally undertake the moral care and physical custody of a girl; consequently, he sought the Salvation Army's aid.

For practical reasons, he could not personally gain acceptance as a bona fide buyer in that squalid market; consequently he sought, through social workers, for a buying agent who would be more familiar to—and with—prospective sellers.

Thus it had come about that Mrs. Jarrett (recently reclaimed from her ways of vice, and willing to assist Stead as "an act of reparation") ostensibly assumed her old role of procuress, and returned to her old hunting-grounds adjoining Lisson Grove.

It was far from being a difficult assignment. Stead's depressing beliefs were amply justified. In the purlieus of that characteristic nineteenth-century slum—a tangle of drunkenness, over-crowding, unemployment, pawn shops, illiteracy, wife-beating—a normal sense of right and wrong easily atrophied.

Mrs. Jarrett had only to call on her erstwhile—and, as yet, unreclaimed—colleague, Mrs. Broughton; from her window she could inspect the parade of likely starters, and from her vocational gossip she could assess the current form.

That was how she got Eliza Armstrong.

The child came into the house—of her own accord—after Mrs. Jarrett had been there for some hours, and had already talked to several girls about a supposedly vacant post for a maid at her own home.

Each girl had been rejected ("too old" or "too big"); but they had speedily spread abroad the visitor's requirements, and, among youngsters used as unpaid drudges, living with eight or nine others in one room, the urge to escape is inevitably strong.

"Mrs. Broughton, I'll go to the service," Eliza Armstrong said.

Mrs. Broughton glanced at Mrs. Jarrett, who gave an almost imperceptible nod.

"Where's your mother?" Mrs. Broughton asked.

"She's out," replied Eliza.

"You mustn't go without her permission," said Mrs. Broughton virtuously. . . .

Mother duly responded to this implied summons. In Eliza's presence the fiction of "service" was preserved (Stead had deeply impressed on Mrs. Jarrett that "the innocent medium of the experimental demonstration" should be guarded from any "contaminating suspicion"). But in

Eliza's absence the three ladies spoke in different terms. There were ancillary winks, significant nods, the passing of loose coins; at the interview's close, Eliza went off in glee with Mrs. Jarrett and Eliza's mother went off in glee to "The Black Man".

The "experimental demonstration" was performed with thoroughness.

Always under the safe protection of the Salvation Army, better fed, better clothed, far more kindly treated than she had ever been before, Eliza travelled to Paris, then to the South of France—"to show," declared Stead later, "the ease with which a girl may be made to disappear abroad."

When Eliza had disappeared abroad for more than a month, without causing the faintest ripple of disturbance here, Stead judged the "demonstration" had sufficiently succeeded.

He did not forthwith return Eliza to her slum, hoping that in the outcome it would not be necessary. But he did write—minus only names—the full report he had always contemplated, printed it in his paper, and headlined it "A Child of Thirteen Bought for £5."

When Mrs. Armstrong learned of Stead's article she recognized how closely the cap fitted, and took fright. She repaired to the local police court, and with an injured air pressed for an inquiry into her daughter's whereabouts.

The result did not lack irony. Eliza, intact in every sense, was regretfully returned—and her benefactors were threatened with the vengeance of the law.

Did Mrs. Jarrett deceive Eliza's mother, leading her to believe the child was going to honest service? Or is it Mrs. Armstrong who, in maintaining this on oath, now deceives the court?

That constitutes the crux, and to that Charles Russell, nonpareil of cross-examiners, directs the questions he puts for the defence.

"When did you first become uneasy about your child?"

Mrs. Armstrong folds her arms belligerently. She has heard about Russell, and does not intend to be intimidated.

"When I got the *Pall Mall Gazette*," she says.

"You don't ordinarily read the *Pall Mall Gazette*?"

"Never read it before or since."

"Neighbours called your attention to it?" suggests Russell pointedly.

"Yes."

"Had you any anxiety before that?"

"Yes, because I hadn't heard of her."

"But you have just said you were *first* anxious when you saw the *Gazette*. Do you want to correct that answer?"

"Of course I do," says Mrs. Armstrong, as though counsel were to blame, not she.

"Well," says Russell, "we will begin again. *When* did you first begin to be anxious?"

"About a fortnight after she'd gone."

"Did you inquire about her from Mrs. Broughton?"

"Yes."

"What inquiry did you make?"

"Asked if she'd had any letter. She said No."

"That was as far as you went to ascertain where your child was?"

"Yes."

"Did you know her address?"

"No."

"When she left, you didn't ask where she was going?"

"I thought Mrs. Broughton knew all about it," Mrs. Armstrong answers.

"Why didn't you ask Mrs. Broughton for the address?"

"Didn't think it'd be any use." Mrs. Armstrong is now beginning to feel hard-pressed. "Mrs. Jarrett had said her husband was a commercial traveller, so I didn't think they'd have any address."

"At any rate, you didn't ask Mrs. Broughton for it?"

"Yes, I did."

"What, madam?" Russell's voice rings out a warning. "Scarcely a moment ago you told me you did not."

Mrs. Armstrong mumbles angrily.

"Before the *Gazette*," Russell goes on, "had neighbours spoken to you about the disappearance of your child?"

"Two or three of them."

"Did some say you had sold her?"

Mrs. Armstrong guesses that neighbours have been interviewed.

"They said it seemed very much like it after the story in the *Gazette*."

"Didn't some of them say it *before*?"

Mrs. Armstrong, very reluctantly, assents.

"The *Gazette* article described how a child of thirteen was bought for £5?"

"Yes."

"But you *hadn't* sold your child for £5, had you?"

"No. But when Mrs. Broughton admitted having a sovereign, I began to think there was something in it."

"You did?" Russell surveys the witness grimly. "You've been in trouble once or twice, haven't you?"

"For what?"

"Assault?"

"Years ago."

"Drunkenness?"

"Quite likely."

"On the very day Eliza left, weren't you taken up drunk in the street with your baby in your arms?"

"All through my husband," Mrs. Armstrong shouts. "Knocking me about for letting Eliza go."

"Oh?" Russell deliberately pauses. "If she had gone to genuine service, why should he knock you about?"

"I don't know."

"You had another daughter in service?"

"Yes."

"Did he knock you about on *that* occasion?"

"No. . . ."

It would have been pleasant to record that all the parties in this case received their due rewards—Stead and his associates an honourable acquittal, Mrs. Armstrong a trial for perjury.

The facts are less agreeable. All the defendants were committed; most were subsequently convicted; and a sentence of three months' imprisonment on Stead represents a diabolical triumph for Victorian hypocrisy over natural justice.

Mme. Caillaux

IMAGINE that *The Times* had made a venomous personal attack on Philip Snowden while he was Chancellor of the Exchequer; imagine that, in the midst of it, Mrs. Snowden had called and asked to see the editor; imagine that, upon being shown into his room, she had whipped out a revolver that lay hidden in her muff and fired six shots, wounding him mortally—imagine all this, and you have imagined something of a British counterpart of the famous Caillaux drama which rocked France to its foundations.

In 1914 Joseph Caillaux was French Minister of Finance, and acknowledged to be one of the ablest figures in the Government (although—contrasting in this respect with Mr. Snowden—his integrity was not of the same high standard as his mind).

The *Figaro* was a leading Paris newspaper which, throughout the first two and a half months of 1914, published ceaseless accusations against Caillaux—for instance, that he interfered with the processes of justice and timed official statements to suit speculating friends. And this campaign was riding high that mid-March afternoon when Mme. Caillaux—having equipped herself en route at a gunsmith's—walked unaccompanied into the *Figaro* building, where she simultaneously deprived them of their editor and provided them with the lead story for next morning's issue.

First reaction in Paris to this extraordinary event was sheer incredulity; second, when the news proved authentic, partial stupefaction; finally, when the outrage had been more or less assimilated, there was a great wave of anger against Mme. Caillaux.

Paris was broad-minded; it could take any orthodox *crime passionel* in its stride; but murdering an editor because of his proclaimed antagonism to one's husband—really, even Paris thought this was pushing things too far.

However, to be absolutely fair to Mme. Caillaux—and Mme. Caillaux stands in need of all the fairness she can get—there was a more compelling motive for her action than the distress occasioned her by the campaign to date. She was influenced less by resentment for the past than apprehension for the future.

Mme. Caillaux was the Minister's second wife. She had been his mistress while he was still married to his first, and during that period had received from him some letters which were romantically intimate and politically indiscreet.

Indeed, Caillaux later caught fright and procured their return—a move which had the reverse effect of that which he designed. His first wife abstracted three of these letters from his desk and, after divorce and Caillaux's subsequent remarriage, she willingly exhibited them to persons who showed interest.

It might seem incredible that a newspaper of high standing should seriously contemplate even for a moment printing the pilfered private letters of a statesman as ammunition in political polemics. But a French Press vendetta of that era was the journalistic parallel of all-in wrestling. The *Figaro* had already published one of the three letters, so that Mme. Caillaux had good grounds for her fear that the other—more embarrassing—pair would be published in their turn.

That was an explanation—but surely no defence. Indeed, an English advocate, briefed to defend Mme. Caillaux in an English court, might well have come to the conclusion there was no defence at all.

The mere lack of a defence, though, is not necessarily disastrous in France. In other regards, the French are the most civilized of nations, but their system of justice leaves much to be desired, withholding adequate protection from the innocent and furnishing favourable opportunities for the guilty.

Maître Labori, most famous Paris counsel of his day, who undertook the task of representing Mme. Caillaux, would not by any means regard his cause as hopeless.

The trial of Mme. Caillaux, lasting more than a week, was daily attended by fascinated crowds. To say the court became a theatre would be grotesque understatement; it became a circus, a rodeo, a gymkhana. Neither relevance nor order intruded from the start, and angry scenes of uninhibited hysteria occurred so frequently that no one could keep count.

Counsel fulminated; witnesses made impassioned and interminable speeches; judges quarrelled with each other on the Bench (it was rumoured that two of them were going to fight a duel); the spectators bellowed their approval or disgust.

In the box, M. Callaux defended his record as a Minister at a length he could seldom have exceeded on a platform, and in a tub-thumping style reminiscent of the hustings. ("You have seen a man," someone declared when he concluded, "stand on the coffin of the victim of his wife so as to speak to you from a greater height.")

Talk, talk, talk. They talked of everything at the trial of Mme. Caillaux—of elections, of income-tax, of the incident at Agadir—all the French political crises of the past decade. The only thing they hardly ever seemed to get around to was the shooting; the shooting—you remember?—at the *Figaro* office, which was the ostensible reason for the trial.

Now and again, when they did touch upon this topic, it was always with a slightly apologetic air, as if it was not the sort of stuff one liked to introduce.

Madame herself grasped the nettle with most boldness. "With these automatic pistols, it is terrible," she said. "They go off—it is true—they go off on their own accord. . . ."

No shadow of a case was ever made for Mme. Caillaux—not Maître Labori's fault that, there was no case to be made—and the sole question to tease us nowadays is: What was it the jury thought they were deciding?

Whether M. Caillaux was a good and honest Minister? Whether the *Figaro*'s offensive was well-founded? Whether the Press had gone too far for politicians? Whether politicians had gone too far for the Press?

Any of these might account for their decision. It could hardly have been based upon attention to the facts.

Mme. Caillaux was acquitted.

Cheers in the courtroom, riots in the city. Vehement applause from the well-drilled Caillaux claque; violent fury from sensible French citizens who were suddenly wakened up to the truth about their legal system.

Maître Labori did his skilful best to deflect hostility. Mme. Caillaux was tried in July, 1914, on the edge of the abyss, within touching distance of the First World War. In his closing speech for his client, Maître Labori said: "Let us keep our anger for our enemies outside our gates. Let us leave here all determined to march as one against the common danger."

It was a phoney piece of pleading, but it had its undertones—though they were undertones Maître Labori may not have intended.

As a consequence of the shooting Caillaux left the Government; he came back again later, buoyant as a cork; but he was out of office at a time that happened to be vital.

If Mme. Caillaux had not shot the editor of the *Figaro*, if there had not been this compromising trial, the chances are that Caillaux would have been Prime Minister, the dominant force in France during the months of July and August, 1914. And Caillaux was an appeaser before that name had been coined. Ten to one, he would have failed to support

Russia against Germany. Ten to one, he would have disregarded the Entente with England. Ten to one, he would have kow-towed to the Kaiser.

And then? For you and me and all of us—what then?

Perhaps, despite her defects of temperament, there is something to be said for Mme. Caillaux after all.

Sir Roger Casement

THE prisoner's counsel was in considerable distress. That had been growing more apparent now for several minutes. His speech to the jury had lost its fire and even its direction.

The eloquent Irishman was stumbling over words, often repeating himself, getting lost hopelessly in the middle of a sentence.

His voice, normally vibrant, sounded flat and lifeless; his face, entirely drained of any colour, stood out white as chalk in contrast with his full black beard; his brow glistened with beads of sweat that were not caused by heat.

From the bench, the Lord Chief Justice watched him anxiously. No judge has ever been more considerate than Lord Reading, nor better acquainted—through his own great career as Rufus Isaacs—with the harassments and burdens of the Bar.

"Do you think Serjeant Sullivan is well enough to continue?" he whispered to Mr. Justice Avory, sitting at his side.

Seconds later, Serjeant Sullivan himself supplied the answer. He stopped speaking altogether, swayed from side to side, and pressed his fingertips hard against his temples.

"My lord, I have completely broken down," he said.

"Then, of course," said Lord Reading instantly, "we will adjourn until tomorrow."

Serjeant Sullivan dropped back into his seat and rested his head upon his outstretched arms. He knew in his heart that he would not be there tomorrow; that his junior would have to carry on as best he could; that utter and absolute exhaustion had stricken his faculties as with paralysis.

Painful, but not inexplicable or surprising. Great strain always devolves upon an advocate whose duty it is to defend a long capital case. But greater strain than usual developed upon the advocate whose duty it was to defend Sir Roger Casement.

At the time of his trial for high treason, Casement—Irish-born and black-bearded like his counsel—was closely approaching fifty-three. His public record made him appear the unlikeliest of traitors.

As a young man, he had joined the British Consular service in which he carved out a brilliant, even spectacular, career. In 1905 he had been created C.M.G. In 1911 he had been knighted.

In 1913, when he retired on grounds of health, he had joined that small band of pensioned officials who are both sustained and honoured by a grateful England.

Nevertheless—and notwithstanding outward professions of reciprocal gratitude and loyalty—the dominant mood that Casement took with him into retirement was a passionate and overwhelming hatred of the English.

It matters little now from what sources this hatred had sprung: slights fancied or actual, office feuds, disparagement of his qualities. All that matters is—all that ever mattered was—the existence of such hatred; for in this emotion the real roots of his conduct can be found.

Hatred of the English made him a militant Irish separatist. Hatred of the English made him a Germanophile. And it was still basically hatred of the English, not concern for the interests of the Germans *or* the Irish, that made him, during the 1914–18 war, enter Germany in secret and try to seduce captured Irish troops from their allegiance.

With German approval and support, he visited their prison camp, urging them to form themselves into an "Irish Brigade" designed to fight against, instead of on behalf of, England.

His solicitations fell almost entirely on deaf ears. The idea of an "Irish Brigade" was quietly dropped. Other plans, however, apparently went forward, and during the night of 20 April, 1916, Casement landed from a U-boat on the Kerry coast with two companions and an attendant vessel full of guns.

He was seized within hours, and the guns never reached the hands for which they were intended. But on 23 April, exactly three days later, the bloody and terrible Easter Rising detonated in Dublin.

Few in England failed to mark the coincidence of dates; and that, perhaps more than any other single factor, accounts for the exceptional public fury focused upon Casement during the nine weeks which he spent in the Tower of London and at Brixton Prison waiting to be tried.

The Crown, though, did not subsequently seek to prove any connexion between Casement and the Rising. "Whether he conceived of the innocent blood which was so soon to flow," said the Attorney-General (Sir F. E. Smith), "I cannot tell you, for I do not know."

F. E. prudently concentrated his fire on Casement's addresses to the prisoners of war, and as some of these men had been exchanged and were available as witnesses, his position in that respect was virtually secure.

Prejudice rampant, facts unanswerable. With an appeal to reason or to feeling equally unpropitious, what was the wisest course for the hard-pressed defence?

There were three possible alternatives.

Either Casement could stand trial unrepresented, make no attempt at a legal answer to the charge, and deliver instead a political oration aimed at exciting world-wide sympathy for Ireland. That is what Casement himself wanted to do. But it would have meant letting the trial go by default.

Or they could try to get a verdict of guilty but insane. That is what the prosecution wanted them to do. With an apprehensive eye upon opinion in the land of our potential ally, the United States, the English authorities would have looked with favour on that plea. But, save that Casement was a practising homosexual (as disclosed by his own diaries in the Crown's possession), nothing indicated abnormality of mind.

Or they could rely upon a technical point of law, and contend that, upon a proper construction of the statute, treason cannot be committed outside the King's realm. That is what Serjeant Sullivan wanted to do —and as, in his mature professional judgment as defender, that alone offered any chance of complete immunity, it was ultimately agreed that he should do it.

So when, after many hours of strenuous argument, the Lord Chief Justice and his colleagues ruled against him on that issue, Sullivan had seen his last faint hopes depart.

Manfully, though, he had struggled on, like the courageous and conscientious advocate he was. Facing now, not the judges, but the jury, he painted a picture of divided and unhappy Ireland as an explanatory background to his client's acts.

The Ulstermen "illegally arming and drilling" (this with a side-long glance at the Attorney-General, who had been one of Ulster's most aggressive champions); their open challenge to the King and Commons; the fear of southern Irishmen that police and army might prove inadequate for their protection and support.

"During the war," Serjeant Sullivan was asserting, "more arms were coming in to Ulster; and——"

"Where is the evidence of that?" Lord Reading's beautiful voice was quiet but compelling. "I felt so anxious not to intervene while you were making your speech, but you are dealing with matters which have not been stated in evidence."

Sergeant Sullivan reflected, and then bowed.

"My Lord," he said, "if I have been carried away too far, I am exceedingly sorry."

The intervention was justified and courteous, the acknowledgement dignified and handsome. In another case, at another time, the incident would have been trivial; something hardly noticed and immediately forgotten.

But in this case, at this time, its effect on Serjeant Sullivan was out of all proportion to its own importance. It destroyed his mental poise, sapped his last reserves of nervous strength, and with frightening rapidity led to his physical collapse.

Serjeant Sullivan's compulsory withdrawal did not inflict any injury on Casement. His conviction had by then become a certainty. That conviction, moreover, was unquestionably right: so was the decision to refuse him a reprieve. Whether the latter was expedient is another question.

On the morning of Casement's execution, a leading English journal expressed profound regret that ministerial clemency had not been exercised. "Of a man discredited otherwise before the world," it wrote, "they have made a martyr to live long in the traditions of Irishmen."

So Casement has done. And so Casement will.

Horatio Bottomley

THE gift of the gab—that is the English name for it, and we put on a meaning smile whenever we hear the phrase. Not to be fooled, our smile says; we aren't anyone's suckers; no good trying a lot of empty words on *us*.

And yet there is no country in the world where the gift of the gab can exercise more devastating power than in supposedly phlegmatic and unimpressionable England. For proof, I would cite the case of Horatio Bottomley.

Bottomley was the gift of the gab incarnate and personified; there has been nobody quite like him this century. Charming a bird off a tree? He would have found it child's play.

He could charm a bunch of lifelong pacifists into a fierce mob loudly clamouring for uniforms and guns. He could charm a hard-boiled London Special Jury into giving a verdict rooted in emotion, not in facts. He could charm a gathering of cheated shareholders into applauding and finding fresh money for the cheat.

Not only could, but did.

Bottomley spurned none of the material prizes brought within reach by this exceptional gift. In the years immediately following the Armistice, when his career as a public figure reached its height, these prizes constituted a glittering array.

A Riviera villa, a string of race-horses, a yearly champagne bill large enough for a hotel, reflected Bottomley's personal profit out of his promotions.

A widely discussed periodical, *John Bull*, reflected his conquest of the ordinary mind, and served as a valuable vehicle to carry its proprietor's words beyond the scope of even his stentorian voice.

A seat in Parliament—as an Independent for South Hackney— reflected an accession of political prestige.

This enviable position had not been attained, however, without challenges and setbacks on his upward path. In addition to a period as a bankrupt (which did not overwhelmingly affect his living standards) he could already look back on at least two prosecutions respecting some of the companies he launched so readily.

But both prosecutions had ignominiously failed.

Bottomley—a lay lawyer of consummate skill—appeared on each occasion in his own behalf; and, exploiting the latitude always allowed to one who defends in person, he employed his gift of the gab in feats of demagogy aimed at those outside the court as much as at those within. The effect was immense, and after each acquittal Bottomley walked from the shadow of the dock with popularity confirmed and possibly enhanced.

Why therefore should he worry to excess when, in the early part of 1922, he faces criminal proceedings once again?

Objectively, he calculates his assets. He is sixty-two years old and at the summit of his powers. He knows the ropes—both legal and financial—better, far better, than ever he has done. He can draw upon the vast fund of good will he created by his patriotic speeches during the Great War.

They couldn't beat him before. What reason is there to imagine they can beat him now?

So Bottomley—as usual, his own advocate—prepares for battle with jaunty confidence, not sensing that his long run is coming to an end. . . .

The Crown case against him is simple enough in essence: that, having founded a so-called club in connexion with the Government's Victory Loan, he has helped himself freely to that club's subscriptions and turned the money thus abstracted to his private use. Or, in the more technical terms of the indictment, he has committed the offence of fraudulent conversion.

But though simple in essence, in detail it is complex; so intricate are Bottomley's monetary affairs, with a network of companies real and notional, with a chain of bank accounts in this name and that, with cash constantly transferring from one of them to another, that only a steady and penetrating eye can follow the progress of each manipulation.

This gives the cue for Bottomley's tactics before the magistrate. He cross-examines, not to make things clear, but to make them more obscure. He cracks jokes in the hope of distracting attention—jokes at which his trained supporters laugh uproariously. He frequently interrupts Travers Humphreys, prosecuting, especially when a point is being made that cannot be misunderstood or re-interpreted.

"Rubbish," he cries emphatically, as Humphreys contends that part of £5,000 withdrawn from the club's account was wanted for the upkeep of his horses at Ostend.

"Don't interrupt, please," says the magistrate.

"But it is too absurd. It is utter nonsense."

Travers Humphreys—who is going to see this case through to its end in the Court of Criminal Appeal, and who is later to become an outstanding King's Bench judge—does not intend to get involved in mere recrimination.

"I say Mr. Bottomley wanted that money," he goes on conversationally, "for the purpose of keeping up his horses at Ostend because I have that *under Mr. Bottomley's own hand. . . .*"

Indeed he had; in the shape of a declaration necessary—under the old Defence of the Realm Act—before money could be despatched abroad.

The production of this document came as a blow to Bottomley, but there were many others also that Humphreys held in store. Industriously, meticulously, and above all lucidly, he traced money in batches from the coffers of the club to Bottomley's companies, to Bottomley's wine-merchant, to the account of one of Bottomley's lady friends.

These facts could not be screened by clouds of dust. They were proof against the wittiest of jokes. Only one hope remained; and when in due course Bottomley addressed the jury at his trial, he pulled out every stop and let them have it undiluted—not reasoning, not argument, but just the gift of the gab.

"You have got to find," he said, his massive shoulders heaving, "that I had the intention to steal the money of poor devils, such as ex-soldiers, who subscribed to the club." A glance to see how that's going down, and then a rising note: eyes blazing, fist pounding, chest and chin thrust out.

"You have got to find that Horatio Bottomley, editor of *John Bull*, Member of Parliament, the man who wrote and spoke throughout the war"—he won't let them forget that—"with the sole object of inspiring the troops and keeping up the morale of the country"—and now something still more important that they must remember—"who went out *to the Front* to do his best to cheer the lads; you have got to find that that man intended to steal their money."

Dramatically his voice broke. "God forbid!" he murmured huskily. "God forbid!"

At the close of this speech, at least one person wept without restraint. Horatio Bottomley himself.

For others, the gift of the gab seemed to have lost its magic. The jury took only half an hour to find him guilty. The judge—with an acid comment on his "callous effrontery"—took a great deal less to send him down for seven years.

Bottomley flushed from nervous agony and shock. But, at this moment of crisis, the gift did not entirely let him down.

"I was under the impression," he said, "that it is put to an accused person 'Have you anything to say before sentence is passed.'"

"It is not customary," said the judge, "in the case of a misdemeanour like fraudulent conversion."

"Had it been so, my Lord," Bottomley replied. "I would have had something rather offensive to say about your summing-up."

It was the last flicker, the last gift of the gab. The rest of Bottomley's story is one of a dismissed appeal, the purgatory of prison, and an emergence to penury that lasted until death.

The moral is too obvious to formulate in words. I only wonder what the moral would have been had Bottomley died glorious in 1921.

Alfred Dreyfus

AMONG those men and women who have been martyrized by tribunals officially constituted and legally composed, Captain Alfred Dreyfus still holds primacy of place.

The charge of treason launched, in October, 1894, by the French War Office against this completely innocent man owed its genesis to several contributory causes: political (the clash of the new Left with the old Right), racial (hatred of foreigners and Jews following a disastrous military defeat), and social (dislike and envy kindled among his colleagues by Dreyfus's cold manner, swift rise, and private means). The roots of evil in the Dreyfus case ran deep, and frequently they intertwined far below the surface.

I am here concerned, though, not with causes but effects; not with the military clique which *alleged* that Dreyfus was a traitor but with the evidence they produced in their attempt to *prove* it; not with the whisperings in the corridor but with the proceedings in the court—for the army officers who purported to try Dreyfus were technically entitled to that dignified description.

There were seven of them. From their platform they gazed down on the thirty-five-year-old prisoner who looked like a pallid phantom of his former self—the Captain Dreyfus who, two months ago, in compliance with an order, waited upon Commandant du Paty at the War Office "for general inspection, *in civilian clothes.*"

Dreyfus had been rather puzzled when du Paty—who was on the staff at General Headquarters, like himself—asked him to take down a letter from dictation ("I have a sore finger," the commandant explained). He had been yet more puzzled by the material dictated to him; it appeared to form a covering note for unspecified information about the French possession Madagascar, troop movements, and guns.

It certainly never dawned on him that the commandant's real object was to acquire a sample of his subordinate's handwriting (especially the way he wrote certain sentences and words) for expert comparison with a document which has since established its niche in history as The

Bordereau—a document of very similar theme and content, procured by a counter-espionage agent from a waste-paper basket at the German Embassy.

Still less did Dreyfus anticipate that, before the ink could dry, du Paty would snatch the sheet of paper from him, and—without at that stage even giving it a glance—arrest him and consign him to the Cherche-Midi jail.

Since then Dreyfus had been kept in a dungeon rather than a cell. He had been allowed neither contact nor communication with his wife. His warders were forbidden to exchange a word with him. For more than a fortnight he was deliberately left in total ignorance of the basis for the charge (when at last du Paty did confront him with The *Bordereau*, Dreyfus flatly and emphatically disowned it).

It is in the very highest degree conjectural when—if ever—he would have been granted the formality of trial had not the newspapers gained an inkling—no more—of the position, and had they not then proceeded, by inflammatory rumours, to ensure that the mass of public opinion would approve the only verdict the War Office would accept.

But French public opinion is acute as well as volatile, and the authorities were disinclined to risk a public parade of their so-called evidence. Only giving the seven judges time to seat themselves, the prosecutor asked for a trial behind closed doors. "There are other interests at stake," he said elliptically, "than those of the defence and prosecution."

Maître Demange, defending Dreyfus, at once rose to protest.

"There can be no threat here to France's security," he argued. "In view of the fact that the solitary document exhibited——"

The president of the court interrupted sharply.

"So long as we remain in open session, you must refrain from any incursion into the domain of the facts."

"I undertake," replied Demange, "not to *reveal* any document. But it is within my rights to lay before you the facts on which you must decide whether a trial *in camera* is necessary or not. In view of the fact that the only document——"

"I will not permit you to proceed," the president shouted angrily.

Demagne stuck gamely to his hopeless task.

"Since an officer's honour has for weeks past been the subject of public discussion——"

The president rose while counsel was still addressing him.

"The court will now retire," he snapped.

When they returned they ruled that the trial should be held *in camera* —as their superiors had bidden them to do.

Now, sitting in isolated splendour, the seven judges could scrutinize the case that had been so jealously guarded from the scrutiny of others. It consisted in part of irrelevant prejudice—such as the prisoner's alleged relationships with women—that was introduced with a flourish and abandoned with a shrug; in part of vague endeavours to supply a motive—such as the prisoner's alleged heavy gambling losses—that depended upon gossip retailed secondhand; in part of conflicting inferences by Commandant du Paty—"His guilt was betrayed through his agitation"; "His self-control was itself proof of his guilt"—which ended by appearing ludicrous and futile even in the eyes of that partisan tribunal.

But all this was kite-flying or mere decoration. In the last resort, the prosecutor based his case solely and wholly on The *Bordereau*. That is in Dreyfus's handwriting, he claimed, and, one by one, the experts on handwriting were called.

Every student of forensic history knows that this is an extremely dangerous type of evidence. A handwriting expert—unquestionably reputable—sealed the conviction of innocent Adolf Beck. A handwriting expert—unquestionably reputable—imposed the stigma of dishonesty on innocent Archer-Shee. A handwriting expert—acknowledged first in his profession—declared that the famous "Parnell" letters, which Richard Pigott later admitted forging, were actually in the handwriting of Charles Stewart Parnell.

So the testimony of such experts, even when they are apparently cocksure and speak in unison, should always be approached with caution and reserve. But those who testified against Dreyfus were not —save in a single instance—apparently cocksure, and their opinions did not coincide.

One merely "thought" that Dreyfus wrote The *Bordereau*. Another "believed" he did, but, under pressure from Demange, conceded that he would not like to condemn a man on the strength of that belief. A third agreed that The *Bordereau* did not, superficially, resemble Dreyfus's writing—so concluded that he had changed his writing in The *Bordereau*.

These views could have been interesting—in a parlour game. As sole evidence in support of a treason charge, they did not even attain inadequacy. Even the indoctrinated judges felt uneasy, and, as they retired again for the second and last time, may have begun to brood on a forbidden word: Acquittal.

It is certainly clear that this possibility was reported to the War Office by its representatives. For while the judges were still deliberating, while Dreyfus still awaited their disposal of his fate, a dossier, sent post-haste by the War Minister himself, was secretly smuggled into the judges' private room.

At least two of the papers that it contained were forgeries. At least one did not refer to Dreyfus, but to someone else. None could be contested, as the dossier's very existence was unknown to the defence.

Without a doubt, this secret dossier tipped the scale. "I read only one of the papers," said the presiding judge years afterwards, "*but that one paper was sufficient to convince me.*"

Whether he read one or other of the forgeries, or the paper concerning someone else, we shall never know. . . .

Thus began the chain of events—colloquially known throughout France as The Affair—which for many years dominated French political life. All else was to come: Degradation; Devil's Island; the emergence of Esterhazy (self-confessed author of The *Bordereau*); Zola's *J'Accuse*; Zola's trial for libel; the resignation of generals; the fall of Cabinets, and finally, in 1906, at the Palais du Justice, the annulment of Dreyfus's conviction in the nation's highest court.

And all sprang from the act of seven men who placed the desires of their service chiefs above the demands of law.

Maud Allan

IF ever a woman suffered injustice through the processes of law, Maud Allan suffered thus—and in an English court. That court not only failed to accord her any protection against a curiously gross and wholly unfounded libel; it also imposed on her, when in the witness-box, an additional and needless strain of its own clumsy compounding. For once, our admirable legal system did not work; not because of flaws in the machine itself, but because of flaws in the human beings called upon to work it.

Maud Allan was a dancer of world-wide repute.

While training as a pianist under the guidance of Busoni, she had conceived a powerful ambition to revive the art of classic dancing by her own example, and had diverted her versatile talent to that sphere with conspicuous and continuous success.

From her debut in the early years of the present century, her career was marked by a string of glittering triumphs achieved on celebrated stages all over the world; in Vienna, in Paris, in London, in St. Petersburg, and in the great cities of remoter continents.

Although the puritanical often disapproved, and attacked alike her dancing and her costumes, Maud Allan's status with those of broader culture could be deduced from Ministerial tributes and from Royal commands.

Perhaps her most applauded dance was The Vision of Salome. This had no connexion with the play by Oscar Wilde, or with the Dance of the Seven Veils included in that play; nevertheless, when the distinguished impressario, J. T. Grein, decided to produce Wilde's play in the spring of 1918 for private performance at a theatre club, it was natural that Maud Allan should be present to his mind as a highly suitable artist to personate Salome—especially as, unlike the majority of dancers, she could bring professional competence to a speaking part.

It was equally natural, Grein being a respected theatre figure and Salome a coveted theatre role, that Maud Allan should accept his invitation.

It was her great misfortune that announcements of this project caught the fanatical eye of Noel Pemberton-Billing.

Billing, an Independent M.P. then thirty-eight years old, had a bee in his bonnet about sexual perversion.

That he detested perverts, and fought their evil influence, is not—except by perverts—to be placed to his discredit. But Billing had been carried away by his own crusade until he had lost all capacity for judgment; he could see a pervert lurking behind every single tree.

In his propaganda sheet, *The Vigilante*, he lashed out irresponsibly at the highest in the land, maintaining that perversion among the governing class was the cause of their errors in the conduct of the war.

Understandably, specific individuals were not named; but, according to *The Vigilante*, the Germans—who deliberately fostered perversion here—possessed a Black Book with 47,000 names, including that of Cabinet Ministers, Privy Councillors, diplomats and members of His Majesty's Household.

A man obsessed with such chimeras reacted violently to the mere name of Oscar Wilde, and still more to the idea of any woman playing Salome. Perversion had now got a foothold in the theatre, had it? Very well; at least it should not escape exposure.

A blistering article adorned *The Vigilante*, which quite clearly implied that Maud Allan, by reason of her part in the forthcoming production, had demonstrated herself an associate of perverts and had lent herself to the propagation of unnatural practices.

So grave and shocking was this imputation that Maud Allan, instead of seeking damages in the civil courts, instituted proceedings for a criminal libel; and Billing, pleading a guarded justification ("I don't allege," he said, "that Maud Allan is *addicted* to these vices, merely that she *panders* to them") handled his own defence when he came up at the Old Bailey for his trial.

His attack on Maud Allan was more offensive than effective.

"Wasn't your Vision of Salome dance," he asked, "forbidden once in Munich?"

"Yes."

"As the result of a campaign for preservation of public morals?"

"There was a petition," said Maud Allan, "by a club of old men."

"Wasn't your performance objected to in Manchester?"

"Yes."

"By the Watch Committee?"

As guardians of decency, provincial Watch Committees have a record too ludicrous for serious citation.

"Yes, it was the Watch Committee that objected."

"You recognize," said Billing, "that persons who object to your performance may be actuated by high motives?"

"Yes," she said, "but that does not apply to you."

Obviously Maud Allan could look after herself. That was as well, for she was certainly not adequately looked after by the judge.

Defendants who appear on their own behalf are normally permitted greater latitude than are counsel, but Mr. Justice Darling gave Billing altogether too much rope.

As the cross-examination wound its tortuous way along, more and more extraneous prejudice was introduced which—while it did not begin to justify the libel—could only be calculated to inflict the maximum pain.

Baulked, though, of any substantial advantage through such trespasses, Billing reverted to his former tack.

"In your Vision of Salome dance, are you not scantily clad?"

"Only by comparison," Maud Allan replied. "I am a pioneer in art, and the same critics who once said that I was scantily clad would now say that I had too much on."

Present-day patrons of spectacular revue may find interest in Maud Allan's description of her garb. "My gown is of black ninon, very heavily embroidered with gold and jewels. My skirt hangs from my waist to my ankles, and I have a bodice of lined chiffon, with jewels that make it very heavy. My back is exposed with the exception of beads, which come across to hold the dress. . . ."

When Maud Allan stepped down, Billing had made virtually no progress towards a justification of his dreadful calumny. But on opening his defence, he altered his objective.

It was no longer even nominally Maud Allan; it was the community of perverts—and those he supposed perverts—which, in his opinion, dominated and corrupted English life.

The witnesses called by him—Billing did not give evidence—utilized the box to deal out slanders indiscriminately.

Public persons were denounced. Private ones were pilloried. London houses were stigmatized as homosexual brothels. One witness purported to reel off some of the names in the Black Book; they appeared to include Mr. Asquith, Lord Haldane, and—Mr. Justice Darling.

And this wicked farce went on, not for a few minutes or for a few hours, but uninterruptedly over the space of several days.

Of course the judge should have stopped it—and, to be fair, he tried. But Billing intentionally created in that court an atmosphere of uproar with which Darling could not cope.

Clever, charming, and not wanting in courage, he lacked the elemental *power* to enforce his will. "It will take more than you to protect these people, my lord," said Billing once, when Darling rebuked a witness for casting the usual slur on some absent individual; and, unhappily, Billing's jibe was not without foundation.

218

One would have dearly loved to have heard him make that challenge to Lord Goddard. . . .

In all this tumult of irrelevant defamation, poor wronged Maud Allan was practically forgotten.

I question whether the jury thought about her much when they retired. In theory they were to determine whether Billing had any right to say what he had said about Maud Allan. In fact, for them, the case had been allowed to take this form: was Billing right to castigate and wage war on perverts?

Answer, Yes; and so Billing was acquitted and enthusiastically mobbed as he drove away.

No doubt it all showed a healthy British attitude to sexual perversion. But it also showed that even British justice can slip up, and it left an innocent and mistreated dancer to find elsewhere her rightful vindication.

Lord Carrington

THE existence of uninhibited scandal sheets abroad—occasionally floodlit by the glare of court proceedings—tends to induce in us a touch of insular smugness. Britain does not have that kind of thing, we say.

But it did. Or as near as makes no matter. Even the smartest modern operators in printed vilification would have little to teach—and, possibly, something to learn from—a 19th-century London publication, *The Queen's Messenger*. . . .

One doubtful virtue may be granted *The Queen's Messenger*—consistency, both in use of means and choice of ends. Its target was eminence, its weapon calumny; under the guise of fearless public spirit it libelled the living and maligned the dead.

The Royal house, the peerage, the Cabinet, public officials—all were welcome grist to that hard-grinding mill.

As years passed, and *The Queen's Messenger* increased rather than diminished in scurrility, nobody appears to have taken drastic countermeasures.

Legal action, admittedly, might have resulted in giving still greater currency to the very defamation for which redress was sought. Personal action, in the old-fashioned form of physical punishment, usually was impracticable as well as inexpedient; the editorial staff cherished their anonymity.

So the victims bore their sufferings in silence, and *The Queen's Messenger* sailed uninterrupted along its fetid course.

Until Lord Carrington struck out on his own.

Lord Carrington, a very young man in 1869, was scion of a consequential family that had been ennobled by the younger Pitt. Their fame and fortune derived from trade and business; they were born, Lady Bracknell would have said, in the purple of commerce instead of rising from the ranks of the aristocracy.

Such circumstances invite, and generally gain, respect. *The Queen's Messenger*, however, seized upon them as a golden chance for its own brand of abuse.

"To take a bargaining bumpkin," it wrote, "with his pedlar's nature, and give to the rogue two coronets in one year is an outrage upon decency. What can possibly be expected of such a stock except a progeny of lackeys? The very souls of such knaves are crushed out of shape by the load of honour laid on them."

The names and references within which this diatribe was set were so thinly disguised and so maliciously distinctive as to leave no doubt whatever whom the writer meant.

The bumpkins, pedlars, knaves, rogues—those were Lord Carrington's forebears. The progeny of lackeys—those included Lord Carrington himself.

His lordship was a man of spirit as well as a man of honour. The precedents of passive acquiescence were ignored.

He made urgent inquiries about this mysterious paper, and gathered, from what he deemed sound sources, that a Mr. Grenville Murray was its guiding force. Next, he contrived to inspect Mr. Murray's photograph. Finally, he ascertained Mr. Murray's habitual haunts.

Leaving the Conservative Club for his home in Albany, one night the latter was accosted by a stranger.

"Are you Mr. Grenville Murray?"

"Yes."

The stranger promptly lashed him with a whip.

"My name is Lord Carrington," he said, contemptuously striding off. "You know where I am to be found."

The sequel was virtually predetermined. Mr. Murray, with an astonished club porter as his witness, laid complaint against Lord Carrington for assault.

The real defence throughout was that of provocation. Although Lord Carrington entered a not guilty plea, its point and purpose were purely tactical—to compel Mr. Murray's presence in the box so that he could be asked upon his oath whether he was responsible for the offending article.

At Marlborough Street, before the committing magistrate, Mr. Murray repeatedly swore that he was not, and that he had no connexion or concern with *The Queen's Messenger*.

Lord Carrington did not lose heart on being committed. Quite the contrary. He turned the interval that followed to account by charging his accuser with wilful perjury (based on his evidence before the magistrate), and succeeded in getting Mr. Murray committed in his turn.

It is therefore a curious and delicate situation when, the charge of assault duly coming on at Sessions, Sir John Coleridge on Lord Carrington's behalf gets up to cross-examine the chief prosecution witness.

Sir John is bland and charming—and subtly adroit. Mr. Murray is less bland, less charming—but subtly adroit too.

"Have you ever written in *The Queen's Messenger*?" Sir John begins —casually, as if this were a routine question in trials for assault; affably, as if this were a chat between old friends.

But Mr. Murray has been carefully primed, and spots his cue. "I am advised," he says, "to decline answering any questions about *The Queen's Messenger*."

A hint of regret—you could hardly put it higher—temporarily clouds Sir John's urbane expression.

"Why do you decline?"

"Because"—with a swift glance at his own counsel—"because they are trying to convict me of perjury—*on stolen evidence*."

Sir John ignores the bait. "On what ground have you been advised not to answer? You have no right to refuse, you know—except on the ground that it would incriminate you."

The judge murmurs his agreement, and Sir John continues. "Do you believe it would expose you to criminal consequences?"

In face of manifest danger, Mr. Murray hedges. "I don't know," he says.

"I am asking you," Sir John persists, with relentless courtesy, "whether you have ever written in *The Queen's Messenger*—and it is your duty to answer *unless it would incriminate you*."

An answer of sorts Mr. Murray certainly gives—but an answer more theatrical than relevant. "I have come to see," he cries, "what a poor man can do against a rich one."

It must be extremely tempting to retort by referring to the "poor man's" address, clubs, and costly advocate. But Sir John will not be deflected.

"It is a very simple question. Do you know *The Queen's Messenger*?"

"I decline to answer."

"Do you *fear* to answer?"

"Unquestionably I do. How can I not fear when there is so much money against me, while I have not a shilling?"

But again Sir John will not be deflected—merely comes back to his point another way.

"After you had admitted your identity, didn't Lord Carrington say to you, 'You have written against my family in your paper'?"

Mr. Murray perceives the risk in a blank denial. There is the porter. "I think he did say something of the kind."

"Did you know what he meant?"

"I had a vague knowledge."

221

"*What* did you think he meant?"

"You wish to get me round to the old ground," Mr. Murray exclaims —with truth. "I stand here as the representative of the Press, and you shall know nothing about it from me."

This brave declaration of high principle does not conceal the fact that Mr. Murray, despite his talent for obstruction, has been manœuvred into a tight corner—and that Sir John, though in the politest style, is crowding him.

"What paper did you understand Lord Carrington to mean when he said '*Your* paper'?"

"How was I to know?"

"I thought you had vague knowledge," Sir John says, artlessly.

Mr. Murray tries to extricate himself with a sea lawyer's cunning. "Vague knowledge is not evidence," he pronounces.

The judge shifts irritably, but Sir John does not want to waste time on profitless rebukes. "Had you any idea what he meant?"

"I decline to answer."

When did Mr. Murray last "decline to answer"? What was then the immediate subject of inquiry?

Yes, of course.

"Did you believe," says Sir John, artless as before, "that it had anything to do with *The Queen's Messenger*?"

"My belief is not evidence either."

The sea lawyer, however, has made his last desperate throw.

"Have you seen *The Queen's Messenger* placarded all over London?"

"Yes."

"Do you read it?"

"Yes."

"Do you like it?" asks Sir John with sardonic polish, and a gale of laughter drowns the witness's reply. . . .

A refusal to answer, especially if skilfully exploited, can speak with more eloquence than a frank confession. The effect of Mr. Murray's appearance in the box was fully understood and acted on by all.

By the jury who, although reluctantly compelled to record Lord Carrington guilty of assault, added a rider that it had been committed "under circumstances of the greatest provocation."

By the judge who, endorsing that opinion, bound him over with a homily containing as much praise as blame.

And, finally, by Mr. Murray himself who, rather than now face his own impending trial, jumped his bail and fled abroad for good.

Libby Holman

IN a play of theatre life, performed before the war in London, a young actress, rising hope of a famous acting clan, but lately married and devoted to her husband, announces her intention of sacrificing her career for domestic joys.

"After all," she tells the glittering cast who constitute her kinsfolk, "you can't deny it, a woman's place is in the home."

The veteran star, her grandmother, rises wrathfully. "An *actress's* place," she declares, "is on the stage."

To this very day I can hear the dominating tone in which the leading lady delivered that retort. It was imbued not only with technique but with conviction. It proclaimed the born actress's unswerving devotion to her craft; a devotion unaffected by the measure of her gifts.

In vain do such women occasionally protest that they do not differ from the vast majority of professionals; that acting is to them merely a means of livelihood, a bread-and-butter job like dressmaking or typing, to be forsaken any time without a second thought for an agreeable husband and a comfortable home.

They deceive us—or themselves.

Their place is on the stage. The born actress who defies the strongest compulsion of her nature does so at her own peril—and at that of others.

Never was this more curiously or more painfully exemplified than in the tragical events that engulfed Libby Holman. . . .

On Broadway, arena of her greatest triumphs, the name of Libby Holman still evokes a certain magic. In 1931, when young Smith Reynolds, heir to a tobacco fortune, was following her about from place to place proposing marriage, Libby occupied a niche all of her own among the favoured entertainers of New York.

The husky voice, the tall and slender figure, the raven hair that crowned a live and lovely face—all these had contributed to her rapid rise as a vocalist both chic and popular. But the secret of her special fascination lay elsewhere. Within the circumscribed limits of her talent and upon the unpretentious plane of torch songs and of blues, Libby Holman was a born actress in the sense described; she conveyed delight, as she experienced fulfilment, because on the stage she was—strictly—in her element.

Her shrewder friends can hardly have been without misgivings when she stepped out of that element to become Smith Reynolds's wife, and the star of Broadway was transformed into the chatelaine of his luxurious but remote North Carolina home.

Libby herself did not share these misgivings. She was in love with

223

Reynolds: she had confidence in her ability to adapt herself; she meant to make a success of the new life as she had done of the old. And if that old life could not be put quite out of mind, and if its drawing power could not be put quite out of action, at least she would never let these things become apparent; at least they should never cause disharmony or distress.

Though the odds were heavy, she might have succeeded in her aim had Smith Reynolds been less sensitive.

He, not Libby, was the one who suffered torture through gnawing fears that he could not compensate her for everything that, at his persuasion, she had given up. He acquired an almost morbid feeling of responsibility for depriving her of the limelight and the crowds and the applause. He was acutely conscious, too, of his immaturity—twenty, compared with Libby's twenty-six—and also, perhaps, aware that, sexual chemistry apart, nothing bores young women so much as younger men. These obsessions blinded him to the reassuring truth. "He was so worried about my happiness," said Libby afterwards, "and I *was* happy all the time."

Happy—when Reynolds's neurotic bent allowed. For at times in his wretchedness he threatened suicide, and lent his threats point by flourishing a gun. Libby's reaction was invariable. "I pushed the gun away and put my arms around him, so that if it went off the bullet would go through me."

But neither her real love for him—nor his real love for her—could abate the tension these repeated scenes created. For several months they kept it secret to themselves. Then suddenly it exploded with such dramatic violence that their private affairs were laid bare to the world.

That *dénouement* was reserved for a house-party they gathered to celebrate Independence Day in 1932.

This house-party brought Libby Holman echoes from the past. Her former manager came down from New York; so did an actress looking round for a new play. Theatre gossip was exchanged; the latest productions were discussed; scripts were read aloud and their qualities debated. That Libby eagerly joined in there is no doubt. That her harmless pleasure pained her husband there is no doubt either. More than ever—although, quickly responsive to his mood, she went out of her way to show him tenderest attention—he pictured himself with pathological despair as the sole obstacle to Libby's happiness.

While the host silently brooded, the party ran its course. Nothing interrupted the festivities: eating, drinking, canoeing on the lake. Only late in the second evening, when most of the guests had gone, Reynolds spoke strangely to a friend who had stayed on. "I'm going to end it all," he said. "Good night, Ab. I shan't be coming back." Ab, watching him go up to his room where his wife already was, may well have thought it a pointless sort of joke.

Shortly afterwards, the crack of a shot aroused the household. Smith

Reynolds lay dying, with a bullet wound in his head and a pistol close at hand, on the sleeping porch abutting on his room. Near by, Libby lay prostrate and half conscious. . . .

"The first thing I knew after," she told them at the inquest, when at last she had recovered sufficiently to appear in court, "was waking up in a room I didn't know. I found that it was a nursing home, and that two whole days had passed."

Her shoulders were bowed with grief and her eyes swollen with weeping.

"Tell me anything you know," said the coroner, "about the events that led up to the shot being fired."

"I know nothing," Libby Holman said. "I remember nothing after going up at eleven o'clock to bed. Nothing except the flash—that one memory of the flash—that is the only thing."

"Tell us, then of the flash."

"The one picture I have in my mind," Libby went on, "is of Smith standing on the sleeping porch. First he called my name, and then there was this flash—and then that crash of the universe like everything falling around me. And that feeling of his head in my arms, and the warm blood."

The torch singer of Broadway sobbed now in real earnest—sobbed in that low and throaty voice that had won her such renown.

The coroner's jury brought in an open verdict—death from a bullet wound "inflicted by a person or persons unknown"—which seemed unsatisfactorily vague in view of the evidence given by Libby and Reynolds's friend, Ab. But it was a miracle of wisdom when compared with the subsequent proceedings of the local Grand Jury, which—without the faintest justification or excuse—*returned true bills against both Libby and Ab for murder*. For more than three months this most terrible of charges—hardly less so for being utterly unfounded—hung like the shadow of doom over their heads, until the prosecution shamefacedly dropped it "because the evidence we have would lead to an acquittal."

It was a year, almost to the day, since Smith had taken Libby as his bride.

Libby Holman and Smith Reynolds: who can be so hard as not to sympathize with both? Disaster fell in differing degree upon each for no greater sin than the sin against the maxim he knew far too well and she not well enough; the peremptory and uncompromising maxim that an actress's place is on the stage.

Mr. Pigott

FEW forget that Parnell came to ruin through a woman. Few remember, though, after this interval of time, that ruin had stared him in the face before—that he had come within an ace of it as victim of a fraud.

Yet it is the forgotten episode that inspires; the remembered one that sickens and depresses. There is little pleasure or pride to be derived from the spectacle of a man rushing upon destruction; there is much to be derived from the spectacle of a man being saved from destruction by the exertions of another.

And if ever advocate performed such a service for a client, that advocate was Charles Russell and that client Parnell.

It was 1889. The entire British political—and, indeed, social—scene had been dominated for years by the fight for Irish Home Rule. In Ireland itself, that fight was waged with clubs and knives and guns; violent outrage on the one side, ruthless repression on the other.

But Parnell, as leader of the Irish Party in the English House of Commons, officially discountenanced the use of force for an end that they avowedly sought through parliamentary means. When two leading representatives of the British Government had been assassinated in Dublin's Phoenix Park, Parnell had publicly expressed himself as horrified, and had utterly repudiated the doers and the deed.

It could only mean disaster for Parnell and his party if this attitude were proved to be a hypocritical pose. Such an allegation was presently forthcoming—from no less influential a quarter than *The Times*.

That day the eyes of its readers must have popped out of their heads. Long accustomed to closely printed columns unbroken even by a single photograph, they were now confronted with the facsimile of a letter, spread sensationally across a central page.

Beginning "Dear Sir," and signed "Chas. S. Parnell," dated a fortnight after the Phœnix Park assassinations, it sought to excuse Parnell's denunciation of them; pleaded that "to do that promptly was plainly our best policy"; and indicated that, in the writer's view, one of the murdered men at least "got no more than his deserts."

From whom *The Times* had obtained the letter was not then disclosed, and a mere copy in print might have met with scepticism; but the sight of the actual handwriting swept away misgivings—especially when the knowledge spread that it appeared authentic to many familiar with Parnell's.

This letter burst upon the country like a bombshell. The person least excited seemed to be Parnell himself. He told Parliament in plain, but rather off-hand, style that the document was forged—then let the matter drop.

He ignored all advice to sue *The Times* for libel, or take any other step towards judicial vindication. Plagued by ill-health, contemptuous of opinion, increasingly absorbed by an adulterous intrigue, he recoiled from such an addition to his load.

But as *The Times* persisted with and amplified its charge, in the end Parnell was driven into action. He asked for a select committee of inquiry; instead the Government appointed a special commission of three judges to determine the issue between him and *The Times*.

Who should represent the Irish leader before this tribunal?

The ideal choice could hardly be in doubt. Charles Russell was at once an Irish patriot, a supporter of Home Rule, and—beyond dissent or contradiction—premier advocate of the English Bar. Parnell wanted Russell for his counsel. Russell wanted to be counsel for Parnell.

Russell, though, held a general retainer for *The Times*, which was valuable in terms of both money and prestige. He returned it now without a moment's hesitation.

"I am satisfied," wrote *The Times*'s solicitor, not without a trace of anxiety, in response, "that you would not desire to return it in order to be at liberty to represent persons whose interests may be antagonistic to the paper."

Russell did not conceal his indignation at this hint. "I do desire," he wrote back, "to represent 'persons whose interests may be antagonistic to the paper.' In other words, I desire to appear for Mr. Parnell on the Commission, as I conceive I have a right to do."

In that sharp interchange Parnell's triumph was foreshadowed.

The Commission duly sat. They required to know from whom *The Times* obtained the crucial letter. From a Mr. Houston (an Irishman hostile to Parnell). And Mr. Houston had obtained it from . . .? A Mr. Pigott. Mr. Pigott would be called, and would explain the circumstances.

Mr. Pigott was called. Mr. Pigott explained the circumstances. He had bought the letter from an ally of Parnell who had been induced to betray him by a bribe.

So far, so good, for the anti-Parnellites. As Russell rises to cross-examine Pigott—whom he suspects to be the forger, if forgery there be—he has got just one small clue to work upon, and that is a clue that might easily prove false. A word in the letter had been curiously misspelt—"*hesitency*" instead of "*hesitancy*."

It would be easy, of course, to ask Pigott to write the word in court and hope that this mistake would be repeated. But a shrewd witness is unlikely to suppose that counsel's choice of word is entirely accidental; he will carefully examine it for pitfalls; and though he may misspell it when he writes in haste, he may well correct the blunder when placed upon his guard.

How can his attention legitimately be diverted?

"Mr. Pigott," Russell says. "Would you be good enough to write some words on that sheet of paper for me?"

The sheet of paper is handed over, and pen and ink supplied.

"Will you write the word 'livelihood'?"

It is done.

"Just leave a space now. Then will you write the word 'likelihood'?"

It is done.

"Will you write your own name?"

It is done.

"Will you write the word 'proselytism' . . . Done that? And finally, will you write 'Patrick Egan' and 'P. Egan'? *'Patrick Egan' and 'P. Egan'?*"

Russell speaks these last words with tremendous emphasis, as if something of great importance hinged upon them. Then, as Pigott was about to hand the paper back, he added carelessly: "Oh, yes, there is one word I had forgotten. Lower down please, *leaving spaces'*—he paused—"*leaving spaces*, write the word 'hesitancy'."

And then, in a most significant tone: "With a small 'h', Mr. Pigott: with a small 'h'."

Pigott's mind was now so full of Patrick Egan and P. Egan, and so puzzled by the importance attached to leaving spaces, and so watchful for some danger involved in the small 'h', that he proceeded to write the key word without realizing that the catch lay in the spelling. So there it came—'hesitency' once again, and from that moment Russell held him in the hollow of his hand.

Parnell, though, had only a year or so to bask in the newly won affection of the English public, who always take to their hearts a man traduced. His affair with Mrs. O'Shea soon reached an explosive climax, and this time he could seek in vain an instrument of rescue.

Great counsel may expose cheats and smash conspiracies, but they are powerless to aid those who, in the grip of sexual passion, cheat their own judgment and conspire against themselves.

Miss Savidge

IN 1928 there stood at stake a reputation greater than that of any individual. Deep concern arose about the methods being employed by those most essential public guardians—the police.

It began in the most unlikely fashion one fine April evening when a highly respectable lady and a highly respectable gentleman, having dined together at a restaurant in Town, strolled into the leafy darkness of Hyde Park and presently seated themselves upon adjacent chairs.

He was Sir Leo Money, a distinguished economist and formerly a prominent M.P. She was a Miss Savidge.

They had been gossiping thus for a few minutes when, to their utter astonishment and horror, two plain clothes policemen bore roughly down on them and levelled an accusation of indecency. Indignant protests and denials proved of no avail, and later, at the police station, formal charges were preferred.

The prosecution treated it as just another Hyde Park case. But, in court, matters did not work out quite as they intended. After hearing Sir Leo, without so much as calling on Miss Savidge the magistrate dismissed the charges against both, said they should never have been brought, and—to cap it all—awarded costs against the police.

He added a blistering comment, too, on the conduct of the officers, who had not only omitted to get the name and address of a potential witness, but had actually prevented Sir Leo from so doing.

Police cases do occasionally collapse, but seldom in such manifest ruin, or—because of Sir Leo's fame—with such publicity.

The shadow of a perjury trial lay over the officers; in the Home Secretary's view, proceedings against them were "quite likely"; and Chief Inspector Collins, one of the most experienced men at Scotland Yard, was instructed to investigate on behalf of the Director of Public Prosecutions.

His investigation took a questionable form. . . .

One lunch hour, quite unexpectedly, an impressive car containing three policemen and a policewoman, drew up conspicuously at Miss Savidge's place of work. Miss Savidge was "invited" to attend at Scotland Yard, where Inspector Collins awaited her arrival.

At the Yard, the policewoman promptly vanished, and for several hours Miss Savidge was closeted alone with Inspector Collins and a sergeant. She finally signed a "statement", and at eight o'clock that night she was driven home and retired, exhausted, to her bed.

Such things may sometimes pass unremarked even in England, but less easily if the victim has influential friends. Questions were soon being asked in the House of Commons; a passionate debate took place on the adjournment: the Home Secretary found himself assailed from every side.

In the result, a special tribunal was set up—one Conservative M.P. (Mr. Withers) and one Socialist M.P. (Mr. Lees-Smith), presided over by a retired judge (Lord Justice Bankes)—in order to investigate the investigators.

Abuse of the power which is entrusted to the police constitutes the gravest possible threat to civil freedom. Consciousness of that fact pervaded the whole country, and the interest aroused by the tribunal's sessions was not solely due to Miss Savidge's isolated case.

Seeking nothing whatsoever for herself, she had now become—as her counsel, Sir Patrick Hastings, said—a pawn. The question was not a private but a public one—the relations between the police and those they are supposed to serve. If the police could justify their behaviour, well and good; if they could not, fresh safeguards must be sought.

When Sir Patrick got up to cross-examine Inspector Collins, many besides the witness were virtually on trial.

"Did the police car arrive without the slightest notice?"

"Yes."

"Without the slightest indication to Miss Savidge's parents or any of her friends?"

"Yes."

"Was it intended to get that girl to Scotland Yard, if it could possibly be done?"

The police have no right to exert compulsion on a harmless citizen, which Collins knew as well as anyone.

"If she were willing," he answered cautiously.

"*If possible?*"

It is one thing to be high-handed in your office with a frightened girl; it is another in open court with one of the most commanding counsel in the land.

"Very well, sir, yes," Inspector Collins said.

"Why was the policewoman sent?"

"To accompany Miss Savidge."

"Why should there be a policewoman in the car where no questions were asked, and none at Scotland Yard where questions were asked?"

"She was to accompany Miss Savidge," Collins repeated woodenly.

"Was she there," Sir Patrick asked, "to assuage any terrors that this girl might have?"

Collins racked his brains for any other plausible explanation.

"Was that why she was there?"

"I don't know, I'm sure."

Had Miss Savidge then been tricked into going to Scotland Yard by the employment of shock tactics and the use of a decoy? And if such were the preliminaries, what of the interview itself?

Sir Patrick picked up her statement—that statement which so much effort had been expended to obtain.

"According to this, when she described how she was sitting in the Park, she used the expression, 'I was *inclining* towards Sir Leo'?"

"Yes."

"You know Miss Savidge says you put those words into her mouth?"

"I know, but I deny it."

"It would be remarkable, wouldn't it—and it would be very helpful to the two officers whose conduct is in question—if it turned out that Miss Savidge, *of her own accord*, used the exact words they used before the magistrate?"

Collins did not reply.

230

"Do you know that they both used that term—'She was *inclining* towards him'?"

The coincidence seemed startling, to say the least of it. Collins attempted to cover himself—and slipped.

"I didn't refer to the shorthand note of the hearing before the magistrate."

"Oh." Sir Patrick pounced with the speed of lightning. "So you *had* that shorthand note when Miss Savidge made her statement?"

"Yes, but did not refer to it," Inspector Collins insisted.

It was too late, though, to pick up the broken pieces. And Sir Patrick had already begun to hammer at something else.

"Why did you ask for the name and address of Miss Savidge's young man?"

"It's necessary to get every detail that you can."

"What did you want with the young man? To bully him in the same way?"

Collins, already fighting a losing battle, was stung into a most significant answer.

"This was an inquiry into a suspected crime by two police officers," he retorted, "and we were entitled to make inquiries to *disprove* that charge."

Of course, if, instead of an impartial investigation, a campaign had been initiated to extricate these officers, the treatment of Miss Savidge fits neatly into place. . . .

Eventually the tribunal produced two distinct reports. The majority —the ex-judge and the Conservative M.P.—half-heartedly whitewashed the police on the grounds that they had followed "established practice" —but added that "established practice" did not commend itself. This report also recommended that statements should be taken when possible at a person's home; and that when a woman made a statement, and it touched upon her morals, another woman should invariably be present.

The Labour M.P.'s minority report was more courageous, and more in accordance with the evidence. He found that Miss Savidge had been misled about the nature of the inquiry, that she had been asked questions that ought not to have been asked, and that some of her answers had been misrepresented. He discerned "a great peril to private citizens", and squarely laid the principal blame upon Inspector Collins.

None the less, profound relief must have been felt among those primarily affected at the Yard. The majority report excluded drastic measures; no criminal prosecutions, no dismissals. But the Savidge Inquiry did not fail of its purpose. It contributed in substantial measure to those higher standards that have generally prevailed since among the London police.

Fay Marbe

I T was not being an enjoyable dress-rehearsal for Fay Marbe. A damper had descended on her spirits just as she felt within reach of achieving the ambition that had tempted her to England.

As a musical comedy artist in the United States she could command impressive rates of pay. She had no need to search abroad for work in leading parts. But she greatly hankered after a triumph in London— partly for its own sweet sake, partly because it would still further add to her vogue at home.

She had come over to inspect the prospects on the spot, and earned £150 a week in cabaret while she looked around for the right opening on the stage.

That opening seemed to have materialized when Mr. Jimmy White, the boss of Daly's Theatre, invited her to join his production of *Yvonne*.

Yvonne was already running, but not prosperously enough, despite the personal success of its feminine star, Ivy Tresmand, an *ingénue* as delicious and engaging as ever turned the heads of theatre-going males. (I can speak with feeling, for at this time—1926—I myself was madly in love with Miss Tresmand from afar.)

Mr. White proposed to lend fresh strength to *Yvonne* by having one of the minor female roles rewritten and enlarged, endowed with additional numbers, and enacted by Fay Marbe. The salary of one hundred pounds a week he offered was low compared with her American rewards, but Miss Marbe had felt attracted by the opportunity of distinguishing herself on Daly's famous boards.

With this enticing vision uppermost in her mind, she had worked arduously at numerous rehearsals. The whole company had attended these—except the leading lady, who, maybe for some good reason, did not appear.

It was only now, on the very eve of the new version's first night, that Miss Tresmand came upon the scene and met Miss Marbe face to face. And this encounter was the reason for Miss Marbe's dampened spirits. She formed the impression that Miss Tresmand resented her presence in *Yvonne*, and that she was treating her with studied and cold hostility.

Actresses, seldom the most equable of creatures, are often hyper-sensitive at times of acute stress. For all one knows, Miss Tresmand may have formed the impression that Miss Marbe was resentful of, and hostile towards, her—and both ladies may have been equally mistaken.

But when, as soon as the dress rehearsal ended, the Daly's management curtly told Miss Marbe she would not be in the cast either next night or at all, that unhappy artist inevitably regarded this bombshell as a final confirmation of her judgment.

She did not believe for a moment that their decision was unprompted, or that it reflected genuine disappointment with her work. She believed that Miss Tresmand, exerting her considerable power as reigning queen of Daly's, had successfully brought pressure on the management to remove a potential, if temporary, rival for the throne.

Whatever the true cause behind the exclusion of Fay Marbe, the consequences for Daly's Theatre were expensive. As she had been engaged for the London run, and as *Yvonne* contrived to acquire a new lease of life, they were legally bound to send her each week a cheque for a hundred pounds; while she, idle against her wish, brooded over what she felt to be a gross injustice.

Almost certainly, though, she would never have sought redress at law —being unaware that she might have a right to it—for her loss in prestige through deprivation of the part; but Daly's management ultimately overreached themselves.

Tiring of expenditure without equivalent service, and forming a company to take *Yvonne* on tour, they asked Miss Marbe to join it and play the selfsame part—at the same time intimating that, if she refused, the payment of her salary would be forthwith terminated.

Now the *cachet* which the West End bestows upon a player is unobtainable elsewhere in the English theatre. You may be the darling of the reps., the pride of the provinces, the idol of the intellectual groups. But the test of your status is the record of the leading roles you have sustained on stages within a mile of Shaftesbury Avenue.

To ask an actress to go into the provinces after taking her out of the London production for which she had been engaged was indeed heaping insult upon injury. Miss Marbe had no intention of going into the provinces. Instead she consulted lawyers, and that brought things to a head.

Daly's found themselves facing an action in which damages were claimed not only in respect of salary unpaid, but also in respect of injury to reputation and lost publicity.

Any individual challenging a company feels deeply anxious during the weeks awaiting trial. Fay Marbe's anxieties were greatly aggravated through the bullying tactics employed by her opponents.

They wrote asserting that she had deceived them about her profesional prominence in the United States—an assertion they were subsequently driven to withdraw, with the result that Fay Marbe got a hundred pounds for libel. They tried to obtain security for costs, in the hope that she couldn't raise the money for a fight; Fay Marbe countered by retaining Patrick Hastings, one of the most expensive counsel of the day. Meanest of all, they resisted her unanswerable claim for arrears of salary until a day or two before the trial itself, and then paid the total into court with a brazenly belated admission of liability.

Everything considered, it gives no cause for surprise that, by the time the case came up for hearing, Fay Marbe was nourishing a grievance that had become almost insupportable.

White-faced and tense, she heard Sir Patrick say that it was not enough to pay her salary ("People would think they *had* to pay her, good, bad, or indifferent"), and anyway the part was more attractive than the cash. White-faced and tense, she took the oath and gave her evidence, insisting that she had been dismissed not, as Daly's pleaded, because she had proved unsuitable for the part, but because Miss Tresmand did not want her in the show.

Her voice shook; the nervous strain of months was rising to a climax. Unintentionally, opposing counsel touched it off.

"Come, Miss Marbe," he said, in propitiatory tones, "you've been paid a hundred pounds a week for the whole thirty-two weeks of the run; £3,200 that is, and you never once appeared."

You never once appeared. That was her tragedy; that was the wrong that they had done her. Fay Marbe flung up her hands and broke into a storm of passionate tears.

"I'm sorry"—counsel was quite perturbed—"if I said anything to hurt you."

"You did say it; you did," she cried. "I was thrown out—thrown out as if I was less than nothing."

The humiliation she had endured assumed monstrous proportions, and minutes passed before she regained composure. Sir Patrick may have recalled his client's distress when it was his turn to question Jimmy White.

"Miss Tresmand was your leading lady?"

"Yes."

"Isn't it usual for the leading lady to greet a newcomer?"

"It's not my business to introduce them," Jimmy White declared. "You want to go and see what they do on the stage. There are several of them having a free fight every night."

"That is between themselves," returned Sir Patrick. "But hasn't Miss Tresmand influence with you?"

"No one could influence me," said Jimmy White. "Not even you, if you were working for me, my dear Sir Patrick."

"My dear Mr. White," said Sir Patrick coldly, "don't be so affectionate."

But, in the last resort, the jury did not have to determine whether Miss Tresmand had exerted influence or not. As Mr. Justice Horridge pointed out, what actuated the Daly's management was immaterial. They faced simpler questions: did Daly's discard Miss Marbe when they had no business to, and, if so, had she suffered loss?

The jury decided that they did and that she had, and awarded her £3,000 for damage to her reputation in not being allowed to act . . .

Fay Marbe may have returned to the United States with a low opinion of our theatre managements. She would, however, have been singularly ungrateful if she returned with a low opinion of our courts.

Handel Booth

"MY lord, I now call Mr. Handel Booth," says counsel, and with every eye intently fixed upon him, that gentleman calmly makes his way towards the box.

Many people thus spot-lighted forthwith become nervous, falter in speech, even seem to shrink in size. Not so, however, Mr. Handel Booth.

He is an active Member of Parliament, used to public speaking; a shrewd man of business, used to tough negotiation; a person of distinction and repute, used to acknowledgment of his merits and acceptance of his word.

True, the present action, in which he is defendant, strikes a somewhat discordant note in this harmonious blend. He, Handel Booth, M.P., is being sued for fraud; and by a German—yes, a German, if you please— in this year of 1917, when we are fighting the Germans for our very lives.

Only one with Gruban's monumental impudence would have dared appear as plaintiff in a British court, there to heap calumny on a pillar of the State; Gruban, who is every bit as German as the rest, even if he did build up an engineering business here which he at once switched over to munitions when war came.

What was it exactly that Gruban had said yesterday, while he was standing on the spot where Handel Booth now stands?

He had told the jury that, as the war grew fiercer, the growth of anti-German feeling caused him some alarm; that Handel Booth agreed to use his influence with Ministers on behalf of Gruban in exchange for a seat on Gruban's board; that presently (professing to quote the Minister of Munitions) Booth declared that, unless the business was transferred to him, Gruban would be deprived of his property and interned; that on Booth's promise to act as a trustee and pay the income on the shares to Gruban's wife, Gruban acquiesced; that, once having got the business into his own hands, Booth repudiated all liability.

Gruban, moreover, was nevertheless interned, and his advocate had had the temerity to suggest—although without any apparent means of proving it—that Booth had deliberately procured his internment.

An ugly tale, of course, but giving no cause for concern. For it is simply Booth's word against Gruban's, is it not? And who is going to believe an enemy alien rather than an elected British tribune?

So confidently and fluently Handel Booth explains. He joined the company on an appeal from Gruban for finance. Gruban was on bad terms with the Ministry of Munitions. There were articles about his nationality in the papers, and protests against a German manufacturing the vital instruments of war. Finally the Ministry wrote to say Gruban must go.

"He came to me in great distress," Handel Booth asserts. "He said: 'You must take over control, or all the money, we have invested will be lost.'"

"Did you break any agreement you made with him?"

"I did not."

"Did you do anything to promote his internment?"

"I did not."

Handel Booth now feels in really splendid fettle. He is conscious of cutting an impressive figure, in sharp contrast to the figure cut by Gruban; his ease against the other's awkwardness, his fine stature against the other's insignificance, his accomplished cadences against the other's guttural tones. Nor does he fear the imminent clash with Gruban's counsel—not a leading K.C., like the chap they've briefed for him, but a junior barrister, only in his middle thirties; well thought of, he'd gathered, and considered promising; but hardly of the necessary weight for Handel Booth. Didn't they say this was the first big case he'd handled on his own?

The M.P. prepares for battle with absolute assurance.

"Mr. Handel Booth." The name is uttered like a challenge—a characteristic that will remain with Patrick Hastings throughout the brilliant years of success that lie ahead. "Mr. Handel Booth, would it be dishonest for the director of a company to seek for himself a secret commission on the company's earnings?"

"Of course."

"When you were a director of Mr. Gruban's company, did you do that very thing?"

"Never."

"Then take a look, will you, at this piece of paper?"

Handel Booth takes a look, and at once goes very pale.

"Where has this come from?" he says.

"From the waste-paper basket of the boardroom of your company." Hastings lets him study it a moment. "That is your writing?"

"Yes."

"Does the figure in that memorandum correspond exactly with the profit that your company had earned?"

"I couldn't say."

"There is your balance sheet. . . . The figures are the same?"

"Yes."

"Do you know of anyone connected with the company possessing the initials F. H. B. except yourself?"

"No."

"Do you see at the foot of that memorandum the expression 'Full 10 per cent to F.H.B.'?"

The witness turns yet paler.

"What does that expression mean?"

In vain does Handel Booth try to argue his way out. He has been well and truly floored by the first blow—and much of his bounce and aggressiveness have gone as Hastings moved in for the main attack.

"Do you remember the sinking of the Lusitania?"

"Yes."

"Was there not a feeling of great revulsion against the Germans?"

"Yes."

"Did you not know that Mr. Gruban wanted the protection of some powerful man?"

"He didn't ask for it."

"Did you tell Mr. Gruban that certain persons high up in the Government were under an obligation to you?"

"Certainly not," Handel Booth replies. "It isn't true."

"I don't suggest it is," says Hastings drily. "But didn't you tell him you had weight with Ministers?"

Handel Booth hesitates. There is no knowing now what might be up this this young man's sleeve.

"Didn't you tell him that?"

"I may have done."

"When the Ministry said that Gruban must resign, they didn't say that if he failed to do so he would be interned?"

"No."

"Did you tell him that they *had* said so?"

"No."

"Look at your Minute Book." Handel Booth obediently looks. He is a shadow of the man we saw a few minutes ago. "Do you see this entry: 'Interviewed a high official and expressed opinion that in view of Mr. Gruban's retirement there was no necessity he should be interned?' . . . Did you write that?"

Another pause. Then, "Yes."

"What did you mean?"

"I don't know."

"Who was the high official?"

"I've forgotten."

"Do you still say," Hastings asks, "that you said nothing to Gruban about his being interned?"

Handel Booth desperately persists in his denial.

"Do you say you wrote no letter to the Ministry of Munitions just before Mr. Gruban was interned?"

"I do."

"Very well." Hastings turns abruptly to the judge. "My lord, I have subpœnaed the Prime Minister and the Home Secretary. They, or their representatives, must attend the court, and state whether such a letter exists, and, if so, whether they object on any ground to its production. Until they so attend, I shall not say another word."

He shuts up like a clam. There is immense excitement and confusion. Then, in some embarrassment, defendant's counsel speaks.

"Perhaps," he says, "this is a copy of the letter that you want."

The silence beats painfully as Hastings reads aloud.

"*From Handel Booth to Ministry of Munitions. It is quite clear to me, as the new Managing Director, that your instructions have been defied over and over again. My colleagues and myself are amazed that such deceit should have been shown towards the Ministry and ourselves . . .*"

To all intents, the case was over. The court buzzed like a hive. Friends pressed forward to shake Gruban by the hand.

But in the witness-box is not elation, but deflation—one more ego pricked by the cross-examiner's lance.

The consequences of this unusual law-suit were far-reaching. It restored, to the extent of £4,750, the shattered fortunes of the luckless Gruban. It virtually removed Handel Booth from public life. It set Patrick Hastings on the enviable path that leads to the most glittering prizes at the Bar.

But above all, transcending the fate of individuals, it furnished an enduring monument to British justice, which accorded fair play to an individual German even at the very peak and crisis of the war.

The Earl of Durham

THE annual dinner of the Gimcrack Club has long been recognized as an opportunity for responsible racing men to speak in critical vein on current Turf affairs. The third Earl of Durham was notably such a man: vigorous and conscientious and intelligent, with a crusading zeal for the integrity of sport. So when he rose at the Gimcrack dinner of 1887 there were general expectations of a serious discourse which would excite widespread interest and comment. These expectations were in no way belied.

Lord Durham took as his theme the corruption of the Turf, and he did not deal with the subject merely in general terms. He made charges, and—save actual names—his charges were specific.

He spoke of "owners who win large stakes when their horses are successful, but do not lose much when they are beaten"; of "a fashionable and aristocratic stable conspicuous throughout the season for the in-and-out running of its horses, which has disgusted the public and

driven the handicapper to his wits' end to discover their true form";
and of "a notorious jockey" known for his "malpractices".

This was indeed a serious discourse, even by Gimcrack standards,
and made more so still by the reaction of many who heard it, or heard
of it. They believed that the owner so attacked was Sir George Chetwynd, Bart., a member and former steward of the Jockey Club; that
the trainer was Sherrard, who had the care of Sir George's horses; and
that the jockey was Wood, who generally rode them.

What steps, if any, Sherrard and Wood might have been disposed
to take one does not know; but clearly Sir George Chetwynd could not
let the matter pass. He asked Lord Durham bluntly if he had meant to
refer to him, and Lord Durham answered equally bluntly that he had.
Whereupon Sir George, whose notions of securing redress were what
some would call romantic and others primitive, promptly challenged
Lord Durham to a duel.

Lord Durham, with less bravura but more authentic bravery,
furnished the stewards of the Jockey Club with a copy of his speech; and
—to ensure finally against misunderstanding—wrote and signed a letter
that accused Sir George by name.

Sir George retorted with a writ. Whether he wished to litigate or not,
he now could do no other.

There is more than one way to defend a suit for defamation. You
may say you never wrote or spoke the words complained of. You may
say they are without any defamatory meaning. Or you may set out to
justify the words, to show that they were true in substance and in fact.

Most of the great dramatic trials for libel or for slander derive their
drama from a justification plea. For in such trials the plaintiff becomes
the real defendant, and the defendant assumes the role of an accuser—
but subject to heavy penalties should his accusation fail.

Sir George Chetwynd's action fell into this class: Lord Durham
accused him of being an accomplice in the pulling of his horses, and a
fascinated public, both in and out of court, treated the proceedings as
his trial on this indictment.

Neither a judge nor a jury featured in that trial. By agreement of the
parties, the issue had been referred to the three stewards of the Jockey
Club, whose everyday clothes, ironically, appeared incongruous in
their novel situation on the Bench. Distinguished members of the Bar,
however, were present in full glory—and it was noted as a sign of Lord
Durham's resolution to fight this battle out to the end that he had
retained as his leading counsel Sir Charles Russell, most famous—and
most ruthless—cross-examiner of the day.

If you have knowledge that a jockey is dishonest (even though he is
England's foremost jockey, as Wood was), if you are an honest owner
you will not employ him. That was to be one of Russell's major propositions, and his first questions sought to show Sir George possessed that
knowledge.

"Do you know a betting man named Walton?"

"Yes."

"Did you hear that Walton had paid large sums to Wood for information about his mounts?"

"No."

It sounds like a definite and straightforward denial. But Russell has an unerring ear for the spurious answer and a peerless power of extracting the genuine one by domination.

"Do you say you never heard that Walton had paid large sums to Wood?"

"Well," Sir George appears to be considering. "I heard something mentioned about a race in which Wood rode."

"*Do you say you never heard that Walton had paid large sums to Wood?*"

There is no catch in it; no forensic sleight of hand. It is personality matched against personality.

"I only heard of one instance," weakly says Sir George.

That is enough; he has retracted, and the floodgates open.

"Do you think that a jockey should receive money for giving information to outsiders about his mounts?"

"It is difficult to answer."

"Difficult? Do you think it is right, sir?"

"Well, no," says Sir George.

"Would you do it yourself?"

"Well, no," says Sir George.

First item of his knowledge about Wood has been established.

"Were you present," Russell asks, "at the trial of an action brought by Wood against a man named Cox?"

"Yes."

"Didn't every witness called for or against Wood describe him as a man of evil reputation?"

"I don't think. . . ."

"Come, sir," says Russell angrily. "They did so, did they not?"

"Yes, they did," weakly says Sir George.

Second item of his knowledge about Wood has been established.

"Some years ago did rumours reach you about the existence of a jockeys' ring?"

"Yes."

"Does that mean those jockeys put their heads together to back one horse and then divide the proceeds?"

"I don't know," says Sir George. "I should like to be informed."

"Give me *your* idea."

The tone forbids evasion.

"*That* would be my idea," Sir George says hastily.

"Who were the jockeys suspected?"

"A great many."

"Was Wood among them?"

"Yes."

Third item of his knowledge about Wood has been established.

Russell now turns to the running of Sir George's horses, especially one named Fullerton. Sir George agreed that in 1887 the horse was "in and out".

"Ten days before the Lincoln, was he priced at 4 to 1?"

"Yes."

"He wasn't placed?"

"No."

"Did you ever ask your jockey for an explanation?"

"No."

"Was his next time out at Newmarket?"

"Yes."

"Did he win?"

"Yes."

"Did you back him?"

"Yes."

"For how much?"

"I think I won about £1,400."

It would perhaps not be inappropriate to say that Russell gave Sir George Chetwynd a rough ride. But he gave an even rougher ride to Wood, though over a shorter course.

"Do you know a Mr. Peel?" he asked him.

"Yes."

"Has he given you some handsome presents after races?"

"Yes."

"Has he ever given you money when you were riding in a race and told him you thought some other horse would win?"

"No," says Wood, shaking his head.

"Will you swear that?"

"I should think so," Wood says after an awkward pause.

"*I put it to you*," Russell says, "*as plainly as I can.*"

Again that clash of wills and again that same result.

"Well, I might be riding in a race," Wood admits, "and he might ask me what I thought would win, and I might tell him."

Russell steps back the better to scrutinize this jockey whose skill has been admired and acclaimed on every course.

"What is meant by a horse being out for an airing?"

"It might mean that it's backward in condition."

"Not intended to win?"

"No, backward in condition."

"What is meant by a horse being on the job?"

"I suppose it means he's on the job."

That is Wood's first attempt to score. It is his last.

"Have you ever ridden horses out for an airing?"

"Dozens."

"Have you ever ridden a horse on the job?" Russell asks sarcastically.

"Every horse I've ridden," says Wood, "has always been on the job."

Now Russell brings off his coup with the doubled force of contrast.

"In the 1884 Cambridgeshire did you ride a horse named Sandiway?"

"Yes."

"Was the race won by a mare called Florence owned by Mr. Hammond?"

"Yes."

"After the race did Mr. Hammond give you £500?"

Wood puckers.

"I don't know."

"Will you swear he didn't?"

Wood hesitates.

"I can't swear."

"Have you any doubt," Russell thunders, "that you did receive such a present?"

Wood gives up the ghost.

"I cannot say . . ." he says.

The stewards found that Sir George had connived at serious malpractices, but had not actually told his jockey, Wood, to pull his horses. To that extent he had been defamed by the Earl of Durham. They assessed his compensation for this injury at a farthing—with all which that assessment deliberately implies.

It was as well no coin had to be picked for compensating Wood.

Miss Fortescue

ACTING is essentially a feminine accomplishment. Only the female elements in his composition enable any man to act a part at all, and, if acting is by choice his sole activity, his mental attributes must be more female than male. A woman becomes an actress in fulfilment of her nature; a man becomes an actor at the sacrifice of his. That is why, while actors appear like men diminished, actresses appear like women magnified.

But this conception of the actress—which renders her today the most respected of her sex—has only in recent years gained general acceptance.

Formerly—by reason merely of their calling—actors and actresses alike were regarded as proper objects of society's contempt. The absurd lengths to which this doctrine could be carried by persons otherwise intelligent and perceptive was illustrated graphically in 1884 by the sad case of Fortescue versus Garmoyle.

Miss Fortescue at that time was barely twenty-five. She had been born into comfortable circumstances (her advocate stressed that she was brought up "as a lady"—a significant acknowledgment of current prejudice); but her father subsequently failed in business, and Miss Fortescue, with admirable spirit, strove to support her mother and sister by going on the stage.

In this, to her eternal credit, she succeeded; Mr. D'Oyly Carte gave her engagements in his famous operas, and although she did not forthwith become a star she came to play increasingly important minor roles.

Miss Fortescue was very lovely, very charming, very modest. She possessed that effortless poise which marks the girl of breeding. It gives no occasion for surprise that young Viscount Garmoyle, when he met her socially, proceeded to fall most ardently in love.

After a suitable period of courtship he proposed. Miss Fortescue immediately took him to her mother, and both ladies emphasized the propriety and importance of informing the Viscount's parents without the least delay.

Now Lord Garmoyle was no effete scion of a decaying line that might be expected, in any circumstances, to take its tottery stand upon exclusions and taboos. He was heir to Earl Cairns, ex-Lord Chancellor of England and one of the 19th century's greatest legal brains.

This intellectual power, however, apparently had not served to free him from the automatic reactions of his caste. Lady Cairns responded kindly to her son's announcement, and wrote in the friendliest terms to Miss Fortescue. Lord Cairns, though ultimately granting his consent, made it clear that this did not mean that he approved.

Why did Lord Cairns disapprove of Miss Fortescue? Not because a single word could be said against her personally. Miss Fortescue had only one fault; she was an actress, a woman who performed before audiences for pay.

This was an offence that Lord Cairns could not lightly pass over, and his strong views may have prompted Lady Cairns to think again; for presently Lord Garmoyle was explaining with some diffidence to his intended bride that both his parents considered the theatrical profession not merely "frivolous" but "sinful" and "profane".

Miss Fortescue did not hesitate. She had hoped for much from her career, but did not value it more highly than the man who loved her and whom she truly loved. She would give up the stage, she said and something more besides; her plans to train her sister as an actress would be dropped.

Thereafter, on the surface, the sore spot had healed. Miss Fortescue went everywhere as Lord Garmoyle's fiancée, and when the question arose whether he should complete his course at Sandhurst—which would separate them and postpone their prospective marriage—her wishes were punctiliously consulted and expressed.

Her letters to him at Sandhurst—where he continued with her blessing

243

—show the sweetness of her character and the soundness of her sense. "I beg of you not to give me anything else for a little time," she wrote, after gratefully thanking him for some gift. "A man must not be in the habit of thinking a woman a pretty plaything on whom toys and jewels must be lavished and that these things make her happiness.

"You cannot put your income round my neck and arms without getting your affairs into a muddle. All the pretty things you love to give me are, I know, some sort of public witness of your affection for me. But you must give me compliance to my wish in this respect."

The wise head then made way for the young and loving heart. "You know how ambitious I was for myself," she reminded him. "Now my hopes are centred in and upon you. We shall be so happy."

Private letters are a rare clue to personality, and now more than ever one feels satisfied that Lord Garmoyle had bespoken a treasure of a wife—and presented his parents with a treasure of a daughter.

Even treasures, though, are sometimes cast deliberately aside. . . .

The couple had been formally betrothed about six months. Miss Fortescue, firmly installed within the family circle, was preparing for one of her visits to the Cairns's country home. At the very last moment, Lord Garmoyle put her off: "My folk are not so well," he said. Miss Fortescue instead went with her own mother to Brighton; Lord Garmoyle followed and stayed for several days. Never had he been more tender and devoted.

Yet the night he left—"her kisses still warm upon his lips," said counsel—he wrote her a letter that brought all to an end. He retained the deepest love and admiration for her; thought her the finest and most wonderful of beings; but, *looking to her profession*, she would not be acceptable to his relatives and friends. Wherefore "acting in the interests and *on the suggestion of others*" he had no choice but to break off their engagement. . . .

No woman less predatory ever came to court, nor one whose rights were more readily admitted. At all times—in the words of Lord Garmoyle's advocate—her conduct had been that of "a high-minded gentlewoman", and the injuries done her were great and manifest.

Lord Garmoyle, humbly penitent, offered her £10,000. Miss Fortescue, as prop of her close kin, could not refuse. With all her soul she would have wished things otherwise. There are grounds for supposing Lord Garmoyle felt the same. But these two nice and decent people had to go their separate ways; although the lady had renounced that evil life, between them lay the shadow of her histrionic past.

Miss Ashcroft, Miss Wynyard, Miss Leighton, Miss Leigh—on that dizzy peak you so rightly ornament, will you not shed a tear for poor Miss Fortescue?

Dr. Playfair

THE great physician brought his examination to an end. He eyed his pretty patient keenly. His face, over the high Victorian collar, was severe.

"Is it serious, doctor?"

"Not *medically* serious." She stared back at him, perplexed. "You have recently had a miscarriage, that is all."

She sat up. Her eyes blazed with indignation.

"Absurd, doctor. Absolutely absurd. I haven't seen my husband for eighteen months or more—he's been in Australia all the time. You know that very well."

"Yes, I know that very well."

"Then you are mistaken about me, are you not?"

"There is no room for mistake. A novice could tell the signs."

The physician began to pace slowly up and down the room. "I am just considering what ought to be done. Perhaps it will be sufficient if you immediately leave London."

"Leave London—are you mad?"

"I think, ma'am, you are forgetting our relationships." He seated himself on a stiff-backed, upright chair.

"You forget that your husband's sister happens to be my wife. You forget that since you came to England from Australia you have been on familiar terms with her—and her young children. You are now proved to have been guilty of misconduct. I cannot countenance the notion that my family should be in contact with an adulteress. That is why I offer you the chance of leaving London."

"And so seem to admit a sin that I have not committed?"

"It is not open to question," said the physician sternly. "If you insist upon remaining it will be my painful duty to inform my wife of all that has transpired."

Doctor Playfair, who had detected—or, at any rate, believed he had detected—the symptoms of miscarriage upon this examination, was an accoucheur appointed to the Royal house and an outstanding gynæcologist of his day.

He had married the sister of two brothers named Kitson, one of whom—Sir James—was a well-known public man; the other, having gone out to Australia as an agent, there took for wife Dr. Playfair's present patient.

This latter brother proved a ne'er-do-well, and Sir James allowed the wife and children £500 a year.

For some time Mrs. Kitson lived in Australia with her husband; then in September, 1892 she came to England, where she appeared disposed to stay indefinitely. Her health, however, was indifferent and, in January, 1894, on the advice of her local doctor, she sought this ill-starred consultation with her brother-in-law.

The results were more far-reaching than any could have foreseen.

Mrs. Kitson was distressed and scared, but would not fly from London. Thereupon Dr. Playfair communicated his opinion about her to his wife. Thereupon his wife communicated it to Sir James. Thereupon Sir James discontinued his financial help to Mrs. Kitson, offering to resume it only on condition that she quitted English soil.

Thereupon Mrs. Kitson issued a writ for defamation which led to an historic and memorable trial—and to a verdict which, even now, after more than half a century, sometimes sends a shiver down the spines of Harley Street.

The physician's defence was pitched on a lofty ethical plane. He agreed that, in the ordinary course of everyday affairs, professional confidence should be inviolate, knowledge acquired *as a doctor* should be sacrosanct; but pointed out that this rule is subject to "higher claims" —and one such higher claim, he argued, at all times must remain the protection of one's family against contamination.

On that basis he erected the main fabric of his case; that the disclosure by a husband to his wife of an opinion, honestly held, about the morals of a sister-in-law touches upon a matter in which they are bound by common interest—and, becomes, therefore, an occasion privileged at law.

But apart from questions of privilege and honesty, did Dr. Playfair maintain his opinion was *correct*? Not officially, so to speak; his lawyers did not repeat the charge and reassert its truth; they did not ask the jury to find Mrs. Kitson guilty of adultery, only to find that he had been warranted in concluding that she was.

This hair-splitting device, designed to promote the physician's chance of winning without risking an inflation of the damages if he lost, did not survive the withering fire of Lawson Walton, who represented Mrs. Kitson at the trial.

"Dr. Playfair," that distinguished leader asked, when the defendant was in the witness-box, "you formed a view adverse to the plaintiff's honour?"

"Yes," said Dr. Playfair.

"Formed it solely on your examination?"

"Yes," said Dr. Playfair.

"Do you still retain that view?"

Dr. Playfair could not withhold a glance at his own counsel. But witnesses are forced to deal with questions unadvised.

"I have not entered a plea to that effect," he said.

"But, in fact, do you still retain that view?"

"I would much rather not answer; I have not justified."

"That may be," the judge interpolated. "But Mr. Lawson Walton has a perfect right to put the question in cross-examination."

"Do you still retain that view?" Lawson Walton asked again.

It could no longer be avoided.

"I do," said Dr. Playfair.

"Why had you not the courage and manliness to say so in your pleadings?"

The imputation sharply stung the witness.

"I acted upon the advice of eminent counsel," he retorted.

"You thought it more politic?"

"I thought it more judicious."

"But you still persist in your opinion?"

"Yes. . . ."

Those answers, with their apparent flavour of vindictiveness, added heavily to the score of Lawson Walton's client, and surely conduced in substantial measure to the award of £2,000 which she received.

Doctors do not possess—nor, as a rule, profess—infallibility, and it would be easy to sympathize with one that paid so high a price for a diagnosis that was wrong. But it is hard to sympathize with Dr. Playfair, even upon the assumption that he was right.

There may be some excuse for the rigid intolerance of his moral judgments (does an act of adultery, however much to be deplored, of itself transform a woman into a social leper?); doubtless he had contracted the infection of his time. But what right had he, as a doctor dealing with a patient, to traffic in moral judgments of any kind at all?

Had he not been employed by Mrs. Kitson on the same terms as any doctor is employed? Was he not asked to attend her for her health? By what right did he draw moral inferences, and assume the role of a moral inquisitor, and put her under threat of moral sanctions and coercion?

So far as I can learn from modern doctors, none. And no doctor nowadays would dream of claiming such a right.

Which should be well-deserved relief to quite a lot of us.

Miss Violet Douglas-Pennant

"IT is surprising, Miss Douglas-Pennant," says the Chairman, "the accusations that you make, and the inferences you draw."

The distinguished-looking lady who is giving evidence, and to whom this deprecatory observation is addressed, shakes her head slightly to indicate dissent. If you'd only seen what I've seen, her expression signifies; if I could only share my own experience with the court.

It's a court that we're in, yes, but it's no ordinary court. The judges

247

are not robed. Personalities are dispensed with. The very setting seems more like an ordinary room—as indeed it is, a committee room in Parliament.

Dullish place? Certainly, fifty-one weeks of the year. But today the public seats are packed beyond endurance, for here at long last, after months of agitation—Press articles, speeches, questions in the House—Miss Violet Douglas-Pennant has at last gained her inquiry: an inquiry into the reasons for her dismissal from the position of W.R.A.F. Commandant during the 1914–18 war.

Had she been expelled from office—as she alleges—because she was resolved to stamp upon immoral conduct? Did the authorities desire to prevent any such action? Did they fear the Douglas-Pennant searchlight turned upon their camps?

First, let this be said.

In every war that history records, there has been high-level concern about the morals of the troops. It was doubtless a headache to Caesar and to Hannibal. But modern war has made that headache infinitely worse; women, formerly at most camp followers, have been incorporated within the Services, so that they work—and play—as constant comrades of the men.

But Miss Douglas-Pennant very quickly formed the view that immorality in the W.R.A.F. was not sporadic and occasional, but, on the contrary, persistent and endemic; that large numbers of girls were habitually given night passes and were brought back drunk to their station in official cars; that, directly or indirectly, senior male officers were involved who obstructed her efforts, as Commandant, to stop such practices.

Knowing her state of mind, and knowing the feminine bent for emotional rather than rational processes, one can now see a predestined rhythm in the events that followed.

An unremitting moral crusade by Miss Douglas-Pennant; irritation and resentment on the part of colleagues who thought she had a bee in her bonnet (which she had) and was making a fuss about nothing (which is more debatable); a developing personal hostility for which neither side was wholly to blame nor wholly free from blame.

And when, after only a few months' tenure of her post, Miss Douglas-Pennant found herself summarily dismissed (she was not inefficient but unpopular, they said), with absolute inevitability she jumped to the conclusion that this was the upshot of a conspiracy or intrigue by those with a vested interest in suppressing her crusade.

Miss Douglas-Pennant, therefore, departed with a grievance. Had she been an indecisive or uninfluential person she might have sought in vain the requisite means to ventilate it.

But Miss Douglas-Pennant did not remotely square with this description; she had good connexions, powerful friends, a notable record of public work—and an invincible belief in the merits of her case.

So pressure for an investigation came from many quarters; reluctant authority resisted for a year; but in the end she has done it, and she is where we see her now—attempting to justify her various accusations before a sceptical Select Committee of the House of Lords.

The Chairman's comment—signal of the way the wind is blowing—has been interpolated during cross-examination. Patrick Hastings, representing one of the officers she charges, continues his questioning of Miss Douglas-Pennant.

"Do you suggest that my client desired that immorality should prevail in the camps of the W.R.A.F.?"

"Yes," she replies, without a moment's hesitation.

"You agree, it is one of the most terrible imputations you could make against any man?"

"It is very serious," says Miss Douglas-Pennant.

"What evidence have you which warrants your making that very serious imputation?"

"He never gave me any assistance in cleaning up the camps."

"Did you ever say a word to him about immorality in the camps?"

"Indeed I did." Miss Douglas-Pennant is indignant. "He put me off repeatedly and assured me there was nothing in it."

Hastings throws down the gauntlet.

"Do you want it publicly stated that you charge this gentleman with a desire to keep these camps in a state of immorality?"

Put baldly like that, it is a formidable challenge. Miss Douglas-Pennant sidesteps.

"I charge him with being a party to so doing."

Hastings will not allow her to escape.

"Madam, I asked you whether you wanted it publicly stated that you charge this gentleman with a desire to keep these camps in a state of immorality?"

Face to face with it a second time, she turns away—turns towards the group of peers who constitute her judges.

"I ask your Lordships to remember that no evidence has been heard or asked for yet. There will be plenty of evidence," she confidently adds.

But the forecast proved ill-founded. There was a total lack of specific evidence to sustain Miss Douglas-Pennant's allegations. By its subsequent report, the Select Committee rejected every one, and passed "gravest censure" upon her for launching them.

Without in any way reproaching the Select Committee—which simply fulfilled the function for which it was set up—I think that the resulting picture of Miss Douglas-Pennant does her something less than common justice.

In part she was deeply wrong, but in part she was also right. She was right—much emerging since has tended to confirm—in her opinion that immorality flourished in the Service to a far wider extent than could be proved in court. She was wrong when, being balked in general of such proof, and supposing certain colleagues ill-disposed towards her, she branded individuals against whom lay no case.

Her hunch was sound, her judgment faulty. It is the epitome of woman's strength and weakness in command.

Gertie Millar

THE law courts often provide free entertainment; otherwise they would not continue to attract their regular contingent of disinterested spectators. But on this January day of 1907 the presence of an exceptional attraction is attested by the numbers tightly packed into Mr. Justice Darling's court, or loitering, disappointed, in the corridor outside.

There is something more in prospect than the familiar clash between leading counsel and opposing witnesses. There is something more in prospect than that judicial wit for which this judge is famous.

Far surpassing these in popular appeal is the promised appearance of a national idol in the delightful person of Miss Gertie Millar.

At the Gaiety last night an eager crowd gladly paid several hundred pounds to see Miss Millar. At the Gaiety tonight another eager crowd will do the same. But in court today the lucky ones can see this queen of entertainers free of charge—and also, for good measure, see her celebrated manager, Mr. George Edwardes ("The Guv'nor"), and her celebrated husband, Mr. Lionel Monckton, the composer, who are in attendance to lend moral support.

For Miss Millar, of course, has not come here to entertain. True, her personality is such that she could not help delighting people. But that must be distinguished from her present primary purpose: to ventilate a grievance and to ask for its redress.

This grievance is an unwelcome offshoot of her fame.

The Edwardian picture postcard boom principally subsisted upon a regular publication of new issues for which the models were our loveliest musical comedy stars. None was more sought after with this object than Miss Millar. Photographers paid her substantial fees to pose; and her beautiful face and form, in a choice variety of pleasing attitudes, embellished many an album and many a mantelshelf.

Miss Millar was naturally and sensibly content to be a picture postcard favourite under such conditions. She was not content, and indeed was most upset, when she discovered that one firm had produced new pictures of her—pictures of which she heartily disapproved—without her participation, or even her prior knowledge.

Their method had been startlingly simple. They had procured three existing Gertie Millar photographs, extracted the heads, and added to each a body either from a photograph of some other lady or from an imaginative artist's cunning pen. The resulting postcards offered everywhere for sale apparently displayed Miss Millar wearing scant attire: one as a nymph, one in the act of bursting from an egg, and one—most saucily provocative of all—in a nightgown, carrying a light.

There could be no doubt it would be generally believed that the owner of the face was the owner of the body, and that Miss Millar had submitted to being photographed in the costumes and the postures now depicted. This, she felt, reflected on her character and was calculated to detract from her prestige.

Any ordinary woman has a right to choose how and in what fashion her picture shall be taken, especially if it is specifically meant for exhibition. Would they dare to claim that, because she was an actress, she had forfeited that right; that her profession conferred a licence upon all to publish pictures of her partly undressed, utterly regardless of permission and consent?

They could claim what they liked. Actresses were not yet a breed outside the law, deemed to possess neither modesty nor taste . . .

The mere idea has never seemed more ludicrous than at this moment as she stands in the box, giving evidence in her libel suit. Modesty and taste are manifest in her every word and her every gesture, and their combination with such dazzling good looks wins unconcealed and undivided admiration. And when, in answering counsel, it quickly becomes clear that her head is as cool and quick as her smile is warm and tender, even her opponents willingly concede that Gertie Millar is a credit to her calling and her sex.

This, however, does not blunt their onslaught.

"Do ladies on the stage," asks Mr. Powell, K.C., for the defendants, "like to keep themselves in the public eye?"

"I think so," says Miss Millar. "Yes, of course they do."

"And photographs assist?"

"Certainly, they assist."

"You have been photographed, Miss Millar, a great deal?"

"Yes, I have."

"You don't always insist," says counsel craftily, "that your head should appear exactly where it was when the photograph was taken?"

"I always insist that my head should be on my own body."

"A great many people," interpolates the judge, "if they could get another person's head would very much prefer it."

The ripple of laughter immediately dies down. Miss Millar has never yet found any difficulty in retaining more attention than the best comedian.

Mr. Powell now holds up the picture in the nightgown—which, it must be admitted, is not totally displeasing.

"Will you agree that this is pretty?"

251

Miss Millar declines the bait.

"My objection to it," she says, "is that it gives the impression I would be taken in that costume."

"Supposing," asks the judge, "that there was a part on the stage in which it was necessary to dress like that, would you accept that part?"

Miss Millar takes barely a second to consider.

"I have to earn my living, so I probably should."

"But you know"—Mr. Powell picks up the theme—"that in a great many plays actresses have appeared in their nightgowns?"

"No doubt," replies Miss Millar.

"Would you think the worse of a lady who came on to the stage in her nightgown in the part of Lady Macbeth?"

"Certainly not," replies Miss Millar.

"You know that in Othello Desdemona is smothered in bed when she is in her nightgown?"

"Yes."

"You don't suggest that ladies who have played Desdemona and have been photographed in that costume have been defamed thereby?"

"No, I don't."

Mr. Powell wisely leaves the matter there.

"Since these photographs, you are still well received at the theatre, are you not?"

"Yes."

"Always a round of applause upon your entrance?"

"I suppose the public likes my work," says Miss Millar appositely.

"You have never been hissed as a result of these photographs?"

"Certainly not," says Miss Millar, eyes twinkling at the thought.

Mr. Powell girds himself for a decisive thrust.

"The publishers offered to have these photographs withdrawn?"

"Yes, I know they did."

"Regret has been expressed?"

"Yes, I know it has."

"*Then what more do you want?*"

It evokes a response of crushing relevance.

"*I want the public to know that I did not sit for them.*"

After all the decoys and the red herrings, she has restated her case with absolute precision, and thus rounds off her all-round triumph as a witness. . . .

But it was a triumph with a boomerang effect. After Mr. Powell had warned the jury against feeling sympathy for a lady "both popular and pretty," and the judge had urged them not to be affected by her "charm and vivacity and brilliance," they were so busy not being prejudiced in favour of Miss Millar that in the end they did not even do her common justice.

They accepted Mr. Powell's argument that in such a case a difference divides an actress and a private person, and that no injury is suffered by the former if she is pictorially represented in a costume that she might conceivably wear in her work upon the stage.

But that surely is quite beside the point. Is there not a vital distinction to be drawn between adopting a state of undress *necessary to perform a part*, and adopting a state of undress *for its own sake alone?*

Miss Millar, it should be added, showed characteristic poise in her undeserved defeat.

"The Press and public," she was able to write in a letter to the papers, "upheld me in my view that an actress has as good a claim to consider herself defamed by the publication of an unseemly and fictitious photograph of herself as any other woman in the kingdom."

I only hope Miss Millar's view is sounder law than Mr. Powell's. It is certainly sounder sense.

PART FIVE

CASES: (2) SCANDALOUS

Lord Palmerston

THE lawyer's clerk, in his professional capacity, handled divorce petitions by the score. All much of a muchness, he had come to think. The formal title identifying this latest one—"O'Kane versus O'Kane and Another"—did nothing to excite his jaded interest.

He glanced down it perfunctorily. "That your petitioner was on the 2nd day of October, 1851 lawfully married to Margaret Matilda Augusta—"; yes, yes; "that your petitioner lived and cohabited with——" yes, yes; "that there was issue——" yes; yes; "that the said Margaret Matilda Augusta O'Kane committed adultery with——"

It was at this point that the clerk's eyes almost popped out of his head. . . .

He read the words at first with suspended credence, then read them again very slowly; then read them a third time very fast. "That the said Margaret Matilda Augusta O'Kane committed adultery with . . . with one *Henry John Temple, Viscount Palmerston, K.G., First Lord of Her Majesty's Treasury*."

Such was the ground on which obscure Mr. O'Kane, of Bayswater, sought to obtain a decree against his wife. Such, too, was the ground on which he had appended a claim against the co-respondent for £20,000.

The clerk took a long breath, and laid the petition down. A vision arose before his fascinated gaze—a vision of the political giants and the public notables, the society ladies and the aristocratic gentlemen, who would flock to watch a desperate court fight for the good name of the seventy-nine-year-old Prime Minister of England. . . .

It didn't work out quite like that in actuality.

The witness-box remained provokingly unoccupied, and in the end Mr. O'Kane's petition was withdrawn without a question asked—and without an answer given; without a bid for victory—and without admission of defeat.

Despite this forensic anti-climax, though, the O'Kane divorce suit did produce its complement of drama. The difficulty, from the spectator's point of view, is that the drama was played, not on the stage, but in the wings.

Why did Mr. O'Kane abandon his petition?

It had been filed on 19 October, 1863. On 11 November, Mrs. O'Kane filed a flat denial. On 17 November the Prime Minister's representatives obtained from the court an order requiring Mr. O'Kane to furnish more specific particulars of the charges.

So far, so good; the machinery of the law seemed to have got into its usual stride—effective if leisurely, cumbrous but thorough.

Thereafter, however, for two months there was a total standstill.

The machine itself was not at fault; nobody set it in fresh motion.

Why—again, *why?*

In the opinion of Mrs. O'Kane's solicitor, the solution positively stared you in the face. It was a case without merits, brought for the purposes of extortion—in other words, utilizing the court as an instrument of blackmail.

Now, the bluff having been called and Lord Palmerston having rightly refrained from attempts to buy him off, the petitioner found himself deservedly checkmated and chose quiescence as his wisest plan.

During December and January, the months that were so curiously free from legal process, Mr. O'Kane was unquestionably engaged in *some* kind of bargaining.

The existence—though not the nature—of this secret bargaining only came out into the light of day when Mrs. O'Kane, acting as soon as circumstances warranted, requested the court either to enforce a speedy trial, or else to dismiss her husband's suit without one. The petitioner's hand was thereby forced; now, short of a complete capitulation, Mr. O'Kane's dilatoriness would have to be explained.

On the morning of 3 February, a very modish throng—much as one of the minor clerks present had foreseen—besieged the Divorce Court to hear the petitioner's counsel give that eagerly awaited explanation.

They found that the delicate task had been entrusted to a relatively unknown member of the junior Bar, whose stature and prestige did not compete with that of Mr. Digby Seymour, Q.C. (for Mrs. O'Kane), or with that of the Queen's Advocate (for Lord Palmerston). Mr. Browne nevertheless was a proficient barrister, and barristers are trained to be exact in their use of words.

There had been delay, he said, because, soon after the court's order, "negotiations for a settlement were commenced. The law itself," Mr. Browne added, in extenuation, "provides a *pecuniary* remedy, and I therefore know of no reason why a *settlement* shouldn't be made."

A pecuniary settlement.

The disclosure caused a paramount sensation. For, at this point, the situation seemed transparent. Mr. O'Kane had been offered money to call off the proceedings; discussions had followed—perhaps were still in progress—on amount.

Mrs. O'Kane did not even know of them; otherwise she would never have applied for speedy trial. If Mr. O'Kane had taken part in any "negotiation", the other party must surely have been Lord Palmerston.

But the inference was squashed almost before it could be drawn. The Queen's Advocate murmured something, and Mr. Browne went on.

"I wish to make it absolutely plain, my lord," he said, "that no imputation rests upon the lady or the noble co-respondent—no imputation that *either* of them was aware of the settlement being made."

The Queen's Advocate looked satisfied. Mr. Seymour looked neutral. The spectators looked bewildered. If it wasn't Lord Palmerston—then *who?*

The judge may privately have felt as puzzled as the rest.

"I'll take the case the day after tomorrow," he said tersely.

At the appointed time Mr. Browne was again in his place—but with a different duty to discharge. He had been instructed, he said, to withdraw the suit.

An "arrangement"—that was his chosen expression—had been reached, but once more Mr. O'Kane's counsel earnestly absolved the other parties of complicity.

"Then what do you mean by an 'arrangement'?" asked the judge.

"An arrangement, my lord, with persons unconnected with the suit."

"What persons?"

"The petitioner's friends, my lord. There is a letter exhibited illuminating this—a letter from Mr. O'Kane to his solicitor." Mr. Browne flourished the precious document. "It begins: 'Yielding to the advice of my friends, I have decided to drop the suit, solely for the sake of my young children. . . .'"

Of that I do not believe a single word.

Do you "negotiate" for your friends' advice? Would that advice have a "pecuniary" aspect? Could its ultimate acceptance conceivably be described as an "arrangement" or as a "settlement"?

No. There *was* an arrangement, there *was* a settlement, in the ordinary sense of both those terms. And it may well have been brought about by "friends".

Not friends, though, of Mr. O'Kane's; friends of Lord Palmerston's.

We are bound to accept the latter's affirmation—communicated by his counsel to the court—that he was not involved in any compromise.

There must, however, have been ambitious men whose destinies were intertwined with the Prime Minister's; whose political careers were dependent upon his; whose wealth was sufficient to save him—with or without his knowledge—from a national scandal which might destroy them all.

I suspect they did. And Mr. O'Kane's letter—"for the sake of my young children"—was an integral part of the bargain that they struck.

Queen Caroline

THE penalty paid for sexual misconduct is frequently adjusted to the rank of the offender. Adultery by a housewife makes her liable to divorce and to the disapprobation of her virtuous neighbours. Adultery by a statesman makes him liable to the interruption and even termination of his political career. But adultery by a queen is equivalent to treason, and for treason the penalty is death.

Great responsibility, therefore, lay on Henry Brougham when, as counsel for Queen Caroline of England, he rose at the bar of the House of Lords to cross-examine the principal witness called by her accusers. . .

One shares in the passionate sympathy extended to Queen Caroline by the public at the time. History is a long recital of raw deals, but that accorded her takes its place among the rawest. For Caroline was the snubbed, neglected, persecuted consort of the man who tarnished the honourable title of Prince Regent and set the seal upon his infamy as King George IV.

It is the fashion nowadays to reverse former judgments and whitewash George IV; to protest that he has been too censoriously regarded; to claim—in the favoured term of current cant—he was *amusing*. Anyone who finds any material for amusement in the way he treated Princess Caroline of Brunswick would doubtless laugh his head off to see somebody run over.

The marriage treaty, concluded—as was then, of course, a common enough occurrence—before the contracting parties had set eyes upon each other, constituted, on George's side, a cool commercial bargain, the *quid pro quo* being the payment of his debts. Caroline—naïve and unworldly though she was—can hardly have supposed herself the heroine of a love match, but may have expected kindness or at least consideration; in the event, she did not even receive civility.

George hated her with that consuming hatred scoundrels reserve for those whom they have wronged. Having gained the financial benefits he needed, he heaped every kind of insult and humiliation upon the unwanted chattel assigned him in exchange, and when such ill-usage was borne with fortitude, lost patience and summarily dismissed her from his home.

This situation, though, left George dissatisfied. Nothing would content him but the finality of divorce. For a divorce, however, one requires evidence. So as Caroline sought to forget her sufferings by journeying from place to place across the Continent, her doings were observed by a band of hopeful spies.

No wonder that when, after so prolonged a persecution, George's

260

servile Government introduced a Bill with the object of dissolving his marriage on the ground of Caroline's adultery with "a foreigner of low station", popular emotion rallied to the Queen, and the King found himself whole-heartedly condemned long before the strength or weakness of his case was known.

No wonder—but at the same time the fact must be admitted: Caroline had rather asked for it. If not through lack of morals, through lack of common sense.

There are certain things that ladies who are living apart from their husbands should not do if they wish to avoid proceedings for divorce. Above all, they should not lark about with men who are young and handsome and of inferior social rank.

Bergami—"the foreigner of low station"—was all three. His physical attractions were compelling. He was Caroline's junior by more than fifteen years. And his status was that of a servant in her suite; originally engaged as a mere courier, raised by her favour to the post of chamberlain.

For Caroline to live on familiar terms with such a person, to admit him to her table, to dance with him in public—certainly this was the very peak of indiscretion.

But indiscretion does not always mean adultery. Were there grounds for saying it did so here?

That was the King's contention, and his Government's plea, at the hearing in the House of Lords. To support it, they relied mainly on a witness named Majocchi, who had been one of Caroline's lackeys during Bergami's régime.

Majocchi was forthright. Wherever Caroline's suite established quarters, he declared, her room and Bergami's were always close together; he had seen Caroline enter Bergami's room in the middle of the night; he had seen Bergami enter Caroline's room, partially undressed; on a Mediterranean voyage, the pair had occupied the same enclosed tent raised on the ship's deck.

If Majocchi were believed, there was no hope for Caroline. And Majocchi had told this story in the greatest detail, without inconsistency or self-contradiction. Believed he would be, believed he should be, unless his credit failed to weather cross-examination.

Facing him across the crowded chamber, Brougham had no weapon except his own sharp wits. No documents, no record, no secret information. A witness so meticulously specific as Majocchi might or might not be a paragon of truth. Did he speak from recollection of the facts— or of a brief? Was he a keen observer—or an expert, purchased liar?

The test is classical. He recalls perfectly anything that helps to build a case—anything that stigmatizes, that incriminates. But if his evidence is genuine, not faked, he will equally remember surrounding circumstances—circumstances that do not bear directly on the issue, but would not have been forgotten while the others were remembered.

This is the test that Brougham now applies.

A few preliminary questions of a general nature. Then the first sighting shot, heavily disguised.

"At the Queen's house in Naples, the gentlemen of her suite sat at the second table?"

"Yes."

"Didn't Sir William Gell's servant sit at that table too?"

Sir William Gell's servant? What does he matter? What is the point, the relevancy of this?

None—except that Majocchi hesitates; for the first time he appears to be nonplussed.

"*Non mi ricordo*—I don't remember," he replies.

"Didn't Mr. Craven's servant sit at that table too?"

Majocchi hesitates again.

"*Non mi ricordo.*"

The sighting shots have served their purpose. Brougham previously suspected; now he is convinced. Majocchi is no more than an instructed perjurer, and shall be dealt with accordingly until he is exposed.

"Where did Sir William Gell's servant sleep in the Naples house?"

"*Non mi ricordo.*"

"Where did Mr. Craven's servant sleep?"

"*Non mi ricordo.*"

"Was Bergami's child in the house?"

"*Non mi ricordo.*"

The perfect memory has become the perfect blank. The man who knew everything suddenly knows nothing. Where this one ate, where that one slept, arrivals, departures, the position of doors and staircases and windows—"*Non mi ricordo.*"

Brougham, completely confident, comes boldly in from the periphery to the centre.

"This tent on the deck. What sort of sofas were put under it?"

"An ordinary sofa and an iron bedstead."

"Isn't it right that no bedclothes were ever put upon the sofa?"

"*Non mi ricordo.*"

"Or upon the iron bedstead?"

"*Non mi ricordo.*"

"Who removed the bedstead and the sofa in the morning?"

"*Non mi ricordo.*"

"*Will you swear that it was not yourself?*"

And yet again the monotonous response.

"*Non mi ricordo.*"

The job was done, and in due course the Bill was dropped. . . .

That George had tried to frame Caroline there is no doubt. No doubt either, the frame had been exposed by that priceless sword of justice, cross-examination.

What remains obscure is the truth behind the frame. Caroline wasn't caught by Majocchi with Bergami. Was that just sheer good luck; was there anything to catch?

Yes, I should guess, most probably there was. Not that anyone should take too harsh a view of it. Morals are not absolute, they are relative, and George, who was the cause, could not complain of the effect.

Lord Melbourne

S O violent was the waiting throng's eruption into court that it seemed as if the doors must have suddenly given way. Only a fraction of them could be accommodated, and barristers in the case that constituted such a magnet had to force a passage for themselves through those whose hopes were dashed.

Inside the ushers shouted in vain for order, and when Lord Chief Justice Tindal took his seat the utmost confusion and uproar still prevailed.

Counsel, addressing His Lordship, signified a doubt whether it would be possible for the trial to proceed.

The Lord Chief Justice gazed sternly on the unaccustomed scene.

"Let the doors be shut, and let them be kept shut," he said. "Let no one gain admission unless he is subpoenaed." Then, with a minatory glance at the expectant onlookers, he added, "If silence be not kept, I shall adjourn".

Thus upon a note of tension, in an atmosphere of fever, against a background that suggested a fashionable prize-fight, there began the long-anticipated hearing of the action brought by the Honourable George Norton against William Lamb, Viscount Melbourne.

Such conditions, while unwelcome, could occasion no surprise. Because history seldom furnishes an instance of a magistrate suing a Prime Minister in office for injury sustained through the seduction of his wife.

Mrs. Caroline Norton was both beautiful and brilliant; a granddaughter of Sheridan, the dramatist, she herself wrote plentifully and with genuine distinction. She had married Norton—brother and heir-presumptive to Lord Grantley—some nine years before, in 1827, when he was nearly thirty, and she about nineteen. His income did not correspond with his noble rank, so Mrs. Norton wrote to the Home Secretary, Lord Melbourne—whom she did not know, but who had known her father—asking if he could secure her husband some preferment.

In response Lord Melbourne called at their small house in Storey's Gate, and from this first visit flowed substantial consequences; an appointment to the police court bench for the Honourable George, and for his wife the honour of Lord Melbourne's friendship—a friendship which brought him to Storey's Gate almost every afternoon (during the hours when Norton was engaged on his new duties) and that suffered no interruption (but rather grew more intimate) when Melbourne became the first Minister of the Crown.

There is nothing abnormal about mutual attraction between a mature man on the floodtide of success and a lovely young woman with an imaginative mind. Mrs. Norton would doubtless be captivated by Melbourne's assured charm, and flattered by attention from a statesman of his standing; Melbourne would doubtless be captivated by her youthful verve, and flattered by attention from a beauty of her fame.

They would have much to enjoy in each other's company, and the relationship may well have been entirely innocent. But for long Society gossips had whispered otherwise, and now George Norton's counsel contended they were right.

He founded Norton's claim for damages against Melbourne—in those days a necessary initial proceeding when seeking to establish adultery by a wife—upon a series of allegations about the couple's conduct, which, taken in combination, he submitted, could only be consistent with their guilt.

Melbourne always entered the Nortons' house by a secluded entrance in a courtyard at the side instead of the front door. The servants were told to let no one into the house while he was there, and themselves not to enter the drawing-room unless rung for.

During his visits, the drawing-room blinds were often drawn. Mrs. Norton made preparation to receive him by doing her hair and making up afresh. Mrs. Norton had been alone to Melbourne's house. When she was ill, Melbourne had stayed for hours alone with her in her bedroom. Notes—though practically none survived—often passed between the parties. Despite their precautions, they had been seen to kiss and to hold hands.

Witnesses—mostly ex-servants of the Nortons' broken household—testified in full support of counsel's statement.

If those witnesses were to be believed, then, by any standards, the behaviour of Mrs. Norton and Lord Melbourne had been highly suspicious and extremely indiscreet. It might not now be held sufficient proof of adulterous intercourse; but one would not like to assert the same of 1836.

And since—according to the rules prevailing then—Melbourne, as defendant, could not give evidence, and Mrs. Norton, as wife of the plaintiff, could not do so either, the credibility of those ex-servants became a vital issue.

This issue had ripened for immediate decision when a man named Flook stepped up into the box.

He had formerly been a general factotum at the Nortons'; driving the carriage, helping in the house. One day, he told the court, he had

gone into the drawing-room—gone in, for some reason, without preliminary knock; and there he found Lord Melbourne bending over Mrs.
Norton, who was lying on the hearth-rug with her dress disarranged.

There could hardly be any misconstruction about *that*. Others had
only spoken to a series of circumstances from which adultery might—
or might not—he inferred. This was an entirely different proposition;
if the jury accepted Flook's sworn word, the case was at an end.

The Attorney-General, Sir James Campbell, appearing for Lord
Melbourne—Law Officers could then engage in private practice—rises
to begin Flook's cross-examination well aware that the trial is at its
turning point.

Flook admits that, until very recently, he has been living with his
wife and children in a cellar; that he had carried on a business in old
clothes; that he was in debt, and could not pay all that he owed.

"When were you discovered as witness in this case?"

Flook reflects a little.

"About six weeks ago."

"Have you continued to live in the cellar?" asks Mr. Attorney.

"No. I have been to the country," answers Flook.

"Where to?"

"Wonersh."

"Have you been *living* in Wonersh?"

"Yes."

"Oh." Mr. Attorney sounds most interested. "How far from Wonersh
does Lord Grantley live—Lord Grantley, Mr. Norton's elder brother?"

"Lord Grantley lives *at* Wonersh," replies Flook.

"You have not been living in his house, I presume?"

"No. At a public-house."

"Who paid for you there?"

"I paid for myself."

"Who gave you the money?"

"Well." Flook looks down at the floor. "The solicitor gave me
money for my fare."

"How much?"

"Well." Flook looks up at the roof. "Well, about ten pounds."

"Has he given you any money since?"

"No. Oh, no."

"Have you carried on any business at Wonersh?"

"No. Oh no."

"But you have gone on living there ever since, right up till now?"

Flook assents. Next he agrees with Mr. Attorney that when working
for the Nortons he was often drunk, and was actually discharged for
drunkenness.

"Did you think it unjust that you were turned out?"

"Oh," says Flook, grinning, "when Mrs. Norton told Master to do
something, he must do it."

"It was her fault, then?"

"More hers than his."

"Yes," says Mr. Attorney. "And haven't you been around saying that it was that damned bitch, Mrs. Norton, that got you out of your job?"

A look of venom momentarily contorts Flook's cunning face.

"I may have done," he says.

Mr. Attorney has got what he wants. There is only the finishing stroke.

"You expect to make a good thing out of this, don't you, if you win?"

"I don't know," Flook says, "whether we are to win or not."

"But if all goes well?"

"If I were to work," says Flook elliptically, "I should like to be paid for what I've done."

Clearly both a purchased and a vindictive witness. Not only is Flook destroyed, but he drags the rest down with him. There have already been suggestions in regard to other witnesses of subsidies from or through Lord Grantley, and of grievance or of spite. Now disbelief envelops all of them like a cloud, and without leaving their box, the jury find for the defendant. . . .

Immense ovations awaited Mr. Attorney and Lord Melbourne when they returned triumphant from the court to Parliament. Many thought Norton's action was politically inspired, and its dismissal a vindication of the Whigs whom Melbourne led.

Others may prefer the less sophisticated judgment reportedly pronounced by one of Melbourne's female relatives. "Fancy," she said to a friend, "Willie has got away with it."

The Duchess of Kingston

I T is doubtful whether Westminster Hall has ever been so crowded —or ever will be again so long as its historic beams endure. Certainly this moment marks its zenith as a resort of fashion.

There they are, packed together in their thousands: noble ladies and Society fops, friends of Royalty and friends of Royalty's friends, wits like Walpole, actors like Garrick, authors like Hannah More.

All look on with varying degrees of awe and reverence while entering two by two in dignified procession, the massed strength of the House of Lords assembles as a court.

"Serjeant-at-Arms!" The Crown Clerk's thin, pedantic voice falls into the silence like a sharply pointed stone. "Serjeant-at-Arms! Make proclamation for the Gentleman Usher of the Black Rod to bring his prisoner to the bar."

The silence grows deeper as the prisoner is escorted forward, a woman about fifty years old, attired in plain black silk, a hood of mourning on her head. Some few traces still persist of a bygone beauty; but the face is warped by dissipation, the figure flawed by self-indulgence.

"Madame, how say you?" The Lord High Steward speaks from the Woolsack's eminence. "Are you guilty or not guilty of the felony whereof you stand indicted?"

"I am not guilty, my lord."

"How will you be tried?"

The lady places her hand upon her heart.

"By God and by my peers," she says.

The privilege of nobility is thus formally invoked. Their lordships settle themselves for an extended sitting. The Duchess of Kingston's trial for bigamy has begun. . . .

Begun, but at a snail's pace. The preliminary legal arguments dragged on and on. The accused's attention, eager at first, began to stray. The walls grew closer, the roof lower, the light dimmer—and she was back in that tiny church at the end of her cousin's Hampshire garden very late on a summer night more than thirty years before.

She stood, youthfully radiant, before the Reverend Amis. At her right hand, young Mr. Hervey, with whom she was temporarily almost as infatuated as he was with her.

Grouped around, her cousin, Mr. Merrill (at whose house she was staying); his friend, Mr. Mountenay (holding the only taper); her aunt, Mrs. Hanmer (who had been acting as chaperon); and Ann Cradock (Mrs. Hanmer's maid).

These were the witnesses; there was none other present. For circumstances required that this should be a secret marriage; the well-connected but impecunious groom not wishing to forfeit the good will of his father, who confidently relied on him to appropriate an heiress, and the well-connected but unendowed bride not wishing to forfeit her post—reserved for single women—as Maid of Honour to the Princess of Wales.

"Augustus John Hervey, wilt thou take this woman . . .?"

"I will."

"Elizabeth Chudleigh, wilt thou take this man . . .?"

"I will."

The ceremony was both unannounced and unrecorded. There were no entries in a register, there were no marriage lines.

In the event that proved symbolic, for there was virtually no marriage.

After the briefest possible honeymoon—at Mr. Merrill's house—Hervey, a naval officer, had to rejoin his ship and perforce spent the whole of the next two years at sea. But Elizabeth did not pine in his protracted absence.

Her passion for him had been swiftly sated and, on rejoining the Princess's entourage—still as Miss Chudleigh—she confirmed a reputation for profligacy and licentiousness notable even in that profligate and licentious set.

She passed lightly from one promiscuous lover to another and, when Hervey returned from sea at last, ignored or rejected his attempts to assert himself as her husband. Those attempts were finally abandoned, and Elizabeth could put her marriage out of mind as she had always kept it out of sight.

Until, some fifteen years after that clandestine wedding, an extraneous event restored it to her consciousness.

It was noised abroad that the Earl of Bristol lay mortally sick—and, with the passage of time, Hervey became his heir.

Being Mrs. Hervey was one thing; being Countess of Bristol (with its attendant affluence) was another. She was Hervey's lawful wife, of course; but if he should choose to deny it, where, oh where, could she point to the written proof?

Elizabeth thought the matter over; then made a dash for Hampshire and the Reverend Amis.

She tracked him down, and things were quickly put in order. The clergyman made out a declaratory certificate. A memorandum book was specially procured, and in the feeble hand of an old and ailing man, the requisite details were inscribed upon its virgin page.

"The fourth of August, one thousand seven hundred and forty-four, married . . . Hervey, Esq. . . . Chudleigh, daughter of . . . by me, Thomas Amis"—a true, if belated, registration of the rites that had been solemnized so many moons before.

Elizabeth went back to London highly gratified. She had, in fact, acted in the very nick of time. Within weeks, the Reverend Amis died.

The Earl of Bristol, though, made an excellent recovery. . . .

Elizabeth, with no more than a passing pang of disappointment, resumed her gay existence as a notional spinster, locked up the certificate like a long-term investment, and, for a further nine years dismissed her marriage from her thoughts.

But the second reminder, when it came, was sharper and less pleasant. Hervey—who now wanted to marry another woman—sent word of his intentions to press for a divorce.

This proposal did not suit Elizabeth's book at all. She had no objection whatsoever to regaining marital freedom; the same Earl of Bristol was still very much alive, while the Duke of Kingston, her current lover and protector, was more than willing to wed his concubine.

But as guilty party in a divorce she would lose her Maid of Honour's pension and properties she had acquired in the guise of a single woman.

Once again Elizabeth rose to the occasion. She arranged collusive proceedings against Hervey for the legal offence called jactitation of marriage (falsely claiming to be someone else's wife or husband), and thereby obtained—to their mutual satisfaction—a court finding that they had never been joined in matrimony.

Hervey, however, as it turned out, did not seize his chance to "marry". Elizabeth did, and when the Duke of Kingston died. his dowager substantially inherited his wealth.

She could afford to smile indulgently when, shortly afterwards, the Earl of Bristol really did contract a fatal illness, and Hervey succeeded to his coronet.

Thus far her career furnished an object lesson in How To Get Away With It. And thus she might have continued to the end had the Duke's will not treated her so generously.

But his expectant and deprived relatives were bitter; they recalled old rumours (revived by the jactitation case); they cast wide and dug deep in their investigations—till, with one eye on morality and the other on a fortune, they set in motion the machinery of criminal law. . . .

The legal arguments on her behalf have failed, and the Crown has started to call its witnesses. What witnesses? The Reverend Amis is dead. Mr. Merrill is dead. Mr. Mountenay is dead. Mrs. Hanmer is dead.

None, other than the bridegroom and the bride, of those who once assembled in that tiny church survives—save only the maid, Ann Cradock; and she makes an unimpressive appearance in the box, having manifestly peddled her evidence for reward. When it has been paid for, even the truth is suspect.

Ann Cradock goes; her effect is indecisive; if anything, the scale tips a little in the prisoner's favour.

But who is this that follows, frail and elderly, so faint of voice that peers and spectators literally hold their breath as they strain to hear? It is Mrs. Amis. With the damning tale of Elizabeth's dash to see her reverend husband.

And the memorandum book.

Still they had not closed the trap on the elusive bird. As her noble judges rose successively in their places—"Guilty, upon my honour"; "Guilty, upon my honour"—she mastered her fury and waited her turn to speak.

"What have you to allege against judgment being pronounced against you?"

Usually that is the most perfunctory of questions. But this particular felon had plenty to allege. If they said she was not Kingston's widow, then she was Bristol's wife. Duchess or Countess—what difference did it make?—the high prerogatives of peerage remained hers.

"As a peeress, my lords, I plead benefit of clergy, according to the statutes. I claim immunity from any punishment."

Their lordships anxiously conferred with the Chief Justice. They shook their heads in some dismay on hearing his advice.

Once more, the duchess/countess got away with it. . . .

It was the sort of trick she might have been put up to by her lawyers. It was also the sort of trick she might have thought out for herself. A later age would have termed Elizabeth a shrewd cookie—and assuredly Elizabeth would have liked the compliment.

Sir William Wilde

A DOCTOR is in perpetual hazard with his female patients. His relationship with them is, of necessity, much more intimate and personal and private than that which a woman ordinarily maintains with any man except a lover or a husband.

It offers allurement to the frustrated woman, and opportunity to the designing one—as many honourable practitioners have discovered.

But there are also doctors—though infinitely fewer—who exploit the relationship instead of being exploited by it; who use their professional contacts with women to place themselves on terms of wholly unprofessional familiarity.

That was the allegation made in the 1860's against Sir William Wilde at the very peak of his illustrious career.

Sir William Wilde ranked among the most distinguished citizens of Dublin. He was the leading eye specialist in Ireland, with a reputation as a healer that reached other lands. In addition to receiving the honour of a knighthood, he had been appointed Surgeon Oculist-in-Ordinary to the Queen.

Sir William and his wife—a poetess of note—lived in lavish and hospitable style, and were universally recognized as leaders in the intellectual and artistic life of the Irish capital.

A personage so prominently in the public eye cannot hope that his indiscretions will escape attention, especially in a town as gossipy as Dublin.

It was well known—it had been well known for years—that Sir William yielded the palm to none in his pursuit of women; and that, despite his squat and simian appearance, women as a rule responded readily to him. Fame often exerts a magnetism of its own.

Certainly the tally of his intrigues and his bastards had long since grown beyond general computation. If Dubliners viewed the matter tolerantly, doubtless they took into account his services to suffering humanity. Even so, there were those who shook their heads. If he doesn't watch out, he'll get his dues, they said in their own idiom.

270

The instrument through which Sir William ultimately got his dues was a young woman by the name of Mary Travers.

At the age of nineteen Miss Travers had come to him as a patient. Thereafter she had returned for further consultations frequently over a period of years. It is significant that, on her own subsequent admission, she never either paid, or even offered, any fee.

A time came eventually, however, when the free medical advice was discontinued. Miss Travers ceased to see Sir William, and apparently the parting had not been cordial. For Miss Travers wrote and printed and distributed a pamphlet in which, without any real concealment of the fact that the characters concerned were Sir William and herself, she related the story of a doctor violating a female patient in his surgery.

Sir William would have ignored it. Lady Wilde did not. She had become indifferent to her husband's amorous adventures, but not to direct attacks on his professional integrity.

She therefore wrote to Miss Travers's father—himself a practising doctor—deploring his daughter's "disreputable conduct" and attributing to her "the hope of extorting money".

Miss Travers saw the letter and promptly sued for libel.

The ensuing action worked all Dublin up to fever pitch. No one cared much whether Lady Wilde had libelled Mary Travers. A far more important question was involved: Had Sir William sexually assaulted a woman who had reposed her confidence in him as a doctor?

The celebrated surgeon was as assuredly on trial as if he had been literally standing in a dock; and when Miss Travers went into the box she appeared as not only plaintiff, but accuser.

Treading with exquisite verbal delicacy so as not to shock the audience which had assembled to be shocked, her counsel drew from Miss Travers's own lips an account of the occurrence on which she had based her pamphlet.

How one day when Sir William was examining her she fainted; how she recovered consciousness to find she had been "ruined"; how she declared that his behaviour was "an outrage"; how he begged her not to tell anyone what had happened; how he persuaded her to renew her visits; how he pressed gifts upon her.

Through this recital she preserved an air of pained reluctance. But when Serjeant Sullivan got up to cross-examine, it was as if she had suddenly been confronted with Sir William Wilde in person.

Malice and hostility visibly possessed her.

"Now as I understand you," Serjeant Sullivan began, "and as your counsel told the jury when he opened, this one—ah—transaction between you and Sir William occurred in the October of 1862, and nothing of the sort occurred before or after?"

"Not before?"

"Nor after?"

"I consider——"

Serjeant Sullivan, who had thought he was merely clearing the ground, cut in impatiently.

"Did anything occur after—yes or no?"

"I can't say yes or no."

"Can't say yes or no?" The Serjeant's surprise was shared by the murmuring spectators.

"No, I can't." Miss Travers hesitated. So he was asking for it, was he? Very well; here goes. "I can't answer yes or no, because I consider it was attempted."

"The same thing was attempted again?"

"Yes."

"When?"

"In the next July—the July of 1863."

So she's changing her tale in midstream. The Serjeant could hardly credit his good fortune.

"Why did you not say a word about this just now, when you were examined?"

"Because I wasn't asked."

"Not asked? But didn't you draw out all the instructions for this case yourself?"

"I did."

"With your own hand?"

"Yes."

"Every line of them?"

"Yes."

Serjeant Sullivan drew a deep breath of satisfaction.

"Did you hear your counsel mention one—ah—transaction against Sir William, and no more?"

"I did."

"And you now say there was a second attempt upon you in July?"

"I consider there was."

Serjeant Sullivan fished hopefully.

"Was there another after that, now?"

"No."

"Or in the interval?"

Miss Travers could not reject the bait twice running. "I don't know," she said, and the murmuring was renewed.

"You don't know?" Serjeant Sullivan repeated scornfully. "Do you mean to tell me that's your answer? Were there or not attempts made to violate you?"

But Miss Travers did not fancy getting into deeper waters.

"There was rudeness and roughness leading to it," she at last pronounced.

"How often?"

"Two or three times."

Serjeant Sullivan now had more than sufficient for his purpose.

He simply threw Miss Travers's earlier evidence in her teeth.

"Though this was the kind of conduct offered you, you went back time after time to his consulting-room?"

Miss Travers had no option but to answer, "Yes".

"And you took his money?"

"Yes."

"You got tickets for a ball from him?"

"Yes."

"Did you ask for those tickets from the man who violated you?"

"Yes."

"Did you buy a dress for the ball?"

"Yes."

"And did you put it on you?"

"Yes."

"Whose was the money that bought it?"

"His."

The Serjeant smiled sarcastically.

"All that going on with these repeated attempts at violation?"

"Yes," said Miss Travers, malignantly defiant to the last.

She had forfeited all confidence, though, in her unsupported word. It only needed Sir William to give her the lie on oath, and her case would surely crumble in the dust.

But Sir William did not go into the box.

Perhaps he did not fancy the whole truth coming out—that for years Miss Travers had been his acquiescent mistress, and that this was a discarded woman's effort at revenge.

Perhaps he felt it safer to leave things as they were.

The jury, however, neatly resolved the situation. They found for the plaintiff; damages, one farthing.

Thereby they set on lasting record their opinion that Sir William was a goat—and that Miss Travers hadn't minded.

Lady Colin Campbell

LADY COLIN CAMPBELL accused her husband of adultery with a house-maid.

Lord Colin Campbell accused his wife of adultery with General Sir William Butler, with London Fire Chief Captain Shaw, with Mayfair physician Dr. Bird, and with His Grace the Duke of Marlborough.

It was a socially—if not a morally—flattering riposte, and contributed greatly to the chic and scented atmosphere in court during the long trial (nineteen days) of their cross-petitions.

273

If Lord Colin had been larking with the staff—merely piquant. If Lady Campbell had been larking with the Establishment—sensational.

There were other and less colourful elements, however, in the tale that was gradually unfolded before a jury and Mr. Justice Butt. Dismal, sombre, clouded, even tragic—these adjectives more fittingly describe the Campbells' marital and domestic background.

It was not so much a case of a marriage that went wrong as a case of a marriage that could never have gone right.

On the one hand, a gay and high-spirited young woman, with sufficient literary skill to earn rewards for writing, with sufficient vocal talent to draw audiences by singing, with sufficient physical and personal attractions to excite male admiration everywhere she went.

On the other hand, a young man devoid of social gifts, without mental endowments—and continuously debilitated by a discreditable disease.

Either love or the lure of a title—readers can take their choice— must have induced Lady Campbell (then Miss Gertrude Blood) to disregard those first two, manifest, defects.

It is clear, though, that—till marriage—she knew nothing of the third. She could not have remained unaware that her prospective husband's health was less robust than might have been desired. But she certainly did not foresee that a trained nurse would accompany him on their honeymoon; that their union would be ruled by the fiat of doctors, and that, ultimately, she herself would acquire the same infection.

For Lady Campbell, this discovery was the final straw. Up to that point, although deeply and progressively disillusioned, she had been prepared—with certain understandable reservations—to continue living with Lord Colin as his nurse and friend.

But now she invoked the sanction of the law, and in March, 1884, within three years of her wedding, a decree of separation was formally pronounced.

If matters thereafter had been left to Lady Campbell, that decree would have closed the episode. It had been an unhappy matrimonial venture, and she did not wish to rake over the ashes. But Lord Colin reacted differently; he resolved to avenge his judicial reverse by getting his wife convicted of misconduct.

To this end, he had her shadowed by detectives; he tried to persuade the Paris police to arrest her as a prostitute (a step which Mr. Justice Butt characterized as "an outrage"); and, as these measures failed in their effect, he and his agents laboured indefatigably in a retrospective search for "evidence" rooted in the period before the decree.

She was not of the type or temperament to wait passively for a blow to fall.

So when a mutual friend—Lady Miles—disclosed that Lord Colin contemplated proceedings for divorce; and when this same Lady Miles disclosed additionally that she had long known of Lord Colin's own unfaithfulness, had suppressed that knowledge as long as she could bring herself to do so, but now felt constrained to place it at the disposal of a wife who, she believed, was threatened with a grievous wrong—why, Lady Campbell could not dash fast enough to her solicitors.

Her solicitors, in turn, could not dash fast enough to get her petition on to the file before Lord Colin's—an achievement they accomplished with only hours to spare.

Lady Campbell, though, gained nothing from this quickness on the draw, except that her solitary charge could be presented first.

True, Lady Miles told a circumstantial story—that one evening, at Lady Campbell's request, she kept Lord Colin company while his wife was out; that she had remarked on the housemaid's familiarity with her master; that Lord Colin had admitted the girl was "very fond" of him, and did not even deny an imputation that she was his mistress; that Lady Miles had said: "It's a mistake to make love to servants in the house", and Lord Colin had said: "A man can't account for every little thing he does"; that Lady Miles had pretended to leave ("I shut the front door without going out"), and then had shrewdly timed an unheralded re-entry; that Lord Colin and the housemaid had been caught in close embrace.

"They were too well engaged to see me," Lady Miles demurely added.

There seemed to be no valid reason to reject this testimony. But the inference founded on it totally collapsed. Two highly reputable physicians—one the senior consultant at a London Lying-in Hospital—had examined the housemaid on the instructions of Lord Colin's lawyers, and now came forward to declare she was a virgin. . . .

Thus, relatively early in the trial, it became clear that Lady Campbell could not establish a case against her husband. The real battle—waged fiercely and relentlessly—was whether Lord Colin could establish a case against his wife.

In this battle, Lord Colin could fire off a lot of witnesses. Lady Campbell's sole ammunition was her counsel—but that counsel being Sir Charles Russell, at the zenith of his fame, she could not be said to labour under serious disadvantage.

There were indeed those who thought—there are indeed still those who think—that it was better to have Russell on your side than the truth. That I do not believe; but I do believe that it was almost invariably fatal to have Russell on the other side without the truth on yours.

His great powers as a cross-examiner were fully extended only once in the Campbell suit—but that single occasion almost certainly proved decisive. . . .

Notwithstanding the quartet of co-respondents cited, the substantial allegations against Lady Campbell entirely concerned her relations with the Duke. The evidence involving the other three could be written off as nugatory and sometimes frivolous (the strongest item inculpating

General Butler was that Lady Campbell's face had appeared flushed after receiving a visit from him in her drawing-room).

The evidence involving the Duke himself did not always make much more impression (as when a waiter, called to testify that the Duke and Lady Campbell spent a week-end together at a riverside hotel, described the lady of that incident as "fair"—whereas Lady Campbell was conspicuously dark).

But Rose Baer presented a tougher proposition.

For several months, Rose had been Lady Campbell's personal maid. In the box she spoke not only of daily letters from My Lady to the Duke; not only of frequent meetings tête-à-tête; not only of the Duke's presence late at night in her mistress's bedroom when they were guests at a party in a country house.

Though Lord Colin was not there, My Lady had a double bed, and next morning, Rose Baer said: "I could see that there had been two persons in it."

If that was accepted as evidence of truth, the Duke—and Lady Campbell—could give themselves up for lost.

One gleam of light—Rose had been summarily dismissed. That might make her vindictive; that might make her invent. But had it done so, in fact? And, if so, could that fact be demonstrated?

"How long after you left Lady Campbell's service," Russell asked, "did anyone connected with this case approach you?"

"I left in June, 1882," said Rose. "And Lord Colin came to see me in December, 1884."

"How did he know where to find you?"

"I don't know."

"Had you written to him?"

"No."

"*Until December, 1884, you had no communication with Lord Colin —or anyone on his behalf?*"

"No."

"That is clear?"

"Yes."

You didn't have to lie more than once with Russell. Rose Baer, had she but known it, was already trapped; the master girded himself for a spectacular kill.

"When you saw Lord Colin, did you make a statement to him?"

"No. He just asked me if I would give evidence."

"Had you said up to that time that you *could* give evidence?"

"No."

"How did he know you could?"

Rose looked blank.

"Did you *ask* him how he knew?"

"No," Rose said. "I didn't."

"Did he say what the evidence *was to be about*?"

276

"No."

"Did you know what case you were to give evidence in?"

"No."

"Had you then heard of the divorce suits?"

"No."

"But when Lord Colin asked you to give evidence you agreed?"

"Yes."

With one deft gesture Russell pinned her to the wall.

"*So you agreed to give evidence without knowing what it was about?*"

What could Rose Baer say? Helplessly, she said "Yes".

Fourteen questions—and they counted more than anything else that happened during those nineteen days. They did not prove that Rose Baer, in speaking of Lady Campbell's behaviour, had not told the truth. But they proved—it was enough—that she couldn't be relied upon to tell it.

I strongly suspect that Russell's virtuosity saved his client, not from unjust condemnation, but from paying the penalty for her misdemeanours (the jury returning a clean sheet for all).

Personally, I am bound to say that I do not very much mind. It is bad when the sins of the fathers are visited on the children. It is equally bad when the sins of the husbands are visited on the wives.

Sir Charles Dilke

POLITICAL promise is more plentiful than political fulfilment, and ex-future Prime Ministers glut the Parliamentary market. They crowd the House of Commons; they invade the House of Lords; there are even unhappy specimens that have no place in either, and are reduced to soliciting support in the constituencies. No matter how auspicious the omens on any given day, a politician's future is unpredictable.

But even hard-boiled cynics who would never have risked a farthing bet on Gladstone or Disraeli threw their caution to the wind in the early 1880s and staked their reputation on the chance of Sir Charles Dilke.

The very stars in their courses had conspired to favour Dilke.

He had intellect, principle, charm. He had an exceptional grasp of foreign policy at a time when world affairs were fast increasing in importance. He had strongly developed radical inclinations at a time when radicalism was coming into vogue. He nourished—and expressed —unsullied democratic sympathies at a time when democracy was the beacon of the future.

In 1885 Dilke had arrived in his mild-forties and was patently approaching the zenith of his powers. The man, the moment, the dazzling career—all pointed to 10 Downing Street, at no far distant date.

Within a year the man had been broken and the dazzling career had terminated in disgrace.

How? Through a sensational petition for divorce. Why? That is a more complicated question. It will, I suppose, for ever be debated whether Dilke drew ruin upon himself by his own behaviour, or whether, he fell victim to the imaginative lying of a woman.

Virginia Crawford, in whom rests the solution of this puzzle, was wife to one of Dilke's own colleagues in the House. She had married very young; indeed, all the events which invest her name with persisting notoriety were concluded long before she reached the age of twenty-five.

That Virginia was flighty was not subject to doubt, and her flightiness sometimes ended in adultery. Her husband had suspicions of a certain Captain Forster, but Virginia always denied misconduct with him.

Prompted by what seemed to him significant indications, the husband from time to time returned to the attack, and at last Virginia came out with a confession—but a confession other than the one he had expected. Yes, she had been unfaithful but not with Captain Forster. Her lover was Charles Dilke. "He seduced me six months after our marriage," Virginia said, "and I was his mistress ever after."

Crawford accordingly took action for divorce, citing Dilke as co-respondent.

The proceedings—marked, says a contemporary newspaper report, by "a scramble for seats such as has seldom been seen in a court of justice"—did not last unduly long upon this occasion. The husband relied entirely on his wife's confession; there was no other evidence whatever to support it, and Virginia herself did not go into the box.

Now, a person's confession is evidence against that person; it is not evidence against someone else who was not there when it was made. So while the judge could grant Mr. Crawford a divorce, on the grounds of his wife's adultery with Dilke, Dilke was entitled to judgment in his favour. A Gilbertian situation, but one which has not infrequently arisen.

"I agree," said the judge, when Dilke's counsel raised this point. "I cannot see a shadow of a case against your client."

So Dilke was clear, absolutely clear, in law. That was all very well as far as it went, but there were other considerations.

Dilke, after all, was an outstanding public figure. Whatever had been decided in relation to himself, the form of the divorce decree would leave on him a slur. Moreover, Virginia had not spared him in the details; she had portrayed him as a monster of sexual depravity.

Ought he not to have scorned his technical escape and demanded the privilege of refuting her on oath?

His advisers concluded otherwise, and so informed the judge.

"We have decided not to take the responsibility of calling Sir Charles Dilke. In the witness box," declared Sir Charles Russell, his leading counsel, "he might be put through the events of his whole life and"— a sound maxim but curiously employed—"reviewing the life of any man you may find indiscretions."

Russell has been strongly criticized for this decision—a decision in which Dilke, at the very least, acquiesced. Was it not obvious all along, the critics asked, that the majority would make the worst deductions from his silence?

Yes, it was obvious, and to nobody in court would it have been more obvious than to Russell—the legendary Russell, the greatest all-round advocate who has ever adorned the Bar. Russell knew—he must have known—the dangers of this course. Why, then, did he pursue it?

Look at that phrase of Russell's—it was not used casually—"reviewing the life of any man, you may find indiscretions".

What did it mean? Not necessarily, not even probably, that Dilke had committed adultery with Virginia Crawford. The true explanation may become apparent later.

Meanwhile Dilke found himself exposed to the harsh blast. The strict Victorian world assumed the most uncharitable view with satisfaction. Dilke had not spoken; therefore Dilke was guilty. And if Dilke was guilty . . . that was the end of Dilke.

Confronted by this deeply disquieting situation, Dilke worked frantically to undo the mischief. The Queen's Proctor was stirred to intervene, and a fresh inquiry opened, this time before a jury.

The second hearing, which lasted for a week, imposed on Dilke most drastic handicaps.

For practical purposes, he was standing trial. But officially he merely formed part of the case for the Queen's Proctor; he was not a party with a personal interest to protect; he could not, therefore, profit from the shield and spear of counsel; and the onus of proof no longer lay on his accusers, as it always devolves on the Queen's Proctor to establish that the original decree should be rescinded.

These difficulties were increased by a ruling of the court that witnesses whom the Queen's Proctor wished to call—Dilke's secretaries, Dilke's servants, Dilke's dependants, Dilke himself—must take precedence of those called for the husband. Dilke was thus, in a sense, forced to defend before he had been charged, and Virginia—also on this occasion going into the box—secured the inestimable boon of the last word.

She and he were both cross-examined at great length, mostly without determinate result; but two single passages, one with Dilke and one with her, when they are interlinked, to my mind, solve the case.

"Did you tell Mrs. Crawford," Dilke is asked, "that she was like her mother and that that was why you took to her so much?"

"No."

"Were you in fact at one time her mother's lover?"

Everyone expects an immediate negative. Instead Dilke hesitates and visibly turns pale.

"*I decline to answer,*" is his ultimate rejoinder. . . .

When Virginia's turn comes, she is less reserved.

"You told your husband that you had not been unfaithful with Captain Forster?"

"Yes, I did," she says.

"Did you in fact commit adultery with Captain Forster?"

She has denied it up to this very moment; her husband's petition was fought upon that footing. Now perhaps she's scared; or perhaps it suits her to retract.

"*Yes, I did,*" she says.

The picture on both sides promptly becomes clear.

Virginia Crawford implicated Dilke in order to obtain a divorce without implicating Forster. The tale of her affair with Dilke was just a put-up job.

Dilke, though blameless where Virginia was concerned, had had an earlier intimacy with Virgina's mother. That was the "indiscretion" Russell had had in mind—a very dangerous "indiscretion" in the context of the case—and which had led to his advising Dilke to stay out of the box.

This, in my opinion, is the answer to the riddle which has been the cause of so much conflicting speculation. The jury's verdict, upholding the divorce, implicitly recorded their disbelief in Dilke.

But I think he wrote the truth in that mournful, dignified letter to the electors of his constituency on his virtual disappearance from the public scene. "I can only solemnly assure you, as I have with equal solemnity sworn in court, that I am innocent of the charges brought against me, and respectfully and gratefully bid you farewell."

Mabel Normand

"MR. COURTLAND DINES is a friend of mine; an ordinary friend. I went round to his flat at cocktail time on New Year's Day. Edna was there; I expected her to be."

"Edna being Miss Purviance, Mr. Chaplin's leading lady?"

"Yes," says Mabel Normand. "There were just the three of us."

The women who crowd the Los Angeles court room hardly heed her words; their attention is wholly gripped by the innocent beauty of her face—that face which has charmed millions from ten thousand cinema screens.

"What did you do, the three of you, at the flat of Mr. Dines?"

"Talked, and had a drink; then, as arranged, my chauffeur called to fetch me with the car."

"Your chauffeur being Horace Greer, who stands his trial here today for the attempted murder of Mr. Dines?"

She nods, and her eyes stray sympathetically to the wizened little man who finds himself in this unenviable plight after years in the faithful service of a movie queen.

"What happened when Greer called?"

"He came into the sitting-room—I really don't know why; I left him there with Mr. Dines, and went into the bedroom."

"Where was Miss Purviance?"

"She was in the bedroom, too."

"Yes . . . What happened then?"

Mabel Normand's great eyes grow vague and misty.

"I was powdering my nose, and . . ."

"Yes?"

"I heard a noise."

"Yes?"

"So I went—we both went—into the sitting-room."

"Yes?"

"Mr. Dines was lying bleeding on the floor."

Everyone is listening very closely now.

"What was Greer doing?"

"I don't know."

"Did he speak?"

"I can't say."

"Did you see a pistol anywhere?"

"I am unable to remember."

"Can you tell us nothing," says the District Attorney, with some irritation, "about how Mr. Dines came to be lying bleeding on the floor?"

"How can I?" Mabel Normand says, with that look of melting helplessness which has so often bowled them over in the one-and-nines. "How can I when I didn't see it, when I wasn't there?"

The remainder of the evidence is equally deficient. Miss Purviance also didn't see it, wasn't there, doesn't know, can't say, is unable to remember. Even Mr. Dines himself—though three bullet wounds freshly healed, bear witness he was there—seems to have no coherent notion of what happened. "I had been drinking so heavily," he explains. . . .

In the outcome, this universal blankness benefited all the interested parties. It led to an acquittal of the chauffeur Horace Greer, despite the fact that he refrained from going into the box, and that on the night of the shooting he had gone to the Police Department of his own accord and there asserted, "I have just shot a rat"; and it at least restricted inquiry into the private lives of the two beautiful actresses and the wealthy Mr. Dines.

This last consideration was of special importance to both ladies, and to the studios whose valuable property they were.

The effect of *personal* disgrace on a player's *professional* position varies with individual cases. "The theatre thrives on scandal"—so said one of its brightest luminaries recently to me, and certainly in the theatre scandals have been survived that would have wrecked a career in politics or in the Army or at the Bar.

And yet the cinema—at any rate in the twenties, when Miss Normand and Miss Purviance were at their respective peaks—imposed more exacting standards upon its chief performers; any artist—particularly any female artist—publicly caught out in the type of misbehaviour which in Hollywood is assumed to be endemic, thereby forfeits the respect of the exhibitors and, by so doing, easy access to the public.

Mabel Normand had already once experienced the operation of this unofficial veto. Two years earlier an English film producer, Captain W. D. Taylor, had been found shot dead at his Hollywood home; Mabel Normand had been with him barely an hour before.

It was not then suggested that she had shot Taylor, any more than it was now suggested that she had shot Dines; but the consequent investigation gave wide currency to a persistent rumour that she led a wild and wanton life.

Her pictures were thereupon boycotted by the trade; for many months it seemed that her starring days were over; then her old friend, Mack Sennett, gallantly gave her a leading role, in which she did so well that prejudice went by the board and she staged a spectacular come-back which was still the talk of Hollywood on that afternoon she went to visit Courtland Dines.

One shooting, plus attendant gossip, had very nearly ruined her. What would a second shooting, plus attendant gossip, do?

Notwithstanding the uninformative nature of the trial, Mabel Normand felt something close to panic as she prayed it would blow over.

Her misgivings were well founded. It did not blow over. Nor could the clouds that gathered round her for a second time be justly attributed to wholly idle tattle. If few facts had emerged, those few were significant and attracted general notice.

One: when the police arrived at the flat after the shooting they found the wounded Dines clad only in an undervest and a knee-length dressing-gown—an unconventional costume for a gentleman acting as host to two young ladies.

Two: when Mabel Normand was pressed to explain why she had picked that precise moment to withdraw into the bedroom, she said she went to help Edna Purviance fasten up her dress—an explanation that, to say the least, stimulates conjecture about the scene that met the chauffeur's eyes upon his entry.

282

Three: when Greer sought to justify his silence in a trial where the pressure was so great on him to speak, he said, "I would rather risk going into a penitentiary than say anything that would reflect upon Miss Normand"—a sentiment as revealing in its obvious ellipsis as it is touching in its obvious devotion.

These circumstances both confirmed and widened the impression created by Dines's statement that he was very drunk. Belief hardened that, however the shooting had occurred, it had had its roots in what are politely termed excesses, but are more vulgarly and vividly described as goings-on.

Neither actress escaped the lash of public disapproval, but past events ensured that Mabel Normand bore the brunt; and once again that face with the great eyes and innocent beauty vanished from the screen—this time for good and all. . . .

It was not only a human tragedy, but an artistic one. Mabel Normand possessed an attribute rare in studios: talent. She played her own type of comedy with resourcefulness and flair, and had every right to call herself—as few film lovelies have—by the honourable and honoured name of actress.

And yet she proved too much for Hollywood. Or is it possible that Hollywood proved too much for her?

Archdeacon Wakeford

IT is not too much to say that in 1921 Britain consisted of two vast opposing camps: on the one side, those who believed Archdeacon Wakeford guilty; on the other, those who believed him innocent. The latter invoked the law of probabilities.

The Rev. John Wakeford was a cleric of high rank, widely revered for his saint-like disposition. As an indefatigable worker in and for the Church, he excited the admiration of his closest colleagues. As a preacher of unusual eloquence and power, he served as a source of spiritual inspiration to thousands of worshippers up and down the land. He was married to a devoted wife. He was sixty-two.

Could such a man have committed a sordid and shabby and anonymous adultery of the kind that used to be generally linked with dissolute week-ends at Brighton or at Maidenhead?

And even if one regretfully conceded that saints are not entirely immune from moral lapses, would such a man, with his quick intelligence, parade a moral lapse with such fatuity?

For the Archdeacon's offence—if indeed offence occurred—was no affair of secretiveness and stealth; there were no assumed identities, no dark assignations, by which he might at least have hoped to frustrate exposure. The case that his accusers relied upon was this: that in broad daylight, without the least attempt at concealment or disguise, at Peterborough—in the neighbouring diocese to his own at Lincoln— he went *in clerical garb* to a hotel with a young woman, and slept with her there on two separate occasions.

It is understandable that Sir Edward Carson, defending Wakeford, commented: "There is no explanation—except that the Archdeacon is mad."

As no one dared to suggest that the Archdeacon *was* mad, or even simple, a strong argument could be presented by his host of partisans. But a strong argument could also be presented by that other host which thought that for once the law of probabilities played them false.

They invoked instead the sworn evidence of fact, produced at the Archdeacon's first trial in the Bishop's court, and again at his re-trial on appeal before the Privy Council.

There was the manager of the hotel, who swore that on each occasion he had himself greeted the Archdeacon, had complied with his request for a double room, and had noted the self-same lady with him. There was the manager's wife, who swore likewise, and also that she had served the pair in the dining-room, and had seen a night-dress as well as pyjamas on the double bed.

There was the hotel servant, who swore she had escorted them upstairs and lit a fire in their room. There was the police sergeant, who swore that both times he saw them in the hotel together. There was the hotel register, which bore an entry, "J. Wakeford and wife"; the Archdeacon admitted signing his own name, and the subsequent words were in handwriting so similar that it was either his also, or a skilful forgery.

It will be apparent that a measure of common ground existed between accusers and accused. The Archdeacon did not deny his presence in Peterborough, nor his stay at the hotel—nor even that he had walked round the cathedral with a young woman as companion. "I met her near the nave; she was a stranger; we talked about the inscriptions and looked at the choir," he said.

What he did deny, categorically and flatly, was that any woman stayed with him at the hotel. "I went alone," he asserted, "and I remained alone."

Now one thing at least is clear in this perplexing conflict; no room existed for genuine mistake. If the Archdeacon spoke the truth, he had been framed. Ranged against him was a resolute conspiracy of perjurors.

That, indeed, constituted the Archdeacon's case, in which the alleged chief conspirators were named. Two clergymen in the neighbourhood, who nourished a spite against him of long standing: his brother-in-law, the Rev. Herbert Edward Worthington, and the Rev. C. T. Moore.

These men, he maintained, had conceived a plot to bring about his ruin, and had somehow procured the other witnesses' support.

There is no more dramatic defence than that of a sheer concoction. Throughout the seven-day Privy Council hearing, tension never abated, as a well-nigh incredible answer met a well-nigh incredible charge. But the peak was reached when Mr. Worthington mounted the steps up to the box; agreed that *he* had carried the complaint against his sister's husband to the Bishop, *after consultation with the Rev. Moore*; then turned to face the unfriendly gaze of Carson, poised for attack immediately below.

"Do you know that Mr. Moore was very hostile to Archdeacon Wakeford?"

"No," Mr. Worthington said, dubiously. "No."

"Do you not?" A sarcastic lilt embellished the Irish brogue. "Do you not, now? Do you remember when Moore was charged with staying in an immoral house?"

This fierce jab came to the crowded court as a shock and a surprise. But it did not come as a surprise to the Rev. Worthington.

"Yes, I remember."

"You know it was Wakeford who had sent those papers to the Bishop?"

"Yes, I know."

"Did you hear that Moore and Wakeford had a controversy about a church which stood upon some property of Moore's?"

"Yes, I heard."

Carson raised his voice.

"Then you do know, don't you, that Moore was on unfriendly terms with your brother-in-law?"

"Yes," said Mr. Worthington, after an awkward pause.

"And yet when you heard of Wakeford's being at the hotel, you went running to Moore before you went to Wakeford?"

"I never went to Wakeford," Mr. Worthington confessed.

"Were you anxious to prefer this charge against your brother-in-law?"

"Not in the least. Oh no. Not in the least."

"Did you tell your sister there were grave rumours about Wakeford's morals?"

"I did."

"Did you advise her to leave him?"

"I did."

It might have been family affection and concern. But how could that apply to Moore?

"Was it Moore who gave you the statements of the hotel people?"

"It was."

"Did Moore send a detective to give you a helping hand?"

The audience drew a big breath as the witness answered, "Yes."

285

There was no doubt at all, after this cross-examination, that probably Worthington and indubitably Moore laboured with more than ordinary zeal to ensure that Archdeacon Wakeford suffered punishment. But there is a world of difference between that and fabricating the transgression.

Whatever motives might have prompted these two clergymen, what of the others—the police officer and the staff from the hotel? As Lord Birkenhead said in giving judgment, "No suggestion was made that any of them had any personal feeling against Archdeacon Wakeford or indeed had ever seen or heard of him before. And the only possible motive remaining—that they were bribed—is left in the air and unsupported."

One must reluctantly conclude—as did the Privy Council—that the Archdeacon's guilt was satisfactorily proved. The Cloth cannot always discipline the Flesh, nor the inhibitions of religious leadership suppress the sexual impulses that animate the male.

But strangely do we balance the vices and the virtues, and strangely do we deal in rewards and penalties. One wonders whether grave ecclesiastical charges would have been preferred, whether two long trials would have been doggedly fought out, whether irreparable disgrace would have followed a conviction, had Archdeacon Wakeford's sin not been adultery, but cruelty to some helpless animal or child.

Lady Mordaunt

As printed in the Divorce List, it looked prosaic: *Mordaunt v. Mordaunt, Cole, Johnstone and others*. But Society pulsated; at last the day had come. Interest in this case, first roused by the aristocratic derivation of both petitioning husband and respondent wife (he a tenth baronet, she the daughter of a seventh), was fanned to fever heat by the exalted station of those cited as her partners in misconduct.

Viscount Cole, heir to the Earl of Enniskillen; Sir Frederick Johnstone, dashing and fashionable sportsman; most titillating of all, a third and unnamed individual, vaguely described in Sir Charles Mordaunt's Petition as "Some Person".

Vagueness existed, however, only upon paper. Everyone who was anyone knew for a positive fact that the imprecise and noncommittal phrase delicately denoted Queen Victoria's eldest son: the twenty-nine-year-old, dynastically married Prince of Wales. . . .

When the Mordaunt matrimonial imbroglio reached its long anticipated climax in the courts, her lovely ladyship was only twenty-four. Her ladyship's husband was barely thirty-three. Their union initially had not seemed disharmonious. For three years they got on amicably and peaceably, if without any extravagance of romantic passion, until, on 28 February, 1869, Lady Mordaunt gave birth to a child.

Children, in popular belief, cement a marriage. The Mordaunts' infant daughter produced—indirectly—an opposite effect. The act of childbirth wrought a cardinal mental change upon her mother, although its true nature lay wide open to dispute.

Either, under stress of remorse, she was prompted to confess to sins that she had thus far successfully concealed. *Or*, under stress of puerperal disorder, she was prompted to confess to sins that she never had committed.

Whichever the explanation—and established facts excluded any except those—the consequences were momentous and far-reaching. . . .

The first step Lady Mordaunt took towards catastrophe occurred on 2 March during a conversation with the maternity nurse brought in for her confinement.

She had been restless and intermittently agitated for some hours; the nurse had frequently begged her, for her health's sake, to keep quiet. But by evening Lady Mordaunt could no longer be held in check.

"If you don't let me talk," she said, "I will go mad. I have something I must say, and I will tell it you tonight."

Her tone made the nurse suggest fetching Sir Charles, so that his wife might unburden herself to him. That suggestion was summarily dismissed.

"I will tell him another time. I will tell you now. This child is not Sir Charles's. It is Lord Cole's."

"Say no more," pleaded the nurse, "for goodness sake." But Lady Mordaunt—whether plagued by physical malady or inspired by spiritual release—would not call a halt until the details were filled in.

"It took place the last week in June," she went straight on. "Sir Charles was in Norway. Lord Cole visited me."

"Say no more," the nurse pleaded again, uncomfortably recalling that the birth was premature.

For the moment, lightened of her real or fancied guilt, Lady Mordaunt acquiesced, and fell asleep.

None the less, she proved as good as her word. She did "tell him another time"—exactly one week later—and, so far from sparing his feelings, added further shocks. "I have been very wicked, Charlie," she wept. "I've done wrong with others, too."

Sir Charles listened as she quoted the illustrious names, and under pressure of their reiteration over days his disbelief gave way to doubt, his doubt to dawning horror. "I have made him understand at last," Lady Mordaunt said to the nurse; and it is because Sir Charles acted on what he understood—or, at any rate, what he thought he understood—that the big shots of the Bar now take their places for the battle.

It will not, however, be the kind of battle confidently expected by uninformed spectators.

For weeks they have been conjuring up exciting visions of a proud and deeply injured Lady Mordaunt in the box, on oath denying or recanting her confessions—or, at very least, ascribing them to delusion.

But, in the event, adultery is not a direct issue, and Lady Mordaunt will not appear at all. The sole plea raised by her counsel, Dr. Deane, Q.C., consists of a preliminary objection to the trial itself—the plea that when she received first notice of Sir Charles's suit, Lady Mordaunt was (and ever since has been) insane; and that, in consequence, further proceedings against her must be barred.

Lawyers present are highly pleased with this development; such a submission, though familiar in the criminal courts, has never before been enlisted in divorce. Laymen, on the other hand, tend to feel disappointed at the postponement—possibly abandonment—of the theme that originally attracted their attendance.

But soon their disappointment substantially abates.

Serjeant Ballantine, leading counsel for Sir Charles, is a wily old bird and an extremely shrewd tactician. Confronted by an impressive array of doctors testifying that Lady Mordaunt suffers from puerperal mania and is "utterly insane", the Serjeant adroitly modifies his plans.

He will concede, he announces, that she may be insane *now*; will maintain that at an earlier stage she was fit to instruct solicitors; and proposes to demonstrate that her confessions were true—partly as *evidence of her sanity when she made them* ("That was, after all, not long before the petition was served"); partly as *evidence of a motive for feigning insanity when she was still sane.*

Dr. Deane protests to the judge at the injustice threatened to third persons who are not parties to the current investigations.

"That certainly has some force," says Lord Penzance, "but I cannot refuse to allow these matters to be gone into."

Doubtless Serjeant Ballantine has got a valid legal point.

He has also got an inflammatory piece of prejudice—just how inflammatory can be best perceived when, with the jury intently following, he calls Sir Charles.

"Were you aware," the Serjeant asks him, "that the Prince of Wales was an acquaintance of your wife?"

"Yes," replies Sir Charles.

"I believe *you* had no personal acquaintance with His Royal Highness?"

"I have spoken to him," says Sir Charles coldly. "He was never a friend of mine."

"Did he ever come to your house upon your invitation?"

"*Never.*" The emphasis speaks louder than the word.

"Did you ever have a conversation with your wife about him?"

"Yes, I did. I warned her against continuing the acquaintance."

"Can you tell us what you said to her?" Lord Penzance interpolates.

"I said that I had heard from various quarters certain circumstances." As well as an indignant husband, Sir Charles is a loyal liegeman. "I did not enter into full particulars."

"But you did not wish her," says Ballantine, "to retain his acquaintance?"

"I did *not*." Again that significant emphasis.

"Until after your wife's confinement, were you aware of the fact that the Prince of Wales had been a constant visitor to your home?"

"I was not."

"Were you aware that he and your wife had corresponded?"

"I was not."

Ballantine thoughtfully fingers a small bundle of letters, each, it presently transpires, beginning "My dear Lady Mordaunt", and concluding "Yours sincerely, Albert Edward". More harmless letters can never have been penned. But they are now invested with an atmosphere of stealth.

"Were you ever told the Prince had been at your house?"

"On one occasion."

"By Lady Mordaunt?"

"No."

The suspense is heightened by a studied pause.

"Was something said to you by members of your family?"

"Yes."

Very suspicious, underhand, culpable, it sounds. Yet when Dr. Deane counters by calling the Prince as his own witness, Serjeant Ballantyne prudently does not cross-examine. "I am bound to believe His Royal Highness," he declares.

The jury, after only eight minutes' deliberation, found that at all material times Lady Mordaunt was insane. The question of her adultery, therefore, rested in abeyance—until March, 1875. Then a majority of three judges out of five pronounced that a respondent's insanity did not preclude divorce, and—Lady Mordaunt neither appearing nor defending—awarded Sir Charles a decree for her misconduct with Lord Cole.

The majority was right—and Lady Mordaunt's advisers wise.

Apart from her own confession—which a puerperal sufferer was liable to concoct, and was legally evidence only against herself—nothing lay even by moral implication against Sir Frederick Johnstone or the Prince of Wales.

Nothing, that is, unless a tête-à-tête should be treated as tantamount to illicit intercourse.

"I hope," Lord Penzance had said five years before, "that things have not arrived at such a pass that a jury will find a lady and gentleman guilty of adultery merely because the two have dined together."

A daring sentiment from a Victorian judge that may have played an honourable part in prompting the more sensible ethos of our day.

The affair of Lord Cole, however, must be differently regarded.

In Lady Mordaunt's diary for 1869 she had placed a little mark against 3 April, and written "280 days from 27 June". Two hundred and eighty days is the normal term of pregnancy. Lord Cole was with Lady Mordaunt on 27 June. Sir Charles, beyond all controversy, was not.

We have moved a long way in this past century. But the cryptic annotations used in feminine diaries preserve throughout the ages their fixity of purpose.

The Rector of Stiffkey

D URING the early thirties I spent a summer holiday at Blackpool. Among the innumerable exhibitions on that "Golden Mile" which stretches between the north and central piers—relics from Egypt and novelties from Paris, maidens in trances and real-life cannibals, bearded ladies and performing fleas—one show in particular was doing tremendous business.

Queues waited patiently outside the booth all day, and emerged with expressions bordering on beatitude. Eventually I was tempted and went in.

The nature of the spectacle exercising such attraction would certainly have puzzled any uninformed observer. Simply a middle-aged gentleman with clerical collar and features, sitting for some obscure reason in a barrel, apparently engaged in literary pursuits.

But no contemporary observer—if grown-up, wide awake, and capable of reading—could possibly have been uninformed about the source of the clerical gentleman's peculiar drawing power.

This was the Rev. Harold Francis Davidson—more familiarly known by the name of his Rectorship at Stiffkey—whose extra-rectorial activities, lately ventilated in an ecclesiastical court, had made him the subject of more public discussion than any other English clergyman since Wolsey. . . .

Today, when that discussion is virtually closed and the facts which prompted it are virtually forgotten, nothing remains except a vague and shadowy legend—the legend of a monster who took advantage of his cloth to indulge a gluttonous sexual appetite for teen-age girls.

Such certainly was the effect, if not the terminology, of the ecclesiastical court's findings. And yet, in the comparative calm of distant retrospect, it is possible uneasily to wonder whether that court—and hence the resulting legend—did Mr. Davidson something less than justice.

Of course there were grounds for suspicion—great suspicion—suspicion sometimes hovering near the frontier of certainty. But did it ever cross that frontier? Were the "immoral acts and conduct" imputed ever proved?

The great dispute in the Stiffkey case—fought through the spring and summer of 1932 before the Chancellor of the Diocese of Norwich —turned far less upon evidence of the Rector's actual "conduct" than upon the inferences that should be drawn from it.

On either interpretation—his antagonists' or his own—Mr. Davidson could fairly be termed an unorthodox divine. His small country parish, of which he had been incumbent since 1906, was far from enjoying exclusive call upon his energies.

Admittedly, its modest needs could not have kept an active-minded pastor fully occupied. But Mr. Davidson's supplementary interests, and the time he spent on them, and the places where he pursued them, were calculated to attract critical scrutiny.

The Rector appeared in Stiffkey only upon Sundays. From early Monday morning until late on Saturday night, based upon a bed-sitting-room in Shepherd's Bush, he roamed at all hours over the West End, meeting and mixing with young girls—often prostitutes—to whom his attentions were close and unremitting.

There is no question whatsoever that he called on them at their lodgings, let them call on him at his, bought them meals in restaurants, on occasion paid their rent, and sometimes took them to theatres and to cinemas (although he was a bankrupt, chronically hard up, with a wife and several children dependent on his meagre stipend).

There is a question whether he ever kissed and cuddled these companions, or ever housed one in his single room—but both, from the established data, appear probable.

Some direct allegations of more serious misconduct may—in my opinion—be safely disregarded. But still there remains a picture of extreme familiarity bordering on licence.

The case against Mr. Davidson, however, so far as it concerned only his casual associates, was greatly weakened by the notorious unreliability of females who are willing to form casual associations.

On the other hand, the case against him was correspondingly strengthened by witnesses who had never been his associates at all—unimpeachably respectable young women who had declined his matey overtures, but found themselves constantly "pestered" none the less.

For instance, the pretty little waitress from the tea-shop. "You're lovely; I must come again", the Rector had remarked on his first visit. He was as good as his word; and by putting his arm round her shoulders, trying to fondle her hand, paying her crude compliments, and suggesting assignations, he had made her job so disagreeable that the manager requested him to transfer his patronage.

What was Mr. Davidson's explanation for all this?

For his chumminess with the West End girls—rescue work and

charity. True, some of the rescue work might seem over enthusiastic; true, some of the charity might well have begun at home, but wherever the evidence of these girls conflicted with the Rector's, I would rate his oath at least as high as theirs.

The "pestering" of respectable girls, though, posed a more formidable question.

Mr. Davidson's answer to it, in substance, can be simply summarized. I am like that—jolly, free and easy, unconventional, partial to a joke and a bit of harmless horseplay—and you should put the best, not the worst construction on it. I love the society of all my fellow-creatures, and I do not believe in an artificial code dividing men from women.

This last point, at any rate, received abundant confirmation when he was cross-examined.

"If," counsel asked him, "you were to be judged by the standards by which ordinary men are judged, do you not think that you would be convicted?"

"No," said the rector, "except by the bad-minded."

"If an ordinary man took a room for a girl of twenty for six months, and paid thirty shillings a week, do you think it might be inferred that he was keeping her?"

"Not if the matter was explained to the landlady. And I did explain it."

"If an ordinary man took a girl to Paris for a trip, and stayed at the same hotel with her, do you think"—counsel sarcastically inverted his real purport—"that it might be open to misunderstanding?"

It was gathered that Mr. Davidson distinguished between circumstances. A man might take a secretary, or a nurse.

"Did you stay with a girl at a Paris hotel?"

"Yes."

"In what capacity was she? Your secretary, nurse—or mistress?"

"She was my ward," said Mr. Davidson.

No absolute criteria exists for assessing the true significance of social behaviour like that. Behaviour must be read in conjunction with personality.

A squeeze of the hand or arm, the use of verbal endearments (Mr. Davidson favoured "Queen of my heart"), even an apparent recourse to amorous innuendo—all can only be diagnosed as symptoms if first one clearly grasps the psychopathology of the patient.

Was the Rector of immoral or merely bohemian, habits? On that issue—the sole practical issue at his trial—I think he just deserved the benefit of the doubt. In a secular court, I think he would have got it. In the ecclesiastical court, he stood condemned.

It may sound paradoxical to add that, while I regret the conviction, I uphold the penalty: deprivation of his clerical post and status.

But the clergy, by adopting their calling, set themselves apart. A layman may, for example, quite properly proclaim himself an atheist;

a clergyman doing so at the very least commits a basic breach of contract.

So a layman may quite properly display bohemian habits; a clergyman doing so mocks his own vocation. Taking the most generous view of the rector as a man, one still cannot consider him fitted to hold a cure of souls.

Mr. Davidson did not lie down under the court's judgment. He promptly appealed to the Judicial Committee of the Privy Council (it was, he said, to raise funds for that purpose that he went on exhibition "writing his reminiscences").

But the Judicial Committee deals with questions of law only, and his contentions of law were justifiably rejected. No appeal lay on the facts to any terrestrial court.

Lady Dunlo

" A VERDICT for Lady Dunlo," says her counsel, opposing Lord Dunlo's petition for divorced, "will not, perhaps, please her noble father-in-law—but, I venture to think, it will not displease Lord Dunlo."

In that single sentence he pin-points the origin, explains the notoriety, and foreshadows the result of a suit which, during this 1890 London season, has engrossed and enthralled the fashionable world. It is easy to understand—though not always to sympathize with—the motives that actuated the central characters; motives which, expressed through action or inaction, by successive stages brought them all to court.

Young Lord Dunlo, being insufficiently attracted by the stereotyped females of his patrician class, naturally enough fell in love with Miss Belle Bilton, whose undoubted charm and talent adorned the music-halls.

Young Miss Bilton, being translated into Lady Dunlo and relishing both her husband and her newly acquired rank, naturally enough looked forward to a lifelong tenure and clung with equal pertinacity to each.

The Earl of Clancarty, being apprised of his heir's secret marriage and reacting in the tradition of a 19th-century peer, naturally enough longed to liberate his stock from the stigma of a marital alliance with the stage.

In pursuit of their respective purposes, Lord Dunlo did not go far enough; the Earl went much too far; Lady Dunlo sat—as she always looked—extraordinarily pretty. . . .

It had been a register office ceremony in London. Deep in the country, the Earl first learnt that his eldest son was married from the gossip columns of a periodical.

The news came to him as a total surprise and stunning shock. Until that moment he had supposed Lord Dunlo fully occupied preparing to embark on a leisurely voyage around the world in company with an older gentleman chosen by his parents (this as an antidote to the "bad lot" they had heard—and believed—he had mixed up with in town).

The advanced state of this project now seemed to the Earl a providential means of procuring prompt salvation. Get the boy away from her; that's the prime essential; afterwards, we shall see what we shall see.

He sent for Lord Dunlo, and—with many caustic comments on juvenile imprudence—insisted that the world tour should be carried through as planned.

Lord Dunlo was still six months short of his majority. His financial dependence on his father was complete. Reluctantly, he agreed.

Taking fond and tender farewell of his bride, he left these shores, fully intending—as he later told the court—to resume his rights and duties as a husband on return.

Neither Lord Dunlo (because he couldn't) nor the Earl (because he wouldn't) contributed a penny to Lady Dunlo's maintenance. She was fortunate in that her professional earnings were substantial.

Neither Lord Dunlo (because he couldn't) nor the Earl (because he wouldn't) afforded her access to the Clancarty caste. She was fortunate in that her old friends were loyal.

Nevertheless no impartial observer would deny that, under the stress of these unusual conditions, during his lengthy absence Lord Dunlo's lovely wife behaved with something less than absolute discretion.

Liking—as normal women do—male society, lacking the male society that was hers by legal right, she permitted herself to be regularly squired by a former ardent escort and admirer.

Parties and picnics, restaurants and race meetings—once again they were seen together at them all.

Two things, however, must be counted in her favour.

First: she was constrained, by both social and economic pressures, to forgo being Lady Dunlo and continue being Miss Bilton; that is to say, continue living in a circle where conventions—as distinct from morality—were lax.

Second: she was frank about her constant associate in her continuous correspondence with her husband—and drew from him only the mildest of reproofs.

"Don't go out *too* much with W," he wrote. "People will talk. Not that I care. I trust you with all my heart."

Certainly he gave no sign that he did not, or that his feelings had undergone a change. The flow of his letters increased rather than diminished; from one remote region of the globe after another, they carried their messages of fervour and affection. "My own darling wife." "I love you truly." "I do nothing but think of you all day, and dream of you all night."

Lady Dunlo, therefore, could hardly believe her eyes when—utterly unprepared and unsuspecting—she was suddenly served with a petition for divorce, alleging various acts of adultery with W.

Her husband, she knew, was in Australia. Only the day before she had received a letter from him, laden with its customary tribute of endearments.

Only the day after, she received another; not less amatory, equally devoted, but adding—almost as a casual afterthought—that he had been reading a report from his solicitor containing serious reflections on her conduct.

"My darling," Lord Dunlo commented. "I don't believe one word of it."

The date on that letter was later than the date on which he had affixed his signature to the petition. . . .

The hired snoopers have given their tainted testimony; the time W. arrived, the time W. left, a confused oral description of a kiss that somehow—it ultimately transpires—escaped inclusion in their otherwise exhaustive written notes.

Lord Dunlo has given his innocuous and unimportant evidence, with many a boyish glance of manifest distress at the figure of his wife sitting immediately below.

It is only now, though, that the tension rises to its peak as the Earl of Clancarty, father both of the suitor and the suit, ascends—or rather, condescends—to the witness-box.

"Before you read of your son's marriage, had you ever seen his wife?"

It is the first question put to him on behalf of Lady Dunlo by Frank Lockwood, Q.C. in cross-examination.

The Earl shakes his head.

"No, I had not."

"Or heard of her?"—"No, I had not."

By chance the Earl's eyes fell for a moment on his daughter-in-law. He looks straight through her as though she were not there.

"So you knew nothing whatever about her?"—"Only what I read."

"What did you read?"—"That she was a performer on the music-halls."

The distaste, the disdain, the disapprobation.

"Was that all you knew about her when you next saw your son?"—"Yes."

"Did you then tell him," says Lockwood, "that if he remained with her you would have nothing more to do with him?"—"Yes."

"Why?"

The monosyllabic query cracks like a whiplash.

"Because," says the Earl, "I had the impression the lady was likely to . . . go wrong."

"You had formed that impression without seeing her?"—"Yes."

"And without knowing anything about her, except that she was a music-hall artist?"—"Yes."

Lockwood pauses for a moment, then steps up the pace.

"Who consulted the solicitors that now represent Lord Dunlo?"—"I did."

"When?"—"The day my son left England."

"Without his knowledge?"—"Yes."

"And without a shred of evidence against this lady?"

The Earl does not answer. Lockwood repeats the stinging words in measured tones.

"And without a shred of evidence against this lady?"—"Yes."

"Who decided to have her watched?"—"I did."

"When?"—"At about the same time," says the Earl.

"Without Lord Dunlo's knowledge?"—"Yes."

"And without a shred of evidence to justify it?"

As the Earl hesitates, Lockwood adds ironically, "Except, of course, that she was a music-hall artist?"—"Yes."

Lockwood gives no quarter. He has a gravely injured client to protect.

"Did you cause the petition to be drafted?"—"Yes."

"Did you post it to Australia, with a direction that your son should sign?"

The Earl cannot deny it. He is, in tournament terms, unhorsed. But still Lockwood has his finishing stroke to come.

"Immediately after the petition was served," he says, "did you get a letter from Lady Dunlo?"—"Yes."

"Asking for an interview?"—"Yes."

"So that she might clear herself?"—"Yes."

"Did you reply to that letter?"—"No."

"Did you grant her an interview?"—"No."

"Have you ever taken any step of any kind to give her an opportunity of clearing herself?"—"No." . . .

The snoopers had left Lord Dunlo's case extremely shaky. The Earl had left him without a case at all.

"He was a cypher, a puppet in his father's hands." remarked the judge, and the jury spent only minutes in dismissing his petition.

He did not repine. Lockwood's prediction had been strictly accurate, and the Dunlo divorce suit—rare among its species—achieved the satisfying triumph of a happy ending.

The cypher and puppet suddenly sprang to manhood, and was reconciled and reunited with his wife.

In the following year, he succeeded to his father's title. In the following years, she bore him a daughter and four sons.

Madame Rachel

"How old are you, Mrs. Borradaile?"

Counsel defending this grave charge of fraud addresses the witness who claims to have been defrauded. A scraggy woman, wholly devoid of figure; hair dyed bright yellow; face ruddled with paint. Probably more than fifty; but, in dress and speech and manner, making an absurd pretence of juvenility.

"How old are you, Mrs. Barradaile?"

When people put themselves forward as confiding dupes, it is relevant to explore their experience of life. But the cross-examiner meets only an injured silence.

"Mrs. Borradaile." His voice grows sterner. "Will you be good enough to answer—*how old are you?*"

"I refuse to say."

"Why do you refuse?"

"Because, Mr. Seymour," she replies, coyly giggling, "*I think it is a very rude question.*"

Serjeant Ballantine, sitting close to his opponent Seymour, fidgets. In his opening speech for the Crown, he tried to create a favourable atmosphere for their principal witness; while admitting Mrs. Borradaile's "folly" and "vanity", he also projected her as "an estimable character"—an estimable character who had been cruelly wronged.

But these utterly idiotic affectations—why, they could easily lose her the sympathy of the jury—goodness gracious, she is almost losing his.

She must certainly be, Serjeant Ballantine thinks, the silliest woman in London.

Just as the accused must certainly be the wickedest. On that score Serjeant Ballantine has got no doubts at all. He considers—and has so described—this self-styled "Madame Rachel" as a filthy and dangerous moral pest, and has thrown himself with zeal into the task of prosecution.

He now casts a single glance towards the dock, allows his eyes to dwell for a moment on its occupant—a sallow, loose-lipped woman of sixty odd—and his sense of mission, temporarily damped by Mrs. Borradaile, returns.

For the Serjeant knows what the jury do not know—that the twittering and posturing zany in the box is only one of Madame Rachel's victims. And Madame must not be allowed to get away with it. . . .

Most Society and pseudo-Society women had been for years familiar with the name of Madame Rachel. They were not familiar with her real name, Mrs. Levison; nor with her base and sordid origins; nor

297

with the fact that, till her descent on the West End, she had been telling penny fortunes round the East End bars.

They knew her only as proprietor of elegant premises in fashionable Bond Street—premises that signalled their identity with the gold-lettered legend "Beautiful For Ever".

Beautiful For Ever. It was an enticing prospect for ladies whose charms had faded, or had never bloomed.

Madame Rachel operated a racket on these ladies that exploited in turn their weaknesses of temperament and their weakness of position.

First, they were tempted or persuaded to expend fantastic sums on "beauty" preparations: 10, 20, 50, 100 or more guineas on "Circassian Hairwashes" and "Royal Arabian Baths" that would have been more honestly labelled common soap and tap-water.

When prolonged treatment, with such elixirs failed to produce any visible result, Madame Rachel counted on immunity; no client could establish her a criminal without establishing herself a laughing-stock.

If some poor fleeced wretch, in rage and desperation, did seem ready to endure that social martyrdom, Madame need only hint how sorry she would be if compelled—by pangs of conscience—to disclose that her saloon had been used for assignations with a lover.

This blackmailing swindle, with its double insurance for the swindler, regrettably achieved a staggering success.

There was, apparently, in Mayfair and its offshoots an inexhaustible supply of women who did not pause to wonder why the precious secrets of eternal beauty should have done so little for the hideous hag that sold them.

The smart carriages lined up outside Bond Street's door of hope; the Arabs and Circassians were kept working overtime; and when Mrs. Borradaile first called—in 1864—Madame Rachel had grown accustomed to expect a profit of at least £20,000 a year.

Possibly her unbroken run was by then inducing carelessness, sacrificing her discretion to her greed. For with this new and easy prey she over-reached herself.

Mrs. Borradaile was the widow of an Army officer, and herself came of excellent county stock. She was also the possessor of a comfortable little fortune, which she personally controlled.

She was also what would nowadays be called a natural sucker.

All this Madame Rachel either observed or ascertained before getting seriously to work. "You have been very beautiful, Mrs. Borradaile." The emphasis on the past tense was infinitesimal. "And I believe—I feel sure—I could make you beautiful again."

Beautiful—and for ever. It said so on the window. Mrs. Borradaile's heart fluttered. "But . . . the expense," she murmured.

"My fees are necessarily rather high," Madame said, with disarming frankness, "but in your case, I shall be content with £1,000."

A thousand pounds—just like that? Mrs. Borradaile could not—

would not hear of it. And yet . . . beautiful for ever . . . the envy of the women . . . the attention of the men.

Might Madame Rachel reconsider?

Madame might and did. Once get the fly in the web, and it can be devoured by stages. Madame suggested immediate payment of £100 and joint review of the situation later—a suggestion Mrs. Borradaile gratefully accepted.

Her next few weeks were so occupied with unguents, baths, and lotions that a further £100 could be extracted painlessly. But when the weeks became months, and the months bordered on years, without any sign whatever of the promised benefits, even Mrs. Borradaile's credulity was strained.

No more payments were forthcoming, and the fly looked like slipping the web with merely surface wounds.

It was then that Madame Rachel, now well aware that she could go beyond all former limits, gave the web a new twist which secured the fly for good.

She had told Mrs. Borradaile that she had had a visit from Lord Ranelagh (a well-known man about town and eligible *parti*); that Lord Ranelagh had seen Mrs. Borradaile—merely *seen* her—and promptly fallen head over heels in love; that he had asked Madame Rachel to act as intermediary, because—for some reason not precisely specified —personal courtship would, as yet, be imprudent.

"You will be entering one of the greatest families in England," Madame added, "and you will need the youth and beauty only I can give you. But money creates no obstacle, does it, with such a match assured?"

So unsurpassed among gulls was Mrs. Borradaile that she swallowed this story whole on Madame Rachel's word. But Madame constantly reinforced it by handing her letters—"left for you by his Lordship"—to which, through the same post office, Mrs. Borradaile replied.

In her transports of delight the foolish widow failed to acknowledge inconsistencies that would have undeceived a child.

If Lord Ranelagh's declarations of love were singularly misspelt— ah yes, as Madame said, his servant must have written them down at his dictation. If the handwriting varied from one letter to another— ah yes, as Madame said, he employs several servants. And when once Mrs. Borradaile met Lord Ranelagh face to face, and, upon introduction, he was polite but distant—ah yes, as Madame said, he wisely counterfeited. What made this counterfeit imperative still remained obscure.

Now, though, the screws could be tightened to Madame's satisfaction. Mrs. Borradaile followed every injunction of her guardian angel. Beauty treatments—utterly disregarding cost—galore; acquirement of a trousseau and other wedding accessories, all left "for convenience" at Madame's shop; purchase of jewels befitting the future Lady Ranelagh, all deposited "for sure custody" in Madame's safe.

The comfortable little fortune was swiftly drained away, and Mrs. Borradaile reduced to destitution.

When that moment arrived, Madame—one is driven to suppose—lost her head and went berserk. Knowing she had extorted Mrs. Borradaile's last penny, she procured her arrest and committal to jail for debt. The terrified woman at last turned to her relatives and friends; the whole dark matter came under close inquiry; soon they got Mrs. Borradaile out—and put Madame Rachel in. . . .

Judging, though, from this ludicrous scene at the Old Bailey, it is not Madame whom Mrs. Borradaile rates as her chief enemy; it is Mr. Seymour, that impertinent and inquisitive man.

"No, I will *not* say my age," she repeats, and childishly stamps her foot.

"What year were you married?" Seymour asks.

"Eighteen hundred and forty-six."

"How old were you when you married?"

She detects that simple trap. "I won't tell you—no, no no." The coy giggle again, as she volunteers "I will only tell you this—I married *extremely* young."

The crowd cannot contain themselves; they snigger openly. And it is all Mrs. Borradaile's fault—Serjeant Ballantine firmly holds—that the jury, despite overwhelming evidence, disagree.

Only on a second trial does he make London safe—or at least safe for other Mrs. Borradailes—in the next five years to come.

Dr. James Manby Gully

"DOCTOR JAMES MANBY GULLY," says the coroner, and a distinguished-looking man of near seventy picks his way through the packed court towards the witness-box.

Dr. Gully's impressive looks are not deceptive. His professional reputation stands extremely high. As a pioneer of hydropathic treatment, he has contributed more than any to making Malvern the famous spa it is.

Today, though, Dr. Gully appears to feel unwell. His colour is bad, and he sways a little as he takes the oath.

"May he sit down, sir?" asks his counsel.

"Why should he?" cries a juror.

This mannerless interjection excites an unseemly roar of applause from the spectators. Even a few hisses are directed at the witness.

For on this August day of 1876 Dr. Gully is about the best-hated man in England.

All regard him as a sly snake-in-the-grass. Most consider him a vicious libertine. Many think even worse of him than this; they think that he played a sinister part in the death of Charles Bravo, with which the present inquest is officially concerned. . . .

Charles Bravo was a rich young man who had married a rich young widow the previous year. They established for themselves a luxurious *ménage* at the house that the lady already occupied in Balham—butler, footman, three gardeners, six maids, and as housekeeper a certain Mrs. Cox, who had been the widow's companion and devoted confidante.

They had enjoyed four months of uneventful domesticity when, one evening after they had dined at home, Charles Bravo suddenly took ill.

Spasms of vomiting, severe internal pains, a period of deep insensibility followed by a rising pulse and a discharge of blood—the doctors noted the characteristic signs of poisoning. And a statement by Mrs. Cox bore them out in their opinion; Mr. Bravo, she said, had confided to her in his torment that he had taken poison, but entreated her to keep this knowledge from his wife.

Bravo, however, told the doctors he had taken nothing. "I say that," he solemnly affirmed, "fully aware that I am going before my Maker."

His prediction, at least, was wholly accurate. Charles Bravo died— as the post-mortem revealed—from a fatal dose of tartar emetic.

Accident could be virtually discounted. If he was murdered the suspicion must be heavy on Mrs. Bravo, or on Mrs. Cox, or on both— but what could have been the motive actuating either?

For that matter, though, what could have been the motive actuating Charles Bravo to destroy himself?

Each alternative seemed inexplicable—until Mrs. Cox belatedly furnished the authorities with some additional and startling information.

She had been so anxious—she told them—to shield her dear friend, Mrs. Bravo, that she had not repeated Mr. Bravo's words in full. But as things had turned out so serious, she felt bound to do so now.

He had not merely said to her, "I have taken poison". He had said, "I have taken poison *because of Gully*".

Mrs. Cox declared herself the less surprised by this because Mr. Bravo had often voiced his strong suspicion—utterly unfounded, she hastened to point out—that Gully was pursuing an intrigue with his wife.

Mrs. Cox's new disclosure, whether true or false, suggested a plausible motive for Charles Bravo's suicide. But it also suggested—as she apparently did not realize—a plausible motive for Charles Bravo's murder.

The cat might jump either way. Only one thing could be written down as certain: whether the murder or the suicide theory was adopted, Dr. Gully had now been involved in the business right up to his neck. . . .

The coroner and jury have already learned some remarkable facts concerning Dr. Gully. The lawyers—and especially that fashionable solicitor, George Lewis, who represents the dead man's relatives—got them out of Mrs. Bravo when she testified.

She confessed that she had been Dr. Gully's mistress for several years before her second marriage; that he had taken a house in Balham expressly to be near her; that he was still living at that house when Bravo died.

But, she insisted, she had formally broken with him as soon as Charles Bravo began paying her attention. From that day forward, they had never met.

Had he not kept in touch with her, though? they asked. Had he not sent her medicines when she wasn't well? Didn't she know that Mrs. Cox—Mrs. Cox, her dear friend—had admitted this was so?

Ah yes, Mrs. Bravo said; he sent me a bottle of laurel water once; it came after Mrs. Cox had encountered him accidentally on a train and told him I was suffering from insomnia.

It is these revelations that have generated the hostile atmosphere which prevails on Dr. Gully's own appearance. There is hardly a friendly face in court as he regretfully confirms Mrs. Bravo's story, but emphasizes even more urgently than she the finality and completeness of the break. "I even gave orders to my servants," he says, "that Mrs. Bravo and Mrs. Cox were not to be let in."

This is the first point Mr. Lewis fastens on when, with the crowd behind him to a man, he starts on Dr. Gully's cross-examination.

"When did you give those orders to your servants?"

"Immediately after we had separated—about the end of October, 1875."

"Did you ever withdraw those orders?"

"Never."

"When, after Mrs. Bravo's marriage, did you first communicate with Mrs. Cox—accidentally, to use your term and hers?"

"That would be in the March of 1876."

"You then travelled in the same railway carriage with her?"

"By chance," Dr. Gully answers quickly. "I wouldn't have got in if I had known she was there."

"But when you arrived in London from Balham," Mr. Lewis says, "you went into the same carriage in the Underground?"

"Oh yes," Dr. Gully says. "By then I had no reason for doing otherwise."

"Though you had given those orders to your servants?"

It is so much bunkum, Mr. Lewis's tone implies; you and these ladies were still in surreptitious contact.

"Did Mrs. Cox tell you Mrs. Bravo had insomnia?"

"She did."

"Did you ask if she had a doctor attending her at the instance of her husband?"

"No."

"Did you send the bottle of laurel water for Mrs. Bravo through Mrs. Cox at a different address?"

"Yes."

Mr. Lewis's brows contract forbiddingly.

"Were you desirous that it should not be known that you had sent the laurel water?"

"Not the least," says Dr. Gully with some indignation. "But I thought I was forbidden Mrs. Bravo's house in every respect."

"Why didn't you direct the chemist to deliver it there?"

Dr. Gully shakes his handsome head.

"I didn't think of it at all."

Don't pretend to be half-witted, Mr. Lewis's glance implies. Was it really laurel water—or was it tartar emetic?

"You went to Balham," he went on aloud, "simply in order to be near Mrs. Bravo?"

"Yes."

"No other reason?"

"No."

"So when your association ceased, you had no reason to remain?"

Dr. Gully does not answer.

"Is it five minutes' walk," asks Mr. Lewis meaningly, "from your house to that of Mr. Bravo?"

Dr. Gully's counsel springs up to protest.

"This is questioning for questioning's sake," he says. "The distance is known; it has been proved over and over again."

Mr. Lewis grasps his opportunity.

"Yes; it has been proved over and over again," he agrees. "And this gentleman has chosen to stop within five minutes of the house where Mr. Charles Bravo met his death. . . ."

Despite such charges and the jury's patent predilection, they reached an inconclusive verdict in the end. They found that Charles Bravo had been wilfully murdered, but that there was insufficient evidence for them to say by whom.

Myself, I have no doubt that—whatever may be thought about the ladies—Dr. Gully had no connexion whatsoever with any aspect of Charles Bravo's death. But the effect of related emotive words is strong.

Lover, Mistress and Poison proved in combination almost irresistible, and put an old gentleman in peril of his life when his greatest sin had been a masculine weakness for a woman.

The Three Sisters

"ALTHOUGH I say it, members of the jury, in his hearing"— Sir Patrick Hastings is opening the defence in Britain's most sensational breach of promise suit for years—"although I say it in his hearing, one cannot blink the fact that the defendant is a silly old man."

The defendant—active and well-preserved at sixty-seven—shows no signs of disagreement with his famous counsel. Quite the opposite. Rather mournfully, he nods.

But if he is—or, at any rate, has been—silly, certainly he is not in any sense a coward. With substantial wealth at his command, he could have nipped this action in the bud.

A few thousand pounds—two, four, five? Call it five, and he *knows* that Stephanie would have settled. She would have sought advice— she always did—from her slightly older sisters, and the defendant did not doubt the response of Rhoda nor of Fay.

Five thousand pounds—it would not have hurt him in the least.

There need not then have been that painful confession to his wife; there need not then have been those embarrassing explanations to old friends; above all, there need not then have been this present grim exposure of his intimate private life in a crowded public court.

Five thousand pounds—and nobody need ever have known that he was even acquainted with those three fateful sisters; still less that he had long maintained Rhoda as his mistress; still less that lately he had taken Stephanie on too—but without discontinuing his earlier liaison.

The most worldly folk, sparing of moral strictures and accustomed to wink at a little on the side, might regard such a set-up as unsavoury. The defendant has always been acutely aware of that.

Faced with a claim for damages, however, founded on a promise of marriage he could not legally give and is now waiting to swear upon oath he never gave, the defendant resolved to fight at any cost.

Rather than surrender to what he affirmed was blackmail, deliberately he let loose the lashing tongues of scandal.

The result thus far for him has been a nightmare—but a nightmare now increasingly yielding to the light of day.

He had listened, with feelings that verged upon despair, to the introductory speech of Stephanie's counsel. He has heard how— according to that advocate's instructions—his client (aged thirty-four) had known the defendant "socially" since she was twenty-five; how two years ago he had surprised her by proposing marriage, and she had asked for time to talk it over with her sisters; how she had later accepted him when Rhoda and Fay were present; how he had seduced her—an innocent virgin—on the strength and faith of their engagement; how she had finally learned—a dreadful double revelation—that he was both Rhoda's lover and a married man; how she had been "completely crushed" by this discovery, and how the damages ought to be enormous.

He has listened, with horrified fascination, while Stephanie herself confirmed this story in the box.

He has heard her wails, her sobs, her fits of weeping, her piteous appeal, "Do I *have* to talk about these things?" (and Mr. Justice Charles's acid comment, "Of course you do. You brought the action. You brought yourself to court").

He has listened also—with ever-growing relief and hope—to Sir Patrick Hastings's cross-examination. . . .

From the start Hastings had visualized a conspiracy on the part of all three sisters—a conspiracy in which each fulfilled an allotted role.

On this issue he came to grips with Stephanie at once.

"I am going to suggest that you and your two sisters have been arranging this case for many months, and that you dare not put Rhoda in the box?"

"It's not true," Stephanie said, with a marked catch in her voice.

"Where is Rhoda?"

"I don't know."

"Where do you *think* she is?"

"How can I say?"

"Is she in England?"

"Yes."

"Is she in court?"

Stephanie seemed to look very carefully round before replying.

"Yes," she said at last. "Yes, she is in court."

"Where?" Sir Patrick turned towards the onlookers. "Where? Will Rhoda kindly stand up so that we can see her?"

A woman rose from a gangway seat upon a forward row.

"Here I am, darling," she called—not to Sir Patrick, but to Stephanie, who responded with a loving gaze, then gently dabbed her eyes.

"Thank you madam; that will do." Sir Patrick, noting Rhoda's features and where she was installed, quickly refocused his attention on the witness. "You know, don't you, that Rhoda told the old gentleman that if he defended this action he would be charged with attempting to procure an abortion on you?"

"Oh no! Oh no!"

"If your sisters put their heads together and decided upon this, it would be a good way to get money, wouldn't it?"

"Oh, please," Stephanie said, raising her handkerchief afresh.

"Don't cry again, yet," Sir Patrick said, "there will be so much more to cry about presently. Isn't the truth about this so-called seduction that you invited the defendant to your flat and, without anyone breathing a word about marriage, you offered to have intercourse with him on the drawing-room sofa?"

"Oh no! Oh no!"

"And that he did?"

"Oh no! Oh no!"

Sir Patrick moved a step or two nearer to the box—an omen to those familiar with his characteristics. "You say your sisters were present when you accepted the defendant. Is there any other living soul in whose presence he promised to marry you?"

"No."

"Is there any single word in his letters to you about marriage?"

"No."

"Did Rhoda—your loving sister Rhoda, who is sitting over there— did Rhoda ever say to you, 'Don't marry that old man, darling; I've been sleeping with him for years'?"

"I have had two nervous breakdowns," Stephanie pleaded tearfully, "and my brain isn't working properly."

"I suggest it is working very cleverly," said Sir Patrick, "and that you are three scheming adventuresses. You are simply trying to get money out of this old man, aren't you?"

Stephanie indignantly denied it.

"Aren't you? Then why are you here?"

"I want my honour returned," she moaned.

From both the theatrical and artistic point of view, that made an effective climax to the first day's hearing. This morning, it had been sister Fay's turn to take the limelight; but, the defendant could not help noticing, Sir Patrick's interest was not exclusively centred on the witness.

Frequently he cast a sharp glance round the court; and especially in the direction of a particular gangway seat on a forward row.

His first question to Fay made his object manifest. "Have you seen your sister Rhoda this morning?"

"Yes," Fay replied.

"Is she quite well?" Sir Patrick asked, with great solicitude.

"Quite well, thank you." Fay, in contrast to Stephanie, was tough and combative.

"Well enough for her to attend court if she so desires?"

"So far as I know."

"I don't see her in court," said Sir Patrick with another glance at the gangway. "Is she here?"

"No, she is not."

"Where is she?"

Fay hesitated. "She is at the Waldorf Hotel."

"At the Waldorf Hotel?" Sir Patrick's tone was silky. "She is the only person, other than yourself, who can give evidence that the defendant promised to marry Stephanie. Isn't she?"

"Well," Fay said warily.

"Well," Sir Patrick repeated. "Why is she not in court today as she was yesterday?"

"I don't know."

"Don't you? Give it a little more consideration. Can you think of any reason why Rhoda shouldn't go into the box?"

"It's not for me to say."

Sir Patrick moved a step or two nearer. "Is it because it would be very dangerous if she did?"

"Of course not."

"Wouldn't it? Don't you know that she's been writing letters to the defendant containing threats of what will happen if he doesn't pay?"

"I don't know what she has written," Fay said stubbornly.

"Aren't you terribly sorry the jury are not to have a few words from her? Wouldn't you love to see her in the box to say 'I can corroborate my two loving sisters'?"

"If they want her"—Fay didn't specify who 'they' were—"she can be got."

"And meantime she is at the Waldorf Hotel," Sir Patrick said reflectively. "Is she waiting there to get her share if there is anything to split?"

No wonder the defendant can stomach it when Sir Patrick coolly describes him as "a silly old man". He could stomach almost anything from Sir Patrick. For now he really does feel that the nightmare is dissolving. Only remains his own appearance in the box . . . and then . . . surely. . . .

He steels himself for that last ordeal.

But what is this? The jury's heads together; someone's voice— "We've heard enough"; the judge saying something about a conspiracy to extort money and mentioning the Director of Public Prosecutions; Sir Patrick swiftly leaving the packed court for another where he is urgently required; himself surrounded by hand-shaking pals; and Stephanie and Fay going back to break the bad news to Rhoda, still solidly entrenched at the Waldorf Hotel.

Mrs. Bamberger

IN the case of Mrs. Bamberger the King's Proctor did not merely intervene. He practically exploded. It had been such a quiet little divorce, too, up till then. No fuss, no publicity, everything treated with dispatch.

Mrs. Bamberger, a beautiful young wife, had petitioned on grounds of desertion and misconduct. Her stockbroker husband did not defend the suit. She did not ask for the discretion of the court—thus affirming as clearly as if she had shouted it from the house-tops, that there had been no act of misconduct on her part.

Plain sailing and repetitively dull. Pressmen were indifferent, counsel undistinguished, the spectators' benches virtually untenanted when, on commonplace and undisputed evidence, a decree nisi was formally pronounced.

At the second hearing, though, invoked by the King's Proctor with express purpose of cancelling out the first, scene and situation were remarkably transformed.

Reporters sat tensed with pencils ready poised; celebrated Silks jostled for elbow-room; and would-be onlookers, barred from the packed gallery, in disappointment paced the corridor outside.

For the King's Proctor had named not *one* man, but *four*; four different men, each of social standing; four men who—that anonymous functionary alleged—had been Mrs. Bamberger's partners in adultery.

The position of those involved excited interest. Their numbers converted interest to sensation. But it was Mrs. Bamberger's own story, told in the harsh, white spotlight of the box that conferred upon the trial a unique atmosphere and upon the feminine narrator a notoriety which has endured from 1920 to this day.

A touch of melancholy, a hint of patient martyrdom, made Mrs. Bamberger look lovelier than ever as she solemnly raised the book, pledged her truthfulness, and began.

She had married, she said, while still more or less a child. Her husband had never maintained their joint household; almost from the start he had put pressure upon her to get money from susceptible men and then go halves with him.

Again and again he insisted; again and again she refused; but ultimately—"I was seventeen"—her prolonged resistance broke.

She imposed, however, strict limits; she would only go So Far. She acquiesced when her husband, actively prospecting, introduced her to potential gallants as his sister. She accepted gifts of money from such gentlemen; in exchange, yes, she permitted love-making—but not, Mrs. Bamberger delicately explained, *not* the consummation, *not* the final act. She remained technically chaste and physically pure.

The whole sordid business, indeed, was only recalled to show his lordship how her husband's conduct had conduced to adultery—an important point if the judge should hold that she had been guilty of it. If.

But, Mrs. Bamberger protested, she had *not* been guilty of it; neither on those occasions, nor on any other. Not even after the break-up of her marriage; not even between desertion and decree.

That cast no reflection on the witnesses called for the King's Proctor. Pretty nearly everything that they had said was true.

She *had* taken a flat together with a man named Symonds; *had* registered at a London hotel with a British Army major; *had* allowed a lieutenant to sleep at her house when only themselves were present; *had* shared another dwelling with an American flying man.

Oh, yes, yes, yes; they weren't in conflict over that. The facts she admitted; it was the *inference*—the puritanical inference—she denied.

Mr. Symonds? A consumptive she took pity on, and nursed. Unfortunately—Mrs. Bamberger modestly lowered her head—he fell in love with her, grew passionately jealous, and by threats of murder threw her into such a state of fear that she had to call for protection from her friends.

And the Major? The Lieutenant? The American flying man? Chivalrous knights in armour who responded to that call. Sometimes they stayed with her when she was afraid to be alone. Sometimes she stayed with them when she was afraid to be at home.

"They were my big brothers," Mrs. Bamberger said.

An unusual, rather improbable, but not impossible story. It was a question of credit, though, as well as credibility. What confidence should be reposed in Mrs. Bamberger's sworn word?

The issue is still open, the outcome undecided, as Mr. Rawlinson, K.C., representing the King's Proctor, rises to cross-examine.

"Before you married Mr. Bamberger, when you were on your own, did you take a house for yourself at Twyford Mansions?"

One would have expected an immediate answer—yes or no. People don't generally forget where they have lived. But a curious blank expression has come into Mrs. Bamberger's captivating eyes.

"Did you take a house at Twyford Mansions?"—"I can't remember," Mrs. Bamberger replies.

"Can't you? Can't you? Was it not while you were living at Twyford Mansions, before you married Mr. Bamberger"—Rawlinson is clearly laying special stress on this—"that you made the acquaintance of a gentleman named Aguiera?"

"I can't remember," Mrs. Bamberger replies.

"Didn't you meet him at the Alhambra?"

"I don't think so," Mrs. Bamberger says, a trifle primly. "I very seldom go to music halls."

"Didn't you drive with him to Twyford Mansions?"—"I can't remember."

"Weren't you in the police court about it?"

Everyone sits up smartly. Only Mrs. Bamberger, gaze impenetrably void, seems impervious to the sudden shock.

"I can't remember," she replies again, adding that since a motor smash her memory is bad.

"Were you sent to sessions on a charge of stealing from him?"—"I can't remember."

"And at sessions was the charge withdrawn?"—"I can't remember."

But despite her uniformly noncommittal answers, Rawlinson has struck an extremely powerful blow—both at Mrs. Bamberger's indictment of her husband, and (more grave) at Mrs. Bamberger herself.

He launches his next attack from a terrain of strength.

"Where did you meet the American flying man?"—"At a party."

"Who was your host?"—"I can't remember."

"Where did you meet the lieutenant?"—"In a tea shop."

"Who introduced you?"—"I can't remember."

Surely not since the trial of Queen Caroline and Majocchi's constant parrot-cry, "*Non mi ricordo*", has amnesia been so frequently pleaded by any witness in any English court.

"Do you really say that your association with the lieutenant had anything to do with his protecting you from Symonds?"—"Certainly."

The blank expression has entirely gone.

"Look at that letter. Is it from you to Symonds?"

Mrs. Bamberger scrutinizes it carefully. "Yes."

"Dated last May?"—"Yes."

"Long after you had become friendly with the lieutenant?"—"Yes."

"Look down the page, if you please, Mrs. Bamberger. Do you see the sentence 'I am crazy with love for you'?"

"I had to pretend to him," Mrs. Bamberger exclaims. "I went in terror of my life. That letter was a bluff."

"Isn't the whole of your evidence a bluff?" says Rawlinson.

"No," says Mrs. Bamberger, instantly composed again. "It is very sad, and it is very true."

Rawlinson appears neither impressed nor touched. Coldly he passes to her three small slips of paper, each numbered, each bearing a man's name.

"I will refer to them by their numbers only. Number One—haven't you had from him more than a thousand pounds?"

It is not the blank expression that returns; rather it is a dazed one, as at something totally unforeseen.

"I can't remember having so much as that from him," she says.

"From Number Two?"—"About fifty pounds."

"From Number Three?"

Mrs. Bamberger's enchanting mouth is quivering. Some mysterious spell is cast upon her by the sight of a name that we shall never know.

"From Number Three?" Rawlinson repeats.

"Five or six thousand," she half whispers. . . .

The decree nisi was rescinded. The judge found that Mrs. Bamberger had committed adultery with both Symonds and the American flying man.

He termed her "a mistress of the art of fiction", and declared that "she drew with deliberation and skill a cloak over the facts".

He also took a side-swipe at Mr. Bamberger. While acquitting him of

310

responsibility for his wife's misconduct, he thought him "content to live upon its gains".

On that grim note ended the Bamberger divorce suit—so far as it concerned the Law Courts in the Strand. There followed, though, an even grimmer sequel elsewhere—at the Old Bailey, where the beautiful petitioner was tried for perjury and sentenced to nine months.

Few anticipated, and some deplored, that sequel. As Mrs. Bamberger's defender pointed out, since their inception the matrimonial courts had heard some 40,000 defended suits, and not one had given rise to a perjury prosecution—although every loser must have been a perjurer.

Why create a precedent? Why change the form?

The concensus of opinion in fashionable circles—the Divorce Court's most loyal and consistent patrons—deemed Mrs. B. exceedingly ill-starred and the Public Prosecutor exceedingly unsporting.

Mabel Duncan

"Do you still maintain, madam, that your relationship with this young man was innocent?" asks counsel.

"Yes, I do," the lovely actress says.

"Do you still swear you have never been unfaithful to your husband?"

"Yes, I do," the lovely actress says.

"But you admit that the letters you received from this young man were in many, many instances the letters of a lover?"

"Some of them were, more or less so, I suppose."

"And that he told you, in plain words, that he was in love with you?"

"Yes, more or less so, I suppose he did."

"But, despite that declaration and the tenor of those letters, you continued and cemented the association?"

She has never had a part either so dramatic, or so prominent, on the stage.

Musical comedy has been her *métier*; and at the Gaiety Theatre, where she has generally performed, the biggest scenes and the major share of the limelight have been monopolized by celebrated stars. But by far the biggest scene in this protracted drama—which has already occupied the court for several days—is undoubtedly her own appearance in the box. None can hope to steal this scene, though legal stars abound—Edward Carson, Rufus Isaacs, and, not least, Henry Duke, who has now been questioning her remorselessly for hours.

The limelight never shifts from her elevated station, and all eyes focus continually on her.

This is the fruit, however, not of talent, but of folly. And she who has sought such a distinction in the theatre would fain be without that imposed on her in court.

Until the events that led up to the present situation, the career of Mabel Duncan might well have been that of any Gaiety Girl in the best romantic fiction.

Gently bred as well as beautiful, she had known sudden impoverishment through a decamping father, and in consequence, at an extremely youthful age, had set out to make herself a living on the stage.

She was barely seventeen when an aristocratic army aspirant named Francis Bryce became passionately enamoured of her, and proposed.

His family opposed the match, and declined financial aid to the almost penniless couple: whereupon Francis Bryce, with notable resolve, abandoned his military calling for the Stock Exchange, where he soon acquired a status that enabled them to marry, which they did in January, 1898.

A reconciliation followed with the senior Bryces; a steady and substantial rise in Francis Bryce's income led to Mabel's virtual retirement from the theatre, in which at first she had continued working to supplement their needs; and the former Gaiety Girl, with her well-to-do stockbroker husband, now entered that division of fashionable society which for generations has been dubbed The Younger Set.

A man who marries a Gaiety Girl and who joins The Younger Set does not necessarily thereby evince an easy moral standard; fun and propriety need not be incompatible. But he must not expect—and if he does he will be disappointed—that the stuffier conventions will be as rigorously obeyed by his wife and her male friends as though she had taken the veil and they monastic vows.

Nor did Francis Bryce entertain such expectations. He was not disquieted, and he did not object, when rich young Harold Pape, whom they had met at Oxford in Commem Week, thereafter tended to attach himself to them, and to pay Mabel flattering attention.

Upon this score, indeed, Francis Bryce would have found it hard to justify complaint, for he himself was currently paying flattering attention to one whom he afterwards termed his "very good friend"—a girl of seventeen.

We are apt to assume that where things correspond on the surface, they will also correspond in depth. Francis Bryce assumed that Pape's affection for his wife was like his own affection for his "very good friend"—and that light-hearted camaraderie would not go too far.

But there were elements involved besides light-hearted camaraderie, and Harold Pape was going a very great deal further than honourable bachelors should with wedded wives.

He took advantage of Francis Bryce's absence at his office to spend hours alone with Mabel almost daily at her flat. When she went to stay with friends at Windsor, he posted himself at a hotel in the town. When she went to stay with friends in the Isle of Wight, he posted himself at a hotel on the island. And any possibility that these occurrences might be fully explained by him in terms of companionship or coincidence is disposed of by the content and phrasing of his letters.

"I only know I love you, love you, and can't bear to think you are going away from me tomorrow"; "I ought to have stopped myself caring for you, ought never to have told you that I loved you, or shown it"; "I want you tonight awfully, awfully"—whatever conduct may be inferred from these expressions (and that is a prime subject of dispute in court) one thing surely does not call for argument: this is not the language of light-hearted camaraderie.

Francis Bryce most certainly did not think so when these letters and the incidents linked with them came to light. He turned out the wife whom he had so romantically wooed and won, and promptly presented a petition for divorce.

Mabel, in deep distress, resisted and defended. She had done nothing wrong with Harold Pape. She had liked him as a friend; she had accepted him as an escort; she had perhaps basked a little in his obvious admiration. He was sweet on her, but that was where it stopped—she saw to that.

The last thing she wanted was to lose her husband and her home. Could not the suit be dropped? Could not they make it up?

But Francis Bryce was deaf to the appeals of the wife that he thought guilty; and in court he has sat inexorable throughout her long ordeal, although she has twice fainted under Duke's hammer blows.

These do not cease; they are redoubled.

"Did you not think it wrong for you, a married woman, to receive such letters from an unmarried man?"

"I see now it was foolish."

"Did you not consider it dishonourable on his part to make declarations of love to his friend's wife?"

"I do not think so, no."

"Really!" exclaims the judge.

"Will you repeat that?" thunders Duke.

Mabel's lower lip trembles piteously.

"I suppose it *was* dishonourable," she says.

"Was he looking forward to the time when you might be his?"

"I do not know his thoughts," she says.

"Did he desire to possess you?"

"I don't think so," she says.

"Did you doubt it, madam? Did you doubt it?"

She looks helplessly at the formidable figure of the advocate; pathetically at the implacable figure of her husband.

"*I told him,*" she says, "*that his lovemaking must be absolutely harmless,* or I would not see him again. . . ."

There can be very little doubt that she did tell him exactly that. It is a sentiment characteristic of all ladies who want to play with fire without getting themselves burned, who want to keep their beaux and yet keep their virtue too.

Mabel Bryce only partially succeeded. The jury, while severely censuring Harold Pape, pronounced that there had been no adultery. But a heavy toll had been exacted in the process, and the Gaiety Girl quitted the scene of her most spectacular role without the slightest appetite for a repeat performance.

The Gordon Custody Case

I HAVE never felt qualified to pass moral, as distinct from plainly practical, judgments. It should not, therefore, be construed as censure or disparagement if I say that the Gordon custody case evolved a pattern in which the sexual standards of the farmyard intermingled with the family spirit of the jungle.

This is merely straight reporting—reporting based on reliable descriptions of the jungle and on first-hand observation of a farmyard. In the latter, mating is promiscuous and haphazard. In the former, maternal possessiveness is infinite and deadly.

And it was these two elements, transported from their natural habitat to fashionable Mayfair, that occasioned the bitter and unusual dispute which marked the Lent law term of 1903.

This dispute centred upon a lady, widowed young, who had lit a passionate flame in the hearts of two patrician kinsmen: the mature Lord Granville Gordon and his youthful cousin Eric. First she became mistress of the elder, who was married. Then she became wife of the younger, who was not.

The lady afterwards asserted that Eric not only knew of her relations with Lord Granville, but that she had expressly made the match conditional upon his agreement to tolerate their continuance. That allegation Eric emphatically denied.

But there is, at the very least, no doubt of this—her relations with Lord Granville *did* continue, and for a space of years the lady fulfilled her dual role, in wedlock with one cousin, and out of it with the other, while all three remained on terms of easy friendship. It was a design for living anticipating, in plan if not in wit, the Bohemian libertines of Noel Coward's play.

The delicate balance of forces within this tiny group was ultimately disturbed by an external event.

Lady Granville Gordon died.

The sudden revival of Lord Granville's eligible status resulted in the triangle's collapse. Lord Granville desired to sanctify his liaison; the lady desired to discard the sole impediment, her husband; her husband discovered—or decided to act upon—his wife's misconduct. A complete matrimonial re-shuffle supervened, the lady being divorced by Eric and married by his Lordship.

As the ex-husband evinced no disposition to adopt his predecessor's previous role of illicit lover, the trio now presented a more orthodox formation. But if one complex situation had been simplified another almost immediately arose.

The divorce decree gave Eric custody of a child which had been born to his wife during the period of their marriage. The lady maintained that it was in fact Lord Granville's child; that her husband always had been well aware of this; and that they had privately agreed between themselves to treat the custody order as inoperative.

Once again Eric's version was in stark antithesis. So when the lady ignored the order and withheld the child, Eric applied to the court for its enforcement.

Thereby the lady was impaled on the horns of a dilemma.

As the petition for divorce had gone through undefended, only minimal evidence was tendered or required. It had been just as well for what was left of the lady's good repute. In an age when no adulterous woman wholly escaped shame, the circumstances of this particular marital offence—which might well make even indulgent moderns ponder—was such that their disclosure would threaten utter social ruin.

But to defeat Eric Gordon's application and to make herself the legal custodian of her child, the lady could not successfully rely upon an unconfirmed story of an indefinite agreement. She must ask the court to vary its own order.

On what grounds? There could be none—unless Eric was unfit to have the child in his care.

Why should he be unfit? Only one possible reason—if she could prove that he knew at the time of her scandalous goings-on; knew, and accepted them without remonstrance or demur.

Love of the child outweighed her pride, and she embarked upon this course. She went to court to advertise her dishonour to the world; not merely to confess adultery, but to proclaim it; to stress the details of her infidelity; to demonstrate herself devoid of modesty or virtue— think of me as you will; only let me keep my child.

Yes, she insists on it from the witness box, a *ménage à trois* existed throughout her life with Eric—a state of affairs equally accepted by them all. And yes, Eric had always thought the baby Granville's child.

"You were all good and intimate friends?" asks Eric's counsel.

"Yes."

"Your husband and Lord Granville used to go shooting together?"

"Yes."

"Once did they go to Norway together?"

"Yes."

"For six weeks?"

"Yes."

"All this when your husband knew you were Lord Granville's mistress?"

"Yes."

She is poise incarnate, calmness personified; the public exposure affects her not at all; her mind is concentrated on a single aim. Let me keep my child. Let me keep my child.

"During your confinement did your husband's mother visit you?"

"Yes."

"And his sister?"

"Yes."

"Who paid the medical expenses?"

"My husband did."

What, her expression seems to signify, is an accoucheur among friends?

"When did you decide to leave your husband?"

"In 1900, in the autumn."

"Did you write to tell his mother so?"

"I did."

"In that letter did you say that you would send the baby to her?"

"Yes."

"If you were leaving your husband," says counsel, "and going to Lord Granville, there were no more appearances to be kept up. Why, then, send the baby to your husband's mother?"

It is a telling stroke, and it shakes the lady's cool serenity as no indecorous revelations have sufficed to do. Her reply is both obscure and unconvincing.

"Naturally I was not going to say," she said.

Counsel now plays his ace.

"In January, 1901 did you write and ask your husband to come and see you?"

"Yes."

"You thought he would be reluctant?"

"Yes."

"Was the inducement you offered that if he came to see you he could also see the child?"

"It was."

"When you wrote that letter," counsel hammers out each word, "did you think that he believed it was not his child?"

"Yes," she says desperately, but not many are persuaded. . . .

The lady lost her case and was forced to relinquish custody. One cannot be surprised, nor had she just cause to complain.

All the same, it is impossible to refrain from sympathy. She fought for her child with the same singleness of purpose, the same readiness to sacrifice, maybe the same lack of scruple that wild animals exhibit in fighting for their young. And there is much to be said in favour of wild animals.

Index

317

INDEX

Dance of the Seven Veils, 216
Darling, Mr. Justice, 20, 21, 22, 23, 110, 111, 112, 218, 250
Davidson, Rev. Harold Francis (*see* Rector of Stiffkey)
Deane, Q.C., Dr., 288
Demange, Maître, 214, 215
Dickman, John Alexander, 80, 81, 82, 83
Dilke, Sir Charles, 277, 278, 279, 280
Diller, Inspector, 18
Dines, Courtland, 280, 281, 282, 283
Divorce Court, 258, 286, 293, 307, 310
Donald, Jeannie, 50, 51, 52, 53
Don Pat, 137, 138
Douglas, Mr., 147, 148, 149
Douglas, Lord Alfred, 20
Douglas-Pennant, Miss Violet, 247, 248, 249
D'Oyly Carte, Mr., 243
Dreyfus, Capt. Alfred, 213, 214, 215, 216
Duke, Henry, 311, 313
Duncan, Mabel, 311, 312, 313, 314
Dunlo, Lady (Belle Bilton), 293, 294, 295
Dunlo, Lord, 293, 294, 295, 296
Dunne, 31, 32, 33
Durham, Lord, 238, 239, 242

East, Dr., 177, 179, 180
Easter Rising, 208
Eldin, Lord (John Clerk), 46
Elizabeth I, Queen, 120, 121
Ellesmere, Lord, 138
Elliot, K. C., George, 41, 42
Ellison, Frank, 159, 160
Enniskillen, Earl of, 286
Esterhazy, 216

Fay, 304, 305, 306, 307
Figaro, The, 204, 205, 206
Flook, Mr., 264, 265, 266
Forster, Capt., 278, 280
Fortescue, Miss, 242, 243, 244
Fox, Mrs., 129, 130, 132
Fox, Sidney, 117, 129, 130, 131, 132
Fuller, Mr., 39
Fullerton, 241
Fyfe, Sir David Maxwell, 43

Gadda, Mrs., 14, 15, 16
Gaiety Theatre, 311, 312, 314
Gallacher, M.P., William, 101, 103, 104
Gardner, Margery, 173, 174
Garland, James, A., 142
Garmoyle, Lord, 243, 244
Garmoyle, Viscount, 242, 243
Gef, 38
Gell, Sir William, 262
Gentle, Miss, 88, 89
Gill, Sir Charles, 148, 149
Gimcrack Club, 238, 239
Gladstone, Herbert, 43
Goddard, Lord, 23, 25, 26, 219
Goddard, Sergeant, 13, 14, 15, 16, 17
Goodman, Mr. and Mrs., 17, 18, 19
Gordon, Eric, 314, 315
Gordon, Lord George, 181, 182, 183, 184
Gordon, Lady Granville, 314
Gordon, Lord Granville, 314, 315, 316
Grantley, Lord, 263, 265
Greer, Horace, 281, 283
Grein, J. T., 216, 217
Greenglass, David, 113, 114, 115

Gruban, Mr. and Mrs., 235, 236, 237, 238
Gully, Dr. James Manby, 300, 301, 302, 303
Gurrin, Thomas Henry, 159
Guthrie, Lord, 30

Haigh, 187
Hailes, Lord, 45
Haldane, Lord, 218
Hall, Sir Edward Marshall, 57, 58, 59
Hamner, Mrs., 267, 269
Hare, Margaret and William, 174, 175, 176, 177
Harewood, Lord, 138
Hartopp, Sir Charles and Lady, 150, 152
Hastings, Sir Patrick, 24, 25, 26, 38, 39, 40, 50, 138, 139, 153, 154, 155, 229, 230, 231, 233, 234, 236, 237, 238, 249, 304, 305, 306, 307
Haw Haw, Lord (William Joyce), 90, 91, 92, 93, 94
Hawke, Anthony, 173, 174
Hay, William, 181, 182, 183, 184
Heath, Neville, 158, 172, 173
"Helen of Troy", 184, 185, 186, 187
Henriques, William, 160
Hervey, Augustus John, 267, 268, 269
Hewart, Lord Chief Justice, 54, 55, 56
Hiss Alger, 165, 166
Hobbs, William Cooper, 54, 55, 56
Holman, Libby, 223, 224, 225
Hopwood, Superintendent, 181
Horridge, Mr. Justice, 56, 57, 59, 234
Horton, Judge, 64
Houldsworth, Mr., 83
Hubert, Dr., 172, 173, 174
Hudson, Fred (Frederick Nodder), 123
Humphreys, Travers, 211, 212
Humphry, Ozias, 23
Huntington, Mr., 21, 23

Inderwick, K.C., Mr., 151
Inglis, John, 50
Inskip, K.C., Thomas (Lord Chief Justice Caldecote), 118, 119
Irish Brigade, 208

J'Accuse, 216
James II, King, 31
James V, King of Scotland, 120
Jarrett, Rebecca, 200, 201, 202, 203
Jeffreys, Judge, 30, 31, 32, 33
Jenkins, M.P., Roy, 73
Jerome, District Attorney, 141, 142, 143
Jockey Club, 27, 137, 138, 139, 239
John Bull, 210, 212
Johnstone, Sir Frederick, 286
Jowitt, Sir William (Lord Chancellor), 131, 132, 153
Joyce, William (Lord Haw Haw)

Kaye, Emily, 97, 98, 99, 100
Kelly, Miss Renee, 20
Kennyon, Mr., 183, 184
Kingston, Duchess of, 266, 267, 268, 269, 270
Kingston, Duke of, 268
Kitson, Mrs., 245, 246, 247
Kitson, Sir James, 245, 246
Knox, Dr. Robert, 175
Kylsant, Lord, 153, 156

318